LIVES OF INDIAN OFFICERS

LIVES OF INDIAN OFFICERS

JOHN WILLIAM KAYE

IN THREE VOLUMES
VOL. III

Published by

Gyan Publishing House
5, Ansari Road
Daryaganj, New Delhi-110002
Phone: 011-47034999, 9811692060
E-mail: books@gyanbooks.com

Distribution Network
gyanbooks.com
India, USA, Canada, UK, Australia, France

ISBN: 978-81-21-28477-6 (Set)
978-81-212-8474-5 (PB)
First Published, 1869

2nd Impression 2023

Printed at: Gyan Press, Delhi.

LIVES OF INDIAN OFFICERS (VOL. III)
Author: JOHN WILLIAM KAYE

LIVES OF INDIAN OFFICERS

LIVES OF INDIAN OFFICERS

Illustrative of the History of the Civil and Military Service of India

HENRY MARTYN—SIR CHARLES METCALFE—SIR ALEX.
BURNES—CAPTAIN CONOLLY—MAJOR POTTINGER

BY

SIR JOHN WILLIAM KAYE

AUTHOR OF "THE HISTORY OF THE WAR IN AFGHANISTAN," ETC. ETC.

VOL III.

LONDON

DALDY, ISBISTER, & CO

56, LUDGATE HILL

1875

LIVES

OF

INDIAN OFFICERS.

———◦———

THE REV. HENRY MARTYN.

[BORN 1781.—DIED 1812.]

O N the seventh day of February, in the year 1811, in one of the monasteries of Goa, the capital of Portuguese India, two English gentlemen stood before the tomb of Francis Xavier.   Not·that the great apostle of the Gentiles had died there, for he had endured his last earthly pangs far away on the Island of Sancian, at the mouth of the Canton river; but that an admiring people had raised there a monument to his memory, richly ornamented and surrounded with pictures and bronzes, the produce of Italian art.   Of the visitors who stood at that shrine, and listened to the words of the friar who acted as its custodian, one was the statesman, the story of whose life has just been concluded.   The other, a slight, thin-faced man, about thirty years of age, with a hectic flush on his cheek, was a priest of the English Church, then on his way from Calcutta to

Bombay. An enthusiast himself, he could not think without emotion of the grand enthusiasm of the Christian knight, who, more than two centuries and a half before, had left the world behind him and abandoned all things for the love of God. With all the outward grandeur of the Romish Church before him, still, rejoicing in his purer faith, he thought humbly and reproachfully of the little that he had done, measured against the great deeds of that Romish giant. And yet was Henry Martyn, for all his feebleness of frame, cast in the same heroic mould as Francis Xavier.

It has become a mere platitude now, that the world has seen many heroes who have never girded on a sword or listened to the roar of the battle. A truth so accepted needs no demonstrations. Little need is there to show how the courage, the devotion, the self-sacrifice, the grand sense of duty, which make the heroic character, are found beneath the coif of the Priest as beneath the helm of the Warrior. It is given to some to do ; to others only to bear : to some, to strike for the right; to others, to witness to the truth. ‘ Never,’ it has been said, ‘ did the polytheism of ancient or of modern Rome assign a seat among the demigods to a hero of nobler mould or of more exalted magnanimity than Francis Xavier.’ And again the same writer : ‘ Amidst all the discords which agitate the Church of England, her sons are unanimous in extolling the name of Henry Martyn. And with reason ; for it is, in fact, the one heroic name which adorns her annals, from the days of Elizabeth to our own.’ * Fitly, then, in itself, is this ‘ one heroic name ’ in the

* Sir James Stephen.

annals of the Anglican Church placed at the head of this chapter, and more fitly than any other, because it helps at this early stage to illustrate the many-sidedness of the English heroism which has flowered beneath the Indian sun.

Henry Martyn came of a humble stock. In that rich ore country about Truro and Redruth, his father once toiled as a simple miner; but raising himself above the level, by his industry and intelligence, he obtained a seat in a merchant's office, and, appreciating at its true worth the value of that which had done so much for him, he determined to give to his children in early youth that which he had acquired so painfully in adult life, and, by good thrift, provided the means of bestowing upon them the blessings of a good education. But it pleased God, who gave him many children, that there should not be many spared for whom to make this provision. There was a constitutional weakness in the family, and Death laid its hands upon the childhood of the brothers and sisters of Henry Martyn, so that four only of the flock ever lived to see man's estate. And Henry himself was but a weakly, delicate nursling, whose little life needed much care to save it from flickering out in the morning of its existence. But he struggled through infancy and childhood, and went to the Truro Grammar School; and for nine years, under the tutorial care of Dr Cardew, he gathered up the by no means contemptible stock of learning which was accessible to the students in that provincial institution.

The school-days of Henry Martyn were not happy. He was not, indeed, born for happiness. He lacked the puerile robustness and the effervescent animal spirits which make the season of school-life a season of carelessness and joy. There is more or less of tyranny in every school; and Henry Martyn, being of feeble frame and of somewhat petulant temper, was bullied by his stronger schoolfellows. It would have fared still worse with him but for the generous protection of one of the bigger boys, who helped him with his lessons, and fought his battles for him, and often rescued him from the grasp of his juvenile oppressors.

It is not recorded of him that at this time, though he took but little part in the sports and amusements of boyhood, he was inordinately addicted to study. He was docile and quick to learn, but he acquired no very remarkable scholastic reputation. His father, however—a shrewd and discerning man—had always great hopes of him. It was the cherished wish of the elder Martyn's heart that his son should have a college education. So, in the autumn of 1795, when scarcely fifteen years old, he sent Henry to Oxford to try for a Corpus scholarship. Bearing a single letter of introduction to one of the tutors of the University, he set out alone on what was then a long and wearisome, and, for one of his weakness and susceptibility, a somewhat formidable journey. But there was in young Henry Martyn even then a remarkable sense of self-reliance—a remarkable power of self-support. In his quiet, undemonstrative way, he had an immense capacity for going through with anything that he undertook. Thus thrown upon his own resources whilst yet a boy, he acquired confidence in his own strength. Obtaining a set of rooms in Exeter College, without entering as an undergraduate, he prepared himself for the competition; but although he passed an excellent examination, and was much commended, he did not obtain the scholarship. So he went back to Truro, carrying with him his first great disappointment.

But how many of us in after life have the privilege of feeling that, by God's good providence, our first great disappointment has been our first great blessing. Thankfully did Henry Martyn acknowledge this from the very depths of his heart. ' Had I remained (at Oxford),' he wrote, ' and become a member of the University at that time, as I should have done in case of success, the profligate acquaintances I had there would have introduced me to scenes of debauchery in which I must, in all probability, from my extreme youth, have sunk for ever.' But even if he had not sunk into this deep mire, he would never have formed those associations which made him what he was : he would never, as far as we can in our weakness discern the ways of God to man, have been an apostle and a hero.

Cambridge made him what he was. After another year or two at the Truro Grammar School, Henry Martyn entered at St John's College, and took up his residence there in October, 1797. He went to the sister University with a considerably larger store of classical learning than he had carried with him to Oxford, but with small knowledge of mathematics. He had never much addicted himself to the exact sciences ; and even after this Cambridge career had been marked out for him, he spent, according to his own account, more time in shooting birds and reading amusing books than in studying algebra and geometry. It is worthy of notice for the very grotesqueness of the contrast it suggests, that the book which young Henry Martyn on the

threshold of his University life studied most intently, was
Lord Chesterfield's Letters to his Son. Whether accident
threw the book in his way, or whether the son of the Cornish miner thought that he might be wanting in some of
those exterior graces which should fit him to take his place
at the University among men of high birth and high breed-
ing, is not apparent; but assuredly the great master of
worldliness never had a more unworldly pupil. Yet was
there something that he might have learnt from this book.
He, who wrote of the Saviour of mankind, that he was

> ' The first true gentleman that ever lived,'

gave utterance to a practical truth which, I fear, has been
sometimes forgotten by his disciples. In that politeness,
which is the outward expression of charity and love, Henry
Martyn was sometimes wanting.

The commencement of his Cambridge career was not
promising. What conceivable hope is there of an undergraduate who gets up his mathematics by endeavouring to
commit the problems of Euclid to memory? But such was
Henry Martyn's commencement. How at last the power
of demonstration entered into his mind, and took such fast
hold of it, that he whose notion of the exact sciences was of
something to be learnt by rote, at last developed into the
Senior Wrangler of his year, is a chapter of the secret history of the human understanding that will never be revealed
to man. It is something altogether mysterious and surprising. All that we know distinctly about it is, that this
young Cornish undergraduate took to the study of Newton's
Principia, liking it much better than the study of the Bible;

and that in time he came to take delight in what had before been utterly distasteful to him.   Then it dawned upon him that he might take honours; and to that end he began to study with all his might.

It was a happy circumstance, and one not to be omitted from the scanticst record of Henry Martyn's life, that at Cambridge he renewed his acquaintance with his old champion of the Truro Grammar School.   The big boy who had fought his battles for him was now a steady young man, with plenty of good advice for his little friend, and what was better, a good example.   He kept Martyn out of the way of wickedness, and told him that he ought to read hard, 'not for the praise of men, but for the glory of God.'   'This seemed strange,' wrote Martyn, some time afterwards, 'but reasonable.   I resolved, therefore, to maintain this opinion thenceforth; but never designed, that I remember, that it should affect my conduct.'   But such is the inscrutable perverseness of memoir-writers, who so often give us names that we do not want to know, and conceal from us those of the persons who most interest us, that the identity of this excellent friend, who did so much to save Martyn's body at school, and to save his soul at college, is shrouded from the world in the obscurity of the letter K.

Of the undergraduate life of Henry Martyn not much has been recorded or can now be ascertained.   One noticeable incident, however, did occur, which well-nigh brought his academical career to a disastrous close.   He was constitutionally petulant and irritable; and was sometimes wrought even by little things into such a state of excitement as to be scarcely master of himself.   One day, from some cause or

other not chronicled, the vehemence of his anger rose to
such a height, that he flung a knife with all his force at a
friend who had said or done something to cross him.   In
the blindness of his fury he missed his mark, and the knife
entered the opposite wall, where it remained trembling with
the violence of the concussion.   The friend who so narrowly
escaped was Mr Cotterill, afterwards minister of St Paul's,
Sheffield.

In this painfully excitable state, it does not seem that
even the repose of the vacation, the solace of home, and the
kindness of his family, did anything to soothe his troubled
spirit.   During the long vacation of 1799, according to his
own statement, his temper was more unbearable than ever.
'The consummate selfishness and exquisite irritability of my
mind,' he wrote at a later period, 'were displayed in rage,
malice, and envy; in pride and vainglory, and contempt of
all; in the harshest language to my sisters, and even to my
father, if he happened to differ from my wish and will.   Oh,
what an example of patience and mildness was he!'   One
of his sisters, too, was a young woman of signal piety, but her
admonitions were lost upon him.   The sound of the gospel,
conveyed in the admonition of a sister, was, he said, grating
to his ears.   He promised her, however, that he would read
the Bible; but when he returned to college 'Newton engaged all his thoughts.'

And, academically, he worked to good purpose.   At the
Christmas examination of 1799, he was first of his year.
The news delighted his father; but it was the last earthly
solace that he was ever to derive from that source.   The new
year had scarcely dawned when the good old man was stricken

down and laid in his grave. The blow fell heavily on his son—more heavily for the thought that he had sometimes failed in filial duty and respect. The terrible sense of the Irremediable sorely troubled him, and in his trouble he sought a present help which Newton could not extend to his pupil —the One mighty hand and stretched-out arm which alone could lift him out of the deep waters in which he was struggling. ' As at this time,' he recorded at a later period, ' I had no taste for my usual studies, I took up my Bible, thinking that the consideration of religion was rather suitable to this solemn time.' To this he was exhorted by the good human friend who had protected him in the Truro Grammar School and guarded the first footsteps of his University career. So the beginning was made—a faltering, stumbling start in the dark—for he did not take up the Scriptures without some distaste, and he 'began with the Acts, as being the most amusing.' Little by little the light of truth streamed into the obscure tenement of his soul, until he stood in the full broad sunshine of a saving knowledge of the great scheme of redemption. At first, he seems to have been disposed to rejoice in the exceeding goodness of God in sending Christ into the world; but this time of rejoicing soon passed away. There came upon him an overwhelming sense of his own unworthiness; and it may be doubted whether from that time he ever had a day of perfect happiness and peace. His good old friend, who rejoiced as a Christian in the exceeding goodness of God, and delighted to see others happy, endeavoured to persuade him that his despondency was not right. It would seem also that his sister did the same. But Henry Martyn was determined not only to enter in at the strait

gate, but never to emerge into the broad outer-courts of cheerfulness, and serenity, and fear-expelling love.

Whilst this great change was taking place in his heart,
his brain was actively employed, mastering the exact sciences,
the study of which had now become an engrossing pursuit.
It appeared to be peculiarly his lot to illustrate by his own
personal experiences the extraordinary changes and transi-
tions to which by God's providence the human mind, both
in its moral and intellectual aspects, may be subjected.
That he who had begun the study of God's word by select-
ing for perusal the most amusing chapters of the Bible,
should in so short a time have developed into a ripe Christian, with convictions deeply rooted in the true faith, is not
more strange than that one who, under a mortifying sense
of his incapacity to understand them, had committed the
problems of Euclid to memory, should, at his final examination, have been declared the first mathematician of his year.
But so it was.   The great annual contest over, Henry Martyn found himself Senior Wrangler.*   He had gained the
highest object of academical ambition.   But it afforded him
little gratification.   It enhanced the bitterness of the regret
with which he dwelt upon the great loss that he had sustained ; and it made him more than ever suspicious of himself—fearful of stumbling into the pitfalls of human pride.
' I obtained my highest wishes,' he said, ' but was surprise.
to find that I had grasped a shadow.'

* Robert (afterwards Sir Robert) Grant, Governor of Bombay
was third Wrangler, and Charles Grant, afterwards Lord Glenelg,
was fourth.   They were sons of that 'old Charles Grant,' of whom
frequent mention is made in these volumes.

It was in the summer of this year, 1801, that Henry Martyn, having returned to Cambridge during the vacation, made the acquaintance, and soon the true heart's-friendship, of one who was ordained to exercise a remarkable influence over all the future current of his life. Among the fellows of King's College was one, whose inestimable privilege it was, during a long course of years, not only to set his mark upon the religious mind of the University, but to make his presence felt in the remotest regions of the earth. It has been said by one, with the highest authority to be heard upon such a subject,* 'If the section of the Church of England which usually bears that title ("Evangelical") be properly so distinguished, there can be no impropriety in designating as her four Evangelists, John Newton, Thomas Scott, Joseph Milner, and Henry Venn.' But it may be doubted whether the Evangelical influence of Charles Simeon was not more widely diffused than that of any one of these good men ; whether there was in his generation one who did so much for the religion which he professed and taught and illustrated by his great example. The warmth and earnestness of Mr Simeon's preaching had made a great impression on Henry Martyn's mind ; and when the time came, he rejoiced with an exceeding great joy to be admitted to Mr Simeon's college rooms, and there to enjoy the unspeakable benefits of his conversation and advice.

Then there grew up between them a warmth of affection never chilled to the last day of their lives. Mr Simeon delighted in the 'wonderful genius' of his young friend, and

* Sir James Stephen.

took the tenderest interest in the growth of his religious convictions.   To what grand ministerial purposes might not
his fine mind and the earnestness of his nature be turned
under good guidance !   Henry Martyn had determined to
devote himself to the ministry, and Mr Simeon was eager to
have him as a fellow-labourer with him in his own church.
Diligently, conscientiously, with a high sense of the responsibility of the holy office, and a profound conviction
of his own unworthiness, he prepared himself throughout
the year 1802 and the early part of 1803 for holy orders.
At this time he was a fellow of St John's, and he took
pupils ; but the employment did not much please him, and
it may be doubted whether, notwithstanding his eminent
abilities, he was well qualified for the work of tuition.
What his state of mind was at this time may be gathered
from his letters and journals which have been given to the
world : ' Feb. 2, 1803.—In a poor and lukewarm state this
morning.   Resolved to send away two of my pupils, as I
found so much of my time taken up by them of late, instead
of being devoted to reading the Scriptures.'   ' Feb. 4.—But
talk upon what I will, or with whom I will, conversation
leaves me ruffled and discomposed.   From what does this
arise ?   From a want of the sense of God's presence when
I am with others.'   A few days later he records that he is,
' through mere habit, disposed to a cynic flippancy.   Not
quite pleased with the respect and attention shown me by
my friends.'   Then, some ten days afterwards, he says :
' Found myself sarcastic—though without any particular
sensation of pride and bitterness in my heart ; ' and a little
later : ' Much harassed with evil tempers, levity, and dis-

traction of mind.'   Throughout the greater part of March
he was 'in general dejected.'

He would probably have been much worse at this time,
both in spirits and in temper, but for the good and kindly
influence of Mr Simeon, who, though not free from a certain constitutional irritability, was a man by no means of a
morose or gloomy nature.   He was wont to look rather on
the bright side of things, whilst Martyn looked ever at the
darkest.   On the 2nd of April, the latter dined with Mr
Simeon.   Mr Atkinson of Leeds was there.   After this
record, we find in Martyn's journal the significant words:
'The tender pity of our Lord towards Jerusalem, even
when he mentioned so many causes of indignation, was
pressed to my mind strongly as an example.'   It is curious
to observe how at this time a contempt for man and a fear
of man held possession of him at the same time.   On the
22nd of April, he records: 'Was ashamed to confess to
—— that I was to be Mr Simeon's curate—a despicable
fear of man, from which I vainly thought myself free.'
And again, on the 9th of May: 'On Saturday felt great
fear of man, and yet was determined to let slip no proper
occasion of speaking out.'   Then he sets down that he was
'quite fatigued with being so long with——,'   A friend
wisely suggested that this might arise rather from feelings
than from principle; on which Martyn remarks, 'And
this witness is true, for though I could perceive them to be
in the gall of bitterness, I felt little of pity.'   In the month
of June, we have these characteristic entries: 'Read Sir G.
Staunton's "Embassy to China."   I have still the spirit of
worldly men when I read worldly books.   I felt more

curiosity about the manners of this people than love and
pity towards their souls.' 'Was seized with excessive hilarity in company with H. in the afternoon, which rendered
me unfit for serious conversation. This is frequently the
case, especially after severe study either of a temporal or
spiritual kind. It was merely animal, for I would gladly
exchange it for sympathy.' 'D. has heard about a religious
young man of seventeen, who wants to come to College,
but has only £20 a year. He is very clever, and from the
perusal of some poems which he has published, I am much
interested about him. His name is H. K. White.' In
July and September there are these entries : ' Felt the passion
of envy rankle in my bosom on a certain occasion.' Sept.
22.—'Two men from Clare Hall breakfasted with me.
A fear of man, which prevented me from saying grace
before breakfast, brought me into inexpressible confusion of
conscience. Recovered a little by saying it after.' 'In a
gloomy temper, from being vainly concerned about the
appearance of my body.' 'Hezekiah's sin was vanity.
How many times have I fallen into this sin!'

It may be gathered from these passages, which might be
multiplied tenfold, that at that time Henry Martyn was in
no sense in a happy state of mind. Irritable, vain, cen-
sorious, exacting, intolerant, aggressive, he was so eager to
do his duty to God, that he often forgot his duty to his
neighbour. He forgot that without doing the last he could
not thoroughly do the first. 'For he who loveth not his
brother, whom he hath seen, how can he love God whom
he hath not seen?' If he is to be fairly judged by his
journals, he was much wanting in human love—in charity,

in kindness, and in courtesy. His indignation, rather than his compassion, was stirred by what he regarded as the depravity around him. In this respect he much differed from his master. He had learnt much from the teachings of Mr Simeon; it would have been well if had learnt as much from his example. The grand old Fellow of King's was not at all above little things, or scornful of little people. He was one who believed that

> 'The dignity of life is not impaired
> By aught that innocently satisfies
> The humbler cravings of the heart ; and he
> Is a still happier man who for the heights
> Of speculation not unfit, descends,
> And such benign affections cultivates
> Among the inferior kinds.'

But Henry Martyn did not cultivate benign affections among the inferior kinds, or if he did, his biographers have been careful to veil this side of his humanity—ignorant, perhaps, that its weakness may, rightly regarded, be its strength.

It must not, however, be forgotten that Henry Martyn at no time possessed the *mens sana in corpore sano.* Much that appears to be unlovely in his character must be attributed to constitutional infirmity. Want of cheerfulness in him was want of health. Melancholy is only a Greek rendering of black bile; and our English word choler has the same bilious origin. I have a letter now before me, to be quoted more fully hereafter, in which Martyn speaks of the dangerous 'prevalence of bile in his constitution.' It was this that jaundiced all the aspects of human life, and at one time stirred up within him such ungovernable fits of passion.   But it was his glory to wrestle manfully against these infirmities.   The picture of the conflict is before the world—and what a strange picture it is! I do not know another instance of a man at once so self-asserting and so self-denying.   There was a sort of sacrificial egotism in his nature, which had more of the sublime than the beautiful about it.   He was continually watching himself, as though he were eager to catch himself tripping; he was continually in an attitude of offence against himself even more than against others.   Within were conflicts: without were strifes.   He trode down with a remorseless heel all the flowers of this world, lest by cherishing them he should unfit himself for the world to come.   The reader of his journals, believing that they fairly represent all the varying moods of his mind, may lament that the sunshine so seldom entered that godly shrine.   He desired, above all things, to be of the number of the elect.   Yet he did not take to his heart those good words: 'Put on, therefore, as the elect of God, holy and beloved, bowels of mercies, kindness, humbleness of mind, meekness, long-suffering; forbearing one another and forgiving one another, if any man have a quarrel against any; even as Christ forgave you, so also do ye: and above all these things, put on Charity, which is the bond of perfectness; and let the peace of God rule in your hearts, to the which also ye are called in one body; and be ye thankful.'

On the 23rd of October, 1803, Henry Martyn was ordained a Deacon of the Church of England.   It had been arranged that he should assist Mr Simeon in the duties both of the Church of the Holy Trinity and in the neighbouring

parish of Lulworth; and he entered upon these duties with
a solemn sense of the responsibilities he had undertaken, and
a steadfast determination to do his work in the true spirit
of the apostles, without a fear of the reproach or the ridicule
of man. We must go back half a century or more in
imagination to appreciate the force of these last words. At
the present time, they have little special significance. But
in 1803, the University was but just beginning to tolerate
the evangelical earnestness of Mr Simeon. Only a few years
before he had been hooted and howled at, and his ministrations had been interrupted by outrages of the most
violent and indecent character. It demanded some courage
in a young man to stand forth as Mr Simeon's associate;
and Martyn at one time had been assailed by doubts and
anxieties very distressing to his carnal nature. But he
fought them down manfully, and he soon began to take
a lively pleasure in his ministerial work. He had not, however, devoted himself long to the parochial duties of the
ministry, when thoughts of a far different career began
to take shape in his mind. He had some time before
dimly discerned in the distance a hand beckoning to him to
enter upon the glorious fields of missionary adventure. The
perusal of the *Life of David Brainerd* had excited within
him a desire to go forth and do likewise. This desire was
subsequently strengthened by a sermon, in which Mr Simeon
had earnestly discoursed upon the immensity of good that
might be done by a single labourer in the vineyard—the
illustration being derived from the career which the Baptist
apostle, Dr Carey, had commenced in Bengal. This story
fired the enthusiasm of Henry Martyn. Ever intent upon

the thought of some heroic abnegation of self, he sprang up open-armed to embrace this grand idea of a missionary sacrifice. But at this time a misfortune befell him which caused him to consider whether it were not his duty to repress these inclinations and to remain in England. The little property amassed by the industry and intelligence of his father was lost to his family, and his sisters, therefore, became dependent on his exertions. To become a missionary was to become a pauper, and to lose the means of assisting others; so Henry Martyn began to think that it might not be his duty to go forth to preach the gospel to the heathen.

But from these doubts and anxieties there came deliverance from an unexpected quarter. Among the many good men with whom Mr Simeon was in affectionate correspondence were William Wilberforce and Charles Grant. Both were members of the House of Commons; and the latter was a member also of the Court of Directors of the East India Company. They were men of influence—but of influence derived only in part from their position; for they were men, also, of large intelligence, unwearying industry, and of an earnest, many-sided humanity that never rested for a moment. There could be no pleasanter history to write than that which should describe all the great schemes by which they sought to benefit the human race, and for the promotion of which, with Messrs Babington, Stephen, Henry Thornton, and sometimes Lord Teignmouth and Mr Venn, they held a little Parliament of their own, always carrying out its enactments with remarkable promptitude and vigour. To emancipate the enslaved of every kind and degree, whether from the material shackles of the slave-dealer or from the bondage of ignorance and superstition, was the main object of their endeavours. In the conversion of the natives of India to Christianity, Mr Grant, from the nature of his own personal experiences and associations, had an especial interest. Those were times when there were great impediments in the way of direct missionary action in the Company's territories in India; but the Company required chaplains to minister to their servants; and it was thought that if the English clergymen, who were sent out from time to time in this capacity, were wisely chosen, much good directly and indirectly might be done by them for the promotion of Christ's kingdom upon earth. Upon this subject, Mr Simeon and Mr Grant were continually in correspondence; for whilst the latter had the power of providing chaplaincies, the former had the means of supplying, from among the more promising young men of the University, the right persons to fill them. And among these young men who so fit as Henry Martyn? It was soon settled, therefore, that the first Indian chaplaincy at the disposal of Mr Grant should be bestowed upon Mr Simeon's curate. So Henry Martyn went up to town; visited Charles Grant at the India House; was invited by his benefactor to Clapham; and taken by him to dine with Mr Wilberforce. They saw at once that the true spirit of the Apostle was animating the delicate frame of the young minister, and they had great hope of the good to be done by his ministrations.*

* This was on the 26th of January, 1804. Mr Martyn has thus recorded the meeting : 'Walked to the India House to Mr Grant,

In' the long vacation of 1804, Martyn was again in intercourse with those 'godly senators.' On the 9th of July he called on Mr Grant, who told him that ' he had no doubt that there would be a chaplainship vacant before the end of next spring season,' and on the following day he made this characteristic entry in his journal : " July 10, 1804.—Dined with Mr Wilberforce at Palace-yard. It was very agreeable, as there was no one else. Speaking of the slave-trade, I mentioned the words, ' Shall I not visit for these things?'' and found my heart so affected that I could with difficulty refrain from tears. Went with Mr W. to the House of Commons, where I was surprised and charmed with Mr Pitt's eloquence. " Ah," thought I, " if these powers of oratory were now employed in recommending the Gospel!—but as it is, he talks with great seriousness and energy about that which is of no consequence at

who desired I would come down to Clapham. So I went with Mr Grant, and on the road he gave me much information on the state of India. . . . We arrived at Mr Wilberforce's to dinner ; in the evening we conversed about my business. To Mr Wilberforce I went into a detail of my views and the reasons that had operated on my mind. The conversation of Mr Wilberforce and Mr Grant, during the rest of the day, was edifying—what I should think right for two godly senators planning some means of bringing before Parliament propositions for bettering the moral state of the colony of Botany Bay.' It was probably this visit that supplied the original of Sir James Stephen's picture of Charles Grant ' traversing the gorse-covered common attended by a youth, who, but for the fire of his eye and the occasional energy of his bearing, might have passed for some studious and sickly competitor for medals and prize poems.' I cannot find, in Martyn's journals, any other trace of his appearance at Clapham. His visits to Mr Grant were generally paid at his residence in Bedford-square.

all." ' It is not stated that Martyn ever expressed this opinion to Mr Wilberforce, but I can very well imagine the answer that, in such a case, would have been given by the man, of whom it has been said that ' the fusion in him of religious and worldly thoughts enhanced the spirit with which he performed every duty, and the zest with which he welcomed every enjoyment.'*

On the following day, Mr Martyn started on a long coach-journey to Cornwall, where he purposed to take leave of all his beloved friends in the west of England. These were not all members of his family. There was one whom he loved with a deeper affection even than that which he bestowed upon his sisters. Near St Michael's Mount, under the roof of her widowed mother, lived Miss Lydia Grenfell, a young lady whose charms were not wholly confined to the personal piety for which she was so conspicuous. At what period Henry Martyn first imbibed the delicious poison I do not know ; but it was tingling in all his veins at the time when he paid this farewell visit to Cornwall. What were the tenderness of his feelings and the strength of his devotion towards one whom he hoped might some day be the partner of his life, may be gathered from these entries in his journal : ' July 29 (Sunday).—At St Hilary church, in the morning, my thoughts wandered from the service, and I suffered the keenest disappointment. Miss Lydia Grenfell did not come. Yet, in great pain, I blessed God for having kept her away, as she might have been a snare to me. These things would be almost incredible to another, and almost to myself, were I not taught

* Sir James Stephen's ' Essays in Ecclesiastical Biography.'

by daily experience that, whatever the world may say, or
I may think of myself, I am a poor, wretched, contemptible
worm.   Called after tea on Miss Lydia Grenfell, and
walked with her, and * * conversing on spiritual subjects.
All the rest of the evening and night I could not keep her
out of my mind.   I felt too plainly that I loved her pas-
sionately,   The direct opposition of this to my devotedness
to God, in the missionary way, excited no small tumult in
my mind. . . . . At night I continued an hour and a half
in prayer, striving against this attachment.'   On the following day he recorded that he rose in great peace, as God, by
secret influence, seemed to have caused the tempest of self-
will to subside; but at night he said, he found himself to
have backslidden a long way from the life of godliness, and
to have declined very much since his coming to Cornwall,
especially since he went to St Hilary.   It does not appear
that he saw Miss Grenfell again until the end of the following month, when he wrote in his journal (August 27):
'Walked to Marazion, with my heart more delivered
from its idolatry, and enabled to look steadily and peacefully to God.   Reading in the afternoon to Lydia alone
from Dr Watts, there happened to be among other things
a prayer on entire preference of God to the creature.   Now,
thought I, here am I in the presence of God and my idol.
So I used the prayer for myself and addressed to God, who
answered it, I think, for my love was kindled to God and
divine things, and I felt cheerfully resigned to the will of
God to forego the earthly joy, which I had just been desiring with my whole heart in heaven, but every now and
then resting on her.   Parted with Lydia, perhaps for ever

in this life. Walked to St Hilary, determining in great tumult and inward pain to be the servant of the Lord.' But, wrestle as he might against himself, he could not tear out that fair image from his heart. On the following day he wrote in his journal: ' Took leave of St Hilary; walked on, dwelling at large on the excellence of Lydia. A few faint struggles to forget her and delight in God, but they were ineffectual.' And again, next day : ' My mind taken up with Lydia. But once reasoning in this way, if God made me and wills my happiness, as I do not doubt, then he is providing for my good by separating from her.'*

With the vital question yet unspoken Martyn returned to Cambridge, his ' thoughts almost wholly occupied with Lydia, though not in spirit of departure from God.' At the University he reverted to his duties, both as a minister and a tutor, with little zest. He was expecting a summons to London to take up the Indian chaplaincy, and he was eager for any change. The ' dreary scene of college ' appeared to him ' a wilderness after the company of his dear friends in Cornwall.' But month after month passed away, and still the summons did not come. He was endeavouring, all this time, to prepare himself for Indian work by reading missionary publications and mastering the rudiments of the Hindostanee and Bengalee languages. His tuition-work was extremely distasteful to him; and with that strange, morbid obliquity of vision which prevented him ever from taking in the completeness of the Christian life at a glance, he declared that the perusal of the classical

* Wilberforce's Letters and Journals of Henry Martyn.

authors, 'in order to examine a pupil,' was a snare to him. His impatience and quickness of temper with his pupils were really errors to be grieved over ; and they are probably not exaggerated in his journal.

At the beginning of the new year, Henry Martyn went up to London and saw Mr Grant, who told him that he was certainly destined for India, though he had not yet been appointed to a chaplaincy. 'Thus it pleases God,' he wrote, 'to keep me in a certain degree unfixed, and it is but that his own wise purposes should be fulfilled in their time. I find these apparent delays very beneficial to me, as I perceive that God works in providence, as in nature, very slowly, which is a check to human rashness.' On the 12th of January he left London in very low spirits, 'partly from illness and partly from the depression of his thoughts.' On the 15th he wrote in his journal : 'I sat an hour with Mr Simeon, who much reprobated the idea of my being settled at or near Calcutta, as Mr Brown or Buchanan would want me to take their places in the College, and I should be more than half a secular man. He said he wished me to be properly a missionary, one who should be quite dead to this world and living for another.' This passage seems to require some explanation. Mr Simeon was not only a very pious man, and very conscientious in all the affairs of life, but also a very sensible one. He must have known that his young friend and assistant was expecting to be sent to India by the East India Company as a chaplain upon their establishment, and I cannot help thinking that if he coun- selled Henry Martyn to withdraw altogether from secular engagements, and to give himself up wholly to missionary work, he must have counselled him at the same time to give up the English chaplaincy.

In the first week of March, Henry Martyn visited London again, but the chaplaincy was not yet ready for him. Having completed his twenty-fourth year, he was ordained priest at St James's chapel. During this visit to the metropolis he took some lessons in Hindostanee from Mr Gilchrist, who gave him some very sensible advice, which he has thus recorded in his journal: ' March 21.—On my mentioning to Gilchrist my desire of translating some of the Scriptures with him, he advised me by all means to desist till I knew much more of the language by having resided some years in the country. He said it was the rock on which missionaries had split, that they had attempted to write and preach before they knew the language. The Lord's Prayer, he said, was now a common subject of ridicule with the people on account of the manner in which it had been translated. All these are useful hints to me.' Early in the following month he returned to Cambridge, but he was soon again in London, where, on the 24th of April, he 'found from Mr Grant that he was on that day appointed a chaplain to the East India Company, but his particular destination would depend on the Government of India.' *

* It appears that there had been, at one time, some intention of sending him out to Bengal, in attendance on Lord Cornwallis. In an unpublished letter before me, he writes to Mr Grant, saying : ' In a letter I received a few days ago from Major Sandys, he mentions something about my going out with Marquis Cornwallis ; but as he gives no reason at all for expecting such a thing, I suppose it is not worth my thinking about a moment.'

In London he made the acquaintance of those eminent
Christians Mr Cecil and Mr Newton, and he had sometimes
the privilege of occupying the pulpit of the former in the
well-known chapel in John-street, Bedford-row, the ministry of which at a later period was so long held by Mr Baptist Noel.* During this residence in the metropolis, the
emotional parts of his nature appear to have been in a state
of continual activity. He was one day elevated, another
depressed. Any trifling circumstance caused him to burst
into sudden tears. He was moved by a divine compassion
for the souls of men, to go forth to preach the Gospel in a
heathen land; but there was something ever tugging at his
heart-strings, and imploring him to remain at home. ' Shed
tears to night,' he wrote in his journal, ' at the thought of
my departure. I thought of the roaring seas which would
soon be rolling between me and all that is dear to me on
earth.' The conflict in his mind was rendered all the more
severe by the antagonistic opinions of his friends. On the
3rd of June he wrote in his journal : ' Mr Cecil said that I
should be acting like a madman if I went out unmarried.
A wife would supply by her comfort and counsel the entire
want of society, and also be a preservation both to character
and passions in such scenes. . . . If this opinion of so many
pious clergymen had come across me when I was in Cornwall, and so strongly attached to my beloved Lydia, it would
have been a conflict indeed in my heart to oppose so many

* Cecil was by no means pleased with Martyn's style of preaching, which he considered insipid and inanimate. ' Sir,' said he, ' it
is cupola-painting, not miniature, that must be the aim of a man that
harangues a multitude.'

arguments. I am not seeking an excuse for marriage . . .
but I feel my affections kindling to their wonted fond-
ness while I dwell on the circumstances of an union with
Lydia.' But only a few days afterwards another friend
offered to him a totally different opinion. 'Something fell
from Dr F.,' he recorded in his journal on the 7th of June,
'against my marriage, which struck me so forcibly, though
there was nothing particular in it, that I began to see I
should finally give up all thoughts of it. But how great
the conflict! I could not have believed it had such hold
on my affections. . . . Before this I had been writing in
tolerable tranquillity, and walked out in the enjoyment of
a resigned mind, even rejoicing for the most part in God,
and dined at Mr Cecil's, where the arguments I heard were
all in favour of the flesh, and so I was pleased; but Dr F.'s
words gave a new turn to my thoughts, and the tumult
showed me the true state of my heart. How miserable did
life appear without the hope of Lydia! Oh, how has the
discussion of the subject opened all my wounds afresh!' *

Three weeks after this he started for Portsmouth, there
to join the vessel, the *Union,* which was to convey him to
his new field of labour. It was a two days' journey for him;
and it is recorded that at the inn at which he spent the in-
termediate night, he had a fit of convulsions which greatly
alarmed the friends who accompanied him. He continued
his journey in a very depressed state, from which he was
somewhat roused by finding at Portsmouth Mr Simeon and
other friends, who had come to bid him farewell.† On the

* Journals and Letters, Wilberforce.
† Mr Sargent—his biographer—was one of the party assembled

17th, the fleet sailed from Portsmouth. 'Though it was what I had actually been looking forward to so long,' wrote Henry Martyn to Mr Simeon, 'yet the consideration of being parted for ever from my friends almost overcame me; my feelings were those of a man who should be suddenly told that every friend he had in the world was dead. It was only by prayers for them that I could be comforted; and this was indeed a refreshment to my soul, because by meeting them at the Throne of Grace I seemed to be again in their society.'

It happened that the fleet anchored off Falmouth. The ' singularity of the providence of God ' thus ' led him once more into the bosom of his friends.' He thought he had seen the last of all whom he most loved; but now an unforeseen circumstance enabled him again to renew his intercourse with the one whom he loved most of all. The temptation thus presented to him was not to be resisted. So he landed at Falmouth, made his way to Marazion, and passed some days of mingled pleasure and pain in the dear companionship of his beloved. His suit does not seem to have prospered. She had a lingering affection for another man, who appears to have deserted her; and the result of her last meeting with Henry Martyn was, that they parted without a betrothal. But he fully laid bare his heart, and did not meet with such an absolute rejection as forbade him to hope that some day the much-coveted possession might be his. The answer which the young lady gave rather evaded than met the question. It was settled that Henry Martyn should go out to India unmarried—how, at Portsmouth. He has given an interesting account of the parting.

indeed, could it be otherwise?—and that their union at some indefinite period should be left to the Almighty Providence to frustrate or to decree.*

* The entries in his journal run thus : 'July 22.—After much deliberation I determined to go to Marazion on the morrow. Went to bed with much thought about the step I was going to take, and prayed that if it was not the will of God it might be prevented. I arrived in time for breakfast, and met my beloved Lydia. In the course of the morning I walked with her, though not uninterruptedly. With much confusion I declared my affection for her, with the intention of learning whether, if I ever saw it right in India to be married, she would come out ; but she would not declare her sentiments. She said that the shortness of the arrangement was an obstacle, even if all others were removed.' '29th.—The consequence of my Marazion journey is that I am enveloped in gloom ; but past experience assures me it will be removed. . . . . Another consequence of my journey is that I love Lydia more than ever.' '31st.—Went on board this morning in extreme anguish. I could not help saying, " Lord, it is not a sinful attachment in itself, and therefore I may commune more freely with thee about it." . . . . Left England as I supposed for the last time.' The fleet, however, was detained, and Martyn went on shore again ; but he had not been long at Marazion when tidings suddenly reached him that the ship was about to sail. 'August 10.—Apprehensions about the sailing of the fleet made me dreadfully uneasy ; was with Lydia a short time before breakfast ; afterwards I read the 10th Psalm, with Horne's Commentary, to her and to her mother ; she was then just putting into my hand the 10th of Genesis to read, when a servant came in and said a horse was come for me from St Hilary, where a carriage was waiting to convey me to Falmouth. . . . . Lydia was evidently painfully affected by it. She came out, that we might be alone at taking leave, and I then told her that if it should appear to be God's will that I should be married, she must not be offended at receiving a letter from me. In the great hurry, she discovered more of my mind than she intended ; she made no objection whatever to coming out. Thinking, perhaps, I wished to make an engagement with her, she said that we had better go

In thus going on shore, Henry Martyn did as other young men would have done in like circumstances, and often with less excuse. Of course, there were the usual results. He very nearly lost his passage, and he was in dreadfully bad spirits when he returned to the ship. He soon, however, began to rally, and to recover his serenity. Off the Irish coast, he wrote to Mr Grant, saying : ' I cannot leave Europe without assuring you that I bid adieu to it with cheerfulness and joy. The prevalence of bile in my constitution, which I feel particularly oppressive in this mouth, is the only thing that damps my expectations. According to some persons in the ship, the climate in the course of a few years will render me incapable of active exertion. My anxiety does not arise from the fear of an early grave, for many good ends might be answered by such an event, but from a dread lest my present excessive languor should become listlessness and indolence in India. With the apprehension of these things in my mind, I would humbly and earnestly request your prayers for me, and beg that you would occasionally send me such plain admonitions on the subject, that I may be in no danger of being deceived by the bad example of others, or the fancied debility of my own frame. My situation on board is as agreeable as it can be in a ship. I see little reason to prefer my college room to my cabin, except that the former stands still. My sickness, however, has upon the whole been of service to me.

quite free. With this I left her, not knowing yet for what purpose I have been permitted, by an unexpected providence, to enjoy these interviews.'—*Journals and Letters. Edited by Wilberforce.*—Mr Sargent's biography is altogether cloudy upon these points.

. . . . The whole fleet is now under weigh. I therefore bid you adieu. May God bless you, my dear sir, and all your family. This is the sincere wish and earnest prayer of one who honours and loves you in the Lord.'

Another extract from this letter, which was finished on the 31st of August, is equally illustrative of Martyn's character, and of the difficulties with which he had to contend : ' Since writing the above, a few days ago, the commodore has hauled down his blue Peter, and it is now said that we are to be detained until something certain shall be known about the invasion and the combined fleets. The passengers are very dissatisfied, and the captains much more so. It would be proper to make Captain Muter some compensation, on my arrival in India, for the expense occasioned to him by this delay. He continues the same man on board as on shore. He is not, however, a truly religious man. It would be very easy for him to have service more than once on the Sunday, if he had a love for the truth. However, the want of more frequent opportunities of public instruction is supplied by my having free access to the soldiers and sailors. The regimental subalterns dislike my talking to the soldiers and giving them books, and would prevent it if they could ; but the commanding officer begs me to continue my labours among them. So I go on reading and explaining the " Pilgrim's Progress " every day to them on the orlop-deck. Those officers who oppose the truth never speak to me on the subject, but reserve their whole fire for Mackenzie, who, I rejoice to say, is always the advocate of serious piety, and is more than a match for them all. I was lately on board the *Anne,* to see Mr

Thomas. He complained much of his situation, and expressed a determination of leaving the ship if possible. The captain will never allow him to say grace at table, nor even to have service on Sunday, if he can find the least excuse. A few Sundays ago there was no service because the ship was painting. From the tyrannical behaviour of the officers and men, Mr Thomas had no doubt there would be a mutiny, which has accordingly happened. The mutineers, whose plan it was to murder the officers, were on their trial when I was aboard the last time. The boats to and from the shore do not pass near the *William Pitt,* as she lies near the mouth of the harbour; and on that account, I am sorry to say, I have not seen Cecil, though I watch for an opportunity every day. There is a Botany Bay ship lying close to us, which I have visited. There are one hundred and twenty women, and one clergyman, a convict whom I could not see. My indignation was roused at what I saw upon deck between the sailors and the women, and I warned them of the consequence of their wickedness. The men defended their conduct very coolly, and from what they said I conclude that every man in the ship has his mistress. The captain is, I find, a man of bad character. He has promised, however, to dispense some Testaments among them.' *

The voyage to India tried the courage of Henry Martyn. He was on board a troop-ship; and the troop-ship was what troop-ships commonly were sixty years ago. To preach Christ crucified to such a congregation was to bring. down much hatred and contempt upon himself—to endure

* Unpublished correspondence.

hardness of every kind.   He found it up-hill work; but he
toiled upwards manfully, never turning or looking back.
There could scarcely have been a better apprenticeship to
the business of that most unpopular evangelical ministry
to which he was speeding across the ocean; and, though
probably at no period of his life were his sufferings, bodily
and mental, greater than at this time,* there was a little
solace for him in the thought that he was not labouring
wholly in vain.   He spoke to all classes of his fellow-
passengers, freely and earnestly, about the state of their
souls and the great scheme of man's redemption.   To the
officers of the ship and to the officers of the regiment, to
the young cadets, to the soldiers and the sailors, he addressed
himself as they sat or walked on the deck.   The seed often
fell on hard, stony ground, but sometimes it was permitted
to him to hope that it was striking root and fructifying in
good soil.   The voyage was not a common-place one.
Sickness of a bad type broke out on board.   The captain
died.   As they neared the Cape of Good Hope, it became
known that the troops would be landed for active service.
The Cape was to be wrested from the Dutch.   The Fifty-

---

* He suffered greatly from sea-sickness, which was probably
rendered more than ordinarily painful and exhausting by frequent
fasts.   His board-ship journals contain such entries as the following:
'The flesh seemed very unwilling to submit to such self-denial, especially as the bodily frame, from weakness, seems scarcely able to
support it; however, I can but try.   In my walk on deck my flesh
seemed again to shrink very much from fasting and prayer.'   'Had
some thoughts of devoting this day to prayer and fasting, but was un-
decided as to the latter, whether it would be right, in the present
weak state of my body, to omit the meal of dinner.'

ninth had scarcely landed before a battle was fought.
Martyn was then on board, endeavouring to comfort the
ladies. He has himself related how ' a most tremendous fire
of artillery began behind a mountain abreast of the ships.
It seemed as if the mountain itself was torn by intestine
convulsions. The smoke arose from a lesser eminence on
the right of the hill, and, on the top of it, troops were seen
marching down the further declivity. Then came such a
long-drawn fire of musketry, that I could not conceive
anything like it. We all shuddered at considering.what a
multitude of souls must be passing into eternity. The poor
ladies were in a dreadful condition ; every peal seemed to
go through their hearts. I have just been endeavouring to
do what I could to keep up their spirits. The sound is
now retiring, and the enemy are seen retreating along the
low ground on the right towards the town.' * A few hours
afterwards he went on shore, to see what could be done
among the wounded and the dying. ' We found several,'
he wrote in a letter to Mr Simeon, ' but slightly hurt ; and
these we left for a while, after seeing their wounds dressed
by a surgeon. A little onward were three mortally wounded.
One of them, on being asked where he was struck, opened
his shirt and showed a wound in his left breast. The
blood which he was spitting showed that he had been

---

* This was on the 8th of January, 1806, when the Cape fell to
Baird and Popham. A detailed account of this important event will
be found in Theodore Hook's ' Life of Sir David Baird.' In Mr
Sargent's Memoirs, the very interesting letter describing Martyn's
visit to the field of battle is dated *Table Bay, January* 7 ; but this
would seem to be a clerical or typographical error for *January* 9.

shot through the lungs. As I spread my great-coat over him, by the surgeon's desire I spoke of the blessed Gospel, and besought him to look to Jesus Christ for salvation. . . . . . Among several others, some wounded and some dead, was Captain S., who had been shot by a rifleman. We all stopped for a while to gaze in pensive silence on his pale body, and then passed on to witness more proofs of the sin and misery of fallen man.' Leaving the battle-field, he went with the surgeon to some Duch farm-houses in the neighbourhood, which had been converted into temporary hospitals, and where, he said, the wounded presented a more ghastly spectacle than he could have conceived. 'They were ranged without and within the houses in rows, covered with gore. Indeed, it was the blood, which they had not had time to wash off, that made their appearance more dreadful than the reality, for few of their wounds were mortal.' After this, he again visited, with the surgeon, the field of battle, and saw many of the wounded enemy. Here, the surgeon having left him, he was mistaken by a Highland soldier for a Frenchman, and narrowly escaped being shot. 'As I saw that he was rather intoxicated,' wrote Martyn, 'and did not know but that he might actually fire out of mere wantonness, I sprang up towards him and told him, that if he doubted my word he might take me as a prisoner to the English camp, but that I certainly was an English clergyman. This pacified him, and he behaved with great respect.' When evening began to close in, the young minister returned to the shore, intending to regain his ship, but found that she had left her moorings and was

under weigh. 'The sea ran high,' he said, 'our men
were almost spent, and I was faint with hunger, but, after
a long struggle, we reached the Indiaman about midnight.'

Soon after this, the Dutch having capitulated, and
peace being restored, Martyn went on shore and took lodg-
ings in Cape Town.   Like most other English visitors, he
ascended Table Mountain; and he 'thought of the Christian life, what up-hill work it is.'   As he was resting on his
way down, he began to reflect with death-like despondency
on his friendless condition.   'Not that I wanted,' he said,
'any of the comforts of life, but I wanted those kind
friends, who loved me, and in whose company I used to
find such delight after my fatigues.'   He made frequent
visits to the hospitals at this time, and generally preached
on Sundays.   In the second week of February, he rejoined
the vessel, which then continued its voyage to India.   On
the 19th of April, they sighted Ceylon; and on the following Sunday Martyn preached his farewell sermon on board.
Many of his hearers ridiculed and reviled him.   'It pained
me,' he said, 'that they should give a ridiculous turn to
anything on so affecting an occasion as that of parting for
ever in this life.   But such is the unthankful office of a
minister.   Yet I desire to take the ridicule of men with
all meekness and charity, looking forward to another world
for approbation and reward.'   But India was now in sight,
and the long and painful voyage was nearly at an end.

And here something may be said about the state of the
Company's ecclesiastical establishment in India at the time
when the Reverend Henry Martyn, military chaplain, entered the Bay of Bengal.   There were then but few English

clergymen and fewer churches in India. The Protestant faith had done little to assert itself in the East. Not that the Company had been unmindful, even from the first, of their obligations to provide some sort of religious minis- trations for their servants, or that the King's Government had failed to make such provision compulsory upon them. The Directors had generally sent out chaplains on board their ships, and an Act of Parliament had been passed decreeing that the Company should 'in every garrison and superior factory' constantly maintain one minister, and should 'provide or set apart a decent and convenient place for divine service only,' and that 'all such ministers as shall be sent to reside in India, shall be obliged to learn, within one year after their arrival, the Portuguese language, and shall apply themselves to learn the native language of the country where they shall reside, the better to enable them to instruct the Gentoos that shall be the servants or slaves of the said Company or of their agents, in the Protestant religion.' But after a while a succession of various obstruct- ive circumstances, such as the rivalry of the two Com- panies and occasional contentions with the native powers, as well as the conviction that it was not the easiest thing in the world for English clergymen, fresh from home, to instruct the Gentoos in the Protestant religion, caused this Act of Parliament to become little more than a dead letter. The chaplains who went out to India did not remain there very long, or perhaps they found that there was more pro- fitable employment to be had than that of reading prayers to their countrymen and converting the Gentoos. Much depended at that time upon the personal characters of the

chief people of the settlements.   At one time we read of
the President, the Council, and the inferior servants of the
Company walking to church in orderly procession, and at
others of there being an almost total absence of religious
observances at all our settlements.   It will be presumed
that the general thrifty system of the Company with
respect to the pay of their servants was not departed from
in the case of their chaplains.   In the early part of the
seventeenth century the pay of a chaplain was £100 a
year.

It was long a standing complaint against the Company,
that although they could find money to build forts, they
could not find money to build churches.   But the charge
was scarcely a just one; for they had not any greater
predilection for forts than for churches, and the former
were generally constructed without their consent.   When
at last India witnessed the spectacle of an Anglican church,
it was to private not to public beneficence that she was
indebted for the gift.   Towards the end of the seventeenth
century, Sir George Oxenden had striven hard at Bombay
to compass the erection of a church; but he died before
the object was accomplished, and it is stated that one of
his successors in the Presidential chair thought the money
would be better employed if he applied it to his own uses.
So it happened that the first Protestant church was erected,
in the year 1681, not at Bombay but at Madras, whither
a Company's servant named Streynsham Master, who had
served under Oxenden in the former settlement, was sent
as chief of the factory.   In 1715, a church was built by
subscription in Calcutta.   In 1737, the steeple was de-

stroyed in a great hurricane, and in 1756 the entire building was demolished by Surajah Dowlah.   The settlers in
Bengal were then without a church, until a member of
the Danish mission, named Kiernander, whom Lord Clive
invited to Calcutta, built what was long afterwards known
as the Mission Church.   He had married a rich widow,
and devoted a portion of the wealth thus acquired to
Protestant Christianity.   His prosperity, however, was
short-lived.   He fell into trouble.   The church, being
private property, was seized for debt, when Charles Grant
stepped forward and bought it.   In the mean while, however, the first stone of another church had been laid in
1784, when Warren Hastings was Governor-General.   It
was completed in 1787, and is said to have been 'consecrated.'   This building, which was known as the new
church, and afterwards, in early episcopal days, as St John's
Cathedral, was the property of Government, whilst the
old church remained in the hands of trustees.   There was
not much church-going in the time of Warren Hastings.
During the administration of Lord Cornwallis and Sir John
Shore there had been some improvement in this respect, and
Lord Wellesley ever recognized the importance of an outward observance of respect for the religion of his country.
It was in his eyes a matter of policy, as an antidote to the
poison of the French Revolution.   Mr Buchanan, at the
beginning of the century, wrote that 'it became fashionable
to say that religion was a very proper thing, that no civilized state could subsist without it, and it was reckoned
much the same thing to praise the French as to praise
infidelity.'   'The awful history of the French Revolution,'

wrote the Reverend David Brown, from Calcutta, in 1805, 'prepared the minds of our countrymen to support the principles of religion and loyalty which our late Governor-General (Lord Wellesley) considered it his most sacred duty to uphold; he resolved, to use his own words, to make it be seen that the Christian religion was the religion of the State, and, therefore, at different times, he appeared in his place as chief representative of the British nation, attended to church by all the officers of Government, to give the Christian religion the most marked respect of the Governor of the country.' But it was not all statecraft in Lord Wellesley. Mr Brown believed that he promoted and encouraged religion on its own account. 'We lose in Marquis Wellesley,' he wrote in a letter to Mr Grant, now before me, 'the friend of religion and the bulwark of the public morals. I have turned over with him the Holy Scriptures, and I shall ever believe that

'——the tear
Which dropped upon his Bible was sincere.'

He has countenanced and encouraged faithful preaching, treated with kindness and favour those devoted men, Carey and his brethren, and has done much in every way for the truth, and nothing against it. Having been Lord Wellesley's almoner for seven years past, I can speak of his diffusive benevolence. . . . . I have just presented him with *Bishop Horne on the Psalms,* to be his companion on the voyage, believing it to be a work in all respects exactly suited to his Lordship's religious views, genius, and taste.' *

* Manuscript correspondence.

No man had done more to uphold the character of the English Church in India than the writer of this letter; and, in truth, it needed such support, for it had been little honoured in the persons of its representatives in the Eastern world. The chaplains who had been sent out in the latter part of the eighteenth century were, with a few exceptions, men who, if they did not disgrace their religion by their immorality, degraded it by the worldliness of their lives. The prevailing taint of cupidity was upon them as upon their brother settlers, and they grew rich like the rest. It is not uncharitable to surmise that men who, after a few years of ecclesiastical service in India, carried home with them considerable fortunes, did not derive their wealth from the legitimate gains of the ministry. It has been stated, on credible authority, that one chaplain, Mr Blanshard, after a service of little more than twenty years, carried home a fortune of £50,000; that another, Mr Johnson, after thirteen years' service, took with him from Calcutta £35,000; and that a third, Mr Owen, at the end of ten years, had amassed £25,000. At a later period, they were less successful in money-making, but scarcely more profitable as members of the Church and ministers of the Gospel. 'Our clergy, with some exceptions,' wrote Sir John Shore in 1795, 'are not very respectable characters. Their situation, indeed, is arduous, considering the general relaxation of morals, and from which a black -coat is no security.' At a later period—not long before the epoch at which I have arrived in the career of Henry Martyn—Mr Brown concluded a letter to a correspondent in England with the words, 'I might finish with giving you some account of our wicked chaplains. Out of nine (the full complement), four are grossly immoral characters, and two more have neither religion nor learning.' * Between these men and the two devoted ministers, who maintained alike by their lives and their doctrines the sanctity of the English Church, there was an indecorous feud, patent to the whole settlement. 'The doctrine of the Cross,' wrote Mr Brown, in August, 1805, 'has of late years given offence to many who formerly sat under the same ministry. Mr Limrick tried for a long time to side with evangelical principles, but by conforming to the world he lost his good impressions, and, encouraged by the virulent declamations delivered from the pulpit by Dr Stacy and Mr Shepherd, came forward at last to oppose publicly the doctrines of Grace. This induced Mr Buchanan to preach a set of discourses on the Doctrinal Articles of the Church of England, which was attended with good effect.'† But all this increased the bitterness of the majority, and, so worsted in their argumentative strife, they endeavoured to get rid at least of one of their opponents by denying his clerical authority, and threatening to prosecute him for the performance of ecclesiastical duties to which he had not been ordained. Mr Brown was only a deacon of the English Church, and his enemies affected to believe that he had not received episcopal ordination at all. One of their number, therefore, wrote to him demanding a sight of his 'letters of orders,' and another told him that 'a process of law was about to be commenced against him, which, in the first instance, would subject him to legal penalties, and ultimately

* Manuscript correspondence.   † Ibid.

to degradation, and concluded by assuring him that if he would but immediately resign, he was authorized to say that the business would be dropped.' Mr Brown laid the matter at once before Lord Wellesley, who sent, through his private secretary, a kind and encouraging letter to the faithful minister, and commended his determination to treat such threats with contemptuous silence.

Such was the state of the Company's ecclesiastical establishment in Bengal when Henry Martyn arrived at Calcutta.   Lord Wellesley had left India; Lord Cornwallis was dead; Lord Lauderdale was expected; and Sir George Barlow, a Company's civilian of high character, was invested with the powers of the Governor-General.   The mutations of the temporal Government were not a matter of much concern to Mr Martyn, any further than that one ruler might be better disposed than another to give a permissive sanction to missionary efforts, and to afford an example in his own person of piety and godly living and respect for the ordinances of religion.   As for himself, he had gone out to India to be a chaplain on the Company's establishment, for the performance of the duties of which office he was to receive a thousand a year.   He had nothing of the missionary about him except the true missionary spirit.   He was not his own master; he could not choose the place of his ministrations; he was under the orders of the Commander-in-Chief; and was answerable for all his acts to the temporal authorities, as much as if he had been a lieutenant or an assistant-surgeon.   There was much,

doubtless, in this irksome to a man of his eager and enthusiastic nature. The chains must have pressed heavily upon
one who had set David Brainerd before him as his great
exemplar, and who had longed to go forth and do likewise.
But the position had its compensations too; and chief
among them was this: that there had been no greater obstacle to the diffusion of Christianity among the heathens
than the ungodly lives which were commonly led by professing Christians. It was no small thing, then, to be
allowed to convert his own countrymen. He had gone
out to preach, not to the black man, but to the white; and
he saw plainly that if he could but touch the hearts and
reform the lives of the English settlers, he would make a
grand first step towards the propagation of the Gospel in
the East. On board the *Union* he had had some practice
in this good work; he knew how painful it was, but he
was prepared to endure hardness, and he would not shrink
from an encounter with scoffers, let them scoff ever so
bitterly at him. It is nothing now to preach evangelical
truth from a Calcutta pulpit; but the reader who is acquainted with the state of Anglo-Indian society sixty years
ago, knows that at that time it demanded no mean courage
to teach as Simeon taught at Cambridge, or Cecil in Bedford-row.*

* It should be observed, however, that Mr Simeon lived to feel
that he had erred in giving way overmuch to the vehement, denunci-
atory style in his earlier pulpit addresses. His correspondence abounds
with indications of this. Take the following: 'I am arrived at a
time of my life when my views of early habits, particularly in relation
to the ministry, are greatly changed. I see many things in a different light from what I once did, such as the beauty of order, of regu-

But he had some support from his fellow-labourers of the English Church, though not much. As the *Union* was beating up the Hooghly river to Calcutta, another vessel was beating down the river seawards, and that vessel carried Claudius Buchanan to the southern coast. This was a great loss to him; but the venerable David Brown remained to welcome the young priest; to be a father and a friend to him ; to provide him with a home, and to sustain him in all his trials. Mr Brown resided some fifteen miles from Calcutta, at a place on the opposite bank of the river, named Aldeen, not far from the settlement of Serampore, where the Baptist missionaries Carey, Marshman, and Ward lived and laboured. In the grounds attached to this Aldeen house was a deserted idol-temple, upon the margin of the river, the picturesque aspect of which, as it stands out a broad mass of purple shadow against the setting sun, has been noted by thousands of Englishmen passing to and from the great military station of Barrackpore, ignorant of the historical associations which surrounded it. This pagoda had been fitted up as a dwelling-place—one of those convenient guest-houses which, in the old days of Indian hos-

larity, and the wisdom of seeking to win souls by kindness rather than to convert them by harshness, and what I once called " fidelity." '
Again : ' It is not by coarseness of expression, or severity of manner, that we are to win souls, but by speaking the truth in love.'
And again, a third time : ' What is your object—is it to win souls ? If it be, how are you to set about it ? By exciting all manner of prejudices and driving people from the church ? How did our Lord act ? He spake the word in parables, " as many were able to hear it." How did St Paul act ? He fed the babes with milk, and not with strong meat.'

pitality, English residents delighted to have in their gardens for the reception of their friends. This building was now assigned to Henry Martyn, who took up his abode there, with an imagination inflamed by the traditions of the place. He 'felt something like superstitious dread at being in a place once inhabited as it were by devils; but yet felt disposed to be triumphantly joyful that the temple where they were worshipped was become Christ's oratory.'

What his ministerial duties were at this time, and what the hostility to which they exposed him, may be gathered from the following extract from an unpublished letter to his friend and benefactor Mr Grant, which gives a lively picture of the state of society, in its religious or irreligious aspects, at the commencement of the present century. 'The ministerial work assigned me here,' he wrote in September, 1806, 'is to preach every Sabbath evening at the Mission Church, and every third Sunday at the other. With the former I am delighted; the congregation is numerous and attentive, and, as I have heard, there are encouraging appearances of a work of grace among them. At the New Church I am as a wonder unto many. Whether it is they judge of me relatively with the other clergymen who cannot boast of much *physical* strength, or whether I have really recovered from that insipidity so much complained of at St John's chapel, by having exercised my lungs so many months on the quarter-deck, I am called the son of thunder in this place. The Sunday after my first sermon at the New Church, Dr Ward preached vehemently on the opposite side. I was not present at the time, being laid up with a bilious fever, but heard that it was against evangelical persons and things in general. After describing the rise and progress of the sect of evangelical clergymen in the Church, he proceeded to deny one by one all the leading doctrines of the Gospel. The personal abuse of me which his sermon contained gave such offence that he found it necessary to let it be read, since which many have thought better of it. After the second which I preached, Limerick attacked me. He, too, was very personal, and gravely and distinctly denied all the doctrines of the Gospel. As I knew how much carnal people would enjoy a controversy between their teachers, and so elude the force of what was intended for their consciences, I declined making the smallest allusion to what had been said. Notwithstanding this, many stay away from church, because they say *parties are running so high* among the clergymen. Jefferies unites himself with us, and has preached the pure truth; Stacey will not enter the Church till it is purified from our errors. We anxiously await the arrival of Corrie and Parson, whom we expect in the next fleet. When I can see Mr Brown supplied with coadjutors in Mr Buchanan's absence, I shall proceed to my proper work with double pleasure. I rejoice in the dispensation of God in sending me to this country more than ever. Through His mercy I enjoy excellent health, and I feel little doubt of seeing some of these poor people turning to God from idols, which hope is the health of my soul.'

Such was the outer life of Henry Martyn at this time. His inner life is revealed to us with equal distinctness. There was ever going on within him a conflict in which warm human love was contending on one side and a morbid

spiritualism on the other. He could never altogether rid
himself of the thought that the love of the creature must
be antagonistic to the love of the Creator. Mr Cecil had
told him that it was clearly his duty to marry. Mr Simeon
and other friends had been of the same opinion; and just
before he sailed finally for India, he had, it has been seen,
encouraged by the sight of the beloved object, given way
to the natural inclinations of his heart. But on his voyage
he seems to have cast out all hope, and indeed all desire,
and to have reconciled himself to the thought of a solitary
life. On his arrival in India, he 'saw no reasons at first
for supposing that marriage was desirable for a missionary;'
but after a while his 'opinions began to change,' and his
hopes began to revive, and he sat down to write a letter to
Miss Grenfell, inviting her to join him in India. No surprise can be felt by any one who reads this letter, that it
utterly failed to accomplish the desired object. ' From the
account,' he wrote, 'which Mr Simeon received of you
from Mr Thomason, he seemed in his letter to regret that
he had so strongly dissuaded me from thinking about you
at the time of my leaving England. Colonel Sandys spoke
in such terms of you, and of the advantages to result from
your presence in this country, that Mr B[rown] became
very earnest for me to endeavour to prevail upon you.
Your letter to me perfectly delighted him, and induced
him to say that you would be the greatest aid to the Mission I could possibly meet with. I knew my own heart
too well not to be distrustful of it, especially as my affections were again awakened, and accordingly all my labours
and prayers have been directed to check their influence,

that I might see clearly the path of duty. Though I dare
not say that I am under no bias, yet from every view of
the subject I have been able to take, after balancing the
advantages and disadvantages that may ensue to the cause
in which I am engaged, always in prayer for God's direction, my reason is fully convinced of the expediency, I had
almost said the necessity, of having you with me. It is
possible that my reason may still be obscured by passion;
let it suffice, however, to say that now with a safe conscience and the enjoyment of the Divine presence I calmly
and deliberately make the proposal to you.' Perhaps a
little less calmness and deliberation, a little less reason and
a little more love, a little less talk about the advice of his
friends and a little more about his own longing desires,
might have been more successful in the pleading of his
cause. Even the best of women do not like to be reasoned
over and weighed in the scales after this fashion.

The letter to Miss Grenfell, which I have quoted above,
was written on the 30th of July, 1806. At what date it
reached Cornwall is not quite clear; but Miss Grenfell
replied to it on the 5th of March, and it would seem that
in April the subject of it was still under discussion at Marazion, where Mr Simeon visited the Grenfells, and took an
opportunity to talk over 'Mr Martyn's affair' with the
young lady. He found her not much, and her mother not
at all, disposed to favour the proposal for her departure to
India. All the young lady's arguments might have been
summed up in the one cardinal objection, that she did not
love Martyn well enough. Formally, a sort of promise was
given that, if the mother withdrew her objections, the

daughter would go out to India; but Miss Grenfell made this conditional promise to Mr Simeon, knowing that the conditions would never be fulfilled.* The letter which she wrote to Mr Martyn was an unqualified refusal.

It cut him to the heart. He had been endeavouring to persuade himself that it would be better for him to remain

* Mr Simeon's own account of the affair runs thus: 'With her mother's leave Miss Grenfell accompanied us to Colonel Sandys', when I had much conversation with her about Mr Martyn's affair. She stated to me all the obstacles to his proposals : first, her health ; second, the indelicacy of her going out alone to India on such an errand ; third, her former engagement with another person, which had, indeed, been broken off, and he had actually gone up to London two years ago to be married to another woman, but as he was still unmarried, it seemed an obstacle in her mind ; fourth, the certainty that her mother would never consent to it. On these points, I observed that I thought that the last was the only one that was insurmountable ; for that, first, India often agreed best with persons of a delicate constitution, e. g. Mr Martyn himself and Mr Brown. Second, it is common for ladies to go out thither without any previous connection ; how much more, therefore, might one go out with a connection already formed. Were this the only difficulty, I engaged, with the help of Mr Grant and Mr Parry, that she should go under such protection as should obviate all difficulties on this head. Third, the step taken by the other person had set her at perfect liberty. Fourth, the consent of her mother was indispensable ; and that as that appeared impossible, the matter might be committed to God, in this way : if her mother, of her own accord, should express regret that the connection had been prevented from an idea of her being irreconcilably averse to it, and that she would not stand in the way of her daughter's wishes, this should be considered a direction from God in answer to her prayers, and I should instantly be apprized of it by her, in order to communicate it to Mr Martyn. In this she perfectly agreed. I told her, however, that I would mention nothing of this to Mr Martyn, because it would only tend to keep him in painful suspense.'

single—that living in a state of continual self-denial and mortification, he would be better able to fulfil his duty to his God. But the passions of humanity were not to be preached down in this way; and when the day of trial came, he was as little able to withstand the shock as any worldling of six-and-twenty. On the 24th of October the letter arrived—'An unhappy day,' he wrote in his journal. 'Received at last a letter from Lydia, in which she refuses to come, because her mother will not consent to it. Grief and disappointment threw my soul into confusion at first; but gradually, as my disorder subsided, my eyes were opened, and reason resumed its office. I could not but agree with her that it would not be for the glory of God, nor could we expect His blessing, if she acted in disobedience to her mother. As she has said, " They that walk in crooked paths shall not find peace ;" and if she were to come with an uneasy conscience, what happiness could either of us expect ?' On the same day he sat down and wrote to her a long letter, only a portion of which can be given here : ' Alas ! my rebellious heart,' he wrote, after saying that he did not still surrender all hope, ' what a tempest agitates me ! I knew not that I had made so little progress in a spirit of resignation to the Divine will. I am in my chastisement like the bullock unaccustomed to the yoke, like a wild bull in the net, full of the fury of the Lord, the rebuke of my God. The death of my late most beloved sister almost broke my heart; but I hoped it had softened me, and made me willing to suffer. But now my heart is as though destitute of the grace of God, full of misanthropic disgust with the world, sometimes feeling resentment against yourself and

Emma, and Mr Simeon—and, in short, all whom I love
and honour most—sometimes in pride and anger resolving
to write neither to you nor to any one else again. These
are the motions of sin. My love and my better reason
draw me to you again.'

This letter was written from Dinapore, where Martyn
was then stationed.* He was very busy with the translation
of the Scriptures, and in the season of his disappointment
he fell back upon his work as a stimulant and a solace. All
things, he knew, were working together for good, and this
affliction might yet be a blessing to himself and others.
In making the word of God acceptable to heathen and
Mahomedan races, surely he was doing grand missionary
work, though he might sit all day in his bungalow with
his books and papers before him. The entries which he
made in his journal, and the letters which he wrote to his
friends in the following years (1807 to 1809), show how
he was employed. He was continually toiling ; continually
stumbling ; now hoping that he had really done something ;
now finding, to his bitter disappointment, that his translations
were inaccurate, and that he must spend more time in
correcting them than it would take to commence the work
de novo again. As he became better acquainted with the
languages, he began to make a small commencement of
preaching to the natives ;† and he taught in some schools,

---

* Mr Martyn was appointed military chaplain at Dinapore on the
14th of September, 1806. He left Aldeen on the 15th of October,
and reached Dinapore on the 26th of November.

† Henry Martyn records in his journal the progress which he
made in the languages under his native teachers, and sometimes the

so cautiously that he used an account of one of the Avatars
of Vishnu as a text-book, solacing himself with the thought
that it could do no harm, as his pupils could not understand
a word of it.

But these were his voluntary labours. His appointed
duties were of another kind. He was receiving a salary of
a thousand a year as one of the Company's military chaplains.
In this capacity he did his work with conscientious laboriousness; but he does not seem to have regarded it as anything more than a necessary and inconvenient appendage
to the more important functions which he believed had
been delegated to him by God. There was no church at
Dinapore; but he performed the service in a building
devoted to secular purposes, and he preached to such con-
gregations as the heat would allow to attend his ministrations.
He said that there were four hundred soldiers and forty-five

conversations which he held with them. The following appears under
date January 8, 1807 : ' Pundit was telling me to-day, that there
was a prophecy in their books that the English should remain one
hundred years in India, and that forty years were now elapsed of that
period ; that there should be a great change, and that they (the
English) should be driven out by a King's son, who should then be
born. Telling this to Moonshee, he said that about the same time
the Mussulmans expected some great events, such as the coming of
Dujjel, and the spread of Islamism over the earth. The singular
coincidence of the period of the accomplishment of these things, with
the time at which, according to some, the millennium will begin, struck
me very much, and kept that glorious day before my mind all the
day.' This is curious, but there is obviously something wrong in the
chronology. The English had, at that time, been masters of Bengal
not forty, but fifty years ; and the coincidence of which Martyn speaks
really did not exist, the date of the maturity of one prophecy being
1857, the date of the other, 1867.

officers at the station.* The society was by no means congenial to him. He was a plain speaker, much as it pained
him to speak plainly. He looked upon what he regarded
as the duty of vehemently reprobating worldliness of every
kind as one of his especial crosses. He never seems to have
thought that he might have done more good for the souls
of his brethren if he had spoken more mildly to their ears
and more persuasively to their understandings; and yet he
every now and then reproaches himself for conforming too
much to the ways of the world, and giving way to what he
called 'levity' in society. His friend Mr Corrie,† who had
followed him, after a little space, to India, did much more
good than Henry Martyn, because he was more tender and
genial in his ministrations. Corrie seems to have read the
Bible right through; but a mist seems to have gathered
before Martyn's eyes when he approached the most loving
passages of the sacred book.

But in all this there was one consistent stream of the
great heroism of self-abnegation flowing purely, though
disastrously, through his life. Looking upon happiness as
a crime, if he made a spectacle unpleasing to his Maker, he
tortured himself most painfully. Even the duties imposed
upon him by his profession as a military chaplain, such as
attending levées or social gatherings of the officers, he
regarded as offences against God. If they were so, he should
have given up his chaplaincy and his thousand a year, and
have gone into the villages to preach the Gospel of salvation.

* This number was greatly increased afterwards by the arrival of
the Sixty-seventh Regiment.
† The Reverend Daniel—afterwards Bishop—Corrie.

If he could not—I will not say serve God and Mammon at the same time, but—render unto Cæsar the things which are Cæsar's, and unto God the things which are God's, he should have thrown up Cæsar's commission, and freed himself from what he conceived to be the bondage of his soul.

In April, 1809, under orders from the higher authorities, Martyn prepared to betake himself from Dinapore to Cawnpore. The hot winds were blowing like the blasts of a furnace, but with characteristic disregard of his creature comforts, he put himself in a palanquin, wanting all the appliances that could mitigate the painfulness of such a journey, and even scantily provided .with necessary food. The marvel is that it did not kill him outright. He arrived in a state of pitiable weakness, and fainted as soon as he was removed from the palanquin. But in Captain Sherwood and his accomplished wife he had good and hospitable friends, who opened their house to him, and by their affectionate ministrations restored him to such little health as he was ever likely to enjoy in the world; and he was soon again at his work. 'Nothing has occurred this last year,' he wrote in 1810, 'but my removal to Cawnpore, and the commencement of my ministry, as I hope it may be called, among the Gentiles. This, with my endeavours to instruct the servants, has been blessed by the Lord to the improvement of my temper and behaviour towards them.' His ministry among the Gentiles was little more than an occasional address, from the verandah of his house, to a crowd of beggars, who were attracted by the alms that he gave, not by the Gospel that he preached. But he thought that some of the seed he scattered might fall upon good ground.

His professional life at Cawnpore very much resembled
that which he had passed at the Dinapore station. A church
was in course of erection, but, pending its completion, it
was the duty of the military chaplain to perform the service
in a barrack-room, at the General's house, or in the open
air, according to orders.   It was wearisome and dishearten-
ing work, for he made little progress, and there were few who ,
listened to the Word.*   Of the manner in which his week-
days were spent at this time, he has himself given an account in a letter to Lydia Grenfell, who had never ceased
to hold a cherished place in his heart.   'We all live here,'
he wrote, 'in bungalows or thatched houses, on a piece of
enclosed ground.   Next to mine is the church, not yet
opened for public worship, but which we make use of at
night with the men of the Fifty-third.   Corrie lives with
me, and Miss Corrie with the Sherwoods.   We usually rise
at daybreak and breakfast at six.   Immediately after breakfast we pray together, after which I translate into Arabic
with Sabat, who lives in a small bungalow on my ground.
We dine at twelve, and sit recruiting ourselves with talking
a little about dear friends in England.   In the afternoon, I
translate with Mirza Fitrut into Hindostanee, and Corrie
employs himself in teaching some native Christian boys,

* On the 18th of February, 1810, he wrote in his journal : 'My
birthday ; to-day I completed my twenty-ninth year.   How much
had David Brainerd done at this time of life !   I once used to flatter
myself that, when entering my thirtieth year, I might have the happiness of seeing an Indian congregation of saints won to the Gospel
through my preaching.   Alas ! how far is this from being the case ;
scarcely even a European can I fix upon as having been awakened
under my ministry since coming here.'

whom he is educating with great care, in hopes of their
being fit for the office of catechist.   I have also a school
on my premises for natives, but it is not well attended.
There are not above sixteen Hindoo boys in it at present ;
half of them read the Book of Genesis.   At sunset, we ride
or drive, and then meet at the church, where we often
raise the song of praise with as much joy, through the grace
and presence of our Lord, as you do in England.   Thus we
go on.'

   But a change was now about to take place in his way of
life.   His friends had for some time painfully observed that
as he grew in grace, he had waxed more and more feeble
in his physical health.   The ravages of his old family disorder were visible upon a form which had never indicated
strength, and there were those who thought that the approach of death was discernible ' in the fine fading of his
delicate face.'   If Martyn did not see this, he felt it ; and
on the 19th of April, 1810, he wrote to Lydia Grenfell
this touching account of himself : ' I begin my correspondence with my beloved Lydia, not without a fear of its being
soon to end.   Shall I venture to tell you that our family
complaint has again made its appearance in me, with more
unpleasant symptoms than it has ever yet done ?   However,
God, who two years ago redeemed my life from destruction,
may again, for his Church's sake, interpose for my deliverance.   Though, alas!   what am I, that my place should not
instantly be supplied with far more efficient instruments ?
The symptoms I mentioned are chiefly a pain in the chest,
occasioned, I suppose, by over-exertion the two last Sundays, and incapacitating me at present from all public duty,

and even from conversation. You were mistaken in supposing that my former illness originated from study. Study
never makes me ill—scarcely ever fatigues me : but my
lungs—death is seated there ; it is speaking that kills me.
May it give others life ! " Death worketh in us, but life in
you." Nature intended me, as I should judge from the
structure of my frame, for chamber counsel, not for a
pleader at the bar. But the call of Jesus Christ bids me
call aloud. I spare not. As his minister, I am a debtor both
to the Greek and to the Barbarian. How can I be silent
when I have both ever before me, and my debt not paid ? '

From this time a beautiful resignation appears to have
descended upon him, and he grew outwardly more cheerful
in his manners. Most true is it that ' one fire burns out
another's burning.' A deep-seated affection of the lungs
was destroying Henry Martyn, and the biliary disorder
which had rendered him so irritable and so desponding,
seems to have been burnt out by the tubercular disease.
But although sober biography is bound to take account of
this, we may believe that this increase of cheerfulness was
in part the growth of a sustaining sense of his good work,
and the comforting reflection that it would soon be said to
him—' Well done, thou good and faithful servant, enter
into thy rest.' He had not altogether given up the thought
of doing real missionary work in the apostolic or sent-forth
sense of the word. But he wrote to a friend, saying : ' To
the hardships of missionaries we are strangers ; yet not
averse, I trust, to encounter them when we are called. My
work at present is evidently to translate ; hereafter I may
itinerate.'

And indeed the time had come for him to ' itinerate ; ' but not in the sense here recognized. It was plain that to remain at Cawnpore would be to die at his post. So, after much reflection and much prayer, he determined that, with the permission of the temporal authorities and with the approval of the recognized ' Patriarch ' of the English Church, David Brown, he would fulfil his long-cherished project of journeying to Persia, there to improve his knowledge of its language, to obtain assistance in the translation of the Scriptures, and to dispute with the Moollahs. So he went down to Calcutta, and, ' after consulting with the Patriarch,' saw the Governor-General, Lord Minto, and the Adjutant-General of the army, and obtained their sanction to his departure on sick leave. ' So it strikes me,' he said in a letter to Mr Corrie, ' a way is opened and an intimation given of the will of God : may my journey be for the prosperity of Zion. My ship has dropped down (the river).'

He was very weak when he reached Calcutta ; and the dear friends, with whom he now again took sweet counsel, after a separation of years, saw plainly that he was fading away. Among these friends was one companion of former years, with whom it was a delight to talk of old Cambridge days and Mr Simeon. This was the Reverend Thomas Thomason, now also a chaplain in the Company's service— one of the best and most lovable of men. When he saw Martyn's wasted frame and his sunken cheeks, he was moved with a great compassion, and he felt that the days of his friend were numbered. Writing to Mr Simeon at this time, he said : ' He (Martyn) is on his way to Arabia, where he is going in pursuit of health and knowledge. You know his genius, and what gigantic strides he takes in everything. He has some great plan in his mind, of which I am no competent judge, but as far as I do understand it, the object is far too grand for one short life, and much beyond his feeble and exhausted frame. Feeble it is, indeed! How fallen and changed. His complaint lies in his lungs, and appears to be an incipient consumption. . . . In all other respects he is exactly the same as he was. He shines in all the dignity of love, and seems to carry about him such a heavenly majesty as impresses the mind beyond description. But, if he talks much, though in a low voice, he sinks, and you are reminded of his very "dust and ashes." '

Yet, for all this, he could not be persuaded to spare himself. He wanted rest, and a total cessation, at all events, from all physical labour; but he over-exerted and strained himself by preaching every Sunday, during his stay in Calcutta, in a spacious church, with scarcely voice enough to fill an ordinary room.

I have already narrated, in a previous Memoir, how Henry Martyn sailed to Bombay with Mountstuart Elphinstone as his fellow-passenger. As on the voyage from England, he suffered greatly from sea-sickness as the vessel tossed down the Bay of Bengal.* Then sitting very help-

* See the Journals and Correspondence, edited by Bishop Wilberforce. ' January 10 to 12.—Sea-sickness incapacitated me for everything; was, as usual in such cases, very low-spirited; felt perfectly weary of travelling,' &c. ' 13th.—Was too sick to have divine service, but at night, in cabin, read to and prayed with the captain and passengers.' ' 14th to 17th.—Generally so sick that I could do nothing but sit on the poop. Mr E[lphinstone] kindly entertained me with information about India, with the politics of which he has such

less and miserable on the poop, he derived infinite solace from the instructive conversation of his companion. It was a relief to him, when they reached Ceylon, to be permitted to go on shore. ' At length in the neighbourhood of Ceylon,' he wrote, ' we found smooth water, and came to anchor off Colombo, the principal station in the island. The captain having proposed to his passengers that they should go on shore and refresh themselves with a walk in the cinnamon gardens, Mr E[lphinstone] and myself availed ourselves of the offer, and went off to inhale the cinnamon breeze. The walk was delightful.' On the following day they set sail again and doubled Cape Cormorin. Then as Martyn looked out on the sea-coast and on the churches, which here and there were visible from the deck of the ship, he thought of the coast of Cornwall and of his beloved Lydia, and he sat down in his cabin and wrote to her, saying : ' Was it these maritime situations that recalled to my mind Perran church, or that my thoughts wander too often on the beach to the east of Truro ? You do not tell me whether you ever walk there and imagine the billows that break at your feet to have made their way from India. But why should I wish to know ? Had I observed silence on that day and thenceforward, I should have spared you much trouble and myself much pain. Yet I am far from regret-

opportunities of making himself acquainted. The Afghans, to whom he went as ambassador to negotiate a treaty of alliance, in case of invasion, against the French, possess a tract of country considerably larger than Great Britain, using the Persian and Pushtoo languages. Mr E. has been with Holkar and Scindiah a good deal. Holkar he describes as a little spitfire,' &c. &c.

---

ting that I spoke, since I am persuaded that all things will
work together for good.' And then, as though he were
angry with himself for the expression of so much warmtn
of feeling, he fell back into the old strain of self-deprecia-
tion, and cooled his ardour by every possible kind of dis-
couragement. 'As for what we should be together,' he
added, ' I judge of it from our friends. Are they quite beyond the vexations of common life ? I think not ; still I
do not say that it is a question whether they gained or lost
by marrying. Their affections will live when ours (I should
rather say mine) are dead. Perhaps it may be the effect of
celibacy, but I certainly begin to feel a wonderful indifference to all but myself.'

On the 7th of February they reached Goa, and on the
following day paid that visit to the tomb of Francis Xavier
which has been narrated at the commencement of this Memoir. On the 18th they anchored at Bombay. On the
following day Martyn went on shore, visited Governor
Duncan, and was lodged at Government House. In Bombay he became acquainted with Sir James Mackintosh and
Sir John Malcolm. He appears to have made a different
impression on the minds of these two men ; which may
partly be accounted for by the characteristic variableness of
Martyn's own temperament, and partly by a consideration
of the different temperaments of the lawyer and the soldier.
At all events, Martyn appeared to Malcolm an exceedingly
cheerful person. Of the latter, it is most true that 'a mer-
rier man, within the limits of becoming mirth,' was seldom
seen ; and it would have been difficult to be otherwise than
cheerful under the genial influence of his sunny nature.

Certain at least it is, that he gave the young priest a letter of introduction to the British Minister in Persia (Sir Gore Ouseley), in which he said that Martyn was ' altogether a very learned and cheerful man, but a great enthusiast in his holy calling.' ' I am satisfied,' he added, ' that if you ever see him, you will be pleased with him.   He will give you grace before and after dinner, and admonish such of your party as take the Lord's name in vain ; but his good sense and great learning will delight you, whilst his constant cheerfulness will add to the hilarity of your party.'   Although most men were cheerful in Malcolm's presence, I am inclined to think that causes already stated had done much to increase the habitual cheerfulness of Martyn's temperament, although Mackintosh did speak of him as the saint from Calcutta, whose excessive meekness ' gave a disagreeable impression of effort to conceal the passions of human nature.'

So, cheerfully, he went about his work, and passed from India to the Persian Gulf.   From Muscat he wrote, on the 23rd of April, 1811 : ' I left India on Lady-day, looked at Persia on Easter Sunday, and seven days after found myself in Arabia Felix.   In a small cove, surrounded by bare rocks, heated through, out of the reach of air as well as wind, lies the good ship *Benares,* in the great cabin of which, stretched on a couch, lie I.   But though weak, I am well—relaxed, but not disordered.   Praise to His grace, who fulfils to me a promise, which I have scarcely a right to claim—" I am with thee, and will keep thee in all places whither thou goest." '

On the 30th of May, having obtained the means of
attiring himself in full Persian costume, and having suffered
his beard and moustache to grow, he started for Shiraz.*
The heat was intolerable, and the hardships of the journey
almost killed him. They started in the coolness of the
night, but day had scarcely broken before the summer heats
began to threaten them. 'At sunrise,' he wrote in his
journal, 'we came to our ground at Ahmedee, six parasangs,
and pitched our little tent under a tree; it was the only
shelter we could get. At first the heat was not greater than
we had felt in India, but it soon became so intense as to be
quite alarming. When the thermometer was above 112
degs., fever heat, I began to lose my strength fast; at last
it became quite intolerable. I wrapped myself up in a
blanket and all the warm covering I could get, to defend
myself from the external air; by which means the moisture
was kept a little longer upon the body, and not so speedily

---

* The following is the description of his costume, which he has
recorded in his journal : 'On the 30th of May our Persian dresses
were ready, and we set out for Shiraz. The Persian dress consists of,
first, stockings and shoes in one ; next, a pair of large blue trousers,
or else a pair of huge red boots ; then the shirt ; then the tunic ; and
above it the coat, both of chintz, and a great-coat. I have here
described my own dress, most of which I have on at this moment.
On the head is worn an enormous cone, made of the skin of the black
Tartar sheep, with the wool on. If to this description of my dress I
add that my beard and moustaches have been suffered to vegetate
undisturbed ever since I left India—that I am sitting on a Persian
carpet in a room without tables or chairs—and that I bury my hand
in the pillau without waiting for spoon or plate, you will give me
credit for being already an accomplished Oriental.'—*Sargent's Life
of Martyn.*

evaporated as when the skin was exposed. One of my companions followed my example, and found the benefit of it. But the thermometer still rising, and the moisture of the body being quite exhausted, I grew restless, and thought I should have lost my senses. The thermometer at last stood at 126 deg.; in this state I composed myself, and concluded that, though I might hold out a day or two, death was inevitable. Captain ——, who sat it out, continued to tell the hour and height of the thermometer; and with what pleasure did we hear of its sinking to 120 deg., 118 deg., &c. At last the fierce sun retired, and I crept out, more dead than alive. It was then a difficulty how I could proceed on my journey; for, besides the immediate effects of the heat, I had no opportunity of making up for the last night's want of sleep, and had eaten nothing. However, while they were loading the mules, I got an hour's sleep, and set out, the muleteer leading my horse, and Zachariah, my servant, an Armenian of Ispahan, doing all in his power to encourage me. The cool air of the night restored me wonderfully, so that I arrived at our next munzil with no other derangement than that occasioned by want of sleep. Expecting another such day as the former, we began to make preparation the instant we arrived on the ground. I got a tattie made of the branches of the date-tree, and a Persian peasant to water it; by this means the thermometer did not rise higher than 114 deg. But what completely secured me from heat was a large wet towel, which I wrapped round my head and body, muffling up the lower part in clothes. How could I but be grateful to a gracious Providence for giving me so simple a defence against what, I am persuaded, would have destroyed my life that day. We took care not to go without nourishment as we had done ; the neighbouring village supplied us with curds and milk.'

On the 9th of June he reached his destination, and a few days afterwards he was in the midst of theological discussions with the Moollahs and other learned people of the place. He appears at this time to have enjoyed unusually good health and good spirits. He wrote cheerfully to his friends, with less than the wonted amount of self-abasement in his letters. His thoughts often reverted, not painfully, to the Cornish coast and his 'dearest Lydia.' In one letter, written in June, he says : ' How continually I think of you, and, indeed, converse with you, it is impossible to say. But on the Lord's-day in particular I find you much in my thoughts. . . . On that day I indulge myself with a view of the past, and look over again those happy days when, in company with those I loved, I went up to the house of God with a voice of praise. How, then, should I fail to remember her, who, of all that are dear to me, is the dearest ? It is true that I cannot look back to many days, nor even many hours, passed with you. Would they had been more ! but we have become more acquainted with each other. . . . It was a momentary interview, but the love is lasting—everlasting. . . . Let me here say, with praise to our evergracious heavenly Father, that I am in perfect health ; of my spirits I cannot say much, I fancy they would be better were the beloved Persis by my side. This name, which I once gave you, occurs to me this moment, I suppose, because I am in Persia, intrenched in one of its valleys, separated from Indian friends by chains of mountains and a roaring sea, among a people depraved beyond all belief, in the power of a tyrant guilty of every species of atrocity. Imagine a pale person seated on a Persian carpet, in a room without a table or chair, with a pair of formidable moustaches and habited as a Persian, and you see me.'

'Here I expect to remain six months,' he wrote, a few days afterwards, to the same sweet friend. 'The reason is this : I found, on my arrival here, that our attempts at Persian translation in India were good for nothing ; at the same time, they proposed, with my assistance, to make a new translation. It was an offer I could not refuse, as they speak purest Persian.' But he did not make much progress, and he wrote on the 12th of September to his friend Daniel Corrie : 'I do not find myself improving in Persian ; indeed, I take no pains to speak it well, not perceiving it to be much consequence. India is the land where we can act at present with most effect. It is true that the Persians are more susceptible, but the terrors of an inquisition are always hanging over them. I can now conceive no greater happiness than to be settled for life in India, superintending national schools, as we did at Patna and Chunar. To preach so as to be readily understood by the poor, is a difficulty that appears to me almost insuperable.' To the same old and beloved friend he wrote again in December, saying that he had excited some Mahomedan indignation, and that he had been stoned. 'They continued,' he said, 'throwing stones at me every day, till happening one day to tell Jaffier Ali Khan, my host, how one as big as my fist had hit me in the back, he wrote to the governor, who sent an order to all the gates, that if any one insulted me he should be

bastinadoed ; and the next day came himself in state to pay
me a visit. These measures have had the desired effect ;
they now call me the Feringhee Nabob, and very civilly
offer me the Calean ; but indeed the Persian commonalty are
very brutes. The Soofies declare themselves unable to account for the fierceness of their countrymen, except it be
from the influence of Islam.'

All through the early months of the year 1812 he went
on in the same way, now translating, now studying, now
disputing with the Moollahs, now taking sweet counsel with
his distant friends. His spirits, at this time, seem to have
been sensibly affected by protracted isolation from all his
Christian friends, and he began to long for India and companionship again. 'This is my birthday,' he wrote in his
journal on the 18th of February, 'on which I complete my
thirty-first year. The Persian New Testament has been
begun, and I may say finished in it, as only the last eight
chapters of the Revelation remain. Such a painful year I
never passed, owing to the privations I have been called to
on the one hand, and the spectacle before me of human
depravity on the other. But I hope I have not come to
this seat of Satan in vain. The word of God has found its
way into Persia, and it is not in Satan's power to oppose its
progress, if the Lord hath sent it.' A fortnight afterwards
the work was completed, and he thanked God from the
bottom of his heart.

In the second week of May he left Shiraz in company
with a cafilah.* He was eager to present his translation

* Or caravan. Mr Sargent says he started on the 24th of May,
which is obviously a mistake. His journal shows that he was some
way on his journey by that time.

of the Bible to the King of Persia, and he strove mightily
to this end; but official obstructions in the first instance, and
afterwards utter prostration from illness, baffled his endeavours, and he was obliged to content himself with presenting
it to the Ambassador.   He had enjoyed more than his accustomed amount of health and strength at Shiraz, but the
fatigues of the journey and the alternations of heat and
cold, seem to have affected him severely, and fever and
ague of the worst type seized upon his frail body.   For
some time he lay prostrate and delirious, hovering between
life and death; in intervals of sanity thinking of his beloved
friends in England, and believing that there was little hope
of ever seeing them again.   On the 9th of July, he wrote
from Tabriz: ' My fever never ceased to rage till the 21st,
during all which time every effort was made to subdue it,
till I had lost all my strength, and almost all my reason.
They now administer bark, and it may please God to bless
the tonics, but I seem too far gone; I can only say, " having
a desire to depart and be with Christ, which is far better." '
Three days after, he wrote to Lydia Grenfell: ' I have applied for leave to come on furlough to England.   Perhaps
you will be gratified by this intelligence; but oh, my dear
Lydia, I must faithfully tell you that the probability of my
reaching England alive is but small.'   All through the remainder of that month of July he lay struggling with death,
but early in August he rallied a little, and at the end of the
first week he wrote to Mr Simeon: ' Ever since I wrote,
about a month, I believe, I have been lying upon the bed
of sickness.   For twenty days or more the fever raged with
great violence, and for a long time every species of medicine was used in vain.   After I had given up every hope of

recovery, it pleased God to abate the fever, but incessant headaches succeeded, which allowed me no rest day or night. I was reduced still lower, and am now a mere skeleton; but as they are now less frequent, I suppose it to be the will of God that I should be raised up to life again. I am now sitting in my chair, and wrote the will with a strong hand; but, as you see, I cannot write so now.'

On the 2nd of September, all things being ready, Henry Martyn set out on his long journey of thirteen hundred miles to England, 'carrying letters from Sir Gore Ouseley for the Governors of Erivan, Kars, and Erzeroum, and the Ambassador at Constantinople; from Mr Morier for his father there, and from Cajoo Aratoon, Sir Gore's agent, for the Patriarch, and Bishop Nestus at Echmiazin, and near three hundred tomauns in money.' On the morning of the 11th of September he arrived at Erivan. From Erivan he went on to Echmiazin, where he was most kindly received by the Patriarch and the Bishops, and after a few pleasant days passed in the great Armenian monastery—the last glimpse of pleasure ever permitted to him in this world —he pursued his journey, crossed the Turkish frontier, and on the 21st of September rode into Kars. On the following day, he left this now celebrated place with a Tartar guide, and made his way to Erzeroum, where he halted for three or four days, and then again pressed forward. But there were now symptoms of a return of his malady; he grew weaker and weaker as he went on. The fatigues of the journey were more than he could bear. Riding on rough horses over rough roads, with a half-savage guide who had little compassion for him, he was dragged from place

to place, often through heavy rain, with little rest allowed
to him, until his small remaining strength succumbed to
the hardships and privations of the journey. He still, however, continued to make some entries in his journal, and on
the 2nd of October he wrote: 'Some hours before day, I
sent to tell the Tartar I was ready, but Hassan Aga was for
once riveted to his bed. However, at eight, having got
strong horses, he set off at a great rate, and over the level
ground he made us gallop as fast as the horses would go to
Chifflick, where we arrived at sunset. I was lodged, at my
request, in the stables of the post-house, not liking the scru-
tinizing impudence of the fellows who frequent the coffee-
room. As soon as it began to grow a little cold, the ague
came on and then the fever; after which I had a sleep,
which let me know too plainly the disorder of my frame.
In the night Hassan sent to summon me away, but I was
quite unable to move. Finding me still in bed at the
dawn, he began to storm furiously at my detaining him so
long, but I quietly let him spend his ire, ate my breakfast
composedly, and set out at eight. He seemed determined
to make up for the delay, for we flew over hill and dale to
Sherean, where we changed horses. From thence we
travelled all the rest of the day and all night. It rained
most of the time. Soon after sunset the ague came on
again, which in my wet state was very trying. I hardly
knew how to keep my life in me.' There was, indeed, but
a little feeble flickering life left in his frail body.

He was now dying fast. It had come, indeed, to be
only a question of days. On the 5th of October he wrote
in his journal: 'Preserving mercy made me see the light

of another morning. The sleep had refreshed me, but
was feeble and shaken, yet the merciless Hassan hurried
me off. The munzil, however, not being distant, I reached
it without much difficulty. I was pretty well lodged, and
felt tolerably well till a little after sunset, when the ague
came on with a violence I had never before experienced;
I felt as if in a palsy; my teeth chattering, and my whole
frame violently shaken. Aga Hosyn and another Persian on their way here from Constantinople, going to Abbas Mirza, whom I had just before been visiting, came
hastily to render me assistance, if they could. These
Persians appear quite brotherly after the Turks. While
they pitied me, Hassan sat in perfect indifference, ruminating in the further delay this was likely to occasion. The
cold fit, after continuing two or three hours, was followed
by a fever, which lasted the whole night, and prevented
sleep.' On the following day he wrote: ' No horses being
to be had, I had an unexpected repose. I sat in the or-
chard, and thought with sweet comfort and peace of my
God; in solitude, my companion, my friend and comforter.
Oh! when shall time give place to eternity? when shall
appear that new heaven and new earth wherein dwelleth
righteousness? There, there shall in no wise enter in anything that defileth: none of that wickedness which has
made men worse than wild beasts—none of those corrup-
tions which add still more to the miseries of mortality, shall
be seen or heard of any more.'

These were the last words that he ever wrote. Whether
he sunk under the disorder against which he had so long
been painfully contending, or whether the Plague, which

was then raging, seized him, is not known; but ten days afterwards, at Tokat, Henry Martyn entered into his rest.*

There is little need to dwell upon a character which has illustrated itself so clearly in the passages which I have given from Henry Martyn's own letters and journals. No one has ever laid bare his heart more unsparingly than this young Protestant priest. Evangelical history claims him as a missionary; but he was not a missionary; he was simply an Indian Officer—an officer upon the ecclesiastical establishment of the East India Company—a military chaplain under the orders of the military authorities. That his heart was in the missionary work, with which he supplemented his official duties, not in the business proper of the chaplaincy, is certain; but he was not less a chaplain before the world because his missionary zeal burnt brightly in the sight of Heaven. To what extent his earnestness and self-devotion really contributed, directly or indirectly, to the diffusion of a knowledge of the Gospel through the Eastern world, cannot be rightly estimated; but he takes rank among the apostles of Protestant Christianity, not in accordance with what he did, so much as with what he at-

---

* The date and place of Mr Martyn's death, as given in Mr Sargent's Life, are, I find, officially confirmed by the following extract of a letter from Mr Morier, dated Constantinople, 3rd November, 1812 : 'I am concerned to have to state, for the information of the Honourable the Court of Directors, that the Reverend Henry Martyn, chaplain of Cawnpore, died at Tokat, a town in Asia Minor, on his way hither from Tabriz, about the beginning of last month. I take the liberty of enclosing a letter for his sister, Miss Harriet Martyn, to whom I give the unpleasant intelligence. I have mentioned that the death of the Reverend Mr Martyn happened on the 16th of last month.'

tempted to do ; for he ever strove mightily to accomplish
the great and glorious ends which he had set before him,
and never shrunk from any martyrdom of self.

That much of this martyrdom was a superfluous waste
of that human happiness which, as far as we are enabled to
see things in a glass darkly, is acceptable in the sight of the
Almighty, will appear to most readers of this story. He
seems, as I have already said, to have read one part of the
Christian character with wonderful clearness and distinctness,
but a dim suffusion veiled his eyes when he approached
those other lessons which combine the beautiful with the
sublime of the picture. Truly has it been said, but with
no reference to the subject of this Memoir, by a modern
writer, whose wise and tender utterances have reached me
whilst I have been writing these pages, that 'it is a great
mistake to suppose that God can dispense with the cultivation of any of our powers. The man who systematically
lets mind and body go to wreck whilst he cares exclusively
for what he considers " the interests of his soul," is in a fair
way to spend a joyless and loveless old age, and to lie at
length in a forgotten tomb. Piety is only seen in its true
strength and beauty in the harmony of all the powers.
It sits as queen, but it is cheerless and joyless without its
court. A cleanly, pure, robust body ; a cultivated, well-
stored, and penetrating mind ; a large, tender, and sympa-
thetic heart, as well as a pious, believing spirit, go to make
old age honoured and blest.' * Henry Martyn never
lived to see the autumn of life, and assuredly he has not

* 'The Home Life ; in the Light of its Divine Idea,' by James
Baldwin Brown.

lain in a forgotten tomb. But the cardinal truth contained in this passage is not the less applicable to the story of his life. His errors were heroic, but they were errors. And his career, therefore, must be regarded as much in the light of a warning as of an example.

In the library of the University of Cambridge is to be seen a portrait of Henry Martyn,* the bequest of

* This picture was painted in Calcutta for Mr Simeon, when Martyn was sojourning there in 1810-11, before his embarkation for Persia. It reached England only a few days before he closed his eyes on the world for ever. How deeply Mr Simeon was affected by the first sight of the portrait, he has himself recorded in a letter dated the 12th of October, 1812. 'On Monday I opened and put up the picture of my ever dear and honoured brother, Mr Martyn. I had, indeed, after it was opened at the India House, gone to see it there, and, notwithstanding all that you had said respecting it to prepare my mind, I was so overpowered by the sight, that I could not bear to look upon it, but turned away and went to a distance, covering my face, and, in spite of every effort to the contrary, crying aloud with anguish ; E. was with me ; and all the bystanders said to her, " That, I suppose, is his father." And I think it probable, that if I *had* been his father, or his mother either, I should not have felt more than I did on the occasion. Shall I attempt to describe to you the veneraation and the love with which I look at it ? No words that I can write will convey an adequate idea ; nothing but your own tender mind can exactly conceive what I feel. I remember (indeed, can never forget) the look of a certain lady, when the thought of your going to India was last suggested to her. One might endeavour to describe the mixed emotions that were then depicted in her countenance ; but it must have been seen in order to be understood and appreciated : so I should in vain attempt to describe what I feel, and trust I shall long continue to feel, in looking on that image of my beloved friend. In seeing how much he is worn, I am constrained to call to my relief the thought in *whose service* he has worn himself so much ; and this reconciles me to the idea of weakness, or sickness, or even, if God were so to appoint, of death itself.'

Mr Simeon; and in the chancel of Trinity church is a monumental tablet bearing the following inscription :

THIS TABLET
IS ERECTED TO THE MEMORY OF
THE REV. HENRY MARTYN, B.D.,
FELLOW OF ST JOHN'S COLLEGE,
AND TWO YEARS CURATE OF THIS PARISH.
HE GAINED BY HIS TALENTS THE HIGHEST ACADEMICAL HONOURS ;
BUT COUNTING ALL LOSS FOR CHRIST,
HE LEFT HIS NATIVE COUNTRY, AND WENT INTO THE EAST,
AS A CHAPLAIN OF THE HON. EAST INDIA COMPANY.
THERE, HAVING FAITHFULLY DONE THE WORK OF AN EVANGELIST,
IN PREACHING THE GOSPEL OF A CRUCIFIED REDEEMER,
IN TRANSLATING THE HOLY SCRIPTURES INTO THE ORIENTAL LANGUAGES,
AND IN DEFENDING THE CHRISTIAN FAITH IN THE HEART OF PERSIA
AGAINST THE UNITED TALENTS OF THE MOST LEARNED MAHOMETANS,
HE DIED AT TOKAT, ON THE 16TH OF OCTOBER, 1812,
IN THE 31ST YEAR OF HIS AGE.*
THE CHIEF MONUMENTS WHICH HE LEFT OF HIS PIETY AND TALENTS ARE
TRANSLATIONS OF THE NEW TESTAMENT
INTO THE HINDOSTANEE AND PERSIAN LANGUAGES ; AND
'BY THESE HE, BEING DEAD, YET SPEAKETH.'

'PRAY YE THE LORD OF THE HARVEST,
THAT HE WILL SEND FORTH LABOURERS INTO HIS HARVEST.

* It should have been '32nd year.'

SIR CHARLES METCALFE.

[BORN 1785.—DIED 1846.]

IN the summer of the year 1805, in the neighbourhood
of the city of Muttra, in the Upper Provinces of India,
where a division of Lord Lake's army was posted, two English gentlemen were conversing eagerly together in a tent.
In the papers which lay upon the table, and the frequent
references which were made to them, there were manifest
signs that the intercourse between the two was not merely
of a personal character. Except in respect of a common
earnestness of manner, there was no sort of resemblance
between them. The one was a tall, handsome, soldierly
man in the very meridian of his life. The other was younger
by many years; much shorter and much plainer. The
elder of the two men was Colonel John Malcolm; the
younger was Mr Charles Theophilus Metcalfe—a civilian
upon the Bengal establishment—who had accompanied
Lord Lake's army into the field, in the capacity of Political
Assistant to the Commander-in-Chief.

In the diplomatic service to which the young civilian
was attached, there was, at that time, perhaps, no greater
name than that of John Malcolm. It was the great har-

vest-time of fame. Men seemed to rise, almost by a single bound, from a state of obscure subalternship into the full meridian blaze of historical renown. This had been Malcolm's lot within the six or seven years preceding this meeting with Charles Metcalfe in the camp at Muttra. To the latter, therefore, it was a great event. It stimulated his energies and rekindled his ambition. What the train of thought suggested, and what effect it had upon his actions, may best be told in young Metcalfe's own words. Writing to a cherished friend in Calcutta, he said : 'On the day after his arrival in camp, Colonel Malcolm, to my surprise (for I could scarcely call myself acquainted with him) entered in a full, friendly, and flattering manner into the question of my intentions—with full confidence, he laid open to me the various plans which were in contemplation, gave me admission to all his papers, and by appearing to interest himself in my welfare, prepared me to listen to him with great attention. He expatiated on the great field of political employment now open in Hindostan, the necessity of many appointments and missions, the superiority, as he seems to think, of my claims, and the great risk, if not certain injury, of my quitting the scene of action. By holding out the offer of distinction, he gained the important outwork of.desire, and the citadel of resolve was in danger of falling. It did not immediately yield, however, and notwithstanding all he said, I clung fondly to my rooted and long-indulged intention of returning to Calcutta and of paying my last respects to Lord Wellesley. There was, however, sufficient in what Malcolm said to induce me to reflect seriously on the step I should take. I did not converse with Malcolm

again for five days, and in that period, the subject was ever
in my mind, and I never experienced such irresolution on
any occasion in which I had the power of self-decision.
Exclusive of the reasons suggested by Malcolm for my remaining, others occurred to me which he could not mention. I have long, as you know, looked upon the political
as my line of service, and although I have seen what people
call native courts, and have passed over many countries, I
have had the misfortune of being under men whose talents,
knowledge, and character, or rather want of these, I could
not admire; who gave no encouragement to my desire to
learn; who, on the contrary, rather made me sick of my
pursuit of knowledge. I have felt myself degraded by my
situation, and instead of studying acquaintance with the
natives, I have shrunk from notice as much as possible.
My knowledge, therefore, is only that which I acquired in
the Governor-General's office, and which, though highly
useful, does not in itself qualify a man to be a political
agent. The opportunity of acting under a man of Malcolm's talents and reputation, established knowledge, inquisitive genius, and communicative disposition, promises advantages of the most solid and certain nature and of real
importance. I could not, however, give up my desire to
visit Calcutta, and my second conversation with Malcolm
ended in our agreeing that I should run down to Calcutta
and return quickly. On the same evening, however, he
strongly advised me not to go; and the next day we had a
long conversation, which ended in my being very uncertain
what to do. I think, however, clearly that I shall stay;
but I never did anything with more reluctance. I long to

see our glorious Wellesley before he quits us. Malcolm tells me that I cannot better show my gratitude to Lord Wellesley than by assisting in scenes in which he will always have great interest.'

So after some further doubts and self-questionings he resolved to remain with the army and to take his leave of the 'glorious Wellesley' by letter. 'Malcolm,' he wrote on the 11th of June, 'who will manage all political concerns at head-quarters, has expressed a wish that I should remain on his account, expecting to derive more assistance from me than I fear he will. This subject fills my mind, and it is with very great difficulty that I can reconcile myself to the overthrow of my plans—plans which I have so long ruminated over with anticipated delight. I rest my chief consolation on Malcolm's character, and the useful knowledge that I shall obtain, whilst with him. It is my intention to cultivate his intimacy zealously. His advances to me have been very flattering. I foresee one thing ; he is a likely man to give my mind a turn towards literary pursuits, which have scarcely ever entered my imagination—nay, he already has. He himself is an enthusiast.' And, because he was an enthusiast, he had succeeded nobly in life. Because he was an enthusiast, he had discerned the fine qualities of the young civilian, in whom also there was a pure and generous enthusiasm, waiting only for opportunity to display itself in great and good deeds. There was something thorough about him that especially pleased Malcolm. Young as he was, he expounded his views, in favour of the prosecution of the 'great game,' with all the resolution of a veteran politician. Steeped as he was in admiration of

Lord Wellesley, he was still more ardent in his attachment to the political faith which he cherished, and he could perceive and discuss the shortcomings of the 'glorious little man,' which were then becoming apparent to the war-party in camp. No man knew better than Malcolm the real state of things at Government House, for he was in close and confidential correspondence with Colonel Arthur Wellesley, and the letters which he then received plainly indicated that much toil and trouble and sore vexation had weakened the gallant resolute spirit of the Governor-General, and that he was not now what he had been in the earlier years of his reign. Malcolm and Metcalfe, in close confidential talk, bewailed the change; and still more bitterly lamented that Lord Cornwallis was coming out to India, to undo, as they said, the great work of his predecessor. Greatly as they differed in age, in experience, and in many important points of character, they were bound together by ties of strong political sympathy, and it was a mutual pleasure to them to · discuss unreservedly the past, the present, and the future, of a conjuncture of events at that time unexampled in the history of our Indian Empire.

CHARLES THEOPHILUS METCALFE was then in his twenty-first year. Born in Calcutta on the 30th of January, 1785, he was the second son of Major Metcalfe, an officer of the Company's army, who had amassed a considerable fortune, as fortunes were amassed, rapidly, in the days of Warren Hastings, when a lucrative contract was a sure road to sudden wealth. Having made his fortune, he did as

others did, carried it away to spend in England, and took
his place among the 'nabobs' of the eighteenth century.
He bought an estate in Yorkshire; canvassed, and with
success, for the East India direction; and obtained for himself a seat in Parliament, in the good old days of Toryism
and Pitt. As he always voted with the Minister, and had
money enough to support a respectable position as a country
gentleman, with a house in Portland-place, a baronetcy was
not an unattainable object of ambition. So Major Metcalfe had not been many years in England before he rose
up ' Sir Thomas Metcalfe, Bart. ; ' * and what he owed, in
the first instance, to the accidents of fortune, he afterwards
dignified by his own native worth. He was a man of high
integrity of conduct, endowed with a solid understanding
rather than with any brilliant parts, and if he could not
command the admiration of the world, he always enjoyed
its respect.

In their early boyhood, his two sons, Theophilus and
Charles, were sent to a private school in one of the eastern
suburbs of London—Bromley, beyond Bow, not far from
the frontier-line of Middlesex and Essex; but after they
had received, in worthy Mr Tait's academy, the rudiments
of their education, they were transplanted to Eton, where
they boarded at the house of Dr Goodall, afterwards head-
master and provost of the college. There young Charles,
or, *Academicè*, Metcalfe Minor, applied himself assiduously
to his books rather than to cricket, to boating, or to fives.

---

* These facts are stated without regard to strict chronological
arrangement. Major Metcalfe was not created a baronet until his
son Charles had been some years in India.

Over and above the Latin and Greek, which in those days
were the be-all and end-all of public school education,
Metcalfe Minor read, in his own room, a number of books,
English and French, and improved himself by translating
the latter. From the study of French he proceeded to that
of Italian, and day after day, as his boyish journal declares,
' read Ariosto.' Even then he had promptings of young
ambition, and day-dreams of a great Future. He was
wont to pace the cloisters, and think of the days to come,
in which he might make for himself a place in history as a
great orator, a great statesman, a great soldier, or as the
liberator of an oppressed race.* Of more robust and
athletic pursuits we have no record under his own hand.
But many years afterwards, worthy Dr Goodall recorded
than he ' heard the boys shouting one day, and went out
and saw young Metcalfe riding on a camel. So,' he added,
rather pleasantly than logically, ' you see he was always
orientally inclined.'

* We have this on Charles Metcalfe's own authority. In a letter,
written soon after his arrival in India, to a friend, Mr Sherer (a name
still of high repute in the Indian Services), the young civilian wrote of
the days when he ' heard the echo of his own footsteps in the cloisters of
his much-loved Eton.' ' Ah, Sherer,' he added, ' those were days of
real happiness. In those very cloisters has my youthful and ardent
imagination planned to itself a life of greatness, glory, and virtue—
there have I been the orator, and discussed important topics in the
Senate House—there have I been the statesman, prescribing terms to
the wondering nations of Europe—there have I concluded peaces,
commanded armies, or headed a party struggling for liberty ; or,
descending from these lofty views, there have I fancied myself, in the
enjoyment of domestic happiness, the honoured patron of a neighbouring hamlet.'

That an East India Director should determine to provide for his sons in the East was only in the common order of things. Major Metcalfe had made a fortune in India with no great trouble, and his boys might easily do the same. The best thing of all in those days was ' a China, writership.' The next was a writership in Bengal. So Theophilus was set down for the former, and Charles for the latter. Theophilus was a high-spirited, rather precocious boy ; and having, at a very early age, been allowed to taste the delights of English society, was reluctant in the extreme to be banished to Canton. Charles was not much more eager to go Eastward ; but his unwillingness was of a different kind. He loved Eton ; he was warmly attached to some of his schoolfellows ; he loved his parents and his kindred, and he loved his country. But he could plainly see that there were the best possible reasons for his going to India ; and so he submitted, with a good grace, to the painful decree. At the age of fifteen he was taken from Eton, and sent out to Calcutta. He went, doubtless, because his father had gone there before him ; because Major Metcalfe, being an East India Director, was very properly of opinion that Patronage, like Charity, ' should begin at home.' But if the whole Court of Directors had ransacked England, Scotland, and Ireland, in search of the likeliest boy in the three kingdoms to grow into a serviceable Indian statesman, they could not have found one with more of the right stuff in him than in Charles Metcalfe.

On the 1st day of the year 1801, Charles Metcalfe set foot on Indian soil, and was soon in the full enjoyment of the strenuous idleness of the cold season in Calcutta, He commenced his career at an interesting period of the history of the Indian Civil Service. The great reforms of Lord Cornwallis had purged and purified it. Men had good wages for good work, and they did their duty conscientiously and assiduously to their employers. The East India Company was still a trading company. It had all its commercial privileges intact. The business of providing the investment was still a part of the duty of its servants. But although they were called 'merchants,' 'factors,' and 'writers' (as, indeed, they were long afterwards), the commercial duties of the Company's civil servants were dwarfed by the other responsibilities which had fallen upon them. The traders of Leadenhall-street, sorely against their will, under violent protest, weeping and grimacing at their hard fate, had been beaten by inexorable circumstance into shape as princes and rulers of the land. Greatness had been thrust upon them. They were masters no longer only of certain factories upon the coast, but of three great Presidencies or Governments. They had armies, and councillors, and ambassadors at foreign Courts. The 'pure mercantile bottom,' on which they had been wont to sit, and to which they clung with all the dogged tenacity of their race, had, during the last few years, expanded under this mighty corporation into an imperial throne;

> ' What seemed its head
> The likeness of a kingly crown had on ; '

and sorely bewildered it was sometimes under the pressure of this unlooked-for encumbrance.

The greatest trouble of Leadenhall-street, at this time,

was Lord Wellesley. That ambitious statesman had vast schemes, which were but little appreciated in the City of London. Among them was one for the advancement of learning generally, but more especially among the Company's civil servants. The Directors, as I have already shown,* were very eager to promote the moral welfare of their young people in India ; but as long as they wrote good hands, could cast up accounts with precision, and behaved with due steadiness and discretion, their honourable masters do not appear to have troubled themselves much about the intellectual elevation of the service. They had finished the old century well by sending off a long and well-written despatch, of which Charles Grant, the elder, is commonly supposed to have been the author, protesting against the habitual profanation of the Sabbath, and the general disregard of religion, which were said to mark the proceedings of their servants, and of society generally, in Bengal—most especially in the great metropolis of Calcutta. The charge, I am afraid, was too true. To use the words of a modern writer : ' All the daily concerns of life went on as usual (on Sundays), with the exception, perhaps, that there was somewhat more than the ordinary abandonment to pleasure. At our military stations the flag was hoisted, and they who saw it knew that it was Sunday. But the work-table and the card-table were resorted to as on week-days. Christianity cantered to the races in the morning, and in the evening drove to a nautch.' Against all this—against the habitual extravagance of the Company's servants—against the luxury which had grown up amongst them, and the evil habits of

* *Ante*, Memoir of Lord Cornwallis.

horse-racing, card-playing, and other fashionable indulgences
—there was now a vigorous protest issued under the directing hands of one of the best men who ever sat in Leadenhall-street. 'It is,' said that famous despatch, 'on the
qualities of our servants that the safety of the British possessions in India essentially depends—on their virtue, their
intelligence, their laborious application, their vigilance, and
public spirit. We have seen, and do still with pleasure see,
honourable examples of all these; we are anxious to preserve
and increase such examples, and therefore·cannot contemplate without alarm the excessive growth of fashionable
amusements and show, the tendency of which is to enervate
the mind and impair its nobler qualities—to introduce a
hurtful emulation in expense, to set up false standards of
merit, to confound the different orders in society, and to
beget an aversion to serious occupation.' And then, in a
subsequent paragraph, we have the following—the logic of
which, I confess, is much more convincing than any of the
Leadenhall-street logic which I have quoted in a preceding
Memoir : 'Believing,' says the despatch, 'that the enjoyment
of avowed honourable allowances would tend to promote,
among other honourable effects, a due regulation of expense,
the Company have, from such considerations, strained their
own means to put their servants on the most liberal footing ;
but whilst they feel themselves weighed down by the civil
and military charges of their establishments, they are still
frequently assailed, in one way or another, by new applications
for pecuniary concessions; and yet, at the same time that
we hear of straits and hardships resulting from inadequate
allowances, we not only discern evident marks of increasing

dissipation in the general habits of European society in India, but in some a spirit of gaming publicly showing itself in lotteries and the keen pursuits of the turf.'

Nothing could be better than this; but after-events unhappily proved that there was either a want of sincerity in it, or a want of capacity to view the whole question in a comprehensive spirit. The Governor-General was especially exhorted to look into this matter, and to do everything that possibly could be done to curb the licentiousness of his subordinates. But when he hit upon the best possible device for raising the character of the Company's civil servants, he met only with opposition and reproof.

At that time the Civil Service was recruited with boys fresh from school. A stripling from the fifth form at Eton was suddenly converted, in his teens, into an Indian administrator, and launched at once into a sea of temptation, at an Indian presidency, to sink or to swim, according to the degree of his own strength or of the power of the waves. How he managed 'to fit himself for the public service,' it was hard to say. His education was generally slender, and in its slenderness not of a kind to qualify him for the work of Indian administration. That good or bad angel of EXAMINATION had not at that time flapped his wings over the land. And yet, somehow or other, very good public servants had been, as the Court of Directors acknowledged, reared out of these adverse circumstances. Warren Hastings and John Shore, Jonathan Duncan and George Barlow—the Halheds, the Colebrookes, Neill Edmonstone, and St George Tucker, had ripened under that system; and Mountstuart Elphinstone was growing rapidly, and Butterworth Bayley and Charles Metcalfe where beginning to grow, when it occurred to Lord Wellesley that they would grow stronger and straighter if they were sent to College on their first arrival in India. And thinking of this, and of other palpable wants of the great country which he had been sent to govern, he conceived the idea of the College of Fort William.

It was said of old by one great poet of another, that he 'did all like a man.' Lord Wellesley did all like a man; and with a manliness almost gigantic. It was not in him to do anything on a small scale. When, therefore, he projected a College for the education of the younger servants of Government, he set the stamp of his individuality on such a magnificent design, that it fairly staggered the Company in London—' the ignominious tyrants of Leadenhall-street,' as he called them soon afterwards—the 'generous benefactors' of a later period of his career. But it is not improbable that the Court's despatch, quoted above, actually suggested the idea of the proposed institution. For it was as early as October, 1799, that he wrote to Mr Dundas, saying : 'I think it necessary to apprize you of my intention to adopt, without delay, a plan for the improvement of the Civil Service at Bengal in a most important point. The state of the administration of justice, and even of the collection of the revenue, throughout the provinces, affords a painful example of the inefficiency of the best code of laws to secure the happiness of the people, unless due provision has been made to ensure a proper supply of men qualified to administer those laws in their different branches and departments. This evil is felt severely in every part of this Government, and it rises principally from a defect at the source and fountain-head of the service—I mean the education and early habits of the young gentlemen sent hither in the capacity of writers. My opinion, after full deliberation of the subject, is decided—that the writers, on their first arrival in India, should be subjected for a period of two or three years to the rules and discipline of some collegiate institution at the seat of Government.' Having laid down, in outline, what he proposed to teach—the languages and laws of the country, the regulations of Government, &c., he expressed a hope that, by means of such an institution, habits of activity, regularity, and decency might be formed, instead of those of sloth, indolence, low debauchery, and vulgarity, which he said were 'too apt to grow on those young men, who have been sent at an early age into the interior parts of the country, and have laid the foundation of their life and manners among the coarse vices and indulgences of these countries.'

It was a word and a blow always with Lord Wellesley. He conceived the idea, he wrote a letter, he established the College. He did not wait to realize his magnificent conceptions to the full; he knew the importance of making a beginning. When Charles Metcalfe arrived in India, the great institution was in a crude inchoate state. The original regulations for the foundation of the College of Fort William had been published on the 10th of July, 1800; but Charles Metcalfe, who arrived in India on the first day of 1801, was the first student to sign the statute-book; and he did not sign it until the 27th of April of that year. It would appear from his journals, however, that one great collegiate feature was in existence at an earlier date, for in the preceding months he frequently recorded the fact that he had 'dined at college.' * I conclude that he was the first resident member.

The novelty of Anglo-Indian life, for a time, was pleasing to young Charles Metcalfe, so also was its independence; and all the chief people of the Presidency, the Governor-General and Councillors included, opened their houses to him. But with the hot weather came weariness and exhaustion. The young civilian's spirits failed him; and before the month of June had been gasped out, he had written to his father, telling him that he hated India, and that all his happiness in life depended upon his being permitted to return home and obtain 'a small place in Lord Grenville's office.' Now, if Charles Metcalfe had been the son of a weak-minded mother, it is possible that her entreaties might have prevailed against the paternal judgment; but she was, fortunately, a lady in whom there was as much sound sense as good feeling; she saw at once that her son had written under a temporary depression of spirits, or, in the language of the day, 'vapours,' which would soon pass away; and her expressive answer was—a box of pills. 'You may laugh at my sending them,' she wrote, 'but I think you are bilious, and they will be of great service. . . . . . You study too much. You should dissipate a little. On account of your health you should relax.

* '*January* 13. Dined at college.—*Saturday*, 17. Dined at college, &c. &c. *Monday, April* 27. Read and signed the declaration, and was admitted into college; being the first ever admitted into the College of Fort William.'

Ride on horseback. When intense thinking is joined with the want of exercise, the consequences must be bad.' The answer of Major Metcalfe was drawn from his own book of experience. 'I remember well,' he wrote, 'my own feelings when I was an Ensign, and had been in the country about three months. I one morning (in a fit of bile) waited on the commanding officer with an intention to resign the service and return to England. Fortunately for me, the conversation at breakfast took a pleasant turn, in which I bore an active part, and a hearty fit of laughter got the better of my blue devils. I returned to my quarters with a determination to persevere.' Indeed, it was a very old story. There is no incident with which biography is more familiar, than this early fainting at the outset of the great march to Fame.

It was, perhaps, fortunate for Charles Metcalfe that in those days there were no overland mails. Many months elapsed before he could receive an answer to his appeal; and before the parental replies reached Calcutta, the young civilian had begun to take a more cheerful view of life, and to think that he might do something to distinguish himself in India, though he still clung to the belief that there were better prospects before him in England. Even then his young ambition had been fired. Whilst yet only in his seventeenth year, he wrote in his journal, 'No one possesses more ambition than I do; and am I destined to be great? If I quit this country, I may be; and it is one of the reasons for my desiring it so ardently. I cannot help thinking, should I hereafter be great, of the fervour with which my biographer will seize upon these slight memorandums, and record them to an eager public as a proof of my indulging in youth and in distant climes the idea of becoming a great character on the theatre of the world.' This was written in October; but before the end of the year delivery came in the shape of active employment. Lord Wellesley, who perceived that the youngster had good stuff in him, emancipated him from the control of the College of Fort William, and appointed him an Assistant to the Resident at Scindiah's Court.

On his way to join his appointment, Charles Metcalfe fell in with the camp of the Governor-General, and obtained Lord Wellesley's permission to accompany him to Lucknow. There he caught his first glimpse of the traditional splendour of the East, and found that the reality even exceeded the romance. 'Everything,' he said, 're-called to my memory the "Arabian Nights," for every description of any such procession which I ever met with in history, even the celebrated triumph of Aurelian when he led Zenobia and Tiridates (Tetricus) captives, of which Gibbon gives an account, was completely beggared by it.' From Lucknow, he proceeded to join the camp of the Resident at Scindiah's Court. This high political office was then held by Colonel Collins—an early associate of Metcalfe's father, who spoke of him affectionately as his ' old friend Jack Collins.' But he had another name with the general community, who called him 'King Collins,' for he was a man of an imperious nature and an overbearing temper. Charles Metcalfe did not want temper, but he wanted tact; and he soon quarrelled with his chief. The old soldier resented the clever self-sufficiency of the young civilian, who argued and dogmatized, and was continually rubbing himself against the angularities of King Collins. So there was a rupture. Metcalfe asked permission to resign his appointment, and then returned to Calcutta.

It was well that he did so; for soon after his return to the Presidency, a seat was given to him in what was called 'Lord Wellesley's office.' A little cluster of the most promising young civilians was gathered together in Government House, and did much important confidential work under the superintendence of the Chief Secretaries, or sometimes of the Governor-General himself. It was the best possible nursery for infant statesmen, and there were few who did not profit by the culture. Great events were then taking shape in the womb of Time. We were on the eve of that great conflict of which I have already written—a conflict destined to change the entire aspect of our Eastern Empire, and to make the administration of Lord Wellesley the most momentous in the whole range of our Indian history. It was a great thing for young Charles Metcalfe to take even a humble ministerial part in these great transactions, under the eye of the Governor-General. Lord Wellesley was one to encourage well those who served him well. To the men who did not grudge their work, he did not grudge his praise. A minister, in high place, who is slow to recognize the good services of his subordinates, may be a very clever man, but he is not a great statesman. What this novitiate in Lord Wellesley's office did for Charles Metcalfe, at the turning-point of his career, it is almost impossible to estimate too highly. After a year and a half of this good training, he was thoroughly fit for active service of any kind, and eager above all things to prove his capacity for action. He had ceased to think of the opportumities of Lord Grenville's office.

During this residence in Calcutta, Charles Metcalfe became reverentially attached to Lord Wellesley; and the Governor-General, upon his part, conceived an interest in the young civilian which was never weakened by years. By this time the Governor-General had begun to discern that there was but little sympathy between him and the masters whom he served. His cherished scheme of the Calcutta College * soon excited opposition, which became more vehement as the project developed itself; and soon other acts, little appreciated in Leadenhall-street, increased the bitterness of the feud. But there was at least one man in the Court of Directors who recognized the great qualities of Lord Wellesley, and was well inclined to support him. This was Charles Metcalfe's father; a fact known to the Governor-General, which tended to increase the favour with which he regarded his young assistant. He knew that

---

* The suppression by the East India Company of the College of Fort William, in Bengal, as designed by Lord Wellesley, was followed by the institution of Haileybury College, in Hertfordshire. The majority of the Directors recognized the virtue of the preliminary training, but thought that England was a better place for it than India, and that it would be better for the young writers to go out to India at a more advanced age. But meanwhile the feeling in Calcutta against the opposition of the Court had grown very strong—how strong may be gathered from a letter in the Appendix, addressed by the Reverend David Brown to Mr Charles Grant. They were friends and close correspondents ; but Mr Brown, who had been appointed Principal of the College, was in the matter an earnest Wellesleyite.

Metcalfe was eager to be up and doing; and so, in the full assurance that there was the right stuff in the youth, the Governor-General sent him to the great centre of action in the country between the Jumna and the Ganges.

For the 'great game' had now commenced. General Lake's army had taken the field; and in the spring of 1804, Charles Metcalfe was appointed Political Assistant to the Commander-in-Chief, and despatched to join the army at head-quarters. On his way thither, travelling in a palanquin, he was set upon by a party of armed robbers, who despoiled him of everything that was worth taking, and well nigh deprived him of his life. Abandoned by his bearers, he made an effort single-handed to resist his assailants; but, severely wounded and faint from loss of blood, he was compelled to desist from the encounter. Then staggering into the jungle, he laid himself down on the bank of a river, whilst the thieves were collecting their spoil. He has himself recorded how, as he lay there, he thought of home and of his parents, and how at that very time they might be at Abingdon races. But he recovered strength enough to return to his palanquin to find the robbers departed, and his bearers returned. So he ordered them to proceed to Cawnpore.

There, under the careful and affectionate ministrations of his aunt, Mrs Richardson, he soon recovered from his wounds, and proceeded to join the camp of the Commander-in-Chief. The General was a fine old soldier; but he had his weaknesses, and among them an habitual contempt for civilians; and, indeed, for much penmanship of any kind. He had an emphatic formula by which he expressed to those beneath him his desire that they should mind their fighting and not their writing. The presence in his camp of a boy-civilian, fresh from Government House, rather irritated him; and, perhaps, the members of his Staff humoured the old soldier by sneering at the non-combatant clerk, who shared the pleasant excitements but not the dangers of the campaign. Young Metcalfe got some inkling of this, and quietly bided his time. An opportunity soon came. The army was before the strong fortress of Deeg. The storming party was told off, and the non-combatant clerk volunteered to accompany it. He was one of the first to enter the breach. This excited the admiration of the old General, who made most honourable mention of him in his despatch; and, ever afterwards, throughout the campaign, spoke of him as his ' little stormer.'

It was soon after this that Colonel Malcolm joined the camp of the Commander-in-Chief, and took young Metcalfe into his councils. The war was then nearly over, for the treasury was well-nigh empty, and the Company were on the verge of bankruptcy. There was, however, one last blow to be struck. Holkar was still in an attitude of hostility; but when the British troops drove him, as before narrated, across the Sutlej, and he was at last compelled to accept the terms offered to him by our Government, the ' little stormer' was sent to convey to the Mahratta chief the assurances of our friendship and good will. He spoke modestly of this mission, and said that his task was an easy one; but it required both temper and tact, especially as the celebrated Pathan leader, Ameer Khan, was present at the meeting, and inclined to be insolent to the boyish English diplomatist, who had not by any means an imposing personal presence, and whose countenance could scarcely by any effort be made to discard its habitual expression of cheerfulness and benignity. 'The conduct of Holkar and his chiefs,' he wrote to a young friend in Calcutta, 'was equally expressive of the highest delight, and made my mission a very pleasing and happy business. My task was easy, being in its nature only to convey assurances of friendship. . . . It was my duty to urge his immediate departure from the Punjab on his return to Malwa. I got from him a promise to move on the 13th, which he maintained to my surprise. His appearance is very grave, his countenance expressive, his manners and conversation easy. He had not at all the appearance of the savage we knew him to be. The same countenance, however, which was strongly expressive of joy when I saw him, would look very black under the influence of rage, or any dark passions. A little lap-dog was on his musnud—a strange playfellow for Holkar. The jewels on his neck were invaluably rich. . . . All his chiefs were present. Ameer Khan is a blackguard in his looks, and affected, on the occasion of my reception, to be particularly fierce, by rubbing his coat over with gunpowder, and assuming in every way the air of a common soldier. But for his proximity to Holkar he would have passed for one. I consider his behaviour to have been affectation. He had the impudence to ask from me my name, which must have been known to him ; and his conduct was so evidently designed to bring himself into

notice, that I felt gratification in disappointing the unknown impudent, and, answering plainly to his question,
I turned from him and continued a good-humoured conversation with Holkar and Bhao Buskur. I was better
pleased that I did so, when I learnt his name, for he had
on a late occasion behaved with egregious impertinence.
I have been very much gratified with the accidental mission, because, though of no importance, it is a little distinction. Lord Lake has made use of it to say more in my
favour than I ever deserved, in a despatch to the Governor-
General.'

On the restoration of peace, Mr Metcalfe was appointed
an Assistant to the Resident at Delhi, where the Mogul
Emperor, Shah Allum, old, blind, and infirm, still maintained the shadowy pageantry of a Court. The Resident
was Mr Seton, a civilian of the old school, whose chief
characteristic was an overflowing courtesy and politeness,
which sometimes wholly swept away all the barriers of
sound sense and discretion, and exposed him to not unmerited
derision. In any other man, the strong expressions of admiration with which he spoke of young Metcalfe's genius,
might have been regarded as indications of discernment
and prescience. But on the lips of Seton the language of
flattery was habitual, and Metcalfe attached but little value
to the praise of a superior, who had been represented in a
caricature of the day as saluting Satan with a compliment,
and wishing 'long life and prosperity to His Majesty.'
This weakness had unfortunately free scope for exercise at
Delhi, where exaggerated respect was shown by Seton to
the Mogul. Metcalfe often remonstrated against this, and

by his remonstrances greatly perplexed the Resident, who could not show all the deference he wished both to his old charge and his young friend. Metcalfe was soon sick of the ungenial work, which was even less profitable than it was pleasant. ' I am with respect to health,' he wrote in June, 1807, 'as well as usual, and that, I thank God, is very well; in spirits, too, pretty well; and though the place is very dull, and I myself am no great enlivener of society, never fail to be merry on a favourable opportunity. I am tired of business, and long to have less to do—the nearest to nothing the better. . . . And now comes the dreadful tale. My finances are quite ruined, exhausted beyond any reasonable hope of repair. You know that I am very prudent; prudence is a prominent feature in my character; yet, ever since I came to this Imperial station, I have gradually been losing the ground which I had gained in the world, and at length I find myself considerably lower than the neutral situation of having nothing, and without some unlooked-for and surprising declaration of the fates in my favour, I see nothing but debt, debt, debt, debt after debt before me.' But deliverance soon came. Certain new duties were imposed upon him, and his allowances were consequently increased. As these duties were of an administrative rather than a diplomatic character, the arrangement did not much please him; but he found consolation in the means it afforded him of extricating himself from debt. He determined to convert this addition to his salary into a sinking-fund for the payment of his debts; and resolutely adhering to the design, he paid off his debts to the last sixpence without any foreign aid, and soon laid the foundation of a fortune. He was now on the high road to promotion. Some at least of the day-dreams of the Eton cloisters were about to be realized. There was, or there was supposed to be, a conjuncture which demanded the best services of all the best men in the country. The apprehensions which sent Malcolm to Persia, and Elphinstone to Caubul, suggested the expediency of a mission to Lahore; and Metcalfe was selected to conduct it. In these days, it is no greater feat to go from Delhi to Lahore than to go from London to Scarborough. But in 1808 the Punjab was almost a *terra incognita* to us. We knew little or nothing of the ' strange sect of people called the Sikhs.' Some tidings had reached us of the rising power of a chief named Runjit Singh, who was rapidly consolidating by not the most scrupulous means an empire on the banks of the Hyphasis and the Hydaspes. In pursuance of the comprehensive scheme of defensive policy, which the rumoured designs of the French and Russian Emperors compelled us to initiate, Lord Minto determined to secure the good offices of the ruler of the Punjab, and to bind him to us by treaty-obligations. For this work he selected Mr Metcalfe; and seldom or never before had a mission of so much delicacy and difficulty been intrusted to so young a man.

Charles Metcalfe was only twenty-three years of age— an age at which at the present day many civilians of the new school first set their faces towards the East—when he went forth on his embassy to the Court of Runjit Singh. On the 1st of September, 1808, the mission crossed the Sutlej. On the 12th, Runjit Singh, who had been flitting about in a somewhat erratic fashion, as though he could hardly make up his mind how to act, received the English officers at Kussoor. It is not the custom in these cases to go to business at once. The first visits of Oriental diplomacy are visits of courtesy and congratulation. It is a kind of diplomatic measuring of swords before the conflict commences. 'The Rajah,' wrote Metcalfe, 'met us on the outside of a large enclosure, and having embraced all the gentlemen of the mission, conducted us within, where tents had been prepared for our reception. As a compliment to us, the Rajah, from his own choice, used chairs at this meeting, partly collected from our camp and partly from his own, upon which he and the principal Sirdars present, and the gentlemen of the British mission, were seated. This interview was prolonged by the Rajah beyond the usual time of visits of ceremony; but nothing of consequence passed at it. The Rajah did not enter much into conversation, and made only two observations worthy of remark. One was an expression of regret for the lamented death of Lord Lake, of whom he observed that it would be difficult to find his equal, for that he was as much distinguished by his gentleness, mildness, humanity, and affability as by his greatness as a military character. The other observation was in reply to one of his courtiers, who was remarking that the British Government was celebrated for good faith; upon which Runjit Singh said that he knew well that the word of the British Government included everything.' Great words—and a great fact in those days.

On the 16th Runjit Singh returned the visit of the young English diplomatist; and three days afterwards, at

another meeting, they proceeded to discuss the preliminaries
of business, and on the 22nd negotiations were formally
opened.   In their general features, they very much resembled those which Elphinstone, a few months later, conducted at Peshawur.   The English officer did all that he
could to persuade the Sikh ruler that the British Government were eager to advance his interests, and that the proposed alliance was more to his advantage than to their own ;
and the Sikh ruler regarded this display of disinterested-
ness with some suspicion.   'I opened the conference,'
wrote Metcalfe, ' by stating that the friendship which had
happily existed between the Rajah and the British Government had induced the Governor-General to depute me
to communicate some important intelligence, in which
the Maharajah's interests were materially concerned.   I
then mentioned that his Lordship had received authentic
advices that the French, who were endeavouring to establish
themselves in Persia, had formed the design of invading
these countries, and of seizing Caubul and the Punjab ; that
his Lordship's first care was to give warning to the States
which this intelligence concerned ; that, feeling the interests of the British Government and those of the Rajah to be
the same, his Lordship had commissioned me to negotiate
with the Rajah arrangements for the extirpation of the
common enemy, and had appointed another gentleman to
be Envoy to Caubul for similar purposes with respect to
that country, who would in a short time, with the Rajah's
permission, pass through this country, on his way to the
place of his destination.   I added, that these measures had
been adopted by the Government in the purest spirit of

friendship, and that it was evident that the interests of all the States in this quarter required that they should unite their powers in defence of their dominions, and for the destruction of the common enemy.'

When the young English Envoy had finished his statement, the Rajah asked him how far the British Army would advance to meet the French; and to this Metcalfe replied that it was our practice to seek the enemy, and that ' no doubt the Government would send an army beyond Caubul.' ' But what,' asked Runjit Singh, ' if the King of Caubul should throw himself into the arms of the French ? ' ' Why then,' said Metcalfe, ' we shall attack him as well as the French.' But he added that it was 'improbable that he would be so blind to his own interests; for that the French invariably subjected and oppressed those who joined them; plundered and laid waste their country, and overthrew the Government.' ' In the course of this conversation,' continued the youthful diplomatist, ' I endeavoured, in conformity to the instructions of the Supreme Government, to alarm the Rajah for the safety of his territories, and at the same time to give him confidence in our protection.' To all of this the Rajah made frank and friendly answer; but he said that it was altogether an important subject, that he wanted time to talk it over with his ministers, and that his sentiments would be expressed on the morrow.

So the Sikh statesmen took time to consider the proposals of the British Government, and the more they thought over them, the greater the suspicion with which they regarded them. The big words which Metcalfe had spoken about the dangers to which they were exposed began to

shrivel into insignificance. They could not bring themselves to believe that this remote and conjectural danger
from the ambitious designs of the French was the real
cause of a British mission being sent to the Court of Runjit
Singh. And if it were so, it was not, after all, a matter
that much concerned the Sikhs themselves. Runjit himself
saw clearly that the English had their own objects to gain.
He had his objects, too; and he might turn the British
mission to good account. So he asked Metcalfe whether
the British Government would recognize his sovereignty
over all the Sikh States on both sides of the Sutlej. If the
English wished to preserve their empire, he wished to consolidate his. But Metcalfe only replied that he had no
authority to express the views of his Government on this
subject.

It would be a work of time to narrate all the details of
the protracted negotiations which then ensued. The Sikh
ruler was full of jealousy and suspicion; and, therefore, he
was very wary in his practice. He fenced and evaded with
the greatest skill; and was continually watching for opportunities, which the young English officer never allowed
him, of coming down upon him unawares, or striking him
at a disadvantage. The fact is, that he thought Metcalfe
had entered his country in the character of a spy, and that
the negotiation of a friendly alliance was intended only to
mask some ulterior proceedings of a hostile character. His
conduct was distinguished by an amount of inquietude and
restlessness, which every now and then verged upon dis-
courtesy, if not upon overt insolence to the British mission,
and it is not improbable that many a man in Metcalfe's

place would have resented the strange bearing of the Sikh chief, and have broken up his camp to return to the British frontier.   But, even at that early age, the beautiful patience, which at a later time so perfected in him the true heroic character, displayed itself to his own honour and to his country's good.   He had been sent to perform a certain work, and he was resolute to do it in spite of all temptations to turn aside; and, therefore, he was slow to take offence, feeling that he might attribute to the barbaric ignorance and to the rude impulses of one, who had never known restraint, much which in an European Prince would have been wholly unaccountable and not to be forgiven. When in all courtesy and respect, Runjit ought to have been pursuing to a close the negotiation with the representative of the British Government, he was giving himself up to strong drink and to the unseemly exhibitions of dancing-girls, and giving no sort of heed to the important business before him.   There was method, perhaps, in madness of this kind.   He was evidently anxious to gain time, that he might see what would be written down in the great chapter of accidents, and might be guided to that which would best serve his individual interests.

So the year 1808 was fast wearing away, and Metcalfe still remained at the Court of Runjit Singh—now in one place, now in another.   Runjit was pursuing his schemes of ambition, and meditated the conquest of the lesser Sikh States on the English side of the Sutlej.   But the Government of Lord Minto had determined not to suffer the less powerful chiefs to be sacrificed to Runjit's ambition, and were now making preparations for the advance of a military force to the banks of the river. On the 22nd of December Metcalfe personally communicated these intentions to the Rajah. He received the communication with apparent self-control; but after putting a few questions relating to the strength of the British force, and the position which it was to take up—questions to which Metcalfe was unable to reply—Runjit left the room, descended to the court-yard below, mounted a horse, and began caracolling about with what the young English Envoy described as 'surprising levity.' But it was not levity. He was striving to subdue his strong feelings, and was gaining time to consider the answer he was to give to the British Envoy. After a while he returned to another room and took counsel with his ministers, who, when they rejoined Metcalfe, told him that the Rajah would consent to all the demands of the British Government.

But these were mere words. With characteristic instability, Runjit wished to withdraw them almost as soon as they were uttered. On the same evening he sent a message to Metcalfe, saying that the proposal of the British Government to send troops to the Sutlej was of so strange a character, that he could not finally announce his determination till he had consulted with his chiefs, and that he purposed to proceed for that purpose to Umritsur, and he requested the British Envoy to attend him. But Metcalfe, though habitually of a placid demeanour, fired up at this, and earnestly protested against it as an insult to his Government. His resolute bearing had the desired effect. The negotiations were continued; but it was obvious that Runjit Singh was sorely irritated, and half doubtful at times whether he would try conclusions with the English. He had long been anxious to assure himself with respect to the real military strength of the British Government—most of all, what were the qualities of the trained native soldiers who constituted our Sepoy army. An unexpected incident gave him a glimpse of the knowledge which he sought. The negotiations had been protracted, without any positive results, to the month of February, when one day Metcalfe's escort of British Sepoys came into collision, at Umritsur, with a party of Akalis, or Sikh fanatics—half soldiers and half saints. There was a sharp conflict between them; but, after a little while, the steady discipline of the little band of trained soldiers prevailed, and the Sikhs broke and fled. This appears to have made a great impression on Runjit's mind. He saw clearly that the English, who could make such good soldiers of men not naturally war-like, were a people not to be despised. There were ulterior results of even more importance to history, but that which immediately followed was the conclusion of the treaty, which had been so long in course of negotiation. It was a treaty of general friendship and alliance between the British and the Sikh powers—a plain, straightforward, sensible treaty, unencumbered with details ; and it lasted out the lives both of the Indian chief and the English statesman.

The manner in which Charles Metcalfe had conducted these difficult negotiations placed him at once, notwith-standing the fewness of his years, in the foremost rank of the public servants of the Indian Government.* From

* The thanks of the Government were conveyed to Mr Metcalfe in the following words : ' During the course of your arduous ministry

that time his fortune was made. On Metcalfe's return to India, Lord Minto invited him to Calcutta. The Governor-General was at that time about to proceed to Madras, in consequence of the mutiny of the officers of the Madras Army; and he was so much pleased with Metcalfe, that he invited him to accompany the Government party, as Deputy-Secretary, to the Coast. After a brief sojourn at Madras, Metcalfe went to Mysore to visit his old friend, the Honourable Arthur Cole. In May, 1810, he returned to Calcutta, and was soon afterwards appointed Resident at Scindiah's Court, in succession to Mr Græme Mercer. As he did not like the appointment, it was fortunate that he was not destined long to remain there. After he had resided some ten months at Gwalior, to which the Court had been recently removed from Oujein, Lord Minto offered him the Delhi Residency, in succession to Mr Seton, who had been appointed Governor of Prince of Wales's Island. ' I shall,' wrote the Governor-General to him, ' with (or without) your consent, name you to the Residency of Delhi. I know your martial genius and your

at the Court of Lahore, the Governor-General in Council has repeatedly had occasion to record his testimony to your zeal, ability, and address in the execution of the duties committed to your charge. His Lordship in Council, however, deems it an obligation at the close of your mission, generally to declare the high sense which he entertains of the distinguished merit of your services and exertions in a situation of more than ordinary importance, difficulty, and responsibility, to convey to you the assurance of his high approbation, and to signify to you that the general tenour of your conduct in the arduous negotiations in which you have been engaged has established a peculiar claim to public applause, respect, and esteem.'

love of camps; but, besides that inclination must yield to
duty, this change will appear to fall in, not inopportunely,
with some information and some sentiments conveyed to
me in your letter of the 3rd instant.' And then he added,
in a strain of kindly jocoseness, 'If you ask my reasons for
so extraordinary a choice, I can only say that, notwithstanding your entire ignorance of everything connected with the
business of Delhi—a city which, I believe, you never saw;
and with Cis- and Trans-Sutlej affairs, of which you can
only have read; and notwithstanding your equal deficiency
in all other more general qualifications, I cannot find a
better name in the list of Company's servants; and hope,
therefore, for your indulgence on the occasion.' I have
read a great number of letters from Governors-General,
offering high appointments to the officers of Government,
but never one so pleasant as this—never one that so clearly
indicated the personal affection of the writer for the man
to whom it was addressed.

So, at the age of twenty-six, Charles Metcalfe found
himself in possession of the high dignity and the large
emoluments of an office coveted by men of twice his age
and four times the length of his service. Yet he was by
no means elated by his good fortune. It is hard, perhaps,
to form a just estimate of the habitual feelings of a dweller
in India, so much is a man's cheerfulness affected by the
climate; so great are the vicissitudes from a state of high
animal spirits to one of feebleness and depression. The
biographer should always consider the date of a letter
written in India; but it will be no unfailing guide. The
truth is that, by men who have much official work to do,

private letters to friends in England are commonly written in a state of weariness and exhaustion; and, moreover, there is always something saddening in this communion with the old home; it suggests so many tender regrets and painful yearnings after unattainable bliss. It was not strange, therefore, that Charles Metcalfe should have written to England, from the Delhi Residency, to discourage one of his aunts from sending out her son to India. 'Do not suppose,' he added, ' that I am unhappy or discontented. I have long since reconciled myself to my fate, and am as contented and happy as one far from his friends can be. I do not allow unpleasant thoughts to enter my mind, and if I do not enjoy what is beyond my reach—the inexpressible pleasure of family society—I at least am always cheerful and never unhappy. My father did what he thought best for me ; and it is satisfactory to me to reflect that my career in India, except as to fortune, must have answered his expectations. It has been successful beyond any merits that I am aware of in myself.' As he says, in the next paragraph, that he hopes to save £3000 a year from his salary, I can hardly think that even Sir Thomas Metcalfe could have been much disappointed that his son could not do more financially at the age of six-and-twenty.

As time advanced, his spirits did not rise. He was still subject to fits of depression, if not to an habitual inward gloom. He felt that he was a solitary man. ' I shall never marry,' he said. ' My principal reason for thinking that I positively shall never marry, is the difficulty of two dispositions uniting so exactly as to produce that universal harmony which is requisite to form the perfect happiness that is indispensable to make the married state desirable.' But his affections were very warm. He had already formed some strong friendships in India, which lasted all his life; and now at Delhi, though he had many acquaintances and he was overrun with guests at the Residency (for his hospitality was unstinting), he had no familiar and cherished companions with whom to interchange the inmost feelings of the heart. Some temporary alleviation came in the shape of a visit from his younger brother, Thomas Metcalfe,* who had come out to India in the Bengal Civil Service, and whom, after leaving College, Lord Minto had sent up to Delhi to act as an Assistant to the Resident. But he appears after a while, if his correspondence is to be trusted, to have subsided into his old melancholy ways. The following extracts from letters to his aunt, Mrs Monson, give his own account of the state of his mind : ' I cannot say,' he wrote in one letter, ' that I approve of the plan of sending children out to India for all their lives. There is no other service in which a man does not see his friends sometimes. Here it is perpetual banishment. There was a good reason for sending sons to India when fortunes were made rapidly, and they returned home. But if a man is to slave all his life, he had better do so, in my opinion, in his own country, where he may enjoy the society of his friends, which I call enjoying life. Do not suppose that I am discontented and make myself unhappy. It is my fate, and I am reconciled to it. . . . But can anything be a recompense to me in this world for not seeing my dear and

* Afterwards Sir Thomas Metcalfe, for some time Resident at Delhi.

honoured father, from the days of my boyhood to the day of his death—and, perhaps, the same with regard to my mother? I think not—decidedly not!' Again, in another letter, he said: 'I cannot describe to you how much I am worked, and if I could, there would be no pleasure either to you or me in the detail. I will, therefore, pass over that for a while, and endeavour to forget my plagues. Tom arrived here on the 18th. I am very much pleased with him, and think him a superior young man. Here he and I are together, and here we shall remain for many a long year consoling each other as well as we can for the absence of all other friends. . . . I shall see you, I hope, in eighteen years!' And again, a few months later: 'It is very kind of you to wish me home, and I assure you that I wish myself at home most ardently. Nevertheless, as the sacrifices which a man must make who comes to India have been made for the most part already, I do not mean to return to England to struggle with poverty, or to be forced to draw tight my purse-strings. The sacrifice that I have made, I consider great. The recompense that I propose to myself is to have a competency—not merely for my own expenses, but to enable me to assist others without reluctance or restraint. . . . I am become very unsociable and morose, and feel myself getting more so every day. I lead a vexatious and joyless life; and it is only the hope of home at last that keeps me alive and merry. That thought cheers me, though writing to any of you always makes me sad.' It is not very easy to believe that Charles Metcalfe was ever 'unsociable and morose.'

When Lord Minto returned to England he left Charles

Metcalfe still at the Delhi Residency, and Lord Hastings found him there.   There were stirring times then before the Government of India—the necessary after-growth of the sudden winding-up of the great game of Lord Wellesley's time.   Few men were better acquainted with the politics of Upper India than the Delhi Resident, and the statesmen by whom Lord Hastings was surrounded were eager to obtain an expression of his views.   They were strongly in favour of a 'settlement.'   He knew that until vigorous measures had been taken to crush the Pindarrees, and to place upon a more satisfactory footing our relations with the substantive Mahratta States, there could only be a cry of ' Peace, Peace! ' where there was no peace.   He drew up, therefore, some important State papers for the use of Lord Hastings, and, whether the Governor-General were or were not moved by him, it is very certain that the course pursued was in accordance with the views and recommendations of Charles Metcalfe.

And it is certain that such were the clearness and comprehensiveness of Metcalfe's views, and such the precision with which he expressed them, that the Governor-General saw plainly that it would be to his advantage to have such a statesman at his elbow.   But there was some active diplomatic business yet to be done by the Delhi Resident. In the great political and military transactions which distinguished the administration of Lord Hastings, Metcalfe played an important part.   The task which was set him did not in the sequel involve the rough work which fell to the share of Elphinstone and Malcolm; but it demanded the exercise of no little address.   It was his to bring the great

Patan chief, Ameer Khan, to terms; * to induce him to disband his levies and restore the tracts of country which he had taken from the Rajpoots.   It was his also to bring all the great Rajpoot chiefs into friendly alliance with us; and though the conduct of one or two of them was of a slippery and evasive character, they were all finally persuaded that it was really to their interest that they should be brought under British protection.   This done, and the war concluded, Charles Metcalfe accepted the offer of a place in the Executive Government, which had been made to him by Lord Hastings, and prepared, in the cold weather of 1818-19, to assume the office of Political Secretary, in succession to Mr John Adam, who had been elevated to a seat in Council.

He turned his back upon Delhi with a sigh.   He left behind him many dear friends.   He loved the work that had been intrusted to him, because there was great scope for beneficent action, and he felt that he had not exerted himself in vain.   In after years he looked back with pardonable pride at the results of his administration.   'Capital punishment,' he said, 'was almost wholly abstained from, and without any bad effect.   Corporal punishment was discouraged, and finally abolished.   Swords and other implements of intestine warfare, to which the people were prone, were turned into ploughshares, not figuratively alone, but literally also; villagers being made to give up their arms, which were returned to them in the shape of imple-

* This was the chief on whose pretentious, insolent manner towards Metcalfe, on the occasion of his visit to Holkar's camp in 1805, the young civilian commented in a letter quoted at page 98.

ments of agriculture. Suttees were prohibited. The rights of Government were better maintained than in other provinces, by not being subjected to the irreversible decisions of its judicial servants, with no certain laws for their guidance and control. The rights of the people were better preserved, by the maintenance of the village constitutions, and by avoiding those pernicious sales of lands for arrears of revenue, which in other provinces have tended so much to destroy the hereditary rights of the mass of the agricultural community.'

The Political Secretaryship of the Indian Government is a high and important office; one that had been, and has since been, held by men second to none in the public service. Barlow, Edmonstone, and John Adam had been Metcalfe's predecessors, and had each in turn passed on from the Secretaryship to a seat in the Supreme Council. But those who knew Metcalfe best, doubted whether the place would suit him; and he soon came to doubt it himself. Among others, Sir John Malcolm wrote to him, saying: 'Had I been near you, the King of Delhi should have been dissuaded from becoming an executive officer, and resigning power to jostle for influence. But you acted with high motives, and should not be dissatisfied with yourself.' But Metcalfe was dissatisfied with himself. He had no reason to complain of anything in his intercourse with Lord Hastings, who was always thoroughly a gentleman, with unfailing kindliness of heart and courtesy of manner. Their ministerial relations were of the most friendly, and to Metcalfe of the most flattering, kind; for

if the Governor-General did not always adopt the suggestions, or if he sometimes altered the work of his Secretary,
he explained his reasons, with such urbane consideration
for the feelings of his subordinate, that the most sensitive
mind could not be hurt. Officially he was not tried, as
some men are tried, sorely; and socially his position was
all that could be desired. He had many dear friends in
Calcutta. He renewed his pleasant intimacy with some
old companions of his youth, and he formed some new
connections, which were a solace to him to the end of his
days. But still he did not like this ministerial employment.
He had been King so long that it was irksome to him to
be dwarfed into a Wuzeer.

So he longed to escape from Calcutta, from the
Council-Chamber, and from the elbow of the Governor-
General; and he looked wistfully into the Future. ' I recognize in all your letters,' said Sir John Malcolm, 'the
unaltered Charles Metcalfe with whom I used to pace the
tent at Muttra and build castles; our expenditure on which
was subject neither to the laws of estimate nor the rules of
audit.' And now, though at a distance from each other,
they began castle-building again. Malcolm was meditating
a return to England, and he was eager to make over the
administration of Central India to his friend. Another high
civil officer, who had the charge of a contiguous tract of
country, was also about to retire from his post; and it was
considered whether those two great administrative fields
might not be conjoined and placed together in Metcalfe's
hands. ' The union of Malcolm's charge and Marjoribanks',

he wrote in a rough pencil note on the face of a letter from Mr Adam, 'would be grand indeed, and make me King of the East and the West.'

So, full of this thought, Charles Metcalfe sat down and wrote a long letter to Lord Hastings, in which, after describing the arrangement which might be made, on the resignation by Malcolm and Marjoribanks of their several charges, he said : ' When I reflect on the respectability, emoluments, luxury, comforts, and presumed prospects of my present situation, on the honour of holding a place so near your Lordship's person, combined with the enjoyment of continual intercourse with your Lordship, and on the happiness conferred by your invariable kindness, I cannot satisfy myself that I act wisely in seeking to be deprived of so many advantages in order to undertake arduous duties of fearful responsibility. It is very possible, I think, that if your Lordship should indulge my wishes, I may hereafter repent of them ; but at present I am under the influence of the following considerations.   After a sufficient experience, I feel that the duties of the Secretary's Office are not so congenial to me as those which I have heretofore performed.   I see reasons to doubt my qualifications for this line of service.   I think that many persons might be found who would fill the office more efficiently; and I fancy that I could serve your Lordship better in a situation, such as I have described, nearly resembling that which I formerly held.'   The project was favourably received by the Governor-General, and Metcalfe became so sanguine that ere long it would receive definitive approval, that he wrote to his friend Mr Jenkins, saying that Lord Hastings designed that it should take effect, and inquiring 'the best way of getting speedily to Mhow in November or December.'

But this 'Kingship of the East and the West' was not in store for him. A few weeks passed away, and a new field of labour began to expand itself before him. 'I have given up,' he again wrote to Mr Jenkins, 'the idea of succeeding Malcolm and erecting my standard on the Nerbudda, in order to go to another field, not so extensive, more compact, and more comfortable, and offering a prospect of greater leisure. It is a bad sign, I fear, that for these reasons I think it preferable. I look upon it as a sort of retirement for the rest of my service in India. I have seen enough of the Secretaryship to know that the respectability and satisfaction of those stations depend upon circumstances beyond one's control; and though under some circumstances I should prefer my present situation to any other, I shall quit it without any desire of returning to it, and without much wish of ever having a seat in Council— were it not for the name of the thing, I should say without any wish. This state of feeling I have gained by coming to Calcutta; and it is fortunate that it is so, for I have no chance whatever of a seat in Council at any time.'

There was in all this a great deal of erroneous forecast ; not the least error of all that he was going to a comfortable appointment. The situation before him was that of Resident at Hyderabad, in the Deccan. It was a first-class Political Office, equal in rank and emolument to that which he had quitted in Hindostan. The present incumbent, Mr Henry Russell,* was one of the ablest officers in the service. He

---

* Afterwards Sir Henry Russell. Metcalfe's elder brother had married Mr Russell's cousin.

was a friend connected too by marriage with Metcalfe, and had been for some time endeavouring to persuade the Political Secretary to succeed him. ' I always thought,' wrote Mr Russell, ' that you would regret the change from Delhi to Calcutta. It can hardly be long before you are placed in Council; but if this should not be the case, and you should continue desirous of returning to your own line, I should be delighted to deliver this Residency into your hands. You will find an excellent house, completely furnished; a beautiful country, one of the finest climates in India; and when the business which now presses has been disposed of, abundance of leisure to follow your personal pursuits.' In another letter the same writer said; ' In point of magnitude your situation in Malwah will certainly be superior to this Residency; but you may do as much real good, and acquire as much real importance here, as you could there. The office now proposed will be great, by adding many things together; at Hyderabad it will be compact and considerable in itself, and will afford, for several years to come, an ample field for the exertions of a man of talent and benevolence. As to personal convenience, there can be no comparison. In Malwah you will have no time to yourself, and you will either be wandering about the country, which is always irksome when it is perpetual, or you will have to build and furnish a house, at the expense certainly of not less than a lakh of rupees, out of your private fortune. At Hyderabad, after the first six months, when you have looked thoroughly into everything, you will find, compared with what you have been accustomed to, little to give you trouble; at least half of your time will be at your disposal, and you will step

at once, without care and expense, into a house completely
furnished, and provided with every accommodation.' These
many-sided arguments prevailed. Looking on this picture
and on that, Metcalfe began to incline towards the Hyderabad
Residency. When Mr Russell resigned, the appointment
was offered to him; and he accepted it without much
hesitation.

He parted from Lord Hastings on the best possible
terms. The Governor-General wrote him a letter, expressive both of public and private friendship. 'And now,
my dear sir, for yourself,' he said, after dwelling on political business, 'let me assure you that I have been duly
sensible of your kind and cordial attachment, and that it is
with earnest prayers for your welfare that I wish you all
possible prosperity and comfort. We shall not meet again
in India, and the chances for it in Europe must, considering
my age, be small; but I shall rejoice in hearing from you,
and you will believe that I remain yours, faithfully,
HASTINGS.'

Towards the end of the year 1820, accompanied by a
few young friends who had been appointed his assistants,
Charles Metcalfe set out for Hyderabad. His correspondence
with his predecessor had supplied him with good substantial
information relating to the state of the country. But he
found, upon the spot, that the disorders of which he had
heard were more deeply seated than he had imagined. The
Nizam had borrowed from an extensive banking-house at
Hyderabad large sums of money at high interest, for the
payment of his troops and other current expenses of his
Government. The result was that his ministers were com-

pelled to resort to many acts of oppression and injustice to wring money from the people to keep the machinery of the State from altogether suspending its action. It was plain that the interference of the British Government had long been imperatively demanded. Something had already been done; but something also remained to be done. 'The more I see of the Nizam's country,' wrote Metcalfe, after some six months' experience, ' the more I am convinced that, without our interposition, it must have gone to utter ruin, and that the measures which have been adopted were indispensably necessary for its continued existence as an inhabited territory. As it is, the deterioration has been excessive; and the richest and most easily cultivated soil in the world has been nearly depopulated, chiefly by the oppressions of Government. It will require tender nursing. The settlements are advancing. The moderate revenue, which it has been found necessary to receive in many instances, has greatly disappointed the Government, which, not convinced by the depopulation of villages in consequence of ruinous extortion, would have persisted in the same unprincipled course until the rest were depopulated also. The loss of revenue, if confidence be established by the settlement, will be but temporary. In some of the settlements, on which the assessments for the first year are the lowest, they are doubled and trebled, and in some instances quadrupled and quintupled, in the period—generally five years—for which the settlements are concluded. Such are the productive powers of the soil, that I have no doubt of the propriety of the increase where it occurs to that extent, the assessments for the first year having been made uncommonly low from local circumstances affecting the particular cases. After the conclusion of the settlement, one measure more, and I think only one, will be necessary, and to that I conceive our interference ought to be limited. We must preserve a check on the native officers of the Government, to provide that they do not violate the settlement, otherwise they certainly will; in which case it would be better that it had never been concluded, as it would then, by giving false confidence, furnish the means of additional extortion, and would effectually destroy the very foundation of our probable success, which is the reliance put on our faith and guarantee. I therefore propose, with the assent of the Nizam's Government, to employ the assistants of the Residency and some of the best qualified of the Nizam's officers in different divisions of the Nizam's territory, for the purposes of checking oppression and violation of faith on the part of the officers of Government, securing adherence to settlements, taking cognizance of crimes, and looking after the police, especially on the frontiers, on which point I receive continual complaints from the neighbouring Governments. These officers should take no part in the collection of the revenues, nor in the general administration of the country; neither should the farms of the Nizam's Government be invaded. The officers should not have any peculiar official designation, founded on their duties, lest it should be considered as a partial introduction of our rule; and if at any time, from good schooling or rare goodness, there should be reasonable ground of hope that a district could be managed safely without such a check, I should think it a duty to withdraw the officer from that district, though I have no expectation, I confess, that such is likely to be the case. In order to save expense to the Nizam's Government, the number of divisions should be small—six or seven in all. This would make each of them very extensive, but not, I hope, too much so for the performance of the duty. They ought to be continually in motion (the officers, I mean), and the Resident ought to be frequently in motion also, to observe the state of the several divisions. I hope that this measure will be approved, for on it all my hopes of successful reform in the Nizam's country are built. Without it they will fall to the ground. It appears to me to be the only way of preserving the Nizam's Government in all its parts entire, with the addition of the check of European integrity, which can at any time be removed without damaging any other part of the edifice, if at any time it can be dispensed with. If the Nizam's officers were allowed to go on without some such check, it would soon end, I think, in our being compelled to take the country entirely into our own hands.'

But all the nursing in the world could do nothing, so long as there remained the great cancer of the debt to eat into the very life of the State. The English money-lenders had got fast hold of the Nizam and his minister. They were friends of the Resident and friends of the Governor-General; but the former determined to rescue the country from their grasp. He knew that it could not be done without sore travail; he knew that he would lose many friends and make many enemies; and that the cordial support of the Government was little likely to be obtained. Sir John Malcolm had written to him, saying: 'Every step that you take to ameliorate the condition of the country will be misrepresented by fellows who have objects as incompatible with public virtue and good government as darkness is with light. . . . You have to fight the good fight, and to stand with the resolute but calm feelings such a cause must inspire against all species of attacks that artful and sordid men can make, or that weak and prejudiced men can support. . . . I am quite confident in your ultimate triumph, though I expect that you will have great vexation and annoyance.'

And truly he had; but much as it cost him, he was resolute to go through it to the end. It was the sorest task that he ever set himself, for he was a man of warm affections, and it cut him to the heart to array himself against the personal interests of his friends. But he felt that, in the emergency that had then arisen, the very life of the Hyderabad State hung upon his independent action. He was determined to inquire, where inquiry must of necessity have been exposure, and to cut off the stream from which so much had been poured into the coffers of his friends. It is a long story. The great banking-house of William Palmer and Company suffered greatly by Metcalfe's sturdy uncompromising conduct; and for a while he fell under the displeasure of the Governor-General. But Lord Hastings had too many good qualities of head and heart not at last to do justice to a public servant who had striven only for the public good.

The history of these transactions is recorded in many folio volumes. Never, perhaps, was a greater flood of controversy let loose to bewilder the judgments of men never did partisanship stream forth in more heady currents than when the subject of the Hyderabad Loans was discussed in public papers, in private pamphlets, and on the proprietary platform of the East India Company. This is not the pleasantest part of the story of Metcalfe's life; but there is nothing in the whole of it more illustrative of the sturdy independence and honesty of his character. His private correspondence with Lord Hastings has been published. It cannot be given here in detail; but in the following passage of a letter to the Governor-General, there is so much that bears undoubted witness to the fact that it was a sore trial and travail to the Hyderabad Resident to undermine and to fire the train that was to explode the prosperity of so many of his friends. He was accused of hostility to the house of William Palmer and Company. To this he replied: 'I am at a loss what to say to this, for I know not whence such an idea can have arisen. Excepting Mr. W. Palmer, the European partners of that firm were my friends before I came to Hyderabad. Mr W. Palmer's brother, Mr John Palmer, has been my much-esteemed and warm friend for the last twenty years; and Mr William Palmer himself is one of those men so amiably constituted by nature, that it is impossible to know ever so little of him without feeling one's regard and esteem attracted. There is no family at Hyderabad with which I have so much intercourse as Sir William Rumbold's. Mr Lambe, one of the partners, accompanied me in his medical capacity as acting-surgeon of the Residency during my tour from Hyderabad to this place, and in every respect on the most intimate and confidential footing. Since I came to this place I have accepted, without hesitation, as a personal favour from Mr Hastings Palmer, the head of the branch established at this place, the loan of a house which I occupied till I could otherwise accommodate myself. I may add, that I have lately given my assent to extraordinary exactions, proposed by the Minister, for the purpose of meeting the demands of that firm on the Government, which the Minister would not attempt without my concurrence. All these circumstances, I venture to say, would naturally indicate to the public mind feelings the very reverse of hostile; and I am so unconscious of any appearances that could have justified, in Shroffs or any others, an inference of adverse sentiment, that, notwithstanding the apparent presumption of disputing the accuracy of Sir William Rumbold's apprehension on a point on which he ought to be so well informed, I am much inclined to doubt the existence of such an impression; to ascribe whatever losses the house may have sustained to other causes, and to attribute Sir William Rumbold's persuasion on the subject to artful misrepresentations industriously conveyed to him, for purposes distinct from the concerns or interest of the firm. I could conscientiously deny the existence, on my part, of a shadow of ill will; but I might deceive your Lordship were I to stop here. I cannot help entertaining sentiments regarding the transactions of that firm, which, as being adverse to their own views of their interests, they might possibly charge to the account of ill will. Those sentiments have been slow in growth, but strengthen as I see more of the state of affairs in this country. I lament that Messrs W. Palmer and Company have grasped at such large profits in their negotiations with the Nizam's Government as place his interest and theirs in direct opposition. I lament that they have succeeded in conveying to your Lordship's mind an exaggerated impression of services to the Nizam's Government, which obtains for them on public grounds your Lordship's support, in a degree to which they do not seem to others to be entitled —support which for any ordinary mercantile transactions would be wholly unnecessary. I lament that they are so sensible or fanciful of their weakness on every other ground as to be drawing on your Lordship's personal favour on every occasion in which they apprehend the most distant approach of danger, extending their sensitiveness to the smallest diminution, from whatever cause, of their immediate profits—thus repeatedly forcing on the public the name of your Lordship as the patron of their transactions, whilst these are likened by the world in general to former pecuniary dealings in Oude and the Carnatic. I lament the connection between them and Rajah Chundoo-Lall, because it tends to draw them quite out of their sphere of merchants, and make them political partisans. It is scarcely possible that this can ultimately be beneficial to them. I lament their connection with some of the most profligate and rapacious of the governors of districts, through whom their character, and, what is of more consequence, the British name, has become involved in detestable acts of oppression, extortion, and atrocity. I lament the power which they exercise in the country, through their influence with the Minister; enforcing payment of debts, due to them either originally or by transfer, in an authoritative manner not becoming their mercantile character; acting with the double force of the Nizam's Government and the British name. I lament the continuance of their loan to the Nizam's Government, because it would be a great relief to its finances to discharge it. I lament the terms of the loan, because I think them exorbitant. I lament the concealment of the actual terms of the loan at the time of the transaction, and the delusive prospect held out, by which your Lordship was led to conceive it to be so much more advantageous to the Nizam's Government than it really was. I lament the monopoly established in their favour by the sanction and virtual guarantee of the British Government, because it deprives the Nizam's Government of the power of going into the European money-market, where, with the same sanction, it might borrow money at less than half the rate of interest which it pays to Messrs Palmer and Company. I lament the political influence acquired by the house through the supposed countenance of your Lordship to Sir William Rumbold, because it tends to the perversion of political influence for the purposes of private gain. All these things I lament, not only because they are in themselves evils, but because they must in the end injure the firm itself. Individuals of it may snatch a hasty and splendid harvest, if they do not care for aught else; but the firm itself cannot continue to flourish on such a pinnacle, where it becomes an object for all the shafts of envy, hostility, and unjust opposition, as well as just objection.'

Nothing more manly or more dignified, but within the limits of becoming respect to an official superior, was ever written. It was not lost upon the Governor-General, although it was long before he replied, and then only in a meagre letter. That fidelity which was the strength of Lord Hastings's character was also its weakness.* He was very faithful to his friends; and if he sometimes erred in suffering the man to prevail over the ruler, and supported not wisely but too well those whom he loved and cherished, it was because he lacked the sterner stuff which should have prompted him to restrain the kindliness of his nature and the warmth of his heart, when they were likely to carry him into erratic courses. He was wounded to the quick by Metcalfe's conduct, which he seemed at first not wholly to understand; but afterwards some new light began to dawn upon him and he saw that this matter of the connection of the Hyderabad State with the mercantile house was something far worse than he had suspected. One result of Metcalfe's investigations had been that he had satisfied himself that some of the former members of the British Mission, before his time, had been associated with Messrs William Palmer and Company, in a sort of constructive partnership, which gave them a direct interest in the financial profits of the house. Metcalfe was slow to believe this; but when the conviction came upon him, as it did at last, with irresistible force, he was greatly disturbed in his mind; and he did not doubt that it was his duty to represent the circumstance to

* In the popular literature of my boyhood, the 'Percy Anecdotes,' which appeared from time to time in little pocket volumes, held a distinguished place. The collection was subjectively arranged, and each volume contained a portrait of the individual man or woman supposed to be the brightest exemplar of the particular quality illustrated. I remember that a likeness of Lord Hastings was the frontispiece of the volume devoted to Fidelity.

the Governor-General. In this difficulty he placed himself in confidential communication with two of his friends and brother civilians in Calcutta. The one was Mr John Adam, then a member of the Supreme Council; and the other was Mr George Swinton, who had succeeded Metcalfe in the office of Political Secretary. Both were able and honest men—distinguished members of that new class of Civil Servants, who had by this time nearly displaced altogether the generation by whom private trade and public service were not regarded as incompatible. It was then determined that Mr Adam should, in the first instance, avail himself of a convenient opportunity to make a private statement on this painful subject to the Governor-General; and he did so. Lord Hastings received it, as any honourable man would receive such a revelation; and though, if he felt strongly on the subject, he veiled his emotions at the time, it appears to be certain that the scales then fell from his eyes, and he began from that time to consider, in another light, the conduct of the Hyderabad Resident, and to feel more kindly towards him. The result was a reconciliation. Metcalfe was touched by the altered tone of the Governor-General, as reported to him by Adam and Swinton. He was the least aggressive man in the world. He yearned to be in friendly relations with the whole human family. His own particular weakness was a propensity to serve his friends. He was very sorry for the pain that he had given to others, although he knew that he had only done his duty. So he grasped eagerly at the opportunity of reconciliation unexpectedly afforded to him by the manner in which Lord Hastings had received his last disclosure of corruption at

Hyderabad. So he sat down and wrote a letter to the Governor-General—not penitential, not submissive; but *frank*, and sorrowful in its frankness, which drew forth fitting response, and the breach between them was closed.

Throughout all this long and most painful controversy, Metcalfe had been much sustained and solaced by pleasant intercourse with the beloved friends who had accompanied him to Hyderabad, and were assisting him in the duties of the Residency.* And when this trouble was at an end he was quite content. He was of a very trusting and affectionate nature, and he infused into his friendships a tenderness and devotedness, if not 'passing the love of woman,' scarcely surpassed by it.† He was so happy, indeed, in these relations, that he was alarmed and disturbed by a rumour that he was likely soon to attain to that great object of general ambition, a seat in the Supreme Council. 'Though

---

* This unfortunate business not only sorely distressed his mind, but also affected his health. He had a very severe illness in 1823, and was compelled to go to Calcutta for surgical and medical advice. Lord Hastings had then left India, and had been succeeded in the Government by Lord Amherst. After a sojourn of a few months at the Presidency he returned to Hyderabad, greatly benefited by the professional skill of Nicolson and Martin.

† 'How the heart,' he wrote to one of his friends at this time, 'rejoices and bounds at the thought of the handwriting of a beloved friend ! And how it overflows with delight, how it warms, expands, and boils over, in reading the affectionate language which one knows to have been poured forth from a congenial heart. There are joys of this kind in the pure love which exists between man and man, which cannot, I think, be surpassed in that more alloyed attachment between the opposite sexes, to which the name of love is generally exclusively applied.'

I do not pretend to be insensible to the honour of a seat in Council,' he wrote to a friend, in October, 1824, ' and the possible result of such an appointment, I should rejoice at the nomination of some other person, to put out of credit those rumours which I am told are on the increase in Calcutta regarding my elevation to that dignity, and of which the realization would remove me from the present home of my affections and the ties formed in this sphere. I cannot think on this subject without pain, knowing as I do by experience that separation and removal to distant scenes, though they may leave unimpaired good will, regard, esteem, friendship, confidence, and even affection, are still fatal to that warmth of feeling, that intimacy of ideas, that delight of close and continual intercourse, which constitute what I call the luxuries of friendship.' But, although in no man were individual partialities stronger than in Charles Metcalfe, there was another side to his overflowing kindliness of heart. He was the most hospitable of men, at a time when hospitality was one of the most prominent virtues of the English in the East. He kept open house at the Residency—often to his inconvenience and disturbance. He lamented, indeed, that he had not a residence a little way in the country, to which he could sometimes withdraw himself, with a few chosen friends.* But he looked upon hospitality as one of

---

* He wrote to a friend in December, 1824, saying : ' I feel the want of a country-house incessantly. As long as I live at the Residency it will be a public-house, and as long as the billiard-table stands the Residency will be a tavern. I wish that I could introduce a nest of white ants secretly, without any one's kenning thereof, if the said ants would devour the said table, and cause it to disappear.

the duties of his high office; and it gave him infinite pleasure to think that he was contributing to the happiness of
others.

But that which contributed most of all to his inward
peace of mind, and to the outward cheerfulness which was
its visible expression, was an habitual sense of the goodness
of God, and an incessant feeling of gratitude to the Almighty
giver. He was continually rejoicing in the Lord and lifting
up his heart in praise and thanksgiving. 'If I am really
the happy man you suppose me to be,' he wrote to one of
his most intimate friends at this time, 'I will tell you, as
far as I know myself, the secret of my happiness. You will
perhaps smile, for I am not sure that your mind has taken
the turn that might induce you to sympathize. But be
assured that I am in earnest. I live in a state of fervent
and incessant gratitude to God for the favours and mercies
which I have experienced throughout my life. The feeling
is so strong that it often overflows in tears, and is so rooted
that I do not think that any misfortune could shake it. It
leads to constant devotion and firm content; and, though
I am not free from those vexations and disturbances to
which the weak temper of man is subject, I am guarded
by that feeling against any lasting depression.' There are
few who will not contrast such psychological manifestations
as these with the gloomy and despairing revelations of the
inmost soul of Henry Martyn. Except in a common devotion to duty, each according to his own light, no two men

But I· do not like, either in deed or word, to make any attack on
an instrument of amusement which is so much relished by some of
us, who do not observe the consequences to which it leads.'

were ever more unlike each other than the chaplain and
the civilian who meet together in this little gallery of por-
traits.   The one delighted to suffer and to grieve; the other
rejoiced in the Lord always, and was glad.

From the tranquil pleasures of the last year at the Hyderabad Residency, the turmoil and excitement over, Metcalfe was aroused by a summons to repair to a different part
of the country, and to take upon himself the burden and the
responsibility of more exciting business.   The British Government in India were now again at war with their neighbours.   The Burmese campaign was then in full progress;
and in another part of the country preparations were being
made for an offensive movement, on a grand scale, against
the great Ját fortress of Bhurtpore, which, twenty years
before, had successfully defied the British Army under Lord
Lake.   Lord Amherst was Governor-General; Lord Combermere was Commander-in-Chief.   The political control
of the expedition fell naturally under the Delhi Resident-
ship.   In that important diplomatic office, Sir David Ochterlony had succeeded Mr Charles Metcalfe at Delhi.   Notwithstanding the difference of their ages, they had been
fast friends for many years.   The veteran soldier looked
upon the rising civilian as a beloved son in whose prosperity
he rejoiced, and of whose reputation he was proud.   Metcalfe, upon his part, not unmindful of the old man's weaknesses, regarded him with tender affection, and admired his
many noble qualities.   In the emergency which had arisen,
Ochterlony, without instructions from Government, had
acted with a promptitude which they called precipitancy;
they had repudiated his authority, and had arrested the for-

ward movement which he had made to overawe the enemy, with insufficient means at his disposal. The brave old man had thought to accomplish by a sudden blow what in the opinion of the highest authorities demanded the utmost deliberation and all the resources of scientific warfare. This indiscretion was his ruin. It was determined that he was not the man for the crisis; and Metcalfe, therefore, was requested to proceed to Delhi and to take his place. ' Much as your services,' wrote Lord Amherst to him, ' are still demanded at Hyderabad, a nobler field opens for them in the scene of your former residence and employment, and I flatter myself that, unless there should be some impediment of which I am not aware to your proceeding to Delhi, you will readily afford your services in a quarter where they are now most urgently required, and where, I hesitate not to say, you can of all men in India most benefit your Government and your country.' And, on the same day, his friend, Secretary Swinton, wrote to him, saying : ' To prevent any misconception on your part, I am directed to state to you distinctly that the question of Sir David Ochterlony's retirement does not depend on your accepting or declining the proposal now made to you. If Government should be disappointed in its wish to avail itself of your services as his successor, it must then look to the next best man.' Metcalfe felt, and was afterwards fully assured, that if anything could reconcile Ochterlony to his removal from office, it would be the fact that Charles Metcalfe was to be his successor.*

So Metcalfe accepted the offer that was made to him;

* Ochterlony did not live to see his successor installed. He died, broken-hearted, before Metcalfe reached Delhi.

but he did so with a heavy heart. 'I am out of spirits,' he wrote to one of his chosen friends, 'at the change in my prospects. I looked forward to the assemblage of all I love and a happy time during the rains—our labours in the country to be afterwards resumed. I cannot say that I shall be here for a month, as I must be prepared to start at a moment's notice—then to leave all behind. I wish that I could take you all with me, and then, although I should still regret our desertion of the fate of this country, my personal regrets would be converted into joyful anticipations.' He said, in another letter, that he ' wished he could have been allowed to rest in peace in the quarter that had become the home of his heart.' He was enabled, however, to take one of his beloved friends * with him to Delhi ; and two others afterwards followed him to that place.

When Metcalfe left Hyderabad, he was Sir Charles Metcalfe, Baronet. His elder brother Theophilus had died, two or three years before, in England, leaving only a daughter ; so the title and the paternal estate of Fern Hill in Berkshire, had passed to the second son of Sir Thomas Metcalfe. The change was a very distressing one to him, for he was fondly attached to his brother. It is by this designation of ' Sir Charles Metcalfe ' that he is best known to history and to the world; and India claims him by no other.

I do not purpose to write in detail of the siege and capture of Bhurtpore, or of the events which preceded it. It is sufficient to state that on the 16th of September a formal

* John Sutherland, afterwards Colonel Sutherland, one of our most distinguished political officers.

resolution was passed by the Government of India, declaring that, ' impressed with a full conviction that the existing disturbance at Bhurtpore, if not speedily quieted, would produce general commotion and interruption of the public tranquillity in Upper India, and feeling convinced that it was their solemn duty, no less than their right, as the paramount power and conservators of the general peace, to interfere for the prevention of these evils, and that these evils would be best prevented by the maintenance of the succession of the rightful heir to the Raj of Bhurtpore, whilst such a course would be in strict consistency with the uniform practice and policy of the British Government in all analogous cases, the Governor-General in Council resolved that authority be conveyed to Sir C. T. Metcalfe to accomplish the above objects, if practicable, by expostulation and remonstrance, and, should these fail, by a resort to measures of force.' The issues of peace or war were thus placed in his hands. The responsibility cast upon him was great; but no such burden ever oppressed or disquieted him. He knew that there was small chance of expostulation and remonstrance availing in that conjuncture; but he knew also that there was a noble army, under an experienced commander, prepared to march upon Bhurtpore, and he saw clearly the advantages of victorious operations against such a place, at a time when our dubious successes in Burmah were being exaggerated by native rumour into defeats. He did his best to obtain the desired results by diplomacy; but, perhaps, he was not sorry to fail. The letters which he addressed to the recusant chiefs were said, by the Government party in Calcutta, to be ' models of correspondence; ' and there the uses of the letters began and ended. They elicited only un-meaning and evasive answers; and so a proclamation of war was issued, and the word was given for the advance of the army on Bhurtpore.

On the 6th of December, Sir Charles Metcalfe joined the camp of the Commander-in-Chief. On the 10th the Army was before the celebrated Jat fortress. With the deepest interest did the civilian watch the progress of the siege. Years had not subdued his military ardour, but they had brought him increased military experience. For twenty years he had been studying our military policy in India, and speculating on the causes of our successes and our failures. No man had written more emphatically against that arrogant fatuity which so often displays itself in the conduct of difficult and hazardous operations with insuffi-cient means; no man had urged upon the Government more convincingly the wisdom of securing success by the employment of that irresistible combination of science and force which a great European power can always bring against an Asiatic enemy. And now, although fortified at the outset by the knowledge that the army which had ad-vanced against Bhurtpore was sufficiently strong in numbers, that it was adequately equipped with Artillery, and that some of the best Engineer officers in India were in camp, he began to doubt, as the siege advanced, whether too much would not, after the old fashion, be left to chance. ' We are not getting on here as I like,' he wrote on the 6th of January. ' At one time we were, and I had great hopes that the place would be taken scientifically, without risk or loss. I have now no such expectation. We are to storm soon, and with the usual uncertainty. We may succeed, and I hope that we shall; but we may fail, and whether we succeed or fail will depend upon chance. The business will not be made so secure as I thought it would be, and as I conceive it ought to be. What we have brought together our large means for I do not understand, if risk is to be incurred at the end of our operations. It would have been better tried at the beginning. We might have taken the place in the first hour,* and we may take it now. But much as I shall rue it, I shall not be surprised if we fail. It staggers my opinion to find General Nicolls confident, but I cannot surrender my judgment even to his on this point absolutely, and I remain anxious and nervous. My opinion will not be altered by success, for I shall still consider it as the work of chance. We ought not to leave anything to chance, and we are doing it with regard to everything. Either our boasted science is unavailable or unavailing against Indian fortifications, or we are now about to throw away our advantage. I shudder both for Nicolls and for Sutherland. The former, I think, may perish in carrying on his difficult attack, and the ardour of the latter will carry him into unnecessary danger. God preserve them both, and save us from the not improbable consequences of our folly. You will have good news or bad very soon.'

I do not know whether Sir Charles Metcalfe, who was in frequent communication with Lord Combermere, expressed these anxieties to the military chief, but on that

---

* This was said of Sebastopol in 1855, and of Delhi in 1857.

same day the idea of an immediate assault was abandoned.* The breaching-batteries had not opened Bhurtpore sufficiently to admit the storming columns with good hope of success, so it was determined to insure victory by mining. The attack was, therefore, delayed for a further period of twelve days. 'We stormed on the 18th,' wrote Metcalfe, a few days afterwards. 'It was a glorious affair, and our success was most complete. . . . . . Complete as our success has been, we have had a narrow escape from a most disastrous defeat. We can now see that neither the right breach nor the left, both made by battering, was practicable. . . . . Our first mines were bungling, but the latter were very grand. That to the right did a great deal of mischief to ourselves; for the people assembling in the trenches were too near, and the explosion of the mine took effect outwards. It was a grand sight, and was immediately followed by that of the advance of the storming columns up the two great breaches. That on the left advanced first on the signal of the explosion of the mine, and that on the right immediately afterwards. Both mounted the breaches steadily, and as quickly as the loose earth and steepness of the ascent would admit, and attained the summit without opposition. It was a most animating spectacle.' All this is mere history; but it is history written by Metcalfe, who

* In the 'Life of Lord Combermere,' by Lady Combermere and Captain Knollys, there is a letter from the Commander-in-Chief to the Governor-General, dated January 11, which says : 'It having been ascertained that the batteries were not sufficient effectually to break the walls, a mine was commenced on the evening of the 6th,' &c. &c.

saw the events which are here described. He accompanied the Commander-in-Chief into one of the breaches, but, thinking that he could better see what was going on from another position, he had separated himself from Lord Combermere. Soon after this there was an explosion, from which the chief had a very narrow escape. ' I congratulate myself,' wrote Metcalfe, ' for many about the Commander-in-chief were killed or bruised by the explosion of our mine, and his own escape was surprising.'

So Bhurtpore was taken ; and Metcalfe, when the work of war was at an end, placed upon the throne the boy-Prince whom his usurping uncle had endeavoured to thrust out from his rightful inheritance. The usurper was sent, a prisoner, to Allahabad. There was then some further work to be done in the principality of Ulwur, but it did not give much trouble, and Metcalfe returned to Delhi. Public affairs had gone prosperously with him ; but in those which were much nearer and dearer to his heart there had been a fatality of the most distressing character. Within a short space he lost two of his most beloved friends. The first was Captain Barnett; the second was Mr Richard Wells, a young member of the Bengal Civil Service, who had followed him from Hyderabad, and had been appointed an assistant at Delhi. These calamities cut him to the heart. ' You will have heard long before this,' he wrote to Major Moore, then secretary to the Hyderabad Residency, ' of the second blow which, in a short space, it has pleased Almighty God to inflict upon us. One brief month included to us here the death of both Barnett and Wells. . . . We have been thoroughly wretched. The world is fast receding from

me ; for what is the world without the friends of our heart ?
You remember the three friends with whom I arrived at
Hyderabad in 1820—Barnett, Wells, Mackenzie. I loved
them all cordially. Where are they now ? I cannot write
on the subject. But I can hardly think of any other.' In
another letter, speaking of the death of Richard Wells, he
said that he could hardly believe that the anguish of the
desolated widow could be greater than his. ' Were I to
hear at this moment,' he added, ' of my nomination to be
Governor-General of India or Prime Minister of England,
I am sure that the intelligence would create no sensation
but disgust.' Ambition was ever heavy within him, but it
was light in the balance against the great wealth of affection
garnered in that warm human heart.

He had now fairly earned a seat in the Supreme Council, and in 1827 it was conferred upon him. He then took
up his residence in Calcutta, and was the most hospitable
and the most popular of men. In those days the Supreme
Council consisted of the Governor-General, the Command-
er-in- Chief, and two members of the covenanted Civil
Service. Lord Amherst and Lord Combermere still held
office. The civilian colleague, who welcomed Metcalfe
to the Presidency, was his old friend, Mr Butterworth
Bayley—a man whom to know was to reverence and to
love. He had risen to high office after a career of nearly
thirty years of good service, chiefly in the unostentatious
paths of the judicial department. His life had been a far
less stirring one than Metcalfe's ; but he had done his own

particular work so well that few men bore a higher official reputation, whilst his unfailing kindness of heart and suavity of manner endeared him to all who had the privilege of coming within the reach of their genial influences. There was not one of his contemporaries, perhaps, whom Metcalfe would sooner have found at the Board, nor one with whom he was likely to act more amicably in Council, notwithstanding occasional divergences of opinion.

Sir John Malcolm, who was then Governor of Bombay, wrote to Sir Charles Metcalfe, saying, ' If you are my *beau idéal* of a good councillor, you content yourself with reading what comes before you, and writing a full minute now and then, when the subject merits it ; and do not fret yourself and perplex others by making much of small matters. Supposing this to be the case, you must have leisure, and if I find you have, I must now and then intrude upon it.' But Metcalfe complained bitterly of the want of leisure. His life was a great conflict with Time. ' My days,' he wrote to a friend, ' are portioned as much as possible, so as to enable me to do everything that I have to do, but in vain. Thursday and Friday are appropriated to Council, and nothing else can be done upon those days. Monday, Tuesday, and Wednesday are wholly devoted to the reading of papers that come in, and reading and revising those that go out; but all three are not enough. Saturday I take for writing minutes and revising despatches that go out, but find it too little. . . . . You know how little I have written to you, to other correspondents still less ; and yet the number of letters I have to answer is overwhelming. I have been at work for some hours now, but I have still twenty-five letters on my table requiring answers—six or eight from England. The want of time makes me half mad. . . . . To add to my distress, people will have the kindness to breakfast with me. I am six miles away from them, but that is not sufficient. I shut my doors at all other times, come who may. I should be happy in my business if I had more time for the performance of my various duties, but the want of it plagues me. The only resource left is to withdraw from society, and to work at night, but I shall tear my eyes to pieces if I do.'—[*February* 3, 1828.] This systematic distribution of time was not found to answer; and so, a few weeks later, it was changed. 'I have made,' he said, 'a great alteration in my mode of despatching my business. I reserve no day for any particular branch, but get over all, as well as I can, as it comes in. . . . . The bundle of private letters which used to accumulate for the day in the week set apart was quite overwhelming and insurmountable. I now go pell-mell at all in the ring, and, as far as the new method has yet gone, it promises better than the last.'—[*March* 8, 1828.] But the claims of society were more oppressive than the claims of official work. 'It requires,' he wrote, 'a strong conviction of its being a duty to sustain me in keeping up society. Were I to follow my natural or acquired taste, I should fast sink into habits of seclusion when the company of friends is not obtainable. I have nothing to complain of in society, and am happy enough when in it, but the making up of parties, issuing of invitations, &c., are troublesome operations, which harass me, and frequently drive me from my purpose. My conscience is continually reproaching

me with want of hospitality and attention to individuals
entitled to them.   Many a man has come to Calcutta, and
gone from it without once receiving an invitation to my
house, which an indescribable something—anything but
good will—has prevented until it was too late. My house,
although it has more rooms for entertaining than any other
house in Calcutta, is deficient in that kind of room which
is requisite in large parties—the ones which, with respect
to general society, would answer best for me, as killing all
my birds with one stone.   I am thinking of building a
grand ball-room.   It would not, I suppose, cost less, altogether, than 20,000 rupees—a large sum to lay out on another man's property ; but I am not sure that it would not
be cheaper than giving parties in the Town-hall—my other
resource—each of which costs above 8000 rupees, and cannot, therefore, be often repeated. . . . . . I enjoy the society of our house-party very much, retaining, however,
my old habits of seclusion from breakfast to dinner, which
are seldom broken in upon, except by the Bushby's children, who trot up frequently to my loft in the third story
where I have my sitting-room and library as well as bedroom.   It is, in short, the portion of the house which I
keep to myself, and there they make me show them the
pictures, &c., being privileged by infancy to supersede all
affairs of every kind.'—[*May* 18, 1828.]

His distaste for general society seemed to grow stronger
as time advanced, but to the outer world it appeared that
he delighted in crowds.   He gave splendid entertainments
—large dinner-parties and balls—but he regarded these
merely as ' duties proper to his station.'   What he thought

on the subject may be gathered from his correspondence with his familiar friends; but in this I am inclined to think that there is observable a little of the exaggeration of temporary languor and depression of spirit. ' I am withdrawing myself more and more from public intercourse,' he wrote in March, 1829, 'and am only waiting an opportunity to shake off the remaining shackles and become entirely a recluse; since neither is the performance of public duty compatible with a waste of time in society, nor is knowledge of men's characters in general compatible with that respect for them without which society has no pleasure in it. I am becoming every day more and more sour, and morose, and dissatisfied.' Metcalfe had said this before. But he deceived himself to his own disadvantage. It was impossible to look into his kindly expressive face, or to converse with him for a few minutes, without feeling that there was in truth no sourness or moroseness in his nature. The fact is, that he lamented the loss of his old friends, and he had not at that time formed new associations of the same gratifying character. 'The longer I live,' he said, 'the less I like strange faces, or any other faces than those of friends whom I love.' It may be suggested, also, that the depression of spirit often observable in his correspondence at this time is attributable in some measure to his sedentary habits. He took very little exercise. Unlike Malcolm and Elphinstone, he was an exceedingly bad horseman, and everything of an athletic character was entirely out of his line.*

* He occasionally rode out in the early morning within the spacious grounds of his mansion at Alipore, which he occupied during

But, as time advanced, Sir Charles Metcalfe's position in Calcutta became more and more endurable, until he well-nigh regained his old buoyancy and elasticity of mind. In July, 1828, Lord William Bentinck had succeeded Lord Amherst as Governor-General of India. Metcalfe's first impressions of his new colleague were favourable to him, but somehow or other the two did not assimilate, and the councillor, who had some reason to think that Lord William had been prejudiced against him by the Rumbold party at home, said that the new Governor-General did not understand him, and preferred anybody's opinions to his. 'This forces me,' he said, ' to record dissentient opinions in minutes more frequently than would be necessary, if we could co-operate with more sympathy.' And then he added, with that union of candour and modesty which made him so often express mistrust of himself, ' I fear that there is a want of suavity, or a want of blandness, or some other defect about me, that is not palatable.' This was, perhaps, the last cause in the world to which any one else would have assigned the want of cordial co-operation between the two statesmen which marked the first year of their connection. But, whatever the cause, it soon passed away, and with it the effect. Lord William Bentinck and Sir Charles Metcalfe became fast friends and sympathizing workmen. This

the later years of his Calcutta residence. He had a stout cobby white horse, which carried him with tolerable safety, and he generally wore top-boots. These had been for many years a favourite article of attire. I found among his papers a rough pen-and-ink sketch, contrasting the lower extremities of Sir Charles Metcalfe (in tops) with those of Lord Hastings (in hessians), the distinctive difference being by no means confined to the boots.

alone would have made the latter a happier man. But there were favourable circumstances which touched him more nearly. He was gathering around him a cordon of friends. Lord William Bentinck went up the country, and then Mr Bayley became Vice-President in Council and Deputy-Governor of Bengal. His time of office, however, having expired in November, 1830, Sir Charles Metcalfe succeeded him. This enabled him to add to his 'family ' two members who contributed much to his happiness. The one was Captain John Sutherland, of whom I have already spoken; the other was Lieutenant James Higginson,* whose acquaintance he had made at Bhurtpore, and who had afterwards been on the Staff of Lord William Bentinck. The former was now made private secretary, and the latter aide-de-camp, to the Deputy-Governor; and Metcalfe no longer complained that he was cut off from his friends.

As the members of Council were appointed only for five years, Sir Charles Metcalfe's term of office would have expired in August, 1832. But Lord William Bentinck, as the time approached, determined to make an effort to retain his services; so he wrote urgently to the President of the India Board (Mr Charles Grant), saying: 'Sir Charles Metcalfe will be a great loss to me. He quite ranks with Sir Thomas Munro, Sir John Malcolm, and Mr Elphinstone. If it be intended—and the necessity cannot admit of a doubt—to form a second local Government in Bengal, he undoubtedly ought to be at the head. I strongly re-

* Afterwards Sir James Higginson, Governor of the Mauritius. These arrangements were necessarily of a temporary character contingent on the return of the Governor-General to the Presidency.

commend him. Whilst he has always maintained the most perfect independence of character and conduct, he has been to me a most zealous supporter and friendly colleague.' The 'second local Government,' however, was not then ripe. So the Court of Directors, by a special vote, continued Sir Charles Metcalfe's period of service in Council to August, 1834; and so he remained at the Council Board in Calcutta.

There was still higher office in store for him. When under the new Charter it was contemplated to establish a fourth Presidency in Upper India, to embrace very much the tract of country which Metcalfe had spoken of as conferring upon him the ' Kingship of the East and the West,' he was selected to fill the office; and he was nominated also Provisional Governor-General of India, to succeed on the death or resignation of Lord William Bentinck, in the event of an interregnum in the Government. How afterwards the Government of Agra shrivelled down into a Lieutenant-Governorship need not be narrated here. He had scarcely reached Allahabad and assumed the Government, when he received intelligence of the intended departure of Lord William Bentinck. As ' Provisional Governor-General,' therefore, in the absence of any substantive appointment to the high office, it was now Metcalfe's privilege to receive from him the reins of Government. He hastened, therefore, back to the Presidency, and arrived in time to shake the departing ruler by the hand, and to bid God-speed to him and to that pearl of gentlewomen, his admirable wife.

With what sentiments Lord William Bentinck parted

from his colleague may be gathered from his own recorded words. 'My connection,' said the Governor-General, 'with Sir Charles Metcalfe in Council, during more than six years, ought to make me the best of witnesses, unless, indeed, friendship should have blinded me and conquered my detestation of flattery, which, I trust, is not the case. I therefore unhesitatingly declare, that whether in public or private life, I never met with the individual whose integrity, liberality of sentiment, and delicacy of mind, excited in a greater degree my respect and admiration. The State never had a more able or upright councillor, nor any Governor-General a more valuable and independent assistant and friend; and during the same period, any merit that can be claimed for the principles by which the Indian Government has been guided, to Sir Charles must the full share be assigned. Neither has the access which my situation has given me to the public records and to past transactions led me to form a less favourable opinion of his preceding career. I need not enter into particulars. Suffice it to express my sincere impression, that among all the statesmen, who since my first connection with India have best served their country and have most exalted its reputation and interests in the East, Webb, Close, Sir Arthur Wellesley, Elphinstone, Munro, and Malcolm, equal rank and equal honour ought to be given to Sir Charles Metcalfe.'

He had now reached the topmost step of the ladder. The dreams of the Eton cloisters, the air-built castles of the Muttra tent, had become substantial realities. He had said that he would some day be Governor-General of India—

and now the great official crown was upon his head. It might not remain there long, but it was something to be Governor-General even for a day. Some believed that the substantive appointment would be, and all hoped that it might be, conferred upon him.* Metcalfe, however, had

* The Court of Directors, who, as already told, had oscillated between Elphinstone and Malcolm, were, when the former declined to return to India, unwilling to fill up the substantive appointment at once. They wished that Sir Charles Metcalfe should continue as long as possible at the head of the administration, and they believed that the King's Government, who were then adverse to the nomination of a Company's officer, might in time be reconciled to it. The following are the resolutions which were carried by a majority of fifteen to two of the members of the Court :

'That this Court deeply lament that the state of Lord William Bentinck's health should be such as to deprive the Company of his most valuable services ; and this Court deem it proper to record, on the occasion of his Lordship's resignation of the office of Governor-General, their high sense of the distinguished ability, energy, zeal, and integrity with which his Lordship has discharged the arduous duties of his exalted station.

'That, referring to the appointment which has been conferred by the Court, with the approbation of his Majesty, on Sir Charles T. Metcalfe, provisionally, to act as Governor-General of India, upon the death, resignation, or coming away of Lord William Bentinck ; and adverting also to the public character and services of Sir Charles Metcalfe, whose knowledge, experience, and talents eminently qualify him to prosecute successfully the various important measures consequent on the new Charter Act, this Court are of opinion that it would be inexpedient at present to make any other arrangement for supplying the office of Governor-General. And it is resolved, accordingly, that the Chairs be authorized and instructed to communicate this opinion to his Majesty's Ministers through the President of the Board of Commissioners for the Affairs of India.'

Mr Grant was at this time President of the Board of Control. His objections, as given in his letter of October 1, 1834, are worth no expectation of such a result. In the first place, he knew that the influence of the Court and the Cabinet would assuredly prevail against the 'old Indian' party at home; and, in the second, he felt assured that in the eyes of a large section of that party, he had irremediably damaged himself by his conduct at Hyderabad. He was right. But the interregnum was one of unexpected duration. The appointment of Lord Heytesbury, made by the Tories, having been cancelled by the Whigs, there followed much discussion, involving much delay, with respect to the choice of a successor; and so Sir Charles Metcalfe remained at the head of the Indian Government until the spring of 1836.

The interregnum of the Indian civilian was not a barren one. It was rendered famous by an act, which has, perhaps, been more discussed, and with greater variance of opinion, than any single measure of any Governor-General of India. He liberated the Indian Press. Under the

quoting: 'With respect to the appointment to that office of any servant of the Company, however eminent his knowledge, talents, and experience may confessedly be, his Majesty's Ministers agree in the sentiments of Mr Canning, expressed in a letter from him to the Court on the 25th of December, 1820, that the case can hardly be conceived in which it would be expedient that the *highest* office of the Government in India should be filled otherwise than from England, and that that one main link at least between the systems of the Indian and British Governments ought, for the advantage of both, to be invariably maintained. On this principle it has usually been thought proper to act; and in the various important measures consequent on the new Charter Act, his Majesty's Ministers see much to enjoin the continuance of the general practice, but nothing to recommend a deviation from it.' Before Lord Grey's Government had appointed a successor to Lord William Bentinck, there was a ministerial crisis, and Lord Heytesbury was nominated by the Tories.

Government of his predecessor, freedom of speech had been habitually allowed, but the sword of the law still remained in the hand of the civil Government, and at any time it might have been stretched forth to destroy the liberty which was thus exercised. But Metcalfe was not content with this state of things. He desired that the free expression of thought should be the right of all classes of the community. He took his stand boldly upon the broad principle, that to deny this right is to contend 'that the essence of good government is to cover the land with darkness.' 'If their argument,' he added, 'be that the spread of knowledge may eventually be fatal to our rule in India, I close with them on that point, and maintain that, whatever may be the consequence, it is our duty to communicate the benefits of knowledge. If India could be preserved as a part of the British Empire only by keeping its inhabitants in a state of ignorance, our domination would be a curse to the country, and ought to cease. But I see more ground for just apprehension in ignorance itself. I look to the increase of knowledge with a hope that it may strengthen our empire; that it may remove prejudices, soften asperities, and substitute a rational conviction of the benefits of our Government; that it may unite the people and their rulers in sympathy, and that the differences which separate them may be gradually lessened, and ultimately annihilated. Whatever, however, be the will of Almighty Providence respecting the future government of India, it is clearly our duty, as long as the charge be confided to our hands, to execute the trust to the best of our ability for the good of the people.' It would be difficult to gainsay this; but the Court of

Directors of the East India Company had not much sympathy with these 'high-flown notions.' The intelligence of what he had done reached them whilst the question of the Governor-Generalship was still an open one. It may have in some measure influenced the decision, but I scarcely think that it did. At all events, Metcalfe soon heard from England, with some exaggeration, that he had lost the confidence of the Company. Lord Auckland was appointed Governor-General of India; but the provisional appointment which made him the 'second man in India,' was renewed in his favour. The King's Ministers, too, testified their confidence in him by recommending him for the Grand Cross of the Bath. The new Governor-General carried out the insignia, and formally invested him soon after his arrival.

It was now a question earnestly debated in Metcalfe's mind, whether he would take ship for England, or whether he would return to the North-Western Provinces to take charge of the administration which he had quitted to assume the Governor-Generalship. It was no longer the Agra Presidency. It had become a Lieutenant-Governorship, and was formally in the gift of the Governor-General. Lord Auckland was very desirous that he should accept the office, and some of the leading members of the Court of Directors had urged him not to decline the offer. So he made up his mind to remain a little longer yet in harness. There was really as much substantive authority in the new constitution as in the old. 'It is inferior only,' he wrote to his aunt, Mrs Monson, 'in designation, trappings, and allowances. These are not matters which I should think a

sufficient reason for giving, when I am desired to stay by
those whose uniform kindness to me gives them a right to
claim my services.   I feel that I have no excuse for abandoning a post to which I am called by all parties concerned
in the election, and in which I have greater opportunities
of being useful to my country and to mankind than I could
expect to find anywhere else.   The decision, however, costs
me much.   I had been for some time indulging in pleasing
visions of home and the enjoyments of retirement and
affectionate intercourse with relatives and friends.'   He had
now spent thirty-five years in India, without leaving the
country for a day; but his interest in his work was as keen
as in the old days of Lord Wellesley and Lord Minto.

   But he had not long exercised the powers of Lieutenant-
Governor, when renewed reports came to him from England that the Court of Directors regarded him with
dissatisfaction on account of his liberation of the Indian
Press.   This disquieted him greatly, and in his disquietude
he addressed a letter to the official organ of the Company,
in which he requested, that if he had really lost the confidence of the Court, his provisional appointment of Governor-
General might be withdrawn, and that he might resign his
office and retire from the service of the Company.   ' If the
reports,' he wrote to Mr Melvill, ' which have reached this
country from England be true; if I have really lost the
confidence of the Court, and have fallen so low in their
estimation as deliberately to be deemed now unworthy of
the position which they accorded to me three years ago in
the Government of a subordinate Presidency, it is my
earnest entreaty that the Court will withdraw from me the

provisional appointment of Governor-General, or otherwise intimate their pleasure to me, in order that I may resign that appointment, and retire from the service of the Company. I have no wish to retain by forbearance an appointment conferred on me when I was honoured with the confidence of the Court, if that confidence is gone, or to hold my office on mere sufferance, or to serve in any capacity under the stigma of displeasure and distrust. But if I retain the confidence of the Court unimpaired, it will be highly gratifying to me to know that I have been misled by erroneous reports in supposing the possibility of the contrary. In that case I have no desire to retire from the public service. I am proud of the honour conferred by the provisional appointment of Governor-General.. I take a great interest in the duties which I have to perform as Lieutenant-Governor of the North-Western Provinces of India, and am willing to devote myself with all my heart to the service of the State as long as health and faculties enable me to work to any useful purpose. I am aware that I lay myself open to reproof in imagining a want of confidence which has not been authentically announced to me by any of those means which the Court has at command. If I have erred in this respect, and have not had sufficient cause for this address, I trust that the Court will forgive the error. Having received on former occasions marked proofs of confidence and esteem, I could not rest easy under reports, in some degree strengthened by appearances, which indicated the loss of those favourable sentiments.'

Before this letter was written, intelligence had reached Agra that Lord Elphinstone had been appointed Governor

of Madras   Metcalfe had some time before been talked of
for that post; but it had been given to Sir Frederick Adam,
mainly, it was believed, through the interest of Lord
Brougham. This had not in any way disturbed him; and,
in truth, he had no desire to go to Madras. But when
some good-natured friends in London told him that his
appointment to that Government had been again discussed, and that his claims had been set aside as an inten-
tional mark of the Court's displeasure, the case wore a
new aspect. Very different considerations determined the
appointment of Lord Elphinstone; but that the liberation
of the Press had caused Metcalfe to lose caste and credit in
Leadenhall-street was repeated in so many ' Europe letters '
to himself and others, that he could not disbelieve the
story. ' I do not care a straw for the Government of
Madras,' he wrote to his aunt, Mrs Monson, ' and I am
probably better where I am; but I do not mean to serve
in avowed disgrace.' To his friend, Mr Tucker, he wrote
in the same strain : ' The loss of the Madras Government
did not give me any concern, but the asserted dissatisfaction
of the Court distressed me, and I felt that I could not remain in a state of implied disgrace. I therefore wrote as I
did to you, and I am now expecting the Court's reply, on
the receipt of which I shall have to make up my mind as to
the course which I ought to pursue.' In August the
answer came. It was outwardly cold and formal. It
expressed the regret of the Court that Sir Charles Metcalfe
should have thought it necessary to make such a communication, and added that the continuance in him provisionally
of the highest office which the Court had it in its power to

confer, ought to have satisfied him that their confidence had
not been withdrawn.

But Metcalfe was not satisfied; so he forthwith sent in
his resignation, and prepared to return to England. The
letter which he addressed to the Secretary of the East India
Company clearly indicated how painfully he was hurt.
'The Court,' he said in conclusion, 'pronounced that my
letter was altogether unnecessary. With deference, I think
that there was good and sufficient reason to seek an understanding with the Court, for any one who regards the approbation of his superior as an essential condition of his servi-
tude. Either I had lost or I retained the confidence of the
Court. If the latter were the case, a few kind words to
that effect would have assured me that I could continue to
serve without discredit. Instead of which, I receive a
laconic letter, taking no notice whatever of the sentiments
expressed in mine, but conveying a reproof for having
written it, given in a tone which leaves me no reason to
suppose that the Court entertain the least desire for the
continuance of my services. Under all these circumstances,
I must conclude—1st, that I was intentionally disgraced
when I was passed over in the nomination of a Governor
for Madras; 2nd, that the Court retain the sentiments under
which that disgrace was purposely inflicted, and hence no
wish to remove the feelings which it was calculated to
excite; and 3rd, that your letter of the 15th of April, with
reference to mine of the 22nd of August last, could only
produce the effect that it has produced, and, consequently,
that my resignation was contemplated in the despatch of
that letter. I trust that I have sufficiently explained the

causes which compel me reluctantly to retire from the public
service, to which, if I could have remained with honour, I
would willingly have devoted the whole of my life.'

There is no incident of Sir Charles Metcalfe's official
career of which I have thought so much as of this, and regarding which, as the result of this much thought, I feel
such great doubt and uncertainty. One of the shrewdest
and most sagacious men whom I have ever known, with
half a century of experience of public affairs to give weight
to his words, said to me, with reference to this very subject,
'The longer I live, the more convinced I am that over-
sensitiveness is a fault in a public man;' and there is great
truth in the saying. Another very sagacious public servant
has written : 'With regard to hostility evinced towards a
statesman behind his back, and which comes privately to
his knowledge, his best course will be to leave it unnoticed,
and not allow his knowledge of it to transpire.' This also
I believe to be true. I am disposed, therefore, at the present time to think that it would have been a wiser and a
more dignified course to have left the rumours of which I
have spoken wholly unnoticed. No man could have
afforded it better than Metcalfe; no man could more certainly have lived down any temporary discredit in high
places. Every official man—nay, every man who has much
commerce with the world—has, in the course of his career,
to contend with ignorance and misconception, if not with
envy and malice. Every one, indeed, who has done anything better than his fellows must lay his account for this
as one of the inevitable crosses of his life. It is better, in
such a case, 'to bear up and steer right on,' supported by

'the conscience,' than to 'bout ship and go into harbour, when the winds are a little adverse. Life is too short for contests of this kind—too short even for explanations. Metcalfe was fully persuaded in his own mind that what he did was right; and as the superior authorities did not tell him that he was wrong, I think that it would have been better if he had left unnoticed the private reports which reached him from England. No public servant, of any grade or any capacity, can expect all that he does to be approved by higher authority; and if even a declared difference of opinion on one particular point is to afford a sufficient warrant for resignation of office, the public service of the country would be brought to a dead-lock. Nor is it to be forgotten, with reference to more special considerations affecting the individual case, that this question of the liberation of the press was one on which the opinions of thinking men were very much divided, and that some of Metcalfe's staunchest friends and warmest admirers doubted the expediency of what he had done, though they never ceased to repose confidence in his general wisdom as a statesman.

But if some infirmity were apparent in this passage of Metcalfe's life, it was the infirmity of a noble mind, and it detracts nothing from the general admiration to which he is entitled. It arose out of what one who knew him well, from the very commencement of his career, described as his 'very quick and delicate and noble sense of public character.' Some years before, he said that he was getting callous to injustice, and less anxious regarding the opinions of others; * but, in truth, he never ceased to be very sen-

* 'I am getting callous to such injustice. My experience at

sitive on the score of his official reputation, and very eager to repel all assaults upon it.   And that, not from any selfish or egotistical feelings, but from a prevailing sense that by so doing he was maintaining the dignity and the purity of the Public Service.   Indeed, the official sensitiveness, of which I am speaking, marks more distinctly than anything else the great frontier-line between the old and the new race of public servants in India.   It had become a laudable ambition to pass through all the stages of official life without a stain or even a reproach.

No man ever left India, carrying with him such lively regrets and such cordial good wishes from all classes of the community.   I can well remember the season of his departure from Calcutta.   The Presidency was unwontedly enlivened by Metcalfe balls and Metcalfe dinners, and addresses continually pouring in, and deputations both from English and Native Societies.   It would take much of time and much of space to speak of all these; and I must refrain from the attempt to record them.   But it may be mentioned that, on one of these farewell festal occasions, after Metcalfe's health had been drunk in the ordinary way, as a statesman who had conferred great benefits upon the country, and a member of society beloved by all who had come within the circle of his genial influence, another toast was given in the words 'Charles Metcalfe, the soldier of Deeg.'   The story of the 'little stormer,' then but slightly

Hyderabad has taught me some useful lessons; and though it gives me a worse opinion of human nature than I had before, it will make me individually less liable to annoyance, by making me less anxious regarding the opinions of others.'—*Bhurtpore, Feb.* 1826.

known, was told, and well told; and the military enthusiasm of the many officers there present was roused to the
highest pitch.   I shall never forget the applause of the
assembly which greeted this unexpected tribute to the completeness of Sir Charles Metcalfe's character.   All that gay
assemblage in the Town-hall of Calcutta rose to him, with
a common movement, as though there had been but one
heart among them all, and many an eye glistened as women
waved their handkerchiefs and men clapped their hands—
and every one present thought how much he was loved.

During his tenure of these several offices in the Supreme
Government of India, Sir Charles Metcalfe wrote many
very important State papers, officially known as ' Minutes,'
which were always respectfully received by his colleagues,
and very often influenced their opinions in the right direction.   In other shapes, too, he sometimes recorded his
views; and a large selection from his papers has been laid
before the world.   They are distinguished by a remarkable
amount of sagacious common sense, conveyed in most lucid
English.   I do not know a better example of a thoroughly
good official style.   There was in all he wrote a directness
of purpose, a transparent sincerity, which won the admiration of the reader, if it did not convince his judgment.   To
say that he was without his own particular prejudices would
be almost to say that he was perfect.   In many respects he
was before his age; but there were some points with respect to which he was behind it.   He demonstrated, in the
most convincing manner, the earnestness of his desire to

advance the moral progress of the people of India; but it does not appear that he had much sympathy with the efforts which were being made to advance the material progress of the country. He could clearly see what were the benefits to be derived from the diffusion of knowledge among the subjects of the British Government in India; but he was sceptical regarding the profit to be drawn from the improvement of internal and external communications of the country, by means of good roads, and steam vessels to and from England. It puzzled many people at the time, and, doubtless, it has puzzled many since, to understand how one, who had been among the first to recommend the free admission of European settlers into England, should have undervalued such material aids to the promotion of European enterprise.

There was another point upon which he held opinions differing from those of the majority of his contemporaries; but Time has revealed that if he stood alone, in this respect, he stood alone in his wisdom. He often spoke and wrote of the insecurity of our British Empire in India, and predicted that it would some day be imperilled, if not overthrown, by our own Native Army. He expressed himself very strongly in conversation on this subject, sometimes saying that we were sitting on a barrel of gunpowder and never knew when it would explode, and at others declaring that we should wake up some morning and find that we had lost India. He based his opinion on such arguments as the following: 'Our hold is so precarious, that a very little mismanagement might accomplish our expulsion; and the course of events may be of itself sufficient, without any mismanagement. We are, to appearance, more powerful in India now than we ever were. Nevertheless, our downfall may be short work; when it commences, it will, probably, be rapid, and the world will wonder more at the suddenness with which our immense empire may vanish, than it has done at the surprising conquest that we have achieved. The cause of this precariousness is that our power does not rest on actual strength but upon impression. Our whole real strength is in the few European regiments, speaking comparatively, that are scattered singly over the vast space of subjugated India. That is the only portion of our soldiery whose hearts are with us, and whose constancy can be relied on in the hour of trial. All our native establishments, military and civil, are the followers of fortune; they serve us for their livelihood, and generally serve us well. From a sense of what is due to the hand that feeds them—which is one of the virtues that they most extol—they may often display fidelity under trying circumstances; but in their inward feelings they partake more or less of the universal disaffection which prevails against us, not from bad government, but from natural and irresistible antipathy; and were the wind to change—to use a native expression—and to set in steadily against us, we could not expect that their sense of honour, although there might be splendid instances of devotion, would keep the mass on our side in opposition to the common feeling which, with one view, might for a time unite all India from one end to the other. Empires grow old, decay, and perish. Ours in India can hardly be called old, but seems destined to be short-lived. We appear to have passed the brilliancy and vigour of our youth, and it may be that we have reached a premature old age. We have ceased to be the wonder that we were to the natives; the charm which once encompassed us has been dissolved, and our subjects have had time to inquire why they have been subdued. The consequences of the inquiry may appear hereafter. If these speculations are not devoid of foundation, they are useful in diverting our minds to the contemplation of the real nature of our power, and in preventing a delusive belief of its impregnability. Our greatest danger is not from a Russian power, but from the fading of the impression of our invincibility from the minds of the native inhabitants of India. The disaffection which would root us out abundantly exists; the concurrence of circumstances sufficient to call it into general action may at any time happen.' * And again : ' Some say that our empire in India rests on opinion, others on main force. It, in fact, depends on both. We could not keep the country by opinion, if we had not a considerable force; and no force that we could pay would be sufficient, if it were not aided by the opinion of our invincibility. Our force does not operate so much by its actual strength as by the impression which it produces, and that impression is the opinion by which we hold India. Internal insurrection, therefore, is one of the greatest of our dangers, or, rather, becomes so when the means of quelling it are at a distance. It is easy

* This is part of a paper written in reply to some questions propounded in England at the time of the Parliamentary Inquiries of 1832-33, and submitted by Government to the principal authorities on questions of Indian government. Whether this paper was ever officially sent in I do not know. It does not appear in the printed replies to these questions in the parliamentary papers.

to decide it, because insurgents may not have the horse, foot, and artillery of a regular army ; but it becomes serious if we have not those materials at hand.   Nothing can be a stronger proof of our weakness in the absence of a military force, even when it is not far removed, than the history of such insurrections as have occurred.   The civil power, and all semblance of the existence of our government, are instantly swept away by the torrent.'

But although Sir Charles Metcalfe believed that the permanent fidelity of the Sepoy army could not be relied upon, he admitted that the native soldiery were in many respects worthy of admiration, and that it was our policy to maintain large bodies of them, as we could not turn the whole of India into a great European garrison.   'The late Governor-General,' * he wrote, 'condemns our Indian army, in a sweeping sentence, as being the most expensive and least efficient in the world.   If it were so, how should we be here ?   Is it no proof of efficiency that it has conquered all India ?   Is it no proof of efficiency that India is more universally tranquil, owing to our Indian army, than it ever was under any native Government or Governments that we read of ?   If our Indian army be so expensive, why do we not employ European troops alone to maintain India ? Why, but because Europeans are so much more expensive that we could not pay a sufficient number ?   If our Indian army be so inefficient, why do we incur the expense of making soldiers of the natives ?   Why do we not entertain the same number of undisciplined people, who would cost much less ?   Why, but because then we should lose the

* Lord William Bentinck.

country from the inefficiency of our native force? If, therefore, the Indian army be preferable to a European force on account of its cheapness, and to other native troops on account of its efficiency; if we cannot substitute any other force cheaper and more efficient, how can it justly be said to be the most expensive and least efficient army in the world? It enables us to conquer and keep India. If it performs well every duty required of it, hard work in quarters, good service in the field, how can it be subject to the imputation of inefficiency? The proof of its cheapness and of its efficiency is, that we cannot substitute any other description of force at once so cheap and so efficient.'

It was doubtful, in those days, whether India could afford to maintain a permanent European force of thirty thousand men. Sir Charles Metcalfe felt this very strongly; but he could see no other element of safety than the presence of our English regiments, unless our national manhood should take root in the soil by the agency of extensive colonization. ' Considering,' he said, ' the possible disaffection of our native army as our only internal danger, and the want of physical strength and moral energy as rendering them unable to contend with a European enemy, his Lordship proposes that the European portion of our army should be one-fourth, and eventually one-third, in proportion to the strength of our native army. He considers this as requiring a force of thirty thousand Europeans in India. In the expediency of having at least this force of Europeans, even in ordinary times, I entirely concur; that is, if we can pay them. But the limit to this, and every other part of our force, must be regulated by our means. If we attempted

to fix it according to our wants, we should soon be without
the means of maintaining any army. Thirty thousand
European troops would be vastly inadequate for the purpose
of meeting the imagined Russian invasion, for we should
more require European troops in the interior of India at
that time than at any other. To have our army on a footing calculated for that event is impossible. Our army cannot well be greater than it is, owing to want of means. It
cannot well be less, owing to our other wants. Such as it
is in extent, it is our duty to make it as efficient as we can,
with or without the prospect of a Russian invasion ; and
this is the only way in which we can prepare for that or any
other distant and uncertain crisis. On the approach of such
an event we must have reinforcements of European troops
from England to any amount required, and we must increase our native force according to the exigency of the
time. We could not long exist in a state of adequate preparation, as we should be utterly ruined by the expense.'

I may give one more extract from his official papers—it
was written when he was Lieutenant-Governor of the North-
Western Provinces—showing the just and generous sentiments with which he addressed himself to the consideration
of our relations with the Native States of India : ' Several
questions,' he said, ' have lately occurred, in which our interests and those of other powers and individuals are at
variance, and in the decision of which we are likely to be
biased by regard for our own benefit, unless we enter with
a liberal spirit into the claims and feelings of others, and
make justice alone the guide of our conduct. . . . . In all
these cases, the right on our part to come to the decision

apparently most beneficial for our own interests, seems to me to be doubtful. Had our right been clear, I should be far from having any desire to suggest its relinquishment. But when the right is doubtful, when we are to be judges in our own cause, when, from our power, there is little or no probability of any resistance to our decision, it behoves us, I conceive, to be very careful lest we should be unjustly biased in our own favour, and to be liberal only in examining the claims and pretensions of other parties. The Christian precept, " Do as you would be done by," must be right in politics as well as in private life; and even in a self-interested view we should, I believe, gain more by the credit of being just and liberal to others, than by using our power to appropriate to ourselves everything to which we could advance any doubtful pretension.'

So Metcalfe returned to England, in the early part of 1838, after an absence of thirty-eight years. He had no thought of any further employment in the public service, except that which might be entailed upon him by the necessities of a seat in Parliament. He had an abundance of the world's wealth; he was unmarried; and he had done so much work that he might well content himself to be idle at the close of his life. Moreover, there was another and an all-sufficient reason why he should seek this autumnal repose. He had in India enjoyed better health than the majority of his countrymen, although he had taken no especial pains to preserve it. He had worked hard; he had lived well; and he had resorted very freely to the great prophylactic agencies of air and exercise. Still, a naturally robust constitution had carried him through nearly forty years of unbroken work beneath an Indian sun. But the seeds of a painful and a fatal disease had been sown—at what precise time cannot be declared; but the first apparent symptoms manifested themselves at Calcutta, when a friend one day called his attention to a drop of blood on his cheek. It was the first discernible sign of a malignant cancer, which was to eat into his life and make existence a protracted agony. From that day there was perceptible an angry appearance of the skin. But the progress of the malady was so gradual, and it was attended with so little uneasiness, that neither did Metcalfe consult a medical practitioner, nor did the ailment attract the notice of the professional adviser who attended him. But, at the latter end of 1837, the malady had increased so much that he thought it necessary to take advice; the treatment was not effective, and soon afterwards Metcalfe returned to England. There he consulted Sir Benjamin Brodie, who prescribed for him, but without effect. There was, however, little pain, although the disease had assumed the shape of a decided ulcerous affection of the cheek; and so Metcalfe allowed time to pass, and neglected the complaint until no human agency could arrest it.

Of this sad story I must presently write more in detail. Meanwhile, Sir Charles Metcalfe is at Fern Hill, the paternal estate in Berkshire, which he had inherited from his elder brother. It had been his for a quarter of a century, and its revenues had been carefully nursed; for Metcalfe's official salary had been always more than enough for his uses, notwithstanding his overflowing hospitality and the unfailing cheerfulness of his giving.   So he found himself a well-to-do country gentleman, and having carried home all his Indian hospitality, he soon filled his house with relatives and friends. But it was a very unsatisfactory state of life.   He was alone in a crowd; uncomfortable in the midst of luxury; poor though surrounded by all that wealth could purchase; and always in a hurry without having anything to do.   Liberal as he was, and accustomed to a profuse style of living, he was appalled by the extravagance of the servants' hall, and often longed for the self-supporting, rice-eating Khitmudgars and Bearers of the old time.   Many years before, in his previsions of English life, he anticipated this state of things, and declared that he would wrestle against it.   He found it even worse than he expected, and he soon set his face against it.   He had not been many months in England, when he wrote to Mrs Monson : ' I have made up my mind to part with Fern Hill whenever I can make an arrangement for it to my satisfaction.   My reasons for quitting are these : Firstly, the expense of living here is too great ; there being, in my opinion, more satisfactory and better uses for what income I have than spending it all on the mere eating and drinking of a large house and establishment.   Secondly, the life is not suited to my disposition.   I should like greater quiet and retirement, and the occasional enjoyment of affectionate society as a treat.   A continual and incessant succession of company is too much for me.   Thirdly, the only remedy is flight; for neither can I reduce my establishment while I live in this house, nor can I shut my doors whilst I have accommodation for friends.   Elsewhere, if I continue a private man, I can be more retired; and retirement is best suited to my nature. Elsewhere I could live, I think, with sufficient hospitality on a fourth of what I should spend here, and as I have no desire to hoard, the difference may, I trust, be made more beneficial to others than it can be whilst wasted on a lazy, discontented establishment. If I go into Parliament, which I shall do, if I have an opportunity, the only alteration in my present plans will be, that I must reside for seven or eight months in London, and so far deprive myself of retirement for the sake of public duty.'—[*February* 25, 1839.]

For many years this seat in Parliament had been one of his most cherished day-dreams. But now that all outward circumstances seemed to place it within reach, inward obstacles arose to retard his possession of the prize. The sensitiveness and delicacy of his nature caused him to revolt against the ordinary means by which entrance to the great assembly of the nation is obtained. He would neither buy nor beg a seat. Bribery was repugnant, and canvassing was distasteful, to him. His more experienced friends, therefore, assured him that small and large constituencies were equally beyond his reach. He, however, was content to wait. The opportunity of drifting into Parliament blamelessly and pleasantly might some day arise. Meanwhile, he could familiarize himself with the details of European politics, and, by maturing his opinions on all the great questions of the day, strengthen his chance of some day realizing the aspirations of the Eton cloisters and charming a listening Senate. His convictions were mostly those of advanced liberalism. He was against the finality of the Reform Bill; he was eager for the repeal of the Corn-laws, for the overthrow of Protestant ascendancy in Ireland, and for the abolition of Church-rates. He inclined towards Vote by Ballot, Short Parliaments, and the exclusion of the Bishops from the House of Lords. The more he thought of these changes, the more he warmed towards them, and at last his enthusiasm broke out in a pamphlet entitled *Friendly Advice to Conservatives,* in which these views were expounded. But it was not decreed that he should ever stand forth to 'head a party struggling for liberty,' in any other than this literary conflict.*

For soon a new and undreamt-of field of public service lay stretched before him, and he was invited to occupy it by the responsible rulers of the land. Rumour had, ever since his return to England, been very busy with his name. He had been assigned to all sorts of places and appointments, likely and unlikely; but now there was some solid foundation for the story of his re-employment. 'Those who have sent me to Paris or to Ireland,' he wrote to Mrs Monson, 'seem to have been wrong, for the Almighty ruler of all things seems to have ordained that I am to go to Jamaica. Who would have thought of such a destination? This proposal has been made to me, most unexpectedly, of course, on my part, by Lord Normanby, Secretary of State for the Colonies, and the post being one of honour,

---

* He was very nearly presenting himself to the electors of Glasgow in place of his friend Lord William Bentinck, who wished to resign in his favour, but who died before he could vacate the seat. Before this event occurred, Metcalfe's mind had been diverted to other objects.

owing to the difficulties at present besetting it, and the prospect of rendering important service, I have considered it a public duty to undertake the charge, and have accepted it without a moment's hesitation. I have risen in the East, and must set in the West. It is a curious destiny.' To what immediate influences the Indian civilian owed his nomination to a post in the other hemisphere is not very apparent; but I am inclined to think that the nomination is, in part at least, attributable to the strong language of admiration in which Lord William Bentinck had written of his some-time colleague to the Prime Minister, Lord Melbourne. ' No man,' he wrote, at the close of a glowing appeal in his friend's favour,* ' has shown greater rectitude of conduct or more independence of mind. . . . . . We served together for nearly seven years. His behaviour to me was of the noblest kind. He never cavilled upon a trifle, and never yielded to me on a point of importance.'

With what feelings Metcalfe regarded the appointment may be further gathered from what he wrote of it to Sir Charles Trevelyan, who had laid the foundation of his own fame, as an assistant to Metcalfe at Delhi: ' The possibility of serving in the West Indies never entered into my imagination. Neither had I any desire to quit England. The mode in which I was ambitious of devoting my humble services to the country was as an independent Member of Parliament, and it was my intention to embrace any good opportunity of seating myself there. In every other respect I longed for retirement, and was bent on arrangements for

---

* It was written with reference to the question of Metcalfe's liberation of the Indian Press.

securing it in a greater degree than I had previously found practicable.   While in this mind, and with these views, I was surprised by a proposal to undertake the government of Jamaica, and assented without a moment's hesitation, for there was a public duty of importance to be performed, and we are bound, I conceive, to make ourselves useful to our country whenever a prospect of being so presents itself.   If I succeed in reconciling that valuable colony to the mother country, and promoting the welfare of both, I shall be gratified.   The attempt will be a labour of love.   If I fail, I shall have the consolation of having devoted myself heartily to the task, and can again seek the retirement which, with reference exclusively to my own ease and comfort, I prefer to anything else.   I presume that you mean to return to India, and I shall be glad to find that your benevolent zeal and distinguished talent are again at work in that important field.   The immense strides which we have recently taken in our political arrangements and military exertions will either raise our power greatly beyond its former pitch, or by causing our expenses to exceed our resources, will make it more precarious than ever.   In either case our country will require the best exertions of its ablest servants, and your future career, I doubt not, will be even more distinguished than your past.'

Congratulations most cordial, and expressions of pleasure most sincere, poured in upon Metcalfe from all quarters before he took his departure for the West Indian island. But there was not one, perhaps, which more rejoiced his heart than that which he received from his old master— from the statesman at whose feet he had learnt the first

lessons of official life. And no one rejoiced more than
Lord Wellesley in the elevation of his former pupil. 'It
is a matter,' he wrote, 'of cordial joy and affectionate pride
to me to witness the elevation of a personage whose great
talents and virtues have been cultivated under my anxious
care, and directed by my hand to the public service in
India; where, having filled the first station in the Government of that vast empire with universal applause, his merits
and exalted reputation have recommended him to his
Sovereign and his country as the men best qualified to consummate the noblest work of humanity, justice, and piety
ever attempted by any State since the foundation of civilized
society. You have been called to this great charge by the
free, unsolicited choice of your Sovereign; and that choice
is the universal subject of approbation by the voice of her
whole people: no appointment ever received an equal
share of applause. In a letter which I had the honour of
receiving from you, and which is published in my Indian
despatches, you are pleased to say that you were educated
in my school, and that it was the school of virtue, integrity,
and honour. That school has produced much good fruit
for the service of India. You are one of the most distinguished of that produce, and in your example it is a high
satisfaction to me to observe that the benefits of my institution are now extended beyond the limits of that empire for
whose good government it was founded.'

In August, 1839, Sir Charles Metcalfe embarked for
Kingston, and on the 21st of September he assumed charge
of the Government of Jamaica. There were many difficult
problems to solve, for the emancipation of the blacks had

produced a great social and industrial revolution; and the transition-state, which had arisen, required very careful and adroit management.   But he used to say that the work of government would be easy and pleasant to him if it were not for the Baptist missionaries.   He had not been long in the island before a leading minister of that persuasion declared openly that, though their new governor hoped to find Jamaica a bed of roses, they would take care that every rose should have its thorns. ' On my taking charge of the Government,' wrote Metcalfe, 'the course which I laid down for myself was to conciliate all parties, and by the aid of all parties to promote the happiness and welfare of Jamaica.   I have reason to believe that I have succeeded, with the exception of the Baptist missionary party. . . . . I have naturally asked myself why, having apparently succeeded in conciliating all parties, I have failed with respect to that of the Baptist missionaries?   I have conducted myself towards them as I have towards every other denomination of Christian ministers in the island.   I have subscribed with the same readiness to their chapels and schools whenever I have had an opportunity.   I have not allowed the opinions which I have been forced to entertain of their political proceedings to influence my behaviour or demeanour towards them.'   He was driven, therefore, reluctantly to conclude, that the obstacle to his success with this particular section of the community lay in the catholicity of his benevolence.   He loved all men, all races, all classes. He had, during nearly the whole of his adult life, been familiar with dusky faces, and had been ever kindly disposed towards people vulgarly described as of ' black blood.' His heart was as open towards the negro population as towards any other class of her Majesty's subjects in the West Indies; but he could not bring himself to straiten his sympathies in such a manner as to refuse to the white man the hand of brotherhood that he extended to the black. He knew that the latter had once belonged to a downtrodden race, and that it would take years of generous kindness to compensate them for all the injuries which they had borne; but he believed that the best means of insuring for them this generous kindness was to narrow the gulf between the two races—not to keep alive all animosities, old memories of past wrong. But this wise and truly Christian policy was distasteful to the Christians of the Baptist Missionary Society. Metcalfe tried to inculcate the forgiveness of injuries and the extension of brotherly love between the black and the white races. But the Baptists taught other lessons; and a quarter of a century afterwards their ' bloody instructions returned to plague the inventor.' *

Whilst Sir Charles Metcalfe was governing Jamaica, there was a change of government at home. A Conservative ministry was established in Downing-street. Lord Stanley (as I write, Lord Derby) passed into the Colonial Office; but Metcalfe, though a high-pressure Liberal, was not sufficiently a party man to be at all disturbed by the change.

* I gladly break off here from the pursuit of a painful subject. But it ought to be stated that Metcalfe carried with him to Jamaica very strong prepossessions in favour of the Baptist missionaries. He had known many eminent members of that communion in India (including the venerable Dr Carey), and among the farewell addresses he had received at Agra was one from the Baptist missionaries, thanking him for the countenance he had always afforded them.

If he could observe any difference of policy, it was in a
more catholic apprehension of the situation, and a more
generous support of the opinions he had expressed, and the
line of conduct he had desired to follow. Lord Stanley
himself had, ministerially, emancipated the blacks of the
West Indies. He was not likely to close his heart against
the emancipated race; but he was far too good and wise
to take a limited, one-sided view of the obligations of
humanity in such a crisis, and to think that the duties of the
parent State were confined to the protection and encouragement of the coloured population of the colony. When,
therefore, Sir Charles Metcalfe thought that the time had
come when he might consistently lay down the reins of
government, he was very anxious that it should not be
thought that the change of Government had caused him to
hasten the day of his retirement. ' I have given notice to
the new ministers,' he wrote in November, 1841, ' that I
may soon send in my resignation, in order that they may
be prepared for it, and look about for my successor. I have
done this in a manner which will preclude the idea that the
change of ministry is the cause of my retirement, there
being no reason for putting it on any ground but the true
one, which is that, having done what I came to do—by
which I mean the reconciliation of the colony with the
mother country—I see no necessity for staying any longer.'
So Metcalfe prepared himself to return to England, well
satisfied that he had not laboured in vain. What he did in
the West Indian colony has been thus comprehensively
described by himself: ' When,' he wrote in the letter to
the Colonial Secretary referred to above, ' the offer of the

Governorship of this island and its dependencies was conveyed to me, my only inducement in accepting it was the hope of rendering some service to my country by becoming instrumental in the reconciliation of the colony to the mother country. That object was accomplished soon after my arrival by the good sense and good feeling of the colonists, who readily and cordially met the conciliatory disposition which it was my duty to evince towards them. The next subject which attracted my attention was the unsatisfactory feeling of the labouring population towards their employers. This has naturally subsided into a state more consistent with the relations of the parties, and there is no longer any ground of anxiety on that account. Other dissensions in the community, which grew out of the preceding circumstances, have either entirely or in a great degree ceased, and order and harmony, with exceptions which will occasionally occur in every state of society, may be said to prevail.' *

In the following May, a successor having been appointed in the person of Lord Elgin, Sir Charles Metcalfe, amidst a perfect shower of warm-hearted valedictory addresses,

---

* I do not profess, in this account of certain officers of the (East) Indian Services, to give a just narrative of Metcalfe's West Indian, or of his subsequent Canadian administration. I may, however, mention here, in illustration of the military instincts of which I have before spoken, that he devoted himself very assiduously to the improvement of the sanitary condition of the English soldier, especially in respect of his location on the hill country. In this good work Sir William Gomm, who commanded the troops, went hand in hand with him— neither leading and neither following. Perhaps, in a former record of this, I did not sufficiently acknowledge the obligations of humanity to Sir William Gomm.

embarked again for the mother country. When he arrived
in England, the malady of which I have spoken had grown
upon him; he suffered much pain; and it was his first care
now to obtain the best surgical and medical advice. So he
sent at once for his old Calcutta friend and professional adviser, Mr Martin,* who went into consultation on the sub
ject with Sir Benjamin Brodie and Mr Keate. The ulcerous affection of the cheek had been much increased by the
climate of Jamaica, with its attendant plague of flies, and
perhaps by unskilful treatment. But his letters to England
had made no mention of the complaint, and he had generally said that he was in excellent health. It was now
clearly a most formidable disorder, and only to be combated·
by remedies of a most painful character. The diseased
part, it was thought, might be cut out with the knife, or
burnt out with caustic. The latter mode of treatment was
finally approved. Metcalfe was told that it might destroy
' the cheek through and through; ' but he only answered,
' Whatever you determine shall be done at once.' So the
caustic was applied. The agony was intense, but he bore
it without a murmur. His quiet endurance of pain was
something, indeed, almost marvellous.

The success of the operation was greater even than was
expected. The sufferer was removed to Norwood for quiet
and country air, and he wrote thence that the diseased part
looked better than it had done for many years, but that
there was no certainty of a permanent cure. From Norwood he went to Devonshire, where a country-house had

* Now Sir James Ranald Martin.

been taken for him near Honiton, and where he remained for some time in the enjoyment of the affectionate society of his sister, Mrs Smythe. But in the beginning of the new year he was roused from the tranquil pleasures of his country life by reports that it was the intention of Sir Robert Peel's Government to invite him to proceed as Governor-General to Canada. At first he laughed at the credulity of his friends who wrote to him on the subject. 'I have no more idea of going to Canada,' he wrote to Mr Ross Mangles, 'than of flying in the air. . . . . The only thing that I have the least inclination for is a seat in Parliament, of which, in the present predominance of Toryism among the constituencies, there is no chance for a man who is for the Abolition of the Corn-laws, Vote by Ballot, Extension of the Suffrage, Amelioration of the Poor-laws for the benefit of the poor, equal rights to all sects of Christians in matters of religion, and equal rights to all men in civil matters, and everything else that to his understanding seems just and right—and at the same time is totally disqualified to be a demagogue—shrinks like a sensitive plant from public meetings, and cannot bear to be drawn from close retirement, except by what comes in the shape of real or fancied duty to his country.' But little as he thought of it at that time, the claims of duty were even then about to withdraw him from his retirement. Two days after these lines were written, the invitation to proceed to Canada reached him at Deer Park. The letter proposing the arrangement was playfully, but only too truly, described as Lord Stanley's 'fatal missive.' Sir Charles Metcalfe went

to Canada as he went to Jamaica, because he believed that
it was his duty to go; but the arms of death were around
him as he embarked.

Into the history of the troubled politics of Canada at
that time it would be beyond the scope of this Memoir to
enter in detail.   To Metcalfe everything was new and
strange.   There were many perplexing problems, the solution of which was beyond the range of his forty years'
experience of public life.   He had for the first time to cope
with all the difficulties and embarrassments of Government
by Party—or, in other words, by a Parliamentary majority
—and with the complications arising from a conflict of
nationalities in a singularly varied population.   He found,
not much to his surprise, that as the representative of the
monarchical principle of the constitution, he was expected
to suffer himself to dwindle down into a mere cypher.
But he believed that to consent to this would be to abandon
his duty to his sovereign.   ' To the question at issue,' he
wrote to an old friend and fellow-collegian, ' which is,
whether the Governor is to be in some degree what his
title imports, or a mere tool in the hands of the party that
can obtain a majority in the representative body, I am, I
conceive, "vir justus," and I certainly mean to be " tenax
propositi," and hope " si fractus illabatur orbis, impavidum
ferient ruinæ." '   To another old Indian friend he wrote :
' Fancy such a state of things in India, with a Mahomedan
Assembly, and you will have some notion of my position.
On a distinct demand from the Council for stipulations
which would have reduced me to a nonentity, I refused.
They instantly resigned, and were supported by the House

of Assembly. Since then I have not been able to form a Council likely to carry a majority. I have now to strive to obtain a majority in the present Parliament. If I fail in that, I must dissolve and try a new one. I do not know that I shall have a better chance in that; and if I fail then, still I cannot submit, for that would be to surrender the Queen's Government into the hands of rebels, and to become myself their ignominious tool. I know not what the end will be. The only thing certain is that I cannot yield.' A dissolution was imminent. His enemies raged furiously against him. They assailed him with bitterness, which manifested itself in all shapes, from the light language of ridicule to that of vehement indignation. Some called him 'Old Squaretoes' and 'Charles the Simple.' Others denounced him as a designing despot and an unscrupulous tyrant. The crisis was now upon him. An old and dear friend, of whom much has been said in this volume, had written to him from his quiet chambers in the Albany, saying: 'If you think only of your own comfort and content, or were convinced that you were past more useful employment, you might enjoy your repose with as good a conscience as I do; but if I had the energy and ability to fill such a place as yours, I would not give the few months of your approaching crisis for a hundred years of unprofitable engagement.'

No man knew Charles Metcalfe better than Mountstuart Elphinstone—no man was more capable of reading and appreciating his character in all its finest shades and most subtle combinations. When Mr Gibbon Wakefield wrote that remarkable pamphlet on the crisis in Canada, in which there appeared an elaborate portrait of the Governor-

General, highly commendatory of his wonderful patience
and endurance, his almost saint-like temper, and his constant
cheerfulness under the worst trials and provocations,* but
in which some doubt was expressed as to whether the gentleness of his nature did not cause him to be sometimes
regardless of the duty of upholding his personal and official
dignity, Mr Elphinstone wrote to a friend, who had sent
him the book, saying: 'You cannot overrate the pleasure
with which I see justice done to Metcalfe, and I am very
much obliged to you for a publication in which he is so
favourably spoken of. I am not sure, however, that I can
admit that full justice is done to him even in it. The character given of him is admirable, even the part that seems
mere panegyric shows sagacity and discrimination. I cannot
quite agree with the censures, slight as they are. Metcalfe
has unquestionably such a temper as is seldom given to
man, but he surely is capable of indignation when there is
anything to call it forth, and is not likely to invite ill-usage
by showing himself wanting to his own dignity. I should
think he was cautious, almost timid, in deliberating, but
that he would be roused at once by opposition such as appeared to him factious or unreasonable. I agree that he is
not well qualified to use the proper means for managing a

* The following passage is worthy of quotation : 'I never witnessed such patience under provocation. I am speaking now of what I
saw myself, and could not have believed without seeing. It was not
merely quiet endurance, but a constant good-humoured cheerfulness
and lightness of heart in the midst of trouble enough to provoke a
saint or make a strong man ill. To those who, like me, have seen
three Governors of Canada literally worried to death, this was a
glorious spectacle.'

popular government, and that he even despises the use of them ; but I cannot admit that he does not see the end in view, or the relation into which he wishes to bring the Governor and the popular branch of the Legislature.   I think his neglect of the means a misfortune.   It is great weakness to rely on management of individuals and parties (in which Lord Sydenham so much excelled) for the permanent support of a system, but it is requisite for enabling some solid measures to proceed without interruption.   I think it is his over-rating these supposed defects of Metcalfe's that has most led Mr Wakefield to what I cannot but think a wrong conclusion.   I cannot think that the disputes between the Governor-General and his council are to be ascribed to mere 'incompatibility of character,' or to the parties not understanding each other.   Those causes, no doubt, had their influence ; but were there not other grounds of disagreement, which no freedom of communication could have removed ?   Lord Sydenham, it appears, conceded the responsibility of ministers ; Sir C. Bagot carried it into practice, but in this crisis, when the strongest and firmest hand was required to mark the boundary of this new distribution of power, he was incapacitated by sickness from undertaking that work at all.   The whole power fell into the hands of the ministry, and Metcalfe had to reconquer the most indispensable of his rights.   In such circumstances, I doubt if any modification of character, or any skill and experience in parliamentary tactics, could have averted a collision, and I need not say that I most fully concur with Mr Wakefield in thinking that Metcalfe should have the most full, open, and energetic support of Government.   As to the particular sort of support which I understood you to hint at (some distinguished mark of favour on the part of the Crown), however much to be desired, it is, I am afraid, scarcely to be hoped for. A peerage is already due to Metcalfe for his services in Jamaica, and as he has no issue, it would be a very moderate boon; but Peel has from fifty to seventy applicants, many of whom rate even their public services high : he stops their mouths by professing a resolution not to complete the work of the Whigs in swamping the House of Lords; but if he once opens the door, "like to an entered tide they all rush by," and leave room for a new inundation of claimants.'

But rightly to understand what were the heroic constancy and courage of the man in the midst of all this great sea of trouble, we must ever keep before us the fact that he was suffering almost incessant physical pain, and that a lingering and torturing death was before him. The cancer which was eating into his face had destroyed the sight of one eye, and he was threatened with total blindness. He was compelled, therefore, to sit in a darkened room, and to employ an amanuensis, and when he was compelled to go abroad on public business, the windows of his carriage were so screened as to exclude the dust and the glare. Throughout the years 1843 and 1844 the disease had been steadily gaining ground, in spite of all the efforts and appliances of human skill. The Queen's Government had sent out to Canada a young surgical practitioner of high promise, since abundantly fulfilled, recommended by Sir Benjamin Brodie and Mr Martin, who were well acquainted with the case. But neither the skill of Mr Pollock,* nor his assiduous and tender ministrations, could avail more than to palliate, in some small measure, the more painful symptoms of his malady, and by the end of 1844 he had returned to England, assured that the cure of such a disease was beyond the reach of surgery or medicine. Metcalfe had by this time ceased to read or write for himself. At the beginning of 1845, by the help of an amanuensis, he gave the following account of himself to Mr Martin : 'I have three kind letters of yours unanswered. So long as I had the use of my eyes, I hoped that a day would come when I could take up my pen and thank you for them ; but to do that now I am obliged to borrow the aid of another hand, as my right eye is quite blind, and the other cannot be exerted with impunity. I am compelled to abstain almost entirely from reading and writing, both of which operations are performed for me ; thus much is in explanation of my not writing to you with my own hand. Pollock has quitted me on his return to London. I am exceedingly sorry to part with him, not only as a medical adviser, of whose skill and judgment I have a high opinion, and who had acquired considerable

* Mr G. D. Pollock, second son of General Sir George Pollock, now surgeon to the Prince of Wales. Sir Charles Metcalfe thus wrote of him : ' I am most thankful to you and Sir Benjamin Brodie for all your kindness, and I shall be obliged to you if you will tell him that I am very sensible of it. Mr Pollock is arrived. He is very agreeable and winning in his manners ; and his conversation, reputation, and experience afford encouragement. He is about to have a consultation with my other doctors, and will afterwards, I conclude, proceed to business. I shall put myself entirely in his hands, and abide by his judgment and treatment.'

---

experience regarding the state of my complaint, but also as a most agreeable companion, in whose society I had great pleasure. Highly as I think of Pollock, I have lost all faith in chloride of zinc ; that powerful but destructive remedy has been applied over and over again, without efficacy, to the same parts of my cheek. The disease remains uneradicated, and has spread to the eye and taken away its sight. This, at least, is my opinion, although I am bound to hesitate in entertaining it, as I am not sure that Pollock is satisfied of the extension of the actual disease to the eye; but if it be not the disease which has produced the blindness, it must be the remedy. I am inclined, however, to believe that it is in reality the disease, both from appearances and the continual pain. The complaint appears to me to have taken possession of the whole of that side of the face, although the surface is not so much ulcerated as it has heretofore been. I feel pain and tenderness in the head, above the eye and down the right side of the face as far as the chin, the cheek towards the nose and mouth being permanently swelled. I cannot open my mouth to its usual width, and have difficulty in inserting and masticating pieces of food. After all that has been done in vain, I am disposed to believe that a perfect cure is hopeless ; I am, nevertheless, in the hands of a doctor who is inclined to follow Pollock's course, and by whose judgment I shall implicitly abide. Having no hope of a cure, my chief anxiety now regards my remaining eye, which sympathizes so much with the other that I am not without fear of total blindness, which is not a comfortable prospect, although, if it should come, I shall consider it my duty to resign myself to it with cheerfulness. Under these circumstances you will readily imagine that I should be very glad if I could return home, both for the chance of benefit from the medical skill that is to be found in the metropolis, and independently of that, for the sake of retirement and repose, which are requisite for an invalid such as I now am ; but I cannot reconcile it to my own sense of duty to quit my post in the present state of affairs in this country. I have no doubt of the generous readiness of her Majesty's Government to meet any application that I might make for permission to return, but I have myself no inclination to abandon the loyal portion of the community in Canada, who in the recent crisis have made a noble and successful stand in support of her Majesty's Government. Until, therefore, I see a satisfactory state of things so far confirmed as to afford assurance that it will be lasting, notwithstanding my departure, I shall not entertain any idea of my own retirement so long as I have bodily and mental health sufficient for the performance of the duties of my office.'

As the year advanced his sufferings increased. In June he wrote to the same cherished correspondent : ' I have no hope of benefit from anything. The malady is gradually getting worse, although its progress from day to day is imperceptible. I cannot quit my post at present without the certainty of mischievous consequences, and must, therefore, perform my duty by remaining where I am, whatever may be the result to myself personally.' But, although he wrote thus to one who, whether present or absent, had watched the disease in all its stages, he was in the habit of describing his state lightly, and even jestingly, to his relatives and old correspondents. 'A life of perpetual chloride of zinc,' he wrote to one of them, ' is far from an easy one. There are, however, greater pains and afflictions in the world, and I ought to be grateful for the many mercies that I have experienced. . . . . The doctor has just been with me, and says that the face looks very satisfactory. N.B. I can't shut my right one, and after the next application I shall not be able to open my mouth—"very satisfactory." ' But, in spite of all this, he went on unflinchingly at his work. His intellect was never brighter, his courage and resolution never stronger. The despatches which he dictated at this time are amongst the best to which he ever attached his name. But it was plainly not the decree of Providence that he should have human strength to struggle on much longer.

But even then there were great compensations. He felt that he was doing his duty, and he knew that his devotion to the public service was recognized both by the Queen and her ministers. During the space of forty-five years he had toiled unremittingly for the good of the State, in foreign lands and under hostile skies ; he had scarcely known either home or rest. And now he was about to receive his reward. It came in a shape very welcome to him, for the fire of ambition had burnt within him ever since the boyish days when he had paced the Eton cloisters and indulged in day-dreams of future fame. In the midst of a life rendered endurable only by a feeling that he was doing some good to his fellows, and that it was God's will thus to afflict him, letters came to him from Lord Stanley and Sir Robert Peel, informing him that it was her Majesty's desire to raise him to the Peerage as soon as he had communicated to Government his choice of a title. He elected to be called by his own ancestral name. He appreciated the honour. He accepted it gratefully. But he felt that it was ' too late.'

This honourable recognition of his past services would have sustained and strengthened him, for the stimulus of gratitude was thus added to his other incentives to exertion, if it had been possible for the strong spirit to prevail against the failure of the frail flesh. There were political circumstances which in the early summer of 1845 seemed to render it expedient that Metcalfe should remain at his post. ' It will be seen,' he wrote in May to the Colonial Secretary, ' from the description of parties which I have submitted, that the two parties in Lower and Upper Canada, which I regard as disaffected, have a bitter animosity against me ; and if it should ever become necessary to admit these parties again into power, in preference to standing a collision with the Legislative Assembly, a case would arise in which my presence here might be rather prejudicial than beneficial, as it would be impossible for me to place the slightest confidence in the leaders of these parties. If any such necessity should occur in my time, it would cause an embarrassment much more serious to me than any difficulty that I have hitherto had to encounter. Whatever my duty might dictate I trust I should be ready to perform; but I cannot contemplate the possibility of co-operating with any satisfaction to myself with men of whom I entertain the opinions that I hold with regard to the leaders of these parties. Such an embarrassment will not be impossible if any portion of the present majority fall off or become insensible of the

necessity of adhering together.   It is with a view to avert
such a calamity that I consider my continuance at my post
to be important at the present period, as a change in the
head of the Government might easily lead to the result
which I deprecate, and which it will be my study to prevent
as long as I see any prospect of success.'   So he struggled on all through the summer months, doing the best he
could, but feeling, at the same time, that his public useful-
ness was impaired by his physical condition, and that it was
chiefly the moral influence of his presence in Canada that
enabled him to be of service to the Crown.

'The autumn of that year found him more afflicted and
more helpless than he had ever been before.   Still he was
unwilling to resign, but he believed it to be his duty to
report to the Queen's ministers that his resignation might
soon be inevitable.   On the 13th of October he wrote to
Lord Stanley : 'My disorder has recently made a serious
advance, affecting my articulation and all the functions of
the mouth; there is a hole through the cheek into the interior of the mouth.   My doctors warn me that it may soon
be physically impossible for me to perform the duties of my
office.   If the season were not so far advanced towards the
winter, I should feel myself under the necessity of requesting
your Lordship to relieve me; but as such an arrangement
might require time and deliberation, I propose to struggle
on as well as I can, and will address your Lordship again on
this subject according to any further changes that may occur in my condition; in the mean while, I have considered
it to be my duty to apprize your Lordship of the probable
impossibility of my performing my official functions, in

order that you may be prepared to make such an arrangement as may seem to be most expedient for the public service.' And again on the 29th : ' I continue in the same bodily state that I described by the last mail. I am unable to entertain company or to receive visitors, and my official business with public functionaries is transacted at my residence in the country instead of the apartment assigned for that purpose in the public buildings in town. I am consequently conscious that I am inadequately performing the duties of my office, and if there were time to admit of my being relieved before the setting in of the winter, I should think that the period had arrived when I might, perfectly in consistence with public duty, solicit to be relieved ; but, as the doctors say that I cannot be removed with safety from this place during the winter, and as that season is fast approaching, it becomes a question whether I can best perform my duty to my country by working on at the head of the Government to the best of my ability until the spring, or by delivering over charge to other hands, and remaining here as a private individual until the season may admit of my return to Europe with safety. In this dilemma I have hitherto abstained from submitting my formal resignation of my office, and shall continue to report by each successive mail as to my condition and capability of carrying on the duties of my post.'

To the first of these letters Lord Stanley, whose kindly sympathies and genial praises had cheered Metcalfe alike in seasons of political anxieties and in hours of physical pain, returned the following characteristic answer : ' I have received the Queen's commands to express to your Lordship the deep concern with which her Majesty learns that the state of your health is such as to render it necessary for you to tender to her Majesty the resignation of the high and arduous office the duties of which you have so ably fulfilled. Her Majesty is aware that your devotion to her service has led you, amidst physical suffering beneath which ordinary men would have given way, to remain at your post to the last possible moment. The Queen highly estimates this proof of your public spirit; and in accepting your proffered resignation, which in the present circumstances she feels it impossible to decline, her Majesty has commanded me to express her entire approval of the ability and prudence with which you have conducted the affairs of a very difficult Government, her sense of the loss which the public service is about to sustain by your retirement, and her deep regret for the cause which renders it unavoidable. These sentiments, I assure you, are fully participated in by myself and the other members of her Majesty's Government. I shall take early steps for the selection of your permanent successor, though it is probable that some time must elapse before he may be able to relieve you. In the mean time, you will consider the acceptance of your resignation as taking effect from the period, whenever that may be, at which you see fit to hand over the government provisionally to Earl Cathcart.'

But even then, in his heroic constancy, he would not decide for himself; he would not desert those who had stood by him in the great constitutional conflict which had recently agitated the colony. It was necessary, however, as the autumn advanced, that the decision should be formed, for the setting in of the winter would have closed the navigation of the river and rendered impossible his departure before the spring. So he called his ministry together at the country-house near Montreal, in which he was then residing, and placed the matter wholly in their hands. 'It was a scene,' writes the biographer of Lord Metcalfe, 'never to be forgotten by any who were present, on this memorable occasion, in the Governor-General's sheltered room. Some were dissolved in tears. All were agitated by a strong emotion of sorrow and sympathy, mingled with a sort of wondering admiration of the heroic constancy of their chief. He told them, that if they desired his continuance at the head of the Government,—if they believed that the cause for which they had fought together so manfully would suffer by his departure, and that they therefore counselled him to remain at his post, he would willingly abide by their decision ; but that the Queen had graciously signified her willingness that he should be relieved, and that he doubted much whether the adequate performance of his duties, as the chief ruler of so extensive and important a province, had not almost ceased to be a physical possibility. It need not be said what was their decision. They besought him to depart, and he consented. A nobler spectacle than that of this agonized man resolutely offering to die at his post, the world has seen only once before.'

So Lord Metcalfe returned to England, and before him lay the great object of his ambition—a seat in the Legislative Assembly of the Empire. But he felt that it was not the decree of Providence that he should ever lift up his voice in defence of those cherished principles which lay so near to his heart.   He had written from Canada to his sister, saying : 'There was a time when I should have rejoiced in a peerage, as affording me the privilege of devoting the remainder of my life to the service of my Queen and country in the House of Lords—in my mind a most honourable and independent position ; but I doubt now whether I shall ever be able to undertake that duty with any degree of efficiency.   My gratification, therefore, is confined to the pleasure which must be derived from so distinguished a mark of approbation of my public services, and to that of knowing that some kind hearts will rejoice at my elevation. The mere rank and title, if divested by infirmities of the power of rendering useful service in the House of Lords, will be encumbrance, and will not add one jot to the happiness which I still hope to enjoy in living in retirement with you.'   And now in England, with all the appliances of European science at his command, and amidst all the restorative influences of perfect repose and the gentle ministrations of loving friends, it seemed less than ever to be God's will that he should take his place among the ' orators discussing important topics in the Senate House.'   A few more months of pain and it would all be over.

But with the pain there was no sorrow.   There was infinite peace and a beautiful resignation within him, and his habitual cheerfulness never wholly deserted him.   He could still rejoice in the society of loving friends and in the kind words which came to him from a distance.   Among other compensations of this kind were the public addresses which were voted to him—addresses striving to congratulate, but coming only to console—which greeted him in his retirement. A great meeting of the ' Civil and Military Servants of the East India Company and others personally connected with India' was held at the Oriental Club. Men who had held all kinds of honourable positions in India, from Governor-General downwards, vied with each other in doing honour to the veteran statesman. Among them, as he himself afterwards wrote, were 'some whose public service he had had the honour of superintending, some with whom he had co-operated as colleagues, some who as schoolfellows had known him from boyhood, some who as contemporaries had been engaged in the same field, and many who, without his personal acquaintance, had nevertheless concurred to do him honour.' The names appended to the address were so numerous, that when the parchment was unrolled before him it covered the floor of his room. He received it with deep emotion. ' It is easy,' he said, 'to bear up against ill-usage, but such kindness quite overcomes me.' In the written answer, which he returned to this address, he said : ' Had I retired from the colonial service of my country with health to enable me to discharge other public functions, it would have been the highest satisfaction to me to devote the rest of my life to those duties in the Legislature devolving on the rank to which I have been elevated by our most gracious sovereign ; but as it appears to be the will of the Almighty that sickness and infirmity should be the lot of my remaining days, I shall in that state cherish the recollection of your kindness as one of the greatest blessings I can enjoy. Proud of my relation with the services in India, in which so many eminent men have been formed and are continually rising, it is a source

of indescribable pleasure to me that the approbation accorded
to my efforts in other quarters should meet with sympathy
from those personally connected with that splendid portion
of the British Empire, and that one of the last acts of my
public life should be to convey to you my grateful sense of
the generous sentiments which you entertain.' To an address received about the same time from the inhabitants of
Calcutta, who had built in his honour the Metcalfe Hall,
he replied in a few brief but touching sentences, in which
he spoke of the infirmities which beset him and the hopeless
state of his health, and concluded by saying, ' My anxious
hope that prosperity and every other blessing may attend
you will accompany me to the grave, which lies open at
my foot.'

This was written in July. The end was, indeed, rapidly
approaching. He was then at Malshanger Park, near
Basingstoke. His sister, Mrs Smythe, and other dear
friends were with him. To the last his courage and resolution were conspicuous. He would not be confined to the
sick-room, but moved about, and without help, as long as
motion was possible,* and desired that everything should go

---

* ' On the 4th of September, Lord Metcalfe, for the first time,
did not leave his sleeping apartment. The extreme debility of the
sufferer forbade any exertion. There was little apparent change
except in a disinclination to take the nourishment offered to him. On
the following morning, however, the change was very apparent. It
was obvious that he was sinking fast. Unwilling to be removed to
his bed, he sat for the greater part of the day in a chair, breathing
with great difficulty. In the afternoon he sent for the members of
his family, laid his hands upon their heads as they knelt beside him,
and breathed the blessing which he could not utter. Soon afterwards

on in his house as if no change were approaching.* He
was sensible of increasing weakness; but he was anxious to
hide his sufferings from the eyes of others, and never at any
time was the unselfishness of his nature more apparent than
when the hand of death was upon him. His loving-kind-
ness towards others was as beautiful as the patience which
clothed him as with a garment; and in the extremity of his
own sufferings he had ever a heart to feel for the sufferings
of others, and a hand to help and to relieve. And so, gentle and genial and courteous to the last, he passed away
from the scene, solaced beyond all by the word of God that
was read to him, and by the sweet sounds of his sister's
harp. The bodily anguish which had so long afflicted him
ceased; perfect peace was upon him; and a calm sweet
smile settled down on his long-tortured face, as with an assured belief in the redeeming power of Christ's blood, he
gave back his soul to his Maker.

He was buried in the family vault of the Metcalfes, ir

he was conveyed to his bed. . . . The last sounds which reached him
were the sweet strains of his sister's harp. . . " How sweet those
sounds are ! " he was heard to whisper almost with his dying breath
—*Life of Lord Metcalfe.*

 * ' He seemed unwilling to do or to suffer anything that would
bring the sad truth painfully to the minds of others. He wished,
therefore, that everything should go on in his household as though
his place were not soon to be empty. . . . He would converse cheerfully on all passing topics, public and private, and his keen sense of
humour was unclouded to the last.'—*Life and Correspondence of
Lord Metcalfe.* The biographer adds: ' A friend writing to me
regarding Lord Metcalfe's last days, says : " A month before his
death I have seen him laugh as heartily at a joke in *Punch* as the
stoutest of us." '

the little parish church of Winkfield, near his paternal estate; and there may be seen a tablet to his memory bearing the following inscription, inspired by the genius of Macaulay. Both are summed up, in the monumental record, with so much beauty and truth, it leaves nothing to be said about the career or the character of Charles Metcalfe.

Near this Stone is Laid

CHARLES THEOPHILUS, FIRST AND LAST LORD METCALFE,

A STATESMAN TRIED IN MANY HIGH POSTS AND DIFFICULT CONJUNCTURES,
AND FOUND EQUAL TO ALL.
THE THREE GREATEST DEPENDENCIES OF THE BRITISH CROWN
WERE SUCCESSIVELY INTRUSTED TO HIS CARE.
IN INDIA HIS FORTITUDE, HIS WISDOM, HIS PROBITY, AND HIS
MODERATION
ARE HELD IN HONOURABLE REMEMBRANCE
BY MEN OF MANY RACES, LANGUAGES, AND RELIGIONS.
IN JAMAICA, STILL CONVULSED BY A SOCIAL REVOLUTION,
HE CALMED THE EVIL PASSIONS
WHICH LONG SUFFERING HAD ENGENDERED IN ONE CLASS,
AND LONG DOMINATION IN ANOTHER.
IN CANADA, NOT YET RECOVERED FROM THE CALAMITIES OF CIVIL WAR,
HE RECONCILED CONTENDING FACTIONS
TO EACH OTHER AND TO THE MOTHER COUNTRY.
PUBLIC ESTEEM WAS THE JUST REWARD OF HIS PUBLIC VIRTUE,
BUT THOSE ONLY WHO ENJOYED THE PRIVILEGE OF HIS FRIENDSHIP
COULD APPRECIATE THE WHOLE WORTH OF HIS GENTLE AND
NOBLE NATURE.
COSTLY MONUMENTS IN ASIATIC AND AMERICAN CITIES
ATTEST THE GRATITUDE OF NATIONS WHICH HE RULED ;
THIS TABLET RECORDS THE SORROW AND THE PRIDE
WITH WHICH HIS MEMORY IS CHERISHED BY PRIVATE AFFECTION.

HE WAS BORN THE 30TH DAY OF JANUARY, 1785.
HE DIED THE 5TH DAY OF SEPTEMBER, 1846.

SIR ALEXANDER BURNES.

[BORN 1805.—DIED 1841.]

ENTERING upon the last year of the last century, a
youth from the Scotch borough of Montrose, who
had gone up to London to seek his fortune, wrote to his
mother, saying : ' I have passed many a serious hour,
reflecting on, weighing, examining minutely, the advantages and disadvantages, which are likely to follow my conduct in the different plans proposed, and I find the result in
favour of going to India on the establishment.   Perhaps my
wishes to obtain, or my favourable ideas of, that situation
have biased my judgment, and prevented me from seeing
every circumstance as it ought to have been seen ; so I will
say little more on the subject, except to inform you of what
distresses me greatly, but will perhaps please you—viz. the
uncertainty of succeeding as I could wish.'   The letter,
from which this extract is taken, is signed ' Your loving and
affectionate Son, JOSEPH HUME.'

Twenty years afterwards, the writer, who had been thus
doubtful of his power to obtain an appointment on the
Indian establishment for himself, was able to obtain appointments for others.   He had become a man of great influence

in his native town. He had gone out to India poor, and he had returned rich, whilst still in the very prime of his life. He had returned to take a distinguished part in public affairs, with thirty or forty years of good life and of good service still remaining in him. It was a natural and a laudable ambition that he should seek to represent his native town in the great imperial Parliament, and to do for it and its people all the good that lay in his power ; so he canvassed the borough and its dependencies in the liberal interests, and in 1818 was duly returned.*

The success of Joseph Hume was great encouragement to the youth of Montrose. He had taken his first start from a very humble beginning, and he had risen solely by the force of his own personal energy. Might not others do the same ? Moreover, the success of Joseph Hume was something more than an encouragement to the young men of the borough. It was an assistance to them. He had become an influential member of the Court of Proprietors of East India Stock, and he had, therefore, 'interest at the India House.' It must be admitted that for very many years what was familiarly called 'borough-mongering,' was the main cause of so many doughty young Scots finding their way into the Indian services. Practically, this was a happy circumstance. At all events, it bore good fruit. But for this, the Company's army might have been wanting in that muscular sinewy strength imparted to it by a constant recruiting from the middle classes of

* The Montrose Burghs then included Montrose, Brechin, Arbroath, Bervie, and Aberdeen. Mr Hume had previously represented Weymouth in Parliament.

the North. The Scotch member, in *esse* or in *posse*, may have thought about nothing but his seat; but it was often his good fortune 'to entertain angels unaware,' and to count among the happy circumstances of his life that he had 'sent to India' a Malcolm, an Ochterlony, or a Munro.

Some of these happy circumstances were recalled with pleasure and with gratitude at the close of a well-spent life by Mr Joseph Hume. Of one of them I am now about to write. In the first quarter of the present century there dwelt at Montrose a family bearing the name of Burnes. The family was of the same stock as that from which had sprung the inspired ploughman of Ayrshire, though the two branches of the family were pleased to spell their names after different fashions. The grandfather of Robert Burns, the poet, and the grandfather of James Burnes, writer to the signet, burgess of Montrose, and head of the family of which I am now writing, were brothers. In the first year of the century, James Burnes married a daughter of Adam Glegg, chief magistrate of Montrose, and in due course had fourteen children, nine of whom lived to be adults. Of these nine children the four eldest were sons. The first-born was named James, after his father; the second Adam, after his maternal grandfather; the third Robert; and the fourth Alexander, after whom called I know not, but there could have been no better name for one who was destined to do great things in the countries watered by the Indus and bounded by the Caucasian range. He often used to say, in later days, that he found his name a help to him. In Afghanistan he was always known as 'Sekunder Burnes,' and Sekunder (Alexander) has been a great name in that part of the world ever since the great days of the Greek occupation.

Mr James Burnes was, I have said, a burgess of Montrose. He was a man greatly respected by the townspeople, both for his integrity and ability, and he came to be provost of the borough, and recorder or town-clerk. For many years he took an active part in the local politics of the place, and there were few places in which local politics occupied so much of the time and the thoughts of the good people of a country town. The influence of Provost Burnes was, of course, great in the borough. It was no small thing for a candidate for the representation of Montrose and its dependencies to have the Burnes interest on his side. He was not a man to forsake his principles for gain; but there was no reason why, with four stout clever boys pressing forward for employment, and eager to make their fortunes, he should not endeavour to turn his influence to good account for the benefit of his children. He was very useful to Mr Hume, and Mr Hume, in turn, was well disposed to be useful to the family of Burnes. In truth, the tide of liberal politics was somewhat high and heady at that time; and even the children of the worthy burgess's household were no indifferent observers of passing events, but had their bursts of political excitement like their elders. The acquittal of Queen Caroline produced as great a fervour of exultation in that distant seaport town as it did in Westminster or Hammersmith; and one of the Burnes boys, who had at a very early age habituated himself to keep a diary, then recorded in its pages : ' November 14, 1820. News came of the rejection by the House of Lords of the Bill of Pains and Penalties against the Queen. No schooling on account of it. . . . November 15. A most brilliant illumination took place in Montrose and the surrounding neighbourhood, on account of the glorious triumph the Queen had obtained over her base and abominable accusers. Many devices were exhibited, one in the Town-hall with a green bag all tattered and torn ; in another window, a figure of the Queen, with the word " Triumphant," and above it "C. R." The display of fireworks was unlimited. Two boats were burned, and some tar-barrels, and upon the whole it did great credit to Montrose.'

The writer of this journal was Alexander Burnes, the third surviving son, then fifteen years of age, and a student in the Montrose Academy, the head-master of which, Mr Calvert, had something more than a local reputation as a distinguished classical scholar and a highly successful teacher —as men taught in those days with the book in one hand and the scourge in the other. He was a clever, in some respects, perhaps, a precocious boy ; and had learnt as much in the way, both of classics and of mathematics, as most promising striplings of his age. He had read, too, some books of history, and a few of the masterpieces of English poetry. He belonged to a debating society, and was not altogether unskilled in disputation. Like other high-spirited boys, he had taken part in conflicts of a more dangerous character than mere conflicts of words, and fought some hard battles with the boys of the town. Altogether, though not to be accounted a prodigy, he was a youth of high spirit and good promise, and had in him some of the stuff of which heroes are made.

But I can find nothing in the record of Alexander Burnes's early life to warrant the conclusion that the bent of his mind towards foreign travel was then in any way discernible. What little I can find in his papers rather bears the other way. I have before me a collection, in his own writing, of the speeches he delivered at the ' Montrose Juvenile Debating Society,' the thesis of one of which (proposed by himself) is, ' Whether reading or travelling is most advantageous for the acquisition of knowledge ? ' To this the ' juvenile debater ' replied : ' My opinion on the present subject is, that reading is the most advantageous for the acquisition of knowledge.' And then he proceeded to illustrate this opinion, by reading to the meeting an interesting extract from the recently published travels of the African traveller, Belzoni. Having done this, he said : ' Now, to have it in our power to amuse ourselves any night we please with the book which contains all these disasters, without the labour which has been encountered, shows in the clearest light the advantages derived from that most delightful and pleasing amusement, reading.' This is charmingly illogical. The young debater forgot, in his enthusiastic admiration of the book that had given him so much pleasure, that there could have been no ' reading ' in this case if there had been no ' travelling.' Certainly it would have been difficult to cite a more unfortunate illustration of the views of the juvenile speaker. It is possible that when, in after life, he came to gather up his ideas a little more compactly, he bethought himself of the mistake he had made, and remembered that it is an essential condition to the 'acquisition of knowledge' from books of travel like Belzoni's, that there should be Belzonis to write them.

Neither, indeed, is there anything to indicate that the desires of young Alexander Burnes at that time turned towards a life of military adventure in the eastern or the western worlds. Of the hundreds of cadets who year after year went out to India at that time in the service of the East India Company, only an exceptional few were moved by any impulses of their own to enter the Indian army. The choice was commonly made for them as a matter of convenience by their parents or guardians ; and the case of Alexander Burnes was no exception to the rule. The success of Mr Hume was that which decided the choice of the worthy burgess of Montrose, for it afforded at once a great encouragement and a material aid. The eldest hope of the Burnes family, James, was destined for the medical service—that service in which Mr Hume had so rapidly made a fortune—and was pursuing his studies in London, with a view to an Indian career. Adam, the second, was training for the law in his native burgh. And Alexander, by the assistance of Mr Hume, was to be provided with a cadetship, as soon as he was old enough to take up the appointment. When, therefore, the young student was within a few weeks from the completion of his sixteenth year, he was sent up to London in a Dundee smack ; and having arrived there on the 14th of March, 1821, he was on the following day introduced by Mr Hume to Mr Stanley Clerk, a member of the Court of Directors, and was told that his name had been duly entered for a cadetship of infantry on the establishment of Bombay. He spent two months in London, studying under the well-known Oriental professor, Dr Gilchrist, and watched over by Mr Joseph Hume, who gave him good advice of all kinds, and acted as his banker; and then on the 16th of May—his birthday —he attended at the India House and formally took the oath of allegiance.

It was a matter of pleasant family arrangement that the eldest brother, James Burnes, who had been appointed an assistant-surgeon on the Bombay establishment, should sail in the same vessel with Alexander; so they embarked together, early in June, on board the good ship *Sarah*. Of this voyage there are abundant records in the young cadet's journal, many passages of which exhibit considerable discernment of character, and no slight powers of description. But it must suffice here to state that, after an uneventful voyage, the *Sarah* arrived at her destination, and that, on the 21st of October, 1821, these two young Montrosians found themselves on the beach of Bombay, with very little money in their pockets, and with very slender interest; but with stout hearts, clear heads, and that determination to make for themselves careers in the public service which, in the days of the East India Company, carried so many members of our middle classes in India straight on to fortune and to fame.

The brothers were soon separated. On the 13th of November, James Burnes was gazetted to do duty as an assistant-surgeon with the Artillery at Maloongah. Four

days before this, Alexander's name had appeared in General
Orders, by which he was posted to do duty with the 1st Battalion of the 3rd Regiment of Native Infantry at Bombay.
On the 19th, he recorded in his journal that he had 'commenced his military career,' and appeared on parade. From
that day he made steady progress in his profession. He
applied himself sedulously to the cultivation of the native
languages. He had continued on board ship the studies
which he had commenced under Dr Gilchrist in London,
and now he supplemented his literary pursuits by making
and steadily adhering to the rule, to converse with his native
servants only in Hindostanee; and on the 8th of December
he wrote in his journal : ' Ever since I ordered my servants
to address me in Hindostanee I find my improvement very
great, and I am persuaded that there is no method more
effectual in acquiring the language than the one I am at
present pursuing, for it unites the theoretical and the practical. Having migrated from my own country, and being
rather of a curious and searching disposition, I have begun
to gain as much information concerning the manners,
customs, laws, and religions of this people—a study not
only amusing and interesting, but highly instructive; for
what is it that makes a man, but a knowledge of men and
manners ? ' There was nothing which a man might not
achieve in India, who thus set himself to work in the right
way. There was proof of this even then before the young
' unposted ensign.' He had carried out with him, as most
young men carry out, letters of introduction to the Governor
and other influential people of the Presidency. The Governor at that time was Mr Mountstuart Elphinstone, whose

kindness and affability of manner won the heart of the young soldier at once. 'The Governor,' he wrote home to his family at Montrose, 'received us with great politeness, and invited us to the most splendid fête I had ever beheld, and did not behave in a " How do ? " manner, but was extremely affable and polite, which, among a party of a hundred, and for the most part generals and great men, was a great deal. ... A few weeks ago a grand public ball was given to Sir John Malcolm, on his leaving India,* to which I had the honour of receiving an invitation; but where it came from I know not. It was, if anything, grander than Mr Elphinstone's fête, and held in a house built for the purpose, about the size of the old Council House at Montrose, illuminated with lamps from top to bottom.' There must have been something in all this greatly to inspire and encourage the young Scotch subaltern, for Malcolm himself had risen from the same small beginning, and now his name was in every man's mouth, and all were delighted to do him honour. What might not any young Scot, with the right stuff in him, do in India? In all directions there was encouragement and assurances not likely to be thrown away upon a youth of young Burnes's lively imagination. A Montrose man had sent him out to India; an Edinburgh man was now at the head of the Government of Bombay; a Glasgow man was Governor of the Madras Presidency; and now the son of an Eskdale farmer was receiving the plaudits of all classes of his countrymen, and returning for a while to his native land, a successful soldier and a successful statesman, amidst a whirl of popularity that

* See *ante*, Memoir of Sir John Malcolm, vol. i. page 304.

might have fully satisfied the desires of the most ambitious hero in the world.

But to young Alexander Burnes the encouragements of the future were not greater than the consolations of the present. 'I like the country amazingly,' he wrote to Montrose, 'and as yet am not at all desirous of a return to my own land. Here I have everything to be wished for— plenty of time to myself, a gentlemanly commanding officer, and several very pleasant brother-officers.' But he added, for thoughts of home were still pulling at his heart, 'how dearly should I like to see little Charley or Cecilia trudging into my canvas abode—but, ah! that is far beyond probability. However, I may yet see Charley in India, for he seems a boy made for it.'

Thoughts of active service soon began to stir his mind. There was a prospect of a war with China, and the young soldier was eager to take part in it. 'There has been a most dreadful disturbance,' he wrote to his parents, on the 30th of April, 1822, 'between the powers of China and the East India Company within these few months; so all trade between these countries is now at a stop, and nothing seems more inevitable than war, for it is in everybody's mouth, and every person is anxious to go. I hope I may be sent. If I am not sent along with my regiment, I shall certainly volunteer; for if a man does not push on he will never see service, and, of course, will never be an officer worth anything. What will the poor old maids of Montrose do for want of tea?' But the excitement passed away. There was no war. And so young Alexander Burnes fell back peacefully on his Oriental studies, and with such good

success, that at the beginning of May, 1822, he went up
for an examination in Hindostanee, and found that he
passed for an interpretership. 'I was so delighted,' he
wrote in his journal, 'that I could scarcely contain myself.'
A fortnight before, he had been posted to the 2nd Battalion
of the 11th Regiment of Native Infantry, but as the interpretership of that regiment was not vacant, he applied,
without success, to be removed to another corps. Any disappointment, however, which he might have felt about this
was soon removed by the necessities of action; for a few
days afterwards his regiment was ordered to Poonah, which
a few years before had been the capital of the Peishwah,
and was still in the bloom of its historical associations. It
was with no common interest that he repeatedly visited the
battle-field of Khirkee. 'The plain where the cavalry of
the Peishwah charged I galloped over,' he wrote in his
journal, 'and I can scarcely imagine a better place for cavalry
to act than this, for scarcely a nullah intersects it.' *

The time passed very pleasantly at Poonah. 'It is a
most delightful place,' he wrote, 'and I like the Deccan
amazingly. I have joined the 2nd Battalion of the 11th
Bombay Native Infantry, which in point of discipline is not
surpassed by any regiment in the service. . . . In point of
officers there was never, perhaps, a more gentlemanly and
pleasant set of men assembled together in an Indian Native
Corps—in a word, I have got into a regiment that delights
me, and naturally makes my time pass delightfully. . . .'
Governor Elphinstone was then at Poonah, contributing by
his hospitalities to the general happiness, and stimulating

* See *ante*, Memoir of Mountstuart Elphinstone, vol. i.

the youth of the station, by his example, to deeds of heroic sportsmanship.   Here young Burnes fleshed his maiden spear during a hog-hunt of three days' duration.   Here, too, he began the study of the Persian language.   ' I have been strenuously advised to begin Persian,' he wrote to his friends at Montrose, ' as it will improve my Hindostanee, and, perhaps, add greatly to my future prospects in India; so I have commenced it.'   And he prosecuted the study with such good effect, that, after a few months, he was able to derive intense gratification from the perusal of the Persian poets.   Before the end of the month of September he thus pleasantly reported his progress: ' My bedroom is small, and brings often to my recollection my old little closet in the passage, for as it is my study I spend a great deal of time in it, and have managed to scribble pieces of poetry on its walls also; but they are now of a different language, for I have got quite enamoured of Persian poetry, which is really, for sound and everything, like a beautiful song— instead of *Lallah Rookh* in the English, I have got a *Lallah Rookh* in the Persian—at least a much more beautiful poem.'

In December the regiment quitted Poonah *en route* for Surat.   At Bombay, where they halted, Alexander Burnes again made a push for an interpretership, and this time with good success; for on the 7th of January, 1823, his name appeared in General Orders, gazetted as interpreter of the 1st Extra Battalion, which happened to be posted at Surat.   He was, with one exception, the only ensign in the Bombay Army who held such an appointment.   This was great promotion; but in the following year a brighter prospect still expanded before the young soldier. On the general reorganization of the army, by which each battalion was converted into a separate regiment, with a separate regimental staff, Lieutenant Burnes, then little more than eighteen years old, was offered the regimental adjutancy. The offer excited him greatly, and he wrote : ' Behold your son Alexander the most fortunate man on earth for his years! Behold him Lieutenant and Adjutant Burnes of the 21st Regiment, on an allowance of from five hundred to six hundred rupees a month.' The appointment had been offered to him by his friend Colonel Campbell. ' He did not think,' wrote Burnes to Montrose, ' that I would accept the situation, for my life in India has been so much devoted to study, that he conceived, and correctly too, that I was aiming at some political situation. I soon undeceived him, by telling him that I found my abilities greatly turned to that direction, but that, nevertheless, I was ready for anything else. . . . No man in his sound senses would refuse a situation of fifty or sixty guineas a month.' * The breaking up of the old regiment was, however, a source of no little grief to him, and a like feeling prevailed among all the best officers in the army. ' I could little tolerate this,' said Burnes, ' for I had become in a great degree attached to the men ; but I less regretted it as my brother-officers were all to accompany me.' This re-organization gave a blow to the discipline of the whole army, from which it never recovered.

* In this letter Alexander Burnes again urged his father to send out his brother Charles in the army, and undertook to guarantee the payment of all expenses.

From the journals which he kept in this year, a lively impression may be gained of the young soldier's state of mind. A conviction was growing upon him that, notwithstanding early backwardness, there was some good cultivable ground in his nature, and that some day he would make for himself a name. He had conceived a desire to visit other Eastern countries, and was assiduously studying their languages. Like many others at that dangerous period of dawning manhood, he was haunted with strange doubts concerning both his material and spiritual being, and fancied that he was doomed to die young and to lapse into unbelief. There are few earnest inquiring minds that have not been subjected to that early blight of scepticism. A few passages from his diary will illustrate all these mental and moral phases. ' July 24. . . . I find it frequently the case that dull, or rather middling, boys at school shine more in the world than those who are always at the head, and exquisite scholars. . . . . I am the only illiterate man in my family —all professions but me. Never mind—quite content. A soldier's life permits of much spare time, which I am improving.' 'September 2. I reckon three years more will make me a Persian scholar, and five more will give me a tolerable knowledge of Arabic. Before many . more months elapse, I purpose making a visit to Persia, and, if possible, Arabia; that is to say, if my circumstances will allow, as I feel confident of remaining amongst the inferior class of linguists if I do not go to the country.' ' September 3. I have been ruminating on the probability of accomplishing the above project, and if I continue saving 50 rupees a month, as I do at present, I may in time accumulate something; but it is so expensive studying, that that keeps me from saving what I ought. . . . . I expect to reach the height of preferment in this service, and only think my short life will hinder me from it.' ' September 4. . . . . If a speedy return to my native land (say ten years) be not effected, I can entertain little hopes of living to an aged man. In constitution I may be robust, in body I am very weak, slender, and ill made, and if it be true, as I have often heard them say, " I was born before my time." This they tell me, and as my grandfather's house was the place of my birth, I begin to think so. If this is the case, it accounts for my shape. I was very small when born, and, indeed, so much so, that they baptized me three days after my birth, that I might not die nameless, which, according to superstitious people, is bad. I am different from all around me. I dislike all gymnastic and athletic exercises. I like *argument* much— a *jolly* party only now and then ; much study, and am very partial to history, but dislike novels extremely, even Scott's. My abilities are confined, but as my mind expands they seem to improve. I was very dull at school, and reckoned a *dolt.* I ought not to have been a soldier, although I glory in the profession, for I am too fond of pen and ink.' ' September 21. I have of late been deeply pondering in my own mind the strange opinions I begin to imbibe about religion, and which grow stronger every day. . . . . Would to God my mind were settled on this truly important sub- ject ! Could I be convinced fully of it, I would not believe in a future state, but it is an improbable thing to imagine God has made man gifted with reason, after his own image,

and yet to perish.   It is madness to dream of it.   My ideas
may be very barbarous, but I do not see that a man's happiness can be increased by his knowing there is a tribunal.
. . . . I lead a happy life, much more so than the generality
of my companions, but I entertain different ideas of religion
daily, and am afraid they will end in my having no religion at all.   A fatalist I am, but no atheist.   No, nor even
a deist.   No—what shall I call it?—a sceptical blockhead,
whose head, filled with its own vanities, imagines itself more
capable than it is.'   'October 16. My second year in India
being now on the eve of completion, I think it full time to
remit money to my father in Europe; consequently sent a
hoondee to Bombay for 246 rupees to Messrs R. and Co.,
which, with former remittances, makes up a sum somewhat
short of £50.   This I have desired to be transmitted home
to my father directly, or to J. Hume, Esq., M.P., for him.
. . . . . . I am thinking within myself how very gratifying this will be to my father, who could not certainly
expect much from me, and particularly at present, when I
am on reduced allowances.'

The power of gratifying this laudable desire to remit
money to his family in England was well-nigh checked at
the outset by what might have been a serious misadventure,
for which he would have long reproached himself. In
those days there was still a good deal of gambling in the
army, and in a luckless hour young Burnes was induced to
play at hazard. He thus records the incident in his journal:
'October 17. "I have lost a day." This day my feelings
were put more to the test than any other day during my
existence.   G. and H. called in upon me in the morning,

and as we are all very fond of cards, it was proposed by G. to play at hazard. I declined, on the plea, first, of its being daytime; and secondly, on its being too much of a gambling game for me. The first I gave up, being master of the house, and in the second I yielded, provided the stakes were low. A quarter of a rupee was proposed, and we got on very well for some time, till G., beginning to lose, went very high. This induced me also. I lost 1500 rupees, and it was on the increase every turn up of the cards. It was proposed at this time (it being past the dinner-hour) to give up after our rounds. H. and G. played, and I reduced it to about 800 rupees. My turn came, and I lost. I was upwards of 1000 rupees in arrear. G. proposed once more. I agreed. I gained from H. and G., and when it came to my turn I owed 500 rupees. I dealt out the cards. G. gave me a card, and went 50 rupees on ten cards at table, and lost 350 rupees.' The upshot of the game was, that Burnes regained his money, and found himself with a balance of 13 rupees in his favour But he had won much more than this. ' I have got such a moral lesson,' he added, 'that I never intend handling cards at a round game for some time, and I am ashamed of myself, and shall ever be so. " I've lost a day." I could scarcely place the cards on the table, I got so nervous. No wonder. I had at that time lost my pay for half a year. Had I lost 1500 rupees, where would my prospects of sending money to my dear father have been ? What is more than all, these gamblings derange my head and prevent me bestowing proper attention on my Persian studies.'

He gambled no more after this, but continued to apply

himself steadily to the study of the native languages and to his military duties; and he soon made rapid progress in his profession. In 1825 there were threatenings of war with the Ameers of Sindh. There had been a repetition of those border forays which might have resulted in the devastation of Cutch, and a British force was equipped for the coercion of the marauders. To this force Alexander Burnes was attached as Persian interpreter, and he was afterwards appointed to the Quartermaster-General's department, which permanently removed him from the sphere of regimental duty. Writing from Bhooj to his early friend and patron, Joseph Hume, in July, 1825, he gave the following account of his condition and prospects : * 'You must yourself be well acquainted with the present state of India to the eastward, and I can give you no more favourable accounts regarding the Bombay Presidency, as a

---

* This letter was written primarily to acknowledge the receipt of a letter of introduction to Sir David Ochterlony, which Mr Hume had sent to the writer. As illustrative of a passage at page 135, *ante* (Memoir of Sir Charles Metcalfe), the following may, perhaps, be read with interest : 'I had the pleasure to receive your letter of August, 1824, enclosing one to Sir David Ochterlony, and beg leave to express my sincere thanks for the interest you have taken in my behalf. I took the earliest opportunity to forward it to the General, but his unfortunate quarrel with the Government regarding the propriety of reducing Bhurtpore has given him enough to do, and fully accounts for no answer being received. Sir David is much regretted, and it seems to be the general opinion that it was a very impolitic measure to abandon the campaign when so overwhelming an army was encamped before the fort. Our misfortunes in 1805, when under the walls of Bhurtpore, are still fresh in the recollection of the natives, and this has given them, if possible, additional presumption.'

cessation of hostilities at Burmah can only be the signal
for a declaration of war with the Ameers of Sindh, our
north-western neighbours. I can, perhaps, inform you of
some particulars which may prove interesting regarding
this and the adjacent province of India. About four or
five years ago the nobles of Cutch called in the British
Government to assist them in deposing their Rao (King),
who had rendered himself very odious by the most wanton
cruelty. Their request met with the approbation of our
Government; the Rao was deposed, and his son raised to
the musnud, with a Regency of five persons, of which the
British Resident is one. A subsidiary force of two regiments was established, and the Cutch Durbar agreed to
pay half. In April, 1825, a body of marauders invaded
the province from Sindh, but they were not entirely natives
of that country, many of the discontented of this province
having joined them. Be it sufficient to say that there was
little or no doubt of their having received great support
from Sindh. They plundered the whole of the country
around Bhooj, and, from the insufficiency of our force,
actually cut up six hundred of the Rao's horse within four
miles of camp. There being little doubt but that Sindh
was at the bottom of it, some time elapsed before any
attempt was made to dislodge them, it being considered
prudent to wait the arrival of troops. Another native
regiment and some regular cavalry have been added to the
brigade; and Captain Pottinger, the Resident, has just told
me that a letter has arrived from our agent at Hyderabad
mentioning the march of a division of the Sindhian army,
chiefly composed of Beloochees, and amounting to four or

five thousand men, and every hour confirms the report. A third treaty with this nation may be patched up, but a war is inevitable ere long, and the want of officers and troops will be the cause of much expense to the Company. . . . . I am proud to say that the same good fortune which I had at the commencement of my career seems still to attend me, and that the late disturbances in Cutch have elevated me from the regimental to the general Staff, having been appointed Quartermaster of Brigade to the Cutch Field Force. If you were to inquire of me how this has come about, I could not tell you, for I hardly know myself. The Brigadier of the station (Colonel Dyson) sent for me while I was acting Adjutant in April last, and asked me if I would become his interpreter and Staff, vacating my own acting appointment under the hope of Government confirming his nomination. As I was only an Acting Adjutant, I consented, and fortunately I am confirmed in one of the appointments, which makes my pay and allowances 400 rupees a month. I should have liked the interpretership, but as the Staff is 400 rupees alone, I am very fortunate, and have every probability of retaining the situation for a long time, although it is only styled a temporary arrangement. If Sindh is invaded, an officer in the Quartermaster-General's department has a grand field opened to him. My pecuniary concerns are thus in a very thriving way. I have already sent home £250, and have more at my command. I am £500 better off than any of my shipmates, whose letters of credit were in general five times the amount of mine, but then I have been very fortunate. I am not indebted in any way to the Governor, and the

Commander-in-Chief has deprived me of both Quarter-mastership and Adjutancy, when recommended both times by the Commanding Officer, and the latter time by a Lieutenant-Colonel even. I must confess that chance must have done much for me against such opposition, but I am also greatly indebted to Colonel Leighton, who has always stood by me.'

In a later letter the story is thus resumed : ' I continued my study of the languages,' he wrote to an old schoolfellow in the West Indies, ' and mastered the Persian, which brought me to the notice of Government, and I was selected from the army to be Persian interpreter to a field force of eight thousand men, under orders to cross the Indus and attack the territory of Sindh, which is situated at the delta of that great river. . . . . The force to which I was attached did not advance; the campaign terminated in 1825; but during its continuance I had, in the absence of other duty, devoted my time to surveying and geography, and produced a map of an unknown track, for which Government rewarded me by an appointment to the department of the Quartermaster-General—the most enviable line in the service. It removed me for good and all, before I had been four years in the service, from every sort of regimental duty. I advanced in this department step by step, and was honoured by the approbation of my superiors. In 1828 they raised me to be Assistant-Quartermaster-General of the Army, and transferred me to headquarters at Bombay, on a salary of eight hundred rupees a month. There I met Sir John Malcolm, of whom you may have heard. I knew him not, but I volunteered to explore the Indus from where it is joined by the Punjab down to the ocean, and thus delighted the men in authority. I started at the end of 1829 on this hazardous undertaking, and after I had got half through it, was recalled by Lord Bentinck, as it would have involved political difficulties at the moment. I did, however, so much, that I blush to sound my own praises. The substantial part of them is, that they have removed me entirely to the diplomatic line, as assistant to the Resident in Cutch, which is a foreign state, in alliance with the British, close on the Indus. It is difficult to draw a parallel between European and Indian situations; but, if one is to be made, I am what is called Secretary of Legation, and on the high road, though I say it myself, to office, emolument, and honour. I have now briefly sketched out my career. My pursuits are purely literary, and confined to investigating the antiquities of Asia and the wonders of this people. I have been tracing the magnanimous Alexander on his Quixotic journey to these lands; and I shall set out at the end of 1830 to traverse further regions, which have been untrodden since the Greeks of Macedon followed their leader. Being an accredited agent of the Government, I have their support in all these wanderings; so you see that I have hung the sword in the hall, and entered the Cabinet as a civilian. . . . . My great ambition,' he said, ' is to travel. I am laying by a few spare rupees to feed my innocent wishes, and could I but have a companion like you, how doubly joyous would I roam among the ruins of the capitol, the relics of classic Athens, and the sombre grandeur of Egypt! These, and all the countries near them, are in my mind's eye; I think, I dream of them; and when I journey to my native land, my route will traverse them all. I purpose landing at Berenice on the Red Sea, and, following the Nile in its course across from classic to sacred lands, cross the plains of Syria and Mount Sinai; thence, by Asia Minor to the Hellespont and Greece, Italy, and merry France; and last of all to my native Scotia. I have enough of the good things of this life to start on this projected tour, when my ten years of service are out—that is, on the 31st of October, 1831.'

But it was ordained by Providence that his journeyings should be quite in a different direction. In the early part of 1830, a despatch arrived at Bombay, from the Board of Control, enclosing a letter of compliment from the President, Lord Ellenborough, to Runjeet Singh, the great ruler of the Punjab, together with a batch of horses that were to be forwarded to his Highness as a present from the King of England. It was necessary that the letter and the horses should be forwarded to Lahore, under the charge of a British officer. Sir John Malcolm was at this time Governor of Bombay. He was full of enterprise and enthusiasm; he had himself been a great traveller; and he was the one of all others to appreciate the achievements and to sympathize with the aspirations of such a man as Alexander Burnes. He accordingly recommended the young Bombay Lieutenant for this important duty, and the Supreme Government readily endorsed the recommendation. But although the man had been chosen, and chosen wisely, there was much discussion respecting the manner of the mission and its accompaniments, and very considerable official delay.

'It is part of Sir John Malcolm's plan for the prosecution of my journey,' wrote Burnes to the family at Montrose, in September, 1830, 'that I quit Bombay before the Government make any arrangements for my voyage up the Indus to Lahore.' In these days we know every foot of the ground, and such a journey as Burnes was about to undertake belongs only to the regions of common-place; but when Burnes, at this time, wrote about 'the noble prospects which awaited him in being selected for a delicate and hazardous duty,' he by no means exaggerated the fact. He was emphatically the Pioneer, and he had to cut and clear his way through briary difficulties and obstructions which have long since disappeared. He was not merely sent upon a complimentary mission to the ruler of the Punjab; he was directed also to explore the countries on the Lower Indus, and to this end he was intrusted with presents to the Ameers of Sindh.*

---

* If I were writing history, not biography, I should comment upon the error of this. As it is, I cannot resist quoting the following from a minute of Sir Charles Metcalfe, recorded in October, 1830 : 'The scheme of surveying the Indus, under the pretence of sending a present to Runjeet Singh, seems to me highly objectionable. It is a trick, in my opinion, unworthy of our Government, which cannot fail, when detected, as most probably it will be, to excite the jealousy and indignation of the powers on whom we play it. It is just such a trick as we are often falsely suspected and accused of by the native Princes of India, and this confirmation of their suspicions, generally unjust, will do more injury, by furnishing the ground of merited reproach, than any advantage to be gained by the measure can compensate. It is not impossible that it may lead to war. I hope that so unnecessary and ruinous a calamity may not befall us. Yet, as our officers, in the prosecution of their clandestine pursuits, may meet with insult or ill treatment, which we may choose to resent, that result is possible, however much to be deprecated.' The sagacity

But the Ameers were mistrustful of our designs. They believed that Burnes had come to spy the nakedness of the
land. With all the clearness of prophecy, they saw that
for the English to explore their country, was some day for
them to take it. So they threw all sorts of impediments
in the way of Burnes's advance. 'We quitted Cutch,' he
wrote to Sir John Malcolm, 'on the 20th of January,
1831, and encountered every imaginable difficulty and
opposition from the Ameers of Sindh. They first drove
us forcibly out of the country. On a second attempt they
starved us out. But I was not even then prepared to give
up hopes, and I ultimately gained the objects of pursuit by
protracted negotiations, and voyaged safely and successfully
to Lahore.' After he had once entered the Punjab, his
journey, indeed, was quite an ovation. 'My reception in
this country,' he wrote to his mother, on the last day of
July, 'has been such as was to be expected from a Prince
who has had so high an honour conferred on him as to
receive presents from our gracious Sovereign. Immediately
that I reached his frontier he sent a guard of horsemen as
an honorary escort, and announced my arrival by a salute
of eleven guns from the walls of the fortresses I passed.
But what is this to the chief of Bahwulpore, lower down,
who came all the way to Cutch to meet me, and with
whom I had an interview, announced by eighty guns?'
The mission, which had reached Lahore on the 18th of
July, quitted it on the 14th of August; and Burnes pro-

of this is undeniable ; but it is to be observed that Burnes was in no
degree responsible for the policy here denounced. He had only to
execute the order of the Government.

ceeded to Simlah, to give an account of his embassy in
person to the Governor-General, who was then, with his
secretaries, residing in that pleasant and salubrious retreat.

Lord William Bentinck received the young traveller
with characteristic kindness, and listened with the deepest
interest to the account of his adventures. He listened to
the account, not only of what the young Bombay Lieutenant had done, but also of what he desired to do. Before
he had started on this journey, Burnes had cherished in his
heart the project of a still grander exploration—the exploration which was eventually to achieve for him fame and
fortune. . 'I have a vast ambition,' he wrote from the
banks of the Jheelum to the 'old folks at home,' 'to cross
the Indus and Indian Caucasus, and pass by the route of
Balkh, Bokhara, and Samarcand, to the Aral and Caspian
Seas, to Persia, and thence to return by sea to Bombay.
All this depends upon circumstances; but I suspect that
the magnates of this empire will wish to have the results of
my present journey before I embark upon another.' He
was right. But, having communicated the results of this
journey, he found the Cabinet at Simlah well prepared to
encourage another enterprise of the same character, on a
grander scale. 'The Home Government,' he wrote to his
sister, on the 23rd of September, 1831, 'have got frightened at the designs of Russia, and desired that some intelligent officer should be sent to acquire information in the
countries bordering on the Oxus and the Caspian; and I,
knowing nothing of all this, come forward and volunteer
precisely for what they want. Lord Bentinck jumps at it,
invites me to come and talk personally, and gives me com-

fort in a letter.' 'I quit Loodhianah,' he said, a few weeks
later, 'on the 1st of January, 1832, and proceed by Lahore
to Attock, Caubul, Bameean, Balkh, Bokhara, and Khiva,
to the Caspian Sea, and from thence to Astracan. If I
can but conceal my designs from the officers of the Russian
Government, I shall pass through their territory to England,
and visit my paternal roof in the Bow Butts.'

After a few more weeks of pleasant sojourning with the
vice-regal court, Alexander Burnes started on his long and
hazardous journey. He received his passports at Delhi
two days before Christmas, and on the 3rd of January,
1832, crossed the British frontiers, and shook off Western
civilization. He was accompanied by a young assistant-
surgeon, named Gerard, who had already earned for himself a name by his explorations of the Himalayahs, and by
two native attachés,—the one, Mahomed Ali, in the
capacity of a surveyor; the other, a young Cashmeree Mahomedan, educated at Delhi, named Mohun Lal, who
accompanied him as moonshee, or secretary. Traversing
again the country of the 'five rivers,' and making divers
pleasant and profitable explorations 'in the footsteps of
Alexander the Great,' in the middle of March the travellers forded the Indus, near Attock, took leave of their Sikh
friends, and became guests of the Afghans. There were
at that time no jealousies, no resentments, between the two
nations. The little knowledge that they had of us, derived
from the fast-fading recollections of Mr Elphinstone's
mission, was all in our favour; and we in our turn believed

them to be a cheerful, simple-minded, kind-hearted, hospitable people. Along the whole line of country, from Peshawur to Caubul, which cannot now be even named amongst us without a shudder, the English travellers were welcomed as friends. From the Afghan capital, Burnes wrote on the 10th of May, 1832, to his mother: ' My journey has been more prosperous than my most sanguine expectations could have anticipated ; and, instead of jealousy and suspicion, we have hitherto been caressed and feasted by the chiefs of the country. I thought Peshawur a delightful place, till I came to Caubul: truly this is a Paradise.' His fine animal spirits rose beneath the genial influences of the buoyant bracing climate of Afghanistan. How happy he was at this time—how full of heart and hope—may be gathered from such of his letters as reached his friends. With what a fine gush of youthful enthusiasm, writing to the family at Montrose, to which his heart, untravelled, was ever fondly turning, he describes his travel-life on this new scene of adventure. '. . . . We travel from hence in ten days with a caravan, and shall reach Bokhara by the first of July. . . . . If the road from Bokhara to the Caspian is interrupted by war, of which there is a chance, I shall be obliged to pass into Persia, and in that event must bid farewell to the hope of seeing you, as I must return to India. The countries north of the Oxus are at present in a tranquil state, and I do not despair of reaching Istamboul in safety. They may seize me and sell me for a slave, but no one will attack me for my riches. Never was there a more humble being seen. I have no tent, no chair or table, no bed, and my clothes altogether amount to the value of one pound sterling. You would disown your son if you saw him. My dress is purely Asiatic, and since I came into Caubul has been changed to that of the lowest orders of the people. My head is shaved of its brown locks, and my beard, dyed black, grieves—as the Persian poets have it—for the departed beauty of youth. I now eat my meals with my hands, and greasy digits they are, though I must say, in justification, that I wash before and after meals. . . . . I frequently sleep under a tree, but if a villager will take compassion upon me I enter his house. I never conceal that I am a European, and I have as yet found the character advantageous to my comfort. I might assume all the habits and religion of the Mahomedans, since I can now speak Persian as my own language, but I should have less liberty and less enjoyment in an assumed garb. The people know me by the name of Sekundur, which is the Persian for Alexander, and a magnanimous name it is. With all my assumed poverty, I have a bag of ducats round my waist, and bills for as much money as I choose to draw. I gird my loins, and tie on my sword on all occasions, though I freely admit I would make more use of silver and gold than of cold steel. When I go into a company, I put my hand on my heart and say with all humility to the master of the house, " Peace be unto thee," according to custom, and then I squat myself down on the ground. This familiarity has given me an insight into the character of the people which I never otherwise could have acquired. I tell them about steam-engines, armies, ships, medicine, and all the wonders of Europe, and, in return, they enlighten me regarding the customs of their country, its history, state factions, trade, &c., I all the time appearing indifferent and conversing thereon "pour passer le temps." . . . The people of this country are kind-hearted and hospitable; they have no prejudices against a Christian, and none against our nation. When they ask me if I eat pork, I of course shudder, and say that it is only outcasts who commit such outrages. God forgive me! for I am very fond of bacon, and my mouth waters as I write the word. I wish I had some of it for breakfast, to which I am now about to sit down. At present I am living with a most amiable man, a Newab, named Jubbur Khan, brother to the chief of Caubul, and he feeds me and my companion daily. They understand gastronomy pretty well. Our breakfast consists of pillaw (rice and meat), vegetables, stews, and preserves, and finishes with fruit, of which there is yet abundance, though it is ten months' old. Apples, pears, quinces, and even *melons* are preserved, and as for the grapes, they are delicious. They are kept in small boxes in cotton, and are preserved throughout the year. Our fare, you see, is not so bad as our garb, and like a holy friar, we have sackcloth outside, but better things to line the inside. We have, however, no *sack* or good wine, for I am too much of a politician to drink wine in a Mahomedan country. . . . . I am well mounted on a good horse, in case I should find it necessary to take to my heels. My whole baggage on earth goes on my mule, over which my servant sits supercargo; and with all this long enumeration of my condition, and the entire sacrifice of all the comforts of civilized life, I never was in better spirits, and never less under the influence of *ennui*. . . . . I cannot tell you how my heart leaps, to see all the trees and plants of my native land growing around me in this country.'

When Burnes and his companions quitted Caubul, the Newab Jubbur Khan, who had hospitably entertained them, and had endeavoured to persuade them to protract their sojourn with him, made every possible arrangement for the continuance of their journey in safety and comfort, and bade them 'God speed' with a heavy heart. 'I do not think,' said Burnes, 'I ever took leave of an Asiatic with more regret than I left this worthy man. He seemed to live for every one but himself.' He was known afterwards among our people by the name of 'the Good Newab;' and the humanity of his nature was conspicuous to the last.'

Having quitted Caubul, the English travellers made their way to the foot of the Hindoo-Koosh, or Indian Caucasus, and traversed that stupendous mountain-range to Koondooz, Kooloom, and Balkh. This was the route explored by those unfortunate travellers Moorcroft and Trebeck, of whom Burnes now found many traces, and whose sad history he was enabled to verify and authenticate. It was a relief to the young Englishman to find himself in the territory of the King of Bokhara, whose evil reputation had not been then established. 'As we were now in the territories of a king,' he naïvely recorded in the history of his journey, 'we could tell him our opinions, though it had, perhaps, been more prudent to keep them to ourselves.'

After a sojourn of three days at Balkh, which had many interesting and some painful associations, for it had been the capital of the ancient Bactrian kingdom, and a little way beyond its walls was the grave of Moorcroft, Burnes and his companions made their way to the city of Bokhara, which they reached on the 27th of June.   There they re- sided for a space of nearly four weeks, receiving from the Vizier all possible kindness and hospitality.   ' Sekundur,' said he to Burnes on his departure, ' I have sent for you to ask if any one has molested you in this city, or taken money from you in my name, and if you leave us contented?'   I replied that we had been treated as honoured guests, that our luggage had not even been opened, nor our property taxed, and that I should ever remember with the deepest sense of gratitude the many kindnesses that had been shown to us in the holy Bokhara. . . . . I quitted this worthy man with a full heart, and with sincere wishes (which I still feel) for the prosperity of this country.'   The Vizier gave authoritative instructions to the conductors of the caravan with which Burnes was to travel, and to a Toorko- man chief who was to accompany it with an escort, to guard the lives and properties of the Feringhees, declaring that he would root them from the face of the earth if any accident should befall the travellers ; and the King of Bokhara gave them also a firman of protection bearing the royal seal.   It is instructive to consider all this with the light of after-events to help us to a right understanding of its significance.

From Bokhara the route of the travellers lay across the great Toorkoman desert to Merve and Meshed, thence to Astrabad and the shores of the Caspian ; thence to Teheran, the capital of the dominions of the Shah of Persia, from which point Burnes moved down to the Persian Gulf, took ship there to Bombay, and afterwards proceeded to Calcutta. The story has been told by himself, with an abundance of pleasant detail, and is too well known to need to be repeated. Summing up the whole, he says of it, in a few striking words, 'I saw everything, both ancient and modern, to excite the interest and inflame the imagination—Bactria, Trans-Oxiana, Scythia, and Parthia, Kharasm, Khorasan, and Iran. We had now visited all these countries ; we had retraced the greater part of the route of the Macedonians ; trodden the kingdoms of Porus and Taxiles, sailed on the Hydaspes, crossed the Indian Caucasus, and resided in the celebrated city of Balkh, from which Greek monarchs, far removed from the academies of Corinth and Athens, had once disseminated among mankind a knowledge of the arts and sciences of their own history, and the world. We had beheld the scenes of Alexander's wars, of the rude and savage inroads of Jengis and Timour, as well as of the campaigns and revelries of Baber, as given in the delighful and glowing language of his commentaries. In the journey to the coast, we had marched on the very line of route by which Alexander had pursued Darius, while the voyage to India took us on the coast of Mekran, and the track of the Admiral Nearchus.'

At Calcutta, Alexander Burnes laid before the Governor-General an account of his journey, accompanying it with much grave discourse on the policy which it was expedient for the British Government to pursue towards the different states which he had visited. The result was exactly what he wished. He was sent home to communicate to the authorities in England the information which he had ob-

tained. All this was truly delightful. Never in the midst
of his wanderings in strange places, and among a strange
people, had he forgotten the old home in Montrose, and
the familiar faces of the household there; never had his
heart ceased to yearn for the renewal in the flesh of those
dear old family associations. He liked India; he loved his
work, he gloried in the career before him; but the good
home-feeling was ever fresh in his heart, and he was continually thinking of what was said and thought in Montrose. And in most of our Indian heroes this good home-
feeling was kept alive to the last. It was not weariness of
India; it was not a hankering after England. It was
simply a good healthy desire to revisit the scenes of one's
youth, to see again the faces of one's kindred, and then,
strengthened and refreshed, to return with better heart for
one's work.

On the 4th of November, 1833, Burnes landed at Dart-
mouth, and wrote thence to his mother that he could
scarcely contain himself for joy. On the 6th he was in
London, with his brothers, David and Charles; dining in
the evening with the Court of Directors, who had oppor-
tunely one of their banquets at the London Tavern. Before
the week was out, he was in a whirl of social excitement;
he was fast becoming a lion—only waiting, indeed, for the
commencement of the London season, to be installed as
one of the first magnitude. 'I have been inundated by
visits,' he wrote to his mother, 'from authors, publishers,
societies, and what not. I am requested to be at the Geo-

graphical Society this evening, but I defer it for a fortnight, when I am to have a night to myself. . . . All, all are kind to me. I am a perfect wild beast.—" There's the traveller," " There's Mr Burnes," " There's the Indus Burnes," and what not do I hear. I wish I could hear you and my father, and I would despise all other compliments.' ' I am killed with honours and kindness,' he said, in another letter, ' and it is a more painful death than starvation among the Usbeks.' In all this there was no exaggeration. The magnates of the land were contending for the privilege of a little conversation with ' Bokhara Burnes.' Lord Holland was eager to catch him for Holland House. Lord Lansdowne was bent upon carrying him off to Bowood. Charles Grant, the President of the Board of Control, sent him to the Prime Minister, Lord Grey, who had long confidential conferences with him ; and, to crown all, the King—William the Fourth—commanded the presence of the Bombay Lieutenant at the Brighton Pavilion, and listened to the story of his travels and the exposition of his views for nearly an hour and a half.

The account of the interview, as recorded in his journal, is interesting and amusing : ' Well, I have been an hour and twenty minutes with William the Fourth, and eventful ones they have been. It is not likely that I shall have many interviews with royalty, so I may be prolix in this, the first one. From the Castle Square gate I was taken to Lord Frederic Fitzclarence, who led me to the Chinese Hall, where I sat for twenty minutes till the King transacted his business with Sir Herbert Taylor. " Take a book," said Lord Frederic, " from the shelf and amuse yourself; " and one of the first I pulled down, was—what? "Burnes' Justice." This was ludicrous—was it but justice that I should see the King, or what? "Mr Burnes," cried a page. I passed through two rooms; a large hall was thrown open, and I stood, hat in hand, in the presence of King William. "How do you do, Mr Burnes? I am most glad to see you; come and sit down—take a chair—there, sit down, take a chair." The King stood but I sat, as compliance is politeness. There was no bending of knees, no kissing of hand, no ceremony; I went dressed as to a private gentleman. I expected to find a jolly-looking, laughing man, instead of which, William looks grave, old, careworn, and tired. His Majesty immediately began on my travels, and, desiring me to wheel round a table for him, he pulled his chair and sat down by mine. Hereon I pulled out a map, and said that I hoped his Majesty would permit me to offer the explanation on it. I began, and got along most fluently. I told him of the difficulties in Sindh, the reception by Runjeet, &c., but William the Fourth was all for politics, so I talked of the designs of Russia, her treaties, intrigues, agencies, ambassadors, commerce, &c., the facilities, the obstacles regarding the advance of armies—I flew from Lahore to Caubul, from Caubul to Bokhara and the Caspian, and I answered a hundred questions to his Majesty. The King then got up, took me to a large map, and made me go over all a second time, and turning round to me, asked a great deal about me personally. "Where were you educated?" "In Scotland, Sir." "What is your age?" "Twenty-eight, please your Majesty." "Only twenty-eight! What rank do you hold?" I replied, that I was only a Lieutenant

in the Army, but that my situation was political. " Oh,
that I know. Really, sir," commenced the King, " you
are a wonderful man; you have done more for me in this
hour than any one has ever been able to do; you have
pointed out everything to me. I now see why Lord
William Bentinck places confidence in you; I had heard
that you were an able man, but now I know you are most
able. I trust in God that your life may be spared, that our
Eastern Empire may benefit by the talents and abilities
which you possess. You are intrusted with fearful information : you must take care what you publish. My ministers
have been speaking of you to me, in particular Lord Grey
You will tell his Lordship and Mr Grant all the conversation
you have had with me, and you will tell them what I think
upon the ambition of Russia.'. . . I think, sir, that your
suggestions and those of Lord William Bentinck are most
profound; you will tell Lord William, when you return to
India, of my great gratification at having met so intelligent
a person as yourself, and my satisfaction at his Lordship's
having brought these matters before the Cabinet. Lord
Grey thinks as I do, that you have come home on a mission
of primary importance—second only to the politics of
Russia and Constantinople. . . . Lord Grey tells me that
you have convinced him that our position in Russia is hopeless." So continued King William. I felt quite overcome
with his compliments. He then made me run over my
early services, wondered only I was not a Lieutenant-Colonel if I had been an Assistant-Quartermaster-General,
added that he saw sufficient reason for employing a man of
my talents in the highest situation, and again hoped that I

might be spared for my country's good.   I replied to the
King that I considered it a high honour to have had such
confidential communication with his Majesty.   He stopped
me, and said that " I have been quite unreserved, for I see
and know you deserve it.   I could say many things to you,"
&c. &c.   I have no more time to write.   The King wore
a blue coat with the ribbon of the Garter, and a narrow red
ribbon round his neck, to which a cross was suspended.
" Good morning, sir ; I am truly happy to have seen you.
You don't go to India yet," &c. &c.   I took my departure,
and, while threading the passages, a page ran after me by
desire of the King, to show me the Palace ; but I had
seen it.'

He was now hard at work upon his book.   He had
written many lengthy and valuable official reports ; but he
had little experience of literary composition for a larger
public than that of a bureaucracy, and he was wise enough
to discern that the path to popular favour must be very cautiously trodden.   Mistrusting his own critical judgment, he
submitted portions of his work, before publication, to some
more experienced friends, among whom were Mr James
Baillie Fraser and Mr Mountstuart Elphinstone.   The latter, not oblivious of his own early throes of literary labour,
read the manuscript—painfully, in one sense, owing to the
failure of his sight, but with the greatest interest and delight.
' I never read anything,' he wrote from his chambers in the
Albany to Alexander Burnes, ' with more interest and pleasure ; and although I cannot expect that every reader will be
as much delighted as I have been, yet I shall have a bad
opinion of the people's taste if the narrative is not received

with general favour.' But although Mr Elphinstone bestowed these general praises on the work, he was fain to do his young friend good service by honestly criticizing the work in detail. ' I have made my remarks,' he wrote, ' with the utmost freedom, and the more so, because I hope you will not pay any attention to them when unsupported, but will be guided by the opinion of people who know the taste of this town, and who are familiar with criticism in general literature. I must premise that many of my objections are founded on general principles, and may, therefore, often be brought against passages which in themselves may be beautiful, but which lack the general effect to which you ought always to look. The first of these principles is, that a narrative of this kind should be in the highest degree plain and simple.' The reader who has perused the preceding Memoir of Mr Elphinstone, may remember how, in the preparation of his own book of travels, he had steadfastly adhered to this critical tenet; but whether naturally, or against nature, I do not undertake to say. My own impression is that he had brought his native instincts and appetencies to this state of critical subjection after sore trial and hard conflict, and that he spoke with the authority of a man who had wrestled down some besetting temptations. For naturally he was ardent, enthusiastic, imaginative; and when he first began to write for the public, he might have given way to the exuberance which he afterwards deprecated, if it had not been for the pruning-knife of his friend Richard Jenkins. Critically, he was doubtless right; but when he continued thus to enlarge upon the paramount duty of simplicity, perhaps he did not sufficiently remember that a 'fastidious public' may be a small one. 'To gain the confidence and good will of his reader,' he said, 'a traveller must be perfectly unaffected and unpretending. His whole object must seem to be to state what he has seen in the countries he has visited, without claiming the smallest superiority over his reader in any other description of knowledge or observation. For this reason, every unusual word, every fine sentiment, every general reflection, and every sign of an ambitious style, should be carefully excluded.' A hard lesson this for a young writer; and there was much more of the same kind; sound and excellent advice, altogether past dispute, and in accordance with the best critical canons. But Mr Elphinstone lived to see these severe literary doctrines utterly set at nought by a younger race of writers— lived to see a 'fastidious public' take to its heart *Eothen,* as the most popular book of travels ever published in modern times.

Nor was the only pruning-knife applied to the exuberance of the young writer that which was wielded by the experienced hand of such chastened writers as Mr Elphinstone, the official knife was also applied to the manuscript in the Secret Department of the India House. This was, doubtless, in a literary sense, disadvantageous to the book; but, after undergoing these ordeals, it came out under the auspices of Mr Murray; and Burnes had the honour of presenting a copy to the King at one of his Majesty's levees. 'I know all about this,' said the good natured monarch, mindful of Burnes's visit to him at Brighton. The book was an undoubted success. It was well received by the critics and by the public, for not only was there something

geographically new in it, but something also politically
suggestive. The Russo-phobia was gaining ground in
England. There were many who believed that the time
was fast approaching when the Sepoy and the Cossack
would meet, face to face, some where in Central Asia. It
was a great thing, therefore, just in that momentous epoch,
that some one should appear amongst us to whom the
countries lying between the Indus and the Caspian were
something more than places on the map. As the depository
of so much serviceable information, Burnes was sure to be
welcome everywhere. There was much, too, in the man
himself to increase the interest which his knowledge of these
strange countries excited. He was young in years, but
younger still in appearance and in manner. When he said
that he had been thirteen or fourteen years in India, Lord
Munster said to him, 'Why, that must have been nearly
all your life.' There was a charming freshness and naïveté
about him—the reflection, it may be said, of a warm, true
heart, in which the home affections had never for a moment
been dormant. The greatest happiness which his success
gave him was derived from the thought that it would give
pleasure to his family, and might enable him to help them.
He had striven in vain, and his father had striven also,
through Sir John Malcolm and others, to obtain a cadetship
for his brother Charles; but now this great object was
readily obtainable, and the young man, who had been
waiting so long for this promotion, received, as a just tribute
to his brother, an appointment in the Bombay Army, which
others' influence had failed to procure for him.

He remained at home until the spring of 1835; and

then, with mingled feelings of hope and regret, he set his face again towards the East.*   His sojourn in England had been attended by so many gratifying and flattering circumstances, that to one of his impressionable nature it must have been a continual delight from the first day to the last. Among other honours bestowed on him of which I have not spoken, it may be recorded here that he received the gold medal of our Geographical Society, and the silver medal of the Geographical Society of Paris, and that he was nominated, without ballot, a member of the Athenæum Club—an honour which has been described as the ‘ Blue Riband of Literature.’ In Paris, too, the *savans* of that enlightened city received him with as much enthusiasm as our own people. It would have been strange if, at his early age, his head had not been somewhat ‘ turned ’ by all this success. But if it caused him to set a high value on his own services, it caused him also to strain his energies to the utmost not to disappoint the expectations which had been formed of him by others. A little youthful vanity is not a bad thing to help a man on in the world.

When Burnes returned to Bombay, he was ordered to rejoin his old appointment as assistant to the Resident in Cutch. In the course of the autumn he was despatched by

* He went out overland in charge of despatches from the India House, and proceeded from Suez to Bombay in the *Hugh Lindsay* (pioneer) steamer, from which vessel he sent intelligence to Sir Charles Metcalfe that Lord Heytesbury had been appointed Governor-General of India.

Colonel Pottinger on a mission to Hyderabad, the capital
of the Ameers of Sindh. 'I am doomed,' he wrote, 'to
lead a vagabond life for ever ; but all this is in my way, and
I am in great spirits.' But neither were his habits of so
vagrant a character, nor the necessities of his work so engrossing, as to prevent him from thinking and writing about
what has since been called the ' Condition-of-India Question.'
He was very eager always for the moral elevation of the
people, and he spoke with some bitterness of those who
looked upon India merely as a preserve for the favoured
European services. ' Do not believe,' he wrote to a friend,
' that I wish to supersede Europeans by unfit natives. I
wish gradually to raise their moral standard, now so low, for
which we are, however, more to blame than themselves.
Men will say, " Wait till they are ready." I can only reply,
that if you wait till men are fit for liberty, you will wait
for ever. Somewhere in the *Edinburgh Review* of days of
yore, you will find this sentiment, which is mine : " Will a
man ever learn to swim without going into the water ? " '
After insisting on the duty of encouraging education by
providing profitable employment for the educated classes,
and declaring that we should thus soon cover the country
with educated and thinking people, he continued in this
letter from Hyderabad : ' There is nothing here that I cannot
support by history. Tacitus tells us a similar tale of our
own ancestors, among whom Agricola sowed the seeds of
greatness. That accomplished historian speaks of the superstitions of the Britons—of the ferocity of the hill tribes—of
the degeneracy of those who had been subdued—of the want
of union which had led to it—of the alacrity with which they

paid their tribute, &c. &c. Change the name of Briton to Indian, and what have we but a sketch of this country under our present rule?   And who are we?   The descendants of those savages whom Agricola, by new and wise regulations, educated—we who are now glorious throughout the world.' And again, a few months later, he wrote: 'I look upon the services, one and all, as quite subservient to the great end of governing India; but I seldom meet with any one who looks upon India in any other light than as a place for those services, which is to me so monstrous, that I have, like Descartes, begun "to doubt my own existence, seeing such doubt around me."'   He spoke of this with righteous indignation, but there was a tinge of exaggeration in his words; and he spoke somewhat too strongly even with reference to those times when he said that, 'instead of raising up a glorious monument to our memory, we should impoverish India more thoroughly than Nadir, and become a greater curse to it than were the hordes of Timour.'

But his services were now about to be demanded by the Government in a more independent position. Lord Auckland had proceeded to India as Governor-General. He had met Burnes at Bowood, had been pleased with his conversation, and had formed a high opinion of the energy and ability of the young subaltern.   When, therefore, the first rude scheme of a pacific policy in the countries beyond the Indus took shape in his mind, he recognized at once the fact that Burnes must be one of its chief agents.   So the Cutch Assistant was placed under the orders of the Supreme Government, and directed to hold himself in readiness to undertake what was described at the time, and is still known in history, as a

'Commercial mission' to Caubul.   Commerce, in the vocabulary of the East, is only another name for conquest.   By commerce, the East India Company had become the sovereigns of the great Indian peninsula; and this commercial mission became the cloak of grave political designs. Very soon the cloak was thrown aside as an encumbrance, and, instead of directing his energies to the opening of the navigation of the Indus, the institution of fairs, and the opening of the new commercial routes through the Afghan and Beloochee countries, Alexander Burnes gave up his mind to the great work of check-mating Russia in the East.

'In the latter end of November, 1836, I was directed by the Governor-General of India, the Earl of Auckland, to undertake a mission to Caubul.   Lieutenant (now Major) Robert Leech, of the Bombay Engineers, Lieutenant John Wood, of the Indian Navy, and Percival B. Lord, Esq., M. B., were appointed with me in the undertaking.   The objects of Government were to work out its policy of opening the river Indus to commerce, and establishing on its banks and in the countries beyond it such relations as should contribute to the desired end.   On the 26th of November we sailed from Bombay, and sighting the fine palace at Mandavee on the 6th of December, we finally landed in Sindh on the 13th of the month.   Dr Lord did not join our party till March.' Such is the first page of a book written some years afterwards by Sir Alexander Burnes, in which he tells the story of this visit to Caubul, stripped of all its political apparel.   Neither in its commercial nor its scientific aspects was it wholly a failure.*   Burnes drew up a report on the trade of the Indus,

* Lord Auckland, it should be stated, received this as a legacy

and Wood wrote an excellent paper on its navigation ; but events were developing themselves even faster than the ideas of the travellers; and commerce and science, though not wholly forgotten, soon dwindled into second-rate affairs.

Lord Auckland was not an ambitious man—quiet, sensible, inclined towards peace, he would not have given himself up to the allurements of a greater game, if he had not been stimulated, past all hope of resistance, by evil advisers, who were continually pouring into his ears alarming stories of deep-laid plots and subtle intrigues emanating from the Cabinet of St Petersburg, and of the wide-spread corruption that was to be wrought by Russian gold. It was believed that the King of Persia had become the vassal of the great Muscovite monarch, and that he had been instigated by the Government of the Emperor to march an army to Herat for the capture of that famous frontier city, and for the further extension of his dominions towards the

from Lord William Bentinck, with whom Burnes had been in communication in India, and in correspondence during his residence in England. Whilst at home, Burnes had ceaselessly impressed on the King's ministers, as well as on the Directors of the Company, the importance of not neglecting, either in their commercial or their political aspects, the countries beyond the Indus ; and some of his letters, written at this time, give interesting accounts of his interviews with Lord Grey, Mr Charles Grant, Lord Lansdowne, and other statesmen, on this favourite subject. In one letter to Lord William Bentinck, he wrote that Lord Grey took a too European view of the question, and considered it chiefly ' in connection with the designs of Russia towards Constantinople ; ' whilst Lord Lansdowne, having ' a mind cast in so noble a mould, looked with more interest on the great future of human society than on our immediate relations with those countries.

boundaries of our Indian Empire. The attack upon Herat was a substantial fact; the presence of Russian officers in the Persian territory, as aiders and abettors of the siege of Herat, was also a fact. The dangers which were apprehended were essentially very similar to those which had alarmed us more than a quarter of a century before, and which had caused the despatch of Mr Elphinstone's mission to Afghanistan. But there were some circumstantial differences. Not only had the Russian power taken the place of the French in the great drama of intrigue and aggression, but another actor had appeared upon the scene to take the leading business at Caubul. There had been a revolution, or a succession of revolutions, in Afghanistan. The Suddozye King, Shah Soojah, whom Elphinstone had met at Peshawur, was now a pensioner in the British dominions, and the Barukzye chief, Dost Mahomed, was dominant at Caubul.

This was the man who, in the autumn of 1837, welcomed the English gentlemen to his capital. 'On the 20th of September,' wrote Burnes in his published book, 'we entered Caubul, and were received with great pomp and splendour by a fine body of Afghan cavalry, led by the Ameer's son, Akbar Khan. He did me the honour to place me upon the same elephant on which he himself rode, and conducted us to his father's court, whose reception of us was most cordial. A spacious garden close to the palace, and inside the Balla Hissar of Caubul, was allotted to the mission as their place of residence. On the 21st of September we were admitted to a formal audience by Ameer Dost Mahomed Khan, and I then delivered to

him my credentials from the Governor-General of India.
His reception of them was all that could be desired. I informed him that I had brought with me as presents to his
Highness, some of the rarities of Europe; he promptly
replied that we ourselves were the rarities, the sight of
which best pleased him.' But neither the presents nor the
promises, which Burnes was allowed to make to the Afghans, were of a character that could much gratify them.
The fact is, that we sought much, and that we granted
little. Dost Mahomed was at this time greatly perplexed
and embarrassed. Alarmed by the attitude of the Sikhs
on the one side,* and of the Persians on the other, he
looked to the English for support and assistance in his
troubles. But weeks passed away, and weeks grew into
months. The English gentlemen remained at Caubul, but
he could extract no comfort from them ; and, in the mean
while a Russian agent had appeared upon the scene, less
chary of his consolations. ' To the East,' said Burnes, ' the
fears of Dost Mahomed were allayed; to the West they
were increased. In this state of things his hopes were so
worked upon, that the ultimate result was his estrangement
from the British Government.'

It was our policy to secure the good offices of the Ameer,
and it was the duty of Alexander Burnes to accomplish the

---

* Whilst Burnes and his companion had been moving onward
from Sindh to Afghanistan, through Beloochistan and the Punjab, the
Sikhs and Afghans had been fighting for Peshawur. In May a great
battle was fought at Jumrood, in which the Sikhs were victorious.
The disturbed state of the country had delayed the progress of the
Mission.

object. Left to himself he would have done it. He, who best knew Dost Mahomed, had most faith in him. The Ameer was eager for the British alliance, and nothing was easier than to secure his friendship. But whilst Burnes was striving to accomplish this great object at Caubul, other counsels were prevailing at Simlah—that great hotbed of intrigue on the Himalayan hills—where the Governor-General and his secretaries were refreshing and invigorating themselves, and rising to heights of audacity which they never might have reached in the languid atmosphere of Calcutta. They conceived the idea of reinstituting the old deposed dynasty of Shah Soojah, and they picked him out of the dust of Loodhianah to make him a tool and a puppet, and with the nominal aid of Runjeet Singh, who saw plainly that we were making a mistake which might be turned to his advantage, they determined to replace the vain, weak-minded exile, whom his country had cast out as a hissing and a reproach, on the throne of Afghanistan. It is enough to state the fact. The policy was the policy of the Simlah Cabinet, with which Burnes had nothing to do. It was rank injustice to Dost Mahomed. It was rank injustice to Alexander Burnes. The young English officer, who had been twice the guest of the Barukzye Sirdars of Caubul, who had led them to believe that his Government would support them, and who had good and substantial reason to believe that they would be true to the English alliance, now found that he was fearfully compromised by the conduct of his official superiors. He left Caubul, and made his way to Simlah; and it is said that the secretaries received him with eager entreaties not to spoil the 'great game' by dissuading Lord Auckland from the aggressive policy to which he had reluctantly given his consent.

This was in the summer of 1838. Even if the young Bombay officer could have spoken with 'the tongue of angels,' his words would have been too late. What could he do against a triumvirate of Bengal civilians—the ablest and most accomplished in the country? It is true that he had an intimate acquaintance, practical, personal, with the politics of Afghanistan, whilst all that they knew was derived from the book that he had written, from the writings of Mountstuart Elphinstone, and from another book of travels written by a young cavalry officer named Arthur Conolly, of whom I shall presently give some account in this volume. But they had had the ear of the Governor-General whilst Burnes had been working at Caubul; and so their crude theories prevailed against his practical knowledge. He was not, however, a man of a stubborn and obstinate nature, or one who could work out, with due ministerial activity, only the policy which he himself favoured. It is the sorest trial of official life to be condemned to execute measures, which you have neither recommended nor approved, and then to be identified with them as though they were your own. But every good public servant must consent to bear this burden with all becoming resignation and humility. The State could not be efficiently served, if every subordinate servant were to assume to himself the right of independent judgment. Burnes would have supported Dost Mahomed from the first, but when it was decreed that Shah Soojah

shoula be supported, Burnes endeavoured to reconcile himself to the policy, and did his best to render it successful.*
What his views were may be gathered from the following
letter, which he wrote to Sir John Hobhouse, in December,
1838 : 'The retreat of the Persians from Herat has been
to us all most gratifying intelligence, but the subsequent
proceedings of the Shah raise up in my mind the strongest

* From Simlah he wrote on the 10th of September, 1838, saying : 'I implored the Government to act. His Lordship lauded me
for my abilities, &c., but thought I was travelling too fast, and would
do nothing. Matters got worse hourly. Letters from Russian
agents, promising everything to the Afghan chiefs, fell into my hands.
I founded on them further remonstrances at the supineness of Government ; their eyes were opened ; they begged of me to hold on at
Caubul if I could ; but I knew my duty better to my country, for
meanwhile Russian good offices had been accepted to the exclusion
of the British, and I struck my flag and returned to India, saying :
"Behold what your tardiness has done !" You might think disgrace
would follow such proceedings: far from it—they applauded my
vigour, and twenty thousand men are now under orders to do what a
word might have done earlier, and two millions of money must be
sunk in what I offered to do for two lakhs ! How came this about ?
Persia has been urged by Russia to attack Herat and invade India.
Poor Dost Mahomed is afraid of the Sikhs on one side, and of Persia
on the other. Russia guaranteed him against Persia, and thus he
clung to her instead of us. Sagacity might have led him to act otherwise, but he was placed in difficult circumstances, and we augmented
his difficulties. In the dilemma they asked my views. I replied :
"Self-defence is the first law of nature. If you cannot bring round
Dost Mahomed, whom you have used infamously, you must set up
Shah Soojah as a puppet, and establish a supremacy in Afghanistan, or you will lose India." This is to be done, and we have
drawn closer to Runjeet Singh, who has feathered his nest in our
dilemma, and kept all his Afghan country, under our promise of
support.

doubt of our having brought his Majesty to reason, or done aught but to postpone the evil day for a time. The frontier fortress of Afghanistan—Ghorian—is still garrisoned by Persian troops, and besides a messenger on the part of the Shah now at Candahar and Caubul, the Russian officer, Captain Vicovitch, is at Candahar, and has already distributed 10,000 ducats among the chiefs who have called out their retainers, and are now on their route to invest Herat. The Russian declares on all occasions that Mahomed Shah will return, and that the money he distributes is not Russian gold, but that of the Shah; and further, that if Herat falls into their hands, the Russians will then lead the Afghans to the Attock (Indus). After the gallant defence made by Herat, it might not appear at all possible that the chiefs of Candahar should capture it with their rabble band; but still I have some apprehensions, as well from the reduced and dilapidated state of Herat itself, as from its being now about to be invested by Afghans. In their wars, victory is decided by defection. The minister of Herat is unpopular, and he will not be able to rouse the courage of his people by their fighting against the enemies of their religion, as were the Sheeah Persians. On the raising of the siege of Herat, I wrote at once to Lieutenant Pottinger, sending him 20,000 rupees, and telling him "to draw on me for such a sum as is indispensable to place the walls of Herat in a state of repair, and relieve its suffering inhabitants from want," and I have received the Governor-General's sanction to send him a lakh of rupees; but in a subsequent part of this letter I will point out that we ought to make much larger sacrifices than this, and as Lord Auckland does not as yet know of the extent of this new Russian intrigue, I shall, without hesitation, cash any bill from Herat for money expended as I have stated. Till I received very precise accounts of Vicovitch's proceedings, I could not unravel the object of his intrigue, but I have had a practical proof of it within this week from the chief of Khelat, the first ruler we shall encounter on our way to Candahar, and through whose territory is the great Pass of Bolan. To an invitation sent to this person to co-operate with us, from Lord Auckland, Shah Soojah, and myself, he tells me that he is a friend, and will do all that is wished, but that he wants certain territories restored to him ; that he supports the Shah only to oblige us, and that the chief of Candahar had offered him a part of the Russian gold now and hereafter to side with him. As an alliance between Candahar and Khelat is perfectly out of the question, and Mehrab Khan's (the chief is so called) pretensions, if allowed to take root, would involve serious embarrassment, I have plainly told him that he is either to be a friend or a foe, and I have little doubt that all will go right with him. But it is not the small chiefship of Khelat or its petty politics that would lead me to trouble you with an introduction of them. What is to be said to a regular train of proof now brought to light of Russian intrigue from Khelat to Kokund, or from the sea to the northern portion of Cashmere ! It is clear, and appears to me imperative on the British Government to spare neither expense nor labour to supplant this growing influence. It is, therefore, with every satisfaction that I see the Governor-General resolved upon carrying through his measures, even though Herat be relieved, for we can have no security for the future without rearing a solid fabric westward of the Indus. Our policy there for the last thirty years has been so supine and full of reserve, that we have to thank ourselves only for the evils that have accumulated. It is not fitting in me to say things of what might have been so easily done by us in Caubul and Candahar last year, since, however much the loss of that opportunity is to be regretted, the basis of the present war is self-defence, the first law of nature. On that stable ground the Government can and must defend its measures, and if sympathy and faction united raise up a party to side with Dost Mahomed Khan, they may paint with much colour the hardship of his case (and it is a very hard one), but all faction must sink before the irrefragable evidence that our Indian Empire is endangered by a further perseverance in our late and inert policy. But supposing our plans for placing Shah Soojah on the throne of his ancestors to succeed, it is evident that we shall have a strong under-current of intrigue to work up against, and that Russia will now add to her former means of intriguing through the Persians in Afghanistan, the unseated rulers of Caubul and Candahar. All our energies will, therefore, be called forth, for I consider Persia to be as much subject to Russia as India is to Britain, and we must make up our minds to oppose her, face to face, on the Afghan frontier. My journey to Bokhara in 1832 served to convince me that Russia had ulterior designs eastward, which I expressed as firmly as I believed, but it was not the policy of the day to check them. I did not think that her progress and intrigues would have been so rapid as they have been, and I then believed that we might have injured Russia in these countries by giving encouragement to the Indus commerce and founding fairs, but all these hopes are now vain, without the display of physical power aiding our moral influence. I have urged Lord Auckland to fortify Herat on the principles most approved by engineers. I will give the same advice with reference to Candahar when it falls to us, and I hope in the course of a month to have received from the chief of Northern Sindh (to whose Court I am accredited as Envoy) the fortress of Bukkur. The grand line of route will thus be in our hands, and at Caubul itself we shall have a strong government by supporting the Shah, and a good pledge for his continued friendship in the British officers we have placed in his service.'

When it was determined by Lord Auckland's Government that a great army should be assembled for the invasion of Afghanistan and the restoration of Shah Soojah to the throne of Caubul, the army was to march by the way of the Bolan Pass, through the country ruled by the Ameers of Sindh, and Burnes was to be sent forward to make all necessary arrangements for the passage of our army through those little known and difficult regions to Candahar. If he had formed any expectation of being vested with the supreme political control of the expedition, and afterwards of representing British interests at the Court of Shah Soojah, they were not unreasonable expectations. But Mr Macnaghten was appointed 'Envoy and Minister' at Caubul, whilst Captain Burnes, in the vice-regal programme having no assured place, was to be employed as a wayside emissary. But the sharpness of his disappointment was mitigated by the receipt of letters announcing that the Queen had taken

his services into gracious consideration, and had made him
a Knight, with the military rank of Lieutenant-Colonel.
This sent him about his work with better heart, and he
brought all his energies to bear upon the important duty of
smoothing the road for the march of the army of the
Indus, and the procession of the restored Suddozye monarch
into the heart of the country, which never wanted him,
and which he was wholly incompetent to govern.

Nor were these the only gratifying circumstances which
raised his spirits at this time. He found that the policy
which he would have worked out in Afghanistan, though
thwarted by the Simlah Cabinet, had found favour in high
places at home. Lord Auckland himself frankly acknowledged this, and generously afforded Burnes full license to enjoy his victory. 'I enclose a letter from the Governor-General
himself,' wrote Lieutenant-Colonel Sir Alexander Burnes,
from Shikarpore, on the 4th of December, 'which is a
document very dear to me, and which I told Lord Auckland I prized as high as the honours themselves. The fact
is, I have been playing the boldest game a man ever dared.
I differed entirely with the Governor-General as to his
policy in Afghanistan, told him it would ruin us, cost the
nation millions, when a few lakhs now would keep off
Russia. They would not be guided by me, and sent me a
laudatory wig (reprimand), and as sure as I had been a
prophet, my predictions are verified. Russia is upon us,
and the Home Government has pronounced me right and
his Lordship wrong! This is the greatest hit I have made
in life. Seeing how they had mismanaged all things, they
asked my advice; but, like all timid politicians, they ran

from one extreme to another. An army was necessary, but not so large an army. However, I told Lord Auckland I should do all I could to work out his views, and am doing so. The declaration of war you will see in the papers, and how much has come out of my mission to Caubul.' *

At this time Burnes was employed on a mission to the Ameers of Sindh, with the object of smoothing the way for the advance of the British army, which was to march, by way of the Bolan Pass, to Candahar and Caubul. It was not work that could be accomplished without some harshness and injustice; and there are indications in his correspondence that he did not much like the course, which he was compelled to pursue, in dealing with Meer Roostum of Khyrpore, from whom the cession of Bukkur was to be obtained. But he had a natural taste for diplomacy, and the issues of success sometimes so dazzled his eyes, that he did not see very clearly the true nature of the means of accomplishment. 'I have been travelling to Khyrpore,' he wrote to Percival Lord, on New Year's-day, 1839,

* The following is the text of Lord Auckland's letter : 'Simlah, Nov. 5, 1838.—My dear Sir,—I cordially congratulate you on the public proofs of approbation with which you have been marked at home. My private letters speak in high terms of your proceedings at Caubul, and I may in candour mention that upon the one point upon which there was some difference between us—the proposed advance of money to Candahar—opinions for which I have the highest respect, are in your favour. I do not grudge you this, and am only glad that a just tribute has been paid to your ability and indefatigable zeal. The superscription of this letter will, in case you have not received direct accounts, explain my meaning to you.—Yours, very faithfully, AUCKLAND.'

'treaty-making on a great scale, and, what is well, carrying all before me. I have got the fortress of Bukkur ceded to us on our own terms (which are, that we are to hold it now and during war)—the Khyrpore State to place itself under British protection ; and a clause has been inserted in my treaty paving the way for the abolition of all tolls on the Indus ! Huzza ! See how old Roostum and his minister (the *Boree*, as you christened him) have cut up. You did not expect such a *chef-d'œuvre* as this, which is a fit ending to the Cauhul mission, since by Bukkur the Macedonians bridled the neighbouring nations. All these great doings happened at Christmas, and I wanted your hilarious tones to make the enjoyment of the day complete.'

There was other work, too, for him at this time—other treaties to be thrust down the throats of the Sindh Ameers. Higher up, along the line of our advancing army, Mehrab Khan of Khelat was to be brought to terms. Burnes, who was officially ' Envoy to the Chief of Khelat or other States,' was, of course, sent forward to negotiate the desired treaty, and to obtain, from the Chief, supplies for the troops who were passing through his territory. But they had already devastated his country ; there was no grain to be had, and all the food that could be supplied to our army consisted of some ill-fed sheep. 'The English,' said Mehrab Khan to Burnes, 'have come, and by their march through my country, in different directions, destroyed the crops, poor as they were, and have helped themselves to the water that irrigated my lands, made doubly valuable in this year of scarcity.' 'I might have allied myself,' he added, ' with

Persia and Russia; but I have seen you safely through the great defile of the Bolan, and yet I am unrewarded.' The reward he sought was, that he might be relieved for ever from the mastery of the Suddozye kings; but, instead of this, it was made a condition of any kind of peaceable negotiation with him, that he should pay homage to Shah Soojah in his camp. Reluctantly bowing to the hard necessity, he consented, and the treaty was sealed. The English undertook to pay him an annual subsidy of a lakh and a half of rupees, in return for which he was to do his best to obtain supplies for us, and to keep open the passes for our convoys. Burnes saw clearly that he had to deal in this instance with a man of great shrewdness and ability. He was warned by the chief that the expedition on which the English had embarked had the seeds of failure within it. 'The Khan,' wrote Burnes to Macnaghten, 'with a good deal of earnestness, enlarged upon the undertaking the British had embarked in; declared it to be one of vast magnitude and difficult accomplishment; that instead of relying on the Affghan nation, our Government had cast them aside, and inundated the country with foreign troops; that if it was our end to establish ourselves in Afghanistan, and give Shah Soojah the nominal sovereignty of Caubul and Candahar, we were pursuing an erroneous course; that all the Afghans were discontented with the Shah, and all Mahomedans alarmed and excited at what was passing; that day by day men returned discontented, and we might find ourselves awkwardly situated if we did not point out to Shah Soojah his errors, if the fault originated with him, and alter them if they sprung from ourselves; that the chief of Caubul (Dost Mahomed) was a man of ability and re-source, and though we could easily put him down by Shah Soojah even in our present mode of procedure, we could never win over the Afghan nation by it.' Truer words than these were seldom spoken; and often, doubtless, as events developed themselves. in Afghanistan, did Burnes think over the warnings of that ill-fated Khelat chief.

How the British army entered Afghanistan, how Dost Mahomed was driven out of the country, how the people for a while sullenly acquiesced in the revolution, which was accomplished by the force of British bayonets and the in-fluence of British gold, are matters which belong to history. The further we advanced, the more difficult became the solution of the question, 'What is to be done with Sir Alexander Burnes?' At one time there was some thought of his going to Herat, but this was abandoned. On the 18th of June he wrote from Candahar to one of his brothers, saying: ' In possession of Candahar, the affairs of Herat first engaged our attention, and I was nominated to proceed there with guns and money to make a treaty. After being all ready to go, Macnaghten announced his intention of going back to Simlah, and suggested my going on to Caubul to take charge of the mission. When he went, I at once chose to go to Caubul, for the policy of Government in Herat affairs I do not like. A King at Caubul and another at Herat are "two Kings at Brentford," from which I foresee serious evils. I wished them to put all under Shah Soojah, but after Stoddart had been ejected, young Pottinger allowed himself to be apologized to for their threatening to murder him, and the opportunity was lost.   The wretches have again quarrelled with Pottinger, and cut off a hand of one of his servants; but this also is for the present made up, and Major Todd starts to-morrow for Herat, and I predict can do nothing, for nothing is to be done with them.   Kamran is an imbecile, and the Minister, Yar Mahomed, is a bold but doubtful man. . . . . . The King and I are great friends, but I cannot shut my eyes to the fact that he has nothing in common with the chief of Caubul.   But he is legitimate, and that is a great point; and we are to keep him on the throne, so that I think things will go much better than is generally believed.'

Shah Soojah was restored to the Balla Hissar of Caubul, and Sir Alexander Burnes settled down into a most anomalous and unsatisfactory position.   He had no power and no responsibility.   He gave advice which was seldom taken, and he saw things continually going wrong without any power to set them right.   It is impossible to conceive any more unpleasant situation than that which for more than two years—during the latter part of 1839, and all through 1840 and 1841—he occupied at the Court of Caubul.   If, at that time, he had not been sometimes irritable, and sometimes desponding, he would have been more or less than a man.   He had been taught to believe that Macnaghten had been sent only for a little space into Afghanistan, to be soon removed to a higher office, and then that he himself would be placed in the supreme direction of affairs.   But month after month—nay, year after year— passed, and there was no change; and Burnes began to write somewhat bitterly of the good faith of the Governor-

General, and to contrast his conduct with the soft words of
the man who had spoken so kindly and encouragingly to
him on the ' couch at Bowood.' His correspondence at
this time reflects, as in a glass, a mind altogether unsettled,
if not discontented. He wanted active, stirring work ; and,
save on rare occasions, there was little or none for him.
He was disappointed, too, and perhaps somewhat embittered ;
for a great crop of honours had resulted from this invasion
of Afghanistan. Sir John Keane had been made a Peer,
and Mr Macnaghten a Baronet ; and Burnes thought that
his just claim to further distinction had been ignored. He
might have been reconciled to this, for his own honours were
of very recent growth, if the Governor-General had placed
him in a position of dignity and responsibility. But there
was really nothing to be done for the Political Second-in-
command. It was at one time discussed whether he might
not be appointed ' Resident at Candahar ;' but this scheme
was abandoned ; and at last Burnes came to the conclusion
that it was his special mission to receive three thousand
rupees a month for the mere trouble of drawing the money.

There was not one of his correspondents to whom he
unburdened himself so freely as to his friend Percival Lord
(then employed in the neighbourhood of Bameean, near
the Hindoo-Koosh), to whom he wrote freely, alike on
Afghan politics and on his own personal position. A few
illustrative extracts from this correspondence may be given
here : ' Caubul, November 2, 1839. I have been expecting
to hear from you on this astounding intelligence from
Turkistan. I have letters from Nazir Khan Oollah that
leave no doubt of the Russians having come to Khiva, or

being on the road there. Have they ulterior views or not? Is Herat their end, or Bokhara? It is evident that your presence is required at Bokhara, but that cannot be in the present distracted state of the country; native agency must be employed, and more than spies. Macnaghten has, therefore, resolved on sending Mahomed Hoosein Karkee to tell the King that his proceedings in not answering our letters, in threatening our cossids, in fearing Shah Soojah, are all wrong, with much other matter of that kind. The officials you will get all in due time, but this is to give you notice that Karkee is coming to you to get his final instructions. He is a clever fellow, and has killed his pig with the Dost and the King of Persia, so there is no fear of his taking their part. He may be bribed by Russia, but that we cannot help, and it is but right to give the King of Bokhara a chance. I wish to God you could go yourself, and I know Lord A. wishes it, but he declares that the country is not safe, and that, after Stoddart's fate, he has a great reluctance to put our officers in what the Field-Marshal would call a false position. I for one believe in all the reports of the advance of Russia. Of course her fifty regiments may be but ten; but we had better look out, seeing the Dost is loose, and Herat with its walls unprepared. As a precautionary measure, the Bombay column will be halted after Khelat is settled, till we see what turns up——' 'November 10. Old Toorkistanee as you are, you seem to be quite quiescent about the Russian movement in Orgunje, and do not, I imagine from your silence, believe it, but I assure you it is a serious business. I have a letter from Herat twenty-seven days old confirming it, and giving particulars about the

Vizier, Yar Mahomed Khan, being tampered with by the Russians, all of which seems to have been concealed from Todd. I am most anxious to hear further, and have sent a Hindoo on to Khiva itself, who will pass through your camp in a day or two. I have letters from London explanatory of Vicovitch s death, which Count Nesselrode writes to Lord Palmerston was annoying them, as the Russian Government had blamed Simonich, and not Vicovitch——'

' November 22. Here is a curious anecdote for you; let me have your opinion. A couple of years before our mission arrived at Caubul, Vicovitch (the true Vicovitch) came to Bokhara, called at Ruheem Shah's relative's house, and asked him to send letters to Masson at Caubul for MM. Allard and Vetura. The King of Bokhara took offence at Vicovitch's presence, and the Koosh-Begee sent him off sharp. So the letters were never sent. This shows an earlier intention to intrigue on the part of Russia; but how came Masson not to report this, and if he reported it, how came he to give, years afterwards, twenty-one reasons for Vicovitch not being what he was? I cannot unravel this. I once spoke of this before to you, and to no other man——' ' December 13. How can I say things go wrong? Sheets of foolscap are written in praise of the Shah's contingent, and, as God is my judge, I tremble every time I hear of its being employed that it will compromise its officers. You cannot, then, imagine I would ever advocate a weak and yet undisciplined corps garrisoning Bameean. Your remark about employing Afghans in Koonee and Khyber, as you may well imagine, agrees with my own views, but I am not the Envoy. I see European soldiers sent to look after Khyberees, and as well might they be sent after wild sheep. I see, what is worse, Craigie's corps sent after the disaffected at Koonee, when they are not yet drilled, and when Afghans are quite up to the work. From all this I see that Shah Soojah never can be left without a British army, for his own contingent will never be fit for anything——' ' January 7, 1840. I will send you a letter from Lord Auckland to me, wishing again to make me Resident at Candahar, but not to go there unless it ' pleased' me. I replied to Macnaghten that this useless correspondence had been going on since August, and it was high time to do what had been proposed —to give me Resident's pay. Imprisoning rupees and reading are now my engagements, and I have begun the year with a resolution of making no more suggestions, and of only speaking when spoken to. I do not say this in ill humour—quite the reverse. A screw from Machiavelli supports me. " A man who, instead of acting for the best, acts *as he ought,* seeks rather his ruin than his preservation "——' ' Jan. 11. Lord Auckland took a step in sending an army into this country contrary to his own judgment, and he cares not a sixpence what comes of the policy, so that he gets out of it. All the despatches plainly prove this; and Macnaghten now begins to see his own false position, suggests remedies, and finds himself for the first time snubbed by the very Governor-General whose letters have been hitherto a fulsome tissue of praise. The Envoy sees that Russia is coming on, that Herat is not what it ought to have been—ours, and his dawning experience tells him that, if not for us, it is against us. What says Lord Auckland? " I disagree with you. Yar Mahomed is to be conciliated.

Russia is friendly to England, and I do not credit her advance on us, though she may have an expedition against Khiva. I wonder," adds his Lordship to the Envoy, " that you should countenance attacks on Herat contrary to treaty" (who made that treaty? Macnaghten!); " that you should seek for more troops in Afghanistan. It is your duty to rid Afghanistan of troops." All very fine, but mark the result—calamity, loss of influence, and with it loss of rupees. In these important times, what occupies the King and this Envoy? The cellars of his Majesty's palace have been used as powder-magazines to prevent a mosque being " desecrated." They would have been put in the citadel, but his Majesty objected, as they overlooked his harem! This objection dire necessity has removed, and to the citadel they have gone. Read the enclosures, and see what is said of Colonel Dennie's occupying, not the palace, but a house outside, held formerly by sweepers and Hindoos! From this, in the midst of winter, though Brigadier, he has been ejected; but he declares before God that it shall be the Governor-General alone who turns him out. These are the occupations of the King and Envoy. See what Sir W. Cotton says of it. In Persia, in Egypt, in Muscat, the guests of the Sovereigns occupy palaces, and Shah Soojah declares he will resign his throne if he be so insulted—insulted by the contamination of those men who bled for him and placed him where he is. What, my dear Lord, do I mean by all this? *Ex uno disce omnes.* Be silent, pocket your pay, do nothing but what you are ordered, and you will give high satisfaction. They will sacrifice you and me, or any one, without caring a straw. This does not originate from vice, I believe, but

from ignorance. Drowning men catch at straws, and whenever anything goes wrong, other backs must bear the brand. An *exposé* of the policy from the day we were bound hand and foot at Lahore, till Shah Soojah threatened to resign his throne because of the cellars of his palace being occupied by munitions of war when Russia was on the Oxus, would make a book which all future diplomatists could never in blunder surpass; but why should it be otherwise? The chief priest, ere he started, asked if Khiva were on the Indus! Bah! I blame the Governor-General for little; if he is a timid man, he is a good man. W. hoodwinked him about Caubul when I was here; another now hoodwinks him. The one cost us two millions, the other will cost us ten. His Lordship has just written to me to give him my say on public matters. Am I a fool? He does not want truth; he wants support, and when I can give it I shall do so loudly; when I cannot, I shall be silent——' ' Jan. 26. They have been at me again to write "on the prospects of the restored Government," as I think I told you before. I am no such gaby. If they really wanted truth, I would give it cordially, but it is a chiming-in, a coincidence of views, which they seek; and I can go a good way, but my conscience has not so much stretch as to approve of this dynasty. But, mum—let that be between ourselves——'
' Feb. 18. The Envoy is, or pretends to be, greatly annoyed at my being left out of the list of the honoured, and has written four letters on it; three to me, and one to Nicolson. I am not in the least surprised. Every month brings with it proofs of Lord A.'s hostility or dislike. Serves me right.

I ought never to have come here, or allowed myself to be pleased with fair though false words. As a sample, look; they burked the paragraph on me in Sir John (Baron) Keane's despatch because I was a political. Next fight at Khelat, the paragraph on the political Bean is printed. I bide my time, and I may be set down as highly presumptuous; but if I live, I expect to be a G.C.B. instead of a C.B.——'

'February 28. You tell me to accept the Residency at Candahar; it is well I refused it. The Court of Directors have officially sanctioned it, and Lord Auckland says I am to have Resident's pay, but to be Political Agent! Did you ever? However, my refusal had gone in, backed by Macnaghten, and they make me *Resident at Caubul*, but I expect nothing from them after such base ingratitude. The reasons why I refused Candahar were, that I should be as dependent there as here, with a certainty of collision in Herat affairs, over which I was to have "some control." Now I could not have had that without making my silence my dishonesty, and I resolved on "biding my time" here. I have heard no more of the Shah's move to Candahar; it is necessary on many accounts; but it may not take place on that account——' 'March 4. There is no two days' fixity of purpose —no plan of the future policy, external or internal, on which you can depend a week. The bit-by-bit system prevails. Nothing comprehensive is looked to; the details of the day suffice to fill it up, and the work done is not measured by its importance, but by being work, and this work consists of details and drawing money. We are in a fair way of proving all Mr Elphinstone said in his letter to me, and I

for one begin to think Wade will be the luckiest of us all to
be away from the break-down; for, unless a new leaf is
turned over, break down we shall.'

Though condemned thus painfully to official inactivity,
the restless spirit of Alexander Burnes was continually
embracing all the great questions which the antagonism of
England and Russia in Central Asia were then throwing
up for practical solution. He had made up his own mind
very distinctly upon the subject. He somewhat exaggerated
the aggressive designs of Russia; but, starting from such
premises, he was logically right in contending that our best
policy was to strengthen ourselves in Afghanistan, and not
to endeavour either to oppose by arms or to baffle by
diplomacy the progress of the Muscovite in Central Asia.
There were other British officers, however, in the Afghan
dominions at that time, who, thinking less of Russian
aggressiveness and more of Central Asian provocations, felt
that much good might be effected by peaceful mediation—
especially by the good work of endeavouring to liberate the
Russian subjects, who had been carried off into slavery by
the man-stealers of those barbarous States.* It remained
for a later generation to endorse these views, and to believe
that England and Russia might act harmoniously together
in Central Asia in the interests of universal humanity.
Very steadfastly and persistently did Burnes set his face
against them. His own opinions were stated most emphatically in letters, which he addressed to Sir William Mac-

---

* I touch but cursorily on this subject here, because it will be
illustrated more fully in subsequent Memoirs of Arthur Conolly and
D'Arcy Todd.

naghten in this year : ' I have just received your very interesting letter of the 13th,' he wrote to the Envoy, on the
16th of April, ' with its enclosure, an extract from the Governor-General's letter regarding the designs of Russia.   I
now feel somewhat at ease since his Lordship has become
cognizant of the real state of affairs on our frontier, as we
shall no longer be acting on a blind reliance that the expedition to Khiva was small, and would be unsuccessful, when it
is an army composed of the élite of their empire, and has
made good its lodgment on the delta of the Oxus.   After
the Punic faith which Russia has exhibited, I confess I was
astonished to see Lord Clanricarde put trust in what Count
Nesselrode told him of the strength of the Russian force,
and you may rely upon it that we are better judges of what
Russia is doing in Turkistan than our ambassador at St
Petersburg, and I hope the correctness of all our information
from first to last will now lead to the most implicit reliance
being hereafter placed upon it.   One correspondent may
exaggerate and distort, but it is not in the nature of false-
hood to be consistent; and of inconsistency we have had
none, the cry being that Russia has entered Turkistan with
the design of setting up her influence there, and that
(whether her ruler or ministers admit it or not) her object
is to disturb us in Afghanistan.   European intelligence
confirms all this; and with a failing peculiarly her own,
Russia has, for the present, left the Turkish question to be
settled by England and France, and even in her generosity
agreed to open the Black Sea.   " Timeo Danaos et dona
ferentes."   Firmly impressed with these views, they tincture
all my thoughts and opinions, and, in consequence, lead me

to hope that our every nerve will be strained to consolidate Afghanistan, and that nothing of any kind, political or military, may take place beyond the passes. Had we force sufficient, the occupation of Balkh might not be a bad military move, and one which would, in truth, show " an imposing attitude ; " but with Russia at Khiva, and negotiating for the residence of a permanent ambassador at Bokhara, we shall at once precipitate a collision with her by such a step, and with our present force I consider it hopeless, even if our rear were clear, which it is not. The attitude of the Sikhs towards us is that of undisguised hostility, and on both our front and rear we have cause for deep reflection —I will not say alarm, for I do not admit it ; we have only to play the good game we have begun, and exhibit Shah Soojah as the real King, to triumph over our difficulties. The security from that triumph, however, is not an advance to Turkistan, but first a quieting of our rear, and redress of grievances at home. You will guess, then, what I think of any of our officers going in any capacity to Turkistan, to Khiva, Bokhara, or Kokund. I regarded Abbott's departure to Khiva as the most unhappy step taken during the campaign, and his language at Khiva, which will all be repeated to Russia, places us in a position far more equivocal than Russia was placed in by Vicovitch being here. We had no ground of complaint against Dost Mahomed (till he joined our enemies), and two great European powers merely wished for his friendship ; but Russia has at Khiva just grounds for complaint, and still Captain Abbott tells the Khan that he must have no communication with Russia, but release her slaves, and have done with her.

It is well to remember that Russia has extensive trade passing through Khiva, and that the proclamation of war declares that the object of the expedition is to redress the merchants for exactions. Is England to become security for barbarous hordes some thousands of miles from her frontier? If not, Captain Abbott's promises and speeches must compromise us. I observe you proceed on the supposition that Russia wants only her slaves released, but this is one of ten demands only, and instead of our language, therefore, being pertinent on that head, that we insist on her relief, it means nothing, for Captain Abbott tells us that the Khan had offered to release them all, and I know that the King of Bokhara has made a treaty to that effect, and acts up to it; for Captain A. likewise confirms the information frequently reported, that the King there is bought by Russia. We have in consequence, I think, no business in Khiva, and, however much we may wish it, none in Bokhara. The remaining State is Kokund, and we shall know the probable good of a connection with it. In my letter to A. Conolly, I enclosed some "observations on sending a mission to Khiva," but I did not then discuss the policy of the King. I merely, in reply to Conolly's request for hints, pointed out the difficulties of the road and of communication when there. But my first question is the *cui bono* of this mission in a political point of view? In a geographical one, no one can doubt its high expediency. What are we to get from it? Nothing, I see, but to attach to ourselves just and deserved reproach for interfering with Russia in ground already occupied by her merchants, and ground far beyond our own line of operations. The measure will irritate Russia, who will at once march on Balkh to assert her just position, as she calls it, in Central Asia; and then, indeed, the Governor-General's surmises will be proved. It will give uneasiness to " all surrounding States, and add difficulty to the game which we have to play." But one very serious obstacle to all interference with Turkistan has apparently been overlooked. Russia is not engaged *alone* in the enterprise. She has her ally of Persia, and ambassadors, too, to seek the release of the Persian slaves. Are we prepared to insist on this, and reconstruct the whole fabric of society by marching back some two or three hundred thousand slaves? If not, our proceedings are neither consonant with humanity nor the rights of nations; and if they are, the only chance of success is to leave Russia alone, or to aid her with a military force; the former the only judicious course for us to pursue. I have been thus earnest on this very momentous question from the anxiety which I feel to see our cause flourish, and our good name preserved. It is not the question of Lord or Conolly going. That is a mere trifle, which does not call for a moment's consideration. I believe the deputation of any one to Turkistan at this time to be a serious error. If it is to be, I shall, of course, do all I can by information, and by getting good people to assist the officers sent; but I hope you will excuse my beseeching you to weigh the step well before it is taken. Rely upon it, the English Cabinet can alone settle this question, and it must be at London or St Petersburg, and not at Kokund, Bokhara, or Khiva, that we are to counteract Russia. Let us crown the passes. Let an engineer be forthwith sent to map them, and let grain (as you have just proposed) be stored behind them at Bameean. Let alarm be allayed by our not appearing to stir overmuch; for Caubul is the place for the corps d'armée, and not Bameean, which should be its outwork, and, as such, strengthened. We should have done with dealing with the Oosbegs, for it is time. In Khiva we have our agent detained. At Bokhara, poor Stoddart's captivity reflects seriously upon our character, and damages it here; while in Kokund I see no possible good likely to flow, even from the most splendid success attending the agent, and, on the contrary, much chance of evil.'

Some three or four weeks after this letter was written, Macnaghten orally proposed that Burnes himself should proceed on a mission to the Russian camp. Burnes replied that he would go if he were ordered; and after the interview, having thought well over the matter, he wrote on the same evening a letter to the Envoy, saying: ' With reference to our conversation this morning, when I stated my readiness to proceed to General Peroffski's camp with alacrity, if the Governor-General would but grant to me credentials and powers to act as stated in Lord Palmerston's letter—*i. e.* to tell the Russian General if he sought to subvert the political influence of the Khan of Khiva, after due reparation had been made to him, and did not withdraw his force, Great Britain would consider Russia in the light of an enemy—another view of the subject has since struck me—Will you, as the representative of the British nation, grant to me such credentials and powers ? Lord Auckland requested you to communicate with the Russian General by a messenger, but the interests of the public service have pointed out to you the propriety of deviating from such instructions in so far as to send an officer instead of a messenger. With the explicit views, then, of the British Cabinet transmitted officially to you by the Governor-General, do you feel yourself authorized to draw up credentials empowering me to go as far as the Secretary of State for Foreign Affairs has gone? If so, I am ready, without awaiting the Governor-General's reply, to undertake the mission, as I then see in it a chance of gaining the ends of our Government without risking any little reputation I may have. If, on the other hand, you merely mean to convey to General Peroffski a hope, or request by letter, that he will not exceed the Emperor's instructions, this will be but th · duty of a courier, and as my personal insight would thus fall below zero, I have no desire to undertake the journey; though even then, as I have reported to Conolly and yourself, I will proceed there, if you are of opinion it is desirable, and you think I can advance the public interests. If, however, you do not feel yourself authorized to grant to me the powers which seem necessary, your letter of to-day to Lord Auckland may, perhaps, draw such credentials from his Lordship, and if so, I shall hold myself in readiness on their arrival here to follow Conolly to the Russian camp, taking, if possible, the Oxus as my route, by which I could reach Khiva with great expedition, and to political objects add a knowledge of that river, now so important to us.'

But before there was any necessity to bring this question to the point of practical solution, intelligence was received at Caubul which consigned it to the limbo of vanities and abortions. Another mission had proceeded to the Russian camp—a mission from Heaven in the shape of that great white enemy, which was destined at a later date to put our own armies to confusion. Peroffski's legions were arrested by the destroying snow, and decimated by pestilence and famine. This source of inquietude was, therefore, removed, and Burnes was again driven back into inactivity.* The summer passed quietly over his head, but the autumn found him and all his countrymen at Caubul in a state of extreme excitement. Dost Mahomed was again in arms against the Feringhees, who had driven him from his country. He was coming down from the regions beyond the Hindoo-Koosh, raising the tribes on the way, and calling on the children of the Prophet to expel the usurping unbelievers. A British force was sent into the Kohistan, under the command of Sir Robert Sale ; and Burnes went with it in chief

---

* When men—especially men of active habits—have very little to do, they are frequently disturbed by small troubles, which, at times of greater activity, would pass unnoticed. At this period Burnes was greatly irritated by some comments on Affghan affairs in the Calcutta and Agra papers. With reference to a letter in the Agra *Ukhbar,* which had reflected on some of the proceedings of Dr Lord, Burnes wrote to his friend, saying : 'I think that a simple letter under your name calling the man a cowardly slanderer and a villain, or some such choice word, would be a good mode of rebutting him.' As if truth were to be established by calling men hard names ! In another letter Burnes wrote to Lord : 'You have a viper in your Artillery named Kaye, who writes in the *Hurkaru,*' &c. &c. The viper referred to is the writer of this book. I had, as a young man, perhaps a little too fond of my pen, emphatically protested against our entire policy in Afghanistan, and predicted its speedy collapse—which prediction, in the first flush of success, my countrymen in India, with few exceptions, were wont to deride.

political control of the expedition. How badly everything fared with us at the first may be gathered from the fact that the latter wrote to the Envoy, saying that there was nothing left for our troops but to fall back on Caubul, and there to concentrate all our strength. This was on the 2nd of November—a day of evil omen ; for then Burnes's days were numbered by the days of a single year. He saw the last victorious charge of the Ameer; he saw our troops flying before him ; he saw his friends and associates, Broadfoot and Lord, fall mortally wounded from their horses ; and he himself narrowly escaped. This was but the darkest hour before the dawn. On the following day Dost Mahomed surrendered himself to the British Envoy, and, instead of a formidable enemy, became a harmless State prisoner. Then the spirits of Burnes and of his associates at Caubul began to rise. Writing a few weeks afterwards to one of his brothers, he said : ' Caubul, November 24, 1840. I have been too much occupied these two months past to write to you, and though it has pleased Providence to crown our efforts with success, and to permit me to play a prominent part, I have yet to mourn the loss of two very dear friends, Dr Lord and Lieutenant Broadfoot. How I escaped unscathed God only knows. I have a ball which fell at my feet, and of three political officers, I have alone lived to tell the tale. Make no parade of these facts. My interview with Dost Mahomed Khan was very interesting and very affectionate. He taunted me with nothing, said I was his best friend, and that he had come in on a letter I had written to him. This I disbelieve, for we followed him from house to house, and he was obliged to surrender. On that

letter, however, I hope I shall have got for him an annual
stipend of two lakhs of rupees instead of one. On our
parting, I gave him an Arab horse; and what think you
he gave me? His own, and only sword, and which is
stained with blood. He left this for India some fourteen
days ago, and is to live at Loodiana. In Kohistan I saw a
failure of our artillery to breach, of our European soldiers to
storm, and of our cavalry to charge; and yet God gave us
the victory. And now Kurruck Singh is dead, and Now
Nihal, the new ruler of the Punjab, killed while attending
his father's funeral by a gate falling on him, Shere Singh
reigns in his stead. Read the prediction in my *Travels,*
vol. i., pp. 298-9, second edition, on this head. If we could
turn over a new leaf here, we might soon make Afghanistan
a barrier. You regret about my name and the Russians.
Nine-tenths of what is attributed to me I never said, but I
did say the Russians were coming, and that, too, on 31st of
October, 1839, and come they did; and Lord Auckland
would never believe it till March, 1840! He heard from
London and from Khiva of the failure simultaneously, and
they wonder why we did not hear sooner. We have no mail
coaches here, and hence the explanation. From Orenburg
to London is eighteen days; from Bokhara to Caubul is
thirty. We have no intelligence yet of a second expedition,
and I hope none will come. The state of Afghanistan for
the last year will show you how much reason we had to
fear the Czar's approach.'

After this the horizon was clear for a little space, and
there was a lull in the political atmosphere. But with
the new year came new troubles. There was a crisis at

Herat; and the tribes in Western Afghanistan were rising against the King and his supporters. With these things Burnes had little to do in any active capacity. He wrote letters and minutes, and gave advice, clearly seeing that everything was going wrong. 'I am now a highly paid idler,' he wrote to one of his brothers, 'having no less than 3500 rupees a month, as Resident at Caubul, and being, as the lawyers call it, only counsel, and that, too, a dumb one— by which I mean that I give paper opinions, but do not work them out.' He had, however, become more contented with his lot. He ceased to chafe at what seemed, for a time at least, to be inevitable; and enjoying, as best he could, the blessings of the present, he looked forward to a future, then apparently not very remote, when his energies might find freer scope for action, for it was believed that a higher official post would soon be found for Macnaghten. He was in excellent health at this time, and his fine animal spirits sparkled pleasantly in all his letters to his friends. On the 1st of April he wrote to Montrose, saying : ' We had no sooner got Dost Mahomed Khan into our power than Herat breaks with us, and the Punjab becomes a scene of strife. Out of both contingencies we might extract good —real, solid good; we may restore the lost wings of Afghanistan, Herat and Peshawur, to Shah Soojah, and thus enable him to support himself, free us from the expense of Afghanistan, and what would be better, withdraw our regular army within the Indus, leaving Caubul as an outpost, which we could thus succour with readiness. . . . I lead, however, a very pleasant life, and if rotundity and heartiness be proofs of health, I have them. My house

I taboo at all hours for breakfast, which I have long made a public meal. I have covers laid for eight, and half a dozen of the officers drop in as they feel disposed every morning, discuss a rare Scotch breakfast of smoked fish, salmon grills, devils, and jellies, puff away at their cigars till ten (the hour of assembly being nine), then I am left to myself till evening, when my friend Broadfoot (who is my assistant) and I sit down to our quiet dinner, and discuss with our Port men and manners. Once in every week I give a party of eight, and now and then I have my intimates alone, and as the good river Indus is a channel for luxuries as well as commerce, I can place before my friends at one-third in excess of the Bombay price my champagne, hock, madeira, sherry, port, claret, sauterne, not forgetting a glass of curaçoa and maraschino, and the hermetically sealed salmon and hotch-potch (veritable hotch-potch, all the way frae Aberdeen), for deuced good it is, the peas as big as if they had been soaked for *bristling.* I see James Duke is an alderman of London ; he will be Lord Mayor, and then all the smacks of Montrose will flee to London with *fine young men* for his patronage. A Duke and a Mayor ! These are wonderful changes, but I am glad of it, for he is said to be a real good fellow, and deserves his prosperity. I remember he used to sit before us in the Kirk, and in his hat were written, " Remember the eighth commandment and Golgotha," so he will be a terror to evil-doers assuredly. Bravo, say I. I wish I were provost mysel' here ; I would be as happy as the Lord Mayor.'

It is not improbable that the enforced inactivity of which Alexander Burnes, at this period of his career, so often

wrote, was in one sense greatly to his advantage. It often
happens that men who lead very active and stirring lives
fail, in the midst of their day-to-day excitements, to take
that just view of surrounding circumstances which they
would have taken, with more leisure on their hands and
better opportunities of far-reaching observation. We cannot
' see, as from a tower, the end of all,' when we are wrestling
with a crowd at its base. Burnes, as a looker-on, saw
clearly and distinctly what Macnaghten did not see—that
we were interfering a great deal too much in Afghanistan,
and that the best thing for the restored monarchy would be
that we should take less trouble to support it. After an
outbreak, fatally mismanaged by the Western Ghilzyes, he
wrote to Major Lynch, in June, saying : ' I am not cognizant of all which you relate regarding affairs in your quarter,
but I am sorry to tell you that I am one of those altogether
opposed to any further fighting in this country, and that I
consider we shall never settle Afghanistan at the point of
the bayonet. And this opinion, which I have so long held,
I am glad to see has been at length adopted in Calcutta,
and will be our future guide. As regards the Ghilzyes, indeed, immense allowances ought to be made for them ; they
were, till within three generations, the Kings of Afghanistan,
and carried their victorious arms to the capital of Persia. It
is expecting too much, therefore, to hope for their being at
once peaceful subjects.' And again on the 1st of August,
to another correspondent : ' Pottinger undertakes an awful
risk in China. M'Neill ought not to go to Persia ; he deserves Constantinople, and I hope will get it. Lord Auckland will not pardon poor Todd, and here again I predicted

failure there, and am scowled at for being a true prophet; but certes, if Herat has gone over to Persia we are in a greater mess than ever, but I hope the return of our ambassador to Persia will set all this right. For my part, I would send no one to Persia or to Herat; I would withdraw all but two brigades within the Indus, and these I would withdraw, one in next year, and one in the year after next, and leave the Shah to his own contingent and his Afghans, and I, as Envoy, would stake my character on this—We shall be ruined if this expense goes on.'

At last, in this autumn of 1841, news came that Sir William Macnaghten had been appointed Governor of Bombay; but, even then, there were reports that some veteran political officer would be sent up from the Provinces to occupy his seat. It was a period of distressing doubt and anxiety to the expectant minister. In the midst of his perplexities, he was wont to seek solace in his books. His favourite author was Tacitus, in whose writings he read lessons of wisdom, which, he said, were of infinite service to him in the practical affairs of life. Some extracts from the journal, which he kept in this year, will show how, in the enforced inactivity of his anomalous position, he gathered knowledge from his library, which he might, some day, he thought, turn to good account. At all events, such studies diverted his mind and alleviated the pains of the suspense to which he was condemned: 'Caubul, August 13. Read in the thirteenth and fourteenth books of the Annals of Tacitus. What lessons of wisdom and knowledge—how the human mind and its passions are laid bare! I drink in Tacitus, and, perhaps, with the more relish, that his lessons are of practical use——' 'August 19. Horace Walpole's letters, how inimitable! He is only surpassed by Byron, of all letter-writers I have read; yet Walpole's details of trifles, and trifling on details, are inimitable. I have got a grand edition, and eke out the six volumes, that I may enjoy it all to my full——' 'Aug. 24. Reading Sir Sidney Smith's life. It supports an opinion of mine, that all great men have more or less charlatanerie——' 'Aug. 26. This is assuredly one of the idle stages in my life. I do nothing for the public, unless it be giving advice, but, as I have none to perform, unless it be to receive my 3500 rupees a month. At Bhooj, in 1829, I had similar idleness, and I improved myself. Again, in 1835, I was similarly situated, and since May, 1839, I have been so circumstanced here. I conclude that my pay is assigned to me for past conduct and duties; however, as my Lord Auckland is about to depart, I have little chance of being disturbed in my lair in his day; it may be otherwise. To study Tacitus is as pleasant as to write despatches——' 'Sept. 1. An expression from Macnaghten to-day that Shah Soojah was an old woman, not fit to rule his people, with divers other condemnations. Ay, see my *Travels,* and as far back as 1831—ten years ago. Still I look upon his fitness or unfitness as very immaterial; we are here to govern for him, and must govern——' 'Sept. 10. Somewhat contemplative. This is certainly an important time for me. Of supersession I have no fear, but those in power may still keep Macnaghten over me, and much as he objects to this, it enables Lord Auckland to move off, and evade his promises to me. Alas! I did not believe my first interview

with the long, tall, gaunt man on the couch at Bowood
was to end thus——' 'Sept. 22. The Envoy is afraid of
the King's health. A native predicts his death; he is not
long-lived, I plainly see. If he dies, we were planning the
modus operandi. I offered to go to Candahar, and bring
up the new King Timour, and I predict he will make a
good ruler. I question myself how far I am right in avoiding correspondence with Lord Lansdowne, Mr Elphinstone,
and all my numerous friends in England, or even with
Lord Auckland; yet I believe I am acting an honest part to
Macnaghten and to Government, and yet neither the one
nor the other, I fear, thank me; yet it is clear that if I had
carried on a hot correspondence with Lord Auckland, as
he wished me, I must have injured Macnaghten, and had
I, in this correspondence, evaded those points on which
his Lordship was interested, I should have injured myself
in his eyes, and consequently as a public servant. In after
days I hope to be able to applaud my own discretion in
this my difficult position; but I may fail altogether by my
honesty, though I have always found it the best policy——'
'Sept. 24. I have read with great relish and enjoyment
the first volume of Warren Hastings's Life, and with great
admiration for the man, founded on his many virtues and
noble fortitude, and that, too, on the evidence of his letters,
and not his biography——' 'October 16. I seem hourly
to lose my anxiety for power and place; yet away with
such feelings, for if I be worth anything, they ought to
have no hold of me. I have just read in Guizot's *Life of
Washington :* " In men who are worthy of the destiny (to
govern), all weariness, all sadness, though it be warrantable,

is weakness; their mission is toil; their reward, the success of their works;" but still in toil I shall become weary if employed. Will they venture, after all that has been promised, and all that I have done, to pass me over ? I doubt it much; if so, the past will not fix a stain on me, and the future is dark and doubtful. I have been asking myself if I am altogether so well fitted for the supreme control here as I am disposed to believe. I sometimes think not, but I have never found myself fail in power when unshackled. On one point I am, however, fully convinced, I am unfit for the second place; in it my irritation would mar all business, and in supersession there is evidently no recourse but England. I wish this doubt were solved, for anxiety is painful. One trait of my character is thorough seriousness; I am indifferent about nothing I undertake—in fact, if I undertake a thing I cannot be indifferent.'

The anniversary of his arrival in India came round. Twenty years had passed since he had first set his foot on the strand of Bombay. Seldom altogether free from superstitions and presentiments, he entered upon this 31st of October, 1841, with a vivid impression that it would bring forth something upon which his whole future life would turn. 'Ay! what will this day bring forth?' he wrote in his journal, 'the anniversary of my twenty years' service in India. It will make or mar me, I suppose. Before the sun sets I' shall know whether I go to Europe or succeed Macnaghten.' But the day passed, and the momentous question was not settled. Then November dawned, and neither Burnes nor Macnaghten received the desired letters from Calcutta—only vague newspaper reports, which added

new fuel to the doubts and anxieties of the expectant
Envoy. 'I grow very tired of praise,' he wrote in his
journal, 'and I suppose that I shall get tired of censure in
time.' This was his last entry. There was no more either
of praise or of censure to agitate him in this world. Already
the bitter fruit of folly and injustice had ripened upon the
tree of Retribution, and the nation which had done this
wrong thing was about to be judged by the 'eternal law,
that where crime is, sorrow shall answer it.' The Afghans
are an avaricious and a revengeful people. Our only settled
policy in Afghanistan was based upon the faith that by gratifying the one passion we might hold the other in control. So
money was spent freely in Afghanistan. We bought safety
and peace. But when it was found that this enormous expenditure was impoverishing our Indian Empire, and that
the Afghans were still crying 'Give—give!' we were
driven upon the unpopular necessity of retrenchment, and
it ceased to be worth the while of the people to tolerate
our occupation of the country. First one tribe and then
another rose against us; and at last the people at the
capital began to bestir themselves. Already, on the 1st
of November, were the streets of Caubul seething with
insurrection, and the house of Sir Alexander Burnes was in
the city perilously exposed to attack. His Afghan servants
told him that he was in danger, and exhorted him to withdraw to the cantonments. He said that he had done the
Afghans no injury; why, then, should they injure him?
He could not think that any real danger threatened him,
and he retired to rest at night with little fear of the results
of the morrow. Little fear, I should write, of his own.

personal safety; but he saw with sufficient distinctness that a great national crisis was approaching. When, on that evening, his moonshee, Mohun Lal, who had accompanied him for many years in his wanderings, warned him of the approaching danger, he rose from his chair, and made what to his faithful assistant appeared an 'astonishing speech,' to the effect that the time had arrived for the English to leave the country.* But he could not be induced to adopt any precautions. He said that if he sent for a guard to protect his house, it would seem as though he were afraid.

* I give Mohun Lal's own words, which are all the more interesting for the eccentricities of the phraseology: 'On the 1st of November,' he wrote to Mr Colvin, private secretary to the Governor-General, 'I saw Sir Alexander Burnes, and told him that the confederacy has been grown very high, and we should fear the consequence. He stood up from his chair, sighed, and said, he knows nothing but the time has arrived that we should leave this country.' In a letter to Dr James Burnes, there is a similar statement, with the addition that, upon the same night, an Afghan chief, named Taj Mahomed, called upon Burnes, to no purpose, with a like warning: ' On the first of November I saw him at evening, and informed him, according to the conversation of Mahomed Meerza Khan, our great enemy, that the chiefs are contriving plans to stand against us, and therefore it will not be safe to remain without a sufficient guard in the city. He replied that if he were to ask the Envoy to send him a strong guard, it will show that he was fearing; and at the same (time) he made an astonishing speech, by saying that the time is not far when we must leave this country. Taj Mahomed, son of Gholam Mahomed Khan, the Douranee chief, came at night to him, and informed what the chiefs intended to do, but he turned him out under the pretended aspect that we do not care for such things. Our old friend, Naib Sheriff, came and asked him to allow his son, with one hundred men, to remain day and night in his place, till the Ghilzye affair is settled, but he did not agree.'

So Alexander Burnes laid himself down to rest; and slept. But with the early morrow came the phantoms of new troubles. Plainly the storm was rising. First one, then another, with more or less authority, came to warn him that there was 'death in the pot.' The first, who called before daybreak, was not admitted, and Burnes slept on. But when the Afghan minister, Oosman Khan, came to the house, the servants woke their master, who rose and dressed himself, and went forth to receive the Wuzeer. It was no longer possible to look with incredulity upon the signs and symptoms around him. The streets were alive with insurgents. An excited crowd was gathering round his house. Still there might be time to secure safety by flight. But vainly did Oosman Khan implore Burnes to accompany him to the cantonments. He scorned to quit his post; he believed that he could quell the tumult; and so he rejected the advice that might have saved him.

That the city was in a state of insurrection was certain; but it appeared that a prompt and vigorous demonstration on the part of the British troops in cantonments might quell the tumult; so he wrote to Macnaghten for support, and to some friendly Afghan chiefs for assistance. It was then too late. Before any succour could arrive, the crowd before his house had begun to rage furiously, and it was plain that the insurgents were thirsting for the blood of the English officers. From a gallery which ran along the upper part of the house, Burnes, attended by his brother Charles, and his friend William Broadfoot, addressed himself to the excited mob. They yelled out their execration and defiance in reply, and it was plain that no expostulations or entreaties could turn them aside from their purpose. The enemy had begun to fire upon them, and, hopeless as retaliation and resistance might be, there seemed to be nothing left to the English officers but to sell their lives as dearly as they could. Broadfoot was soon shot dead. Then the insurgents set fire to Burnes's stables, rushed into his garden, and summoned him to come down. All hope of succour from cantonments had now gone. Still he might purchase his own and his brother's safety by appealing to the national avarice of the Afghans. He offered them large sums of money if they would suffer him to escape. Still they called upon him to leave off firing and to come down to the garden. At last he consented, and the brothers, conducted by a Cashmeree Mussulman, who had sworn to protect them, went down to the garden; but no sooner were they in the presence of the mob than their guide cried out, 'Here is Sekundur Burnes!' And straightway the insurgents fell upon them and slew them.

And so, on the 2nd of November, 1841, fell Alexander Burnes, butchered by an Afghan mob. He was only thirty-six years of age. That he was a remarkable man, and had done remarkable things, is not to be doubted. He was sustained, from first to last, by that great enthusiasm, of which Sir John Malcolm has spoken, as the best security for a successful Indian career. He was of an eager, impulsive, romantic temperament; but he had a sufficiency of good strong practical sense to keep him from running into any dangerous excesses. He had courage of a high order; sagacity, penetration, and remarkable quickness of observation. It has been said of him that he was unstable, that his opinions were continually shifting, and that what he said on one day he often contradicted on the next. The fact is, that he was singularly unreserved and outspoken, and was wont to set down in his correspondence with his familiar friends all the fleeting impressions of an active and imaginative mind. But on great questions of Central-Asian policy he was not inconsistent. The confusion was in the minds of others, not in his own mind. He had strong opinions, which he never ceased to express, so long as it was possible to give them practical effect; but, over-ruled by higher authority, and another course of policy substituted for that which he would have pursued, he con-sented to act, in a ministerial or executive capacity, for the furtherance of the great object of national safety which he believed might have been better attained in another way. When he found that his views were not the views of the Government which he served, he offered to withdraw from the scene in favour of some more appreciative agent; but he was told that his services were needed, so he consented to work against the grain.* I have already expressed my

* Burnes often stated this very distinctly in his correspondence, and was very anxious that it should be clearly known and remem-bered.   I give the following, from a letter written at the end of 1839, because it is one of his most emphatic utterances on the sub-ject, and contains also a passage on his increased sense of responsi-bility, written in a more solemn strain than the general bulk of his correspondence : ' All my implorations to Government to act with promptitude and decision had reference to doing something when Dost Mahomed was King, and all this they have made to appear in support of Shah Soojah being set up ! But again, I did advocate the setting up of Shah Soojah, and lent all my aid, name, and know-ledge to do it. But when was this ! When my advice had been

belief that in so doing he did what was right. Doubtless, he had his failings, as all men have. But he died young. And I am inclined to think that, if his life had been spared, he would have attained to much higher distinction; for all that he lacked to qualify him for offices of large responsibility was a greater soberness of judgment, which years would almost certainly have brought. As it was, few men have achieved, at so early an age, so much distinction, by the force of their own personal character, as was achieved by Alexander Burnes.

rejected, and the Government were fairly stranded. I first gave opinions, and then asked leave to withdraw ; but Lord Auckland proved to me that it would be desertion at a critical moment, and I saw so myself ; but I entered upon the support of his policy not as what was best, but what was best under the circumstances which a series of blunders had produced. To have acted otherwise must have been to make myself superior to the Governor-General, and I saw that I had a duty to my country, ill as the representatives of that country in India had behaved to me, and I bore and forbore in consequence. My life has been devoted to my country ; like creeping things, I may have in the outset looked only to personal advantages, but persons have long since given place to things ; I now feel myself, at the age of thirty-five, with an onerous load upon me—the holy and sacred interests of nations ; and much as men may envy me, I begin sometimes to tremble at the giddy eminence I have already attained. In some respects it is indeed not to be envied, and I only hope that no passion may turn me from the path I tread, and that I may feel the awful responsibility which I have brought upon myself.'

CAPTAIN ARTHUR CONOLLY.

[BORN 1807.—DIED 1842.]

I F the reader, who has followed me through the preceding chapters, remembering what I have written
about the characters and the careers of Alexander Burnes
and Henry Martyn, can conceive the idea of a man com-
bining in his own person all that was excellent and loveable
in both, and devoting his life to the pursuit of the objects
which each in his turn sought to attain, the image of
Arthur Conolly will stand in full perfection before him.
For in him the high courage and perseverance of the ex-
plorer were elevated and sublimed by the holy zeal and
enthusiasm of the apostle. Ready to dare everything and
to suffer everything in a good cause; full of faith, and love,
and boundless charity, he strove without ceasing for the
glory of God and for the good of his fellow-men; and in
little things and in great, in the daily interests of a gentle
life, in which the human affections were never dormant,
and in the stern necessities of public service, which for the
honour of the nation, for the good of the human race, and
for the glory of the religion which he professed and acted,
demanded from him the surrender even of that life itself,

manifested all the noblest self-abnegation of the Hero and the Martyr.

Arthur Conolly was the third of the six sons of a gentleman, who, in the latter part of the eighteenth century, went out to India, made a rapid fortune, and returned to spend it in ease and comfort at home. He was born in Portland-place, London, in the year 1807 ; and received his education at Rugby. He was not much happier there than was Henry Martyn at the Truro Grammar School. Shy and sensitive, and of a nature too refined to cope successfully with the rough realities of public school life, he was not happy there; and he often spoke in after-life of the sufferings he endured at ' Mother Bucknell's.' In good time, however, deliverance came.* He was removed

---

* That all this made a strong impression on his mind—an impression which was never effaced—may be gathered from a passage in a letter which he wrote to one of his brothers in 1840, with reference to the education of a son : ' I don't feel anxious to hear,' wrote Arthur, ' that he has been sent to England for his education ; for, judging by the majority of young men who are driven through our schools and colleges from their earliest youth upwards, the system of turning boys out from the affectionately constraining influences of their own homes, as soon as they can run, does not produce the most desirable fruits. . . . . Under his first instructors, a boy works rather from fear than from esteem, and is prevented from thinking for himself, whilst the religion which should be his mainspring is performed before him as a task for mornings and evenings and twice o' Sundays. Societies of little boys certainly teach each other the meannesses which they would learn at home, and as for the knowledge of the world, on which so much stress is laid, it is commonly got by young men through channels which greatly diminish the value of the acquisition. These opinions would make me retain a son as long as possible under what Scripture beautifully terms "the commandment of his father

from Rugby in 1822, and sent to the Military Seminary of the East India Company. His father had large 'interest at the India House,' especially with the Marjoribanks family; so in due course, one after the other, he sent all his boys to India.

Arthur, in the first instance, was designed for one of the scientific branches of the Indian Army, and was sent, therefore, to the Company's Military Seminary. But whilst at Addiscombe,* an offer having been made to him of a commission in the Bengal Cavalry, he accepted it, or it was accepted for him. He left the military seminary on the 7th of May, 1823, and on the 16th of June he quitted England in a vessel bound for Calcutta. There was so much of incident crowded into the latter years of his life, that it is necessary to pass briefly over the chapter of his boyish years.

The ship in which he sailed for India was the Company's

and the law of his mother," even if his home were in England, that he might be kept unspotted from the world, which is the great thing for the happiness of this life as well as for the next.' And he added : ' I hope he is learning to read and write Hindustani, if not Persian. He will find such knowledge of immense advantage to him, if he ever comes out here ; and if he does not, an induction into Oriental idioms will enrich his mother tongue.'

* As this is the first mention, in the pages of this work, of the old Military Seminary, near Croydon, which was once the nursery of so many heroes, I should not have passed over it without notice, if I had not thought that it would receive fitter illustration in the Memoir which next follows. Arthur Conolly can hardly be regarded as an ' Addiscombe man,' as he never completed the course of education, but went out to India with what was called a 'direct appointment.'

ship *Grenville,* which carried Reginald Heber, then newly consecrated Bishop of Calcutta, to his diocese. In those days, the first voyage to India of a young writer or a young cadet often exercised an important influence over his whole after-career. ' Life-long friendships were often made or abiding impressions fixed upon the mind by the opportunities of a life on board ship. It was no small thing for a youth of sixteen, ardent, imaginative, with a vast capacity for good in his nature, to sit daily at the feet of such a man as Bishop Heber. The Bishop has recorded, in one of his letters, the fact that when he was studying the Persian and Hindostanee languages, 'two of the young men on board showed themselves glad to read with him.' Arthur Conolly was one of the two. But he derived better help than this from his distinguished fellow-passenger. The seed of the Word, which then came from the Sower's hand, fell upon good ground and fructified a hundred-fold. In a letter to a friend, Heber wrote, some five weeks after the departure of the *Grenville :* ' Here I have an attentive audience. The exhibition is impressive and interesting, and the opportunities of doing good considerable.' Among his most attentive hearers was young Arthur Conolly, who took to his heart the great truths which were offered to him, and became from that time rooted and grounded in the saving faith.

The first years of his residence in India did not differ greatly from those of the generality of young military officers, who have their profession to learn in the first instance, and in the next to qualify themselves for independent employment. He was attached, as a cornet, to the 6th

Regiment of Bengal Cavalry, and in 1824 and the two following years was stationed first at Keitah, and then at Lohargong. In 1825 he obtained his lieutenancy; and in 1827 he fell sick, and was compelled to obtain a furlough to England on medical certificate.

After a year and a half spent in Europe, he was sufficiently recruited to think of returning to India. In those days, it was the ordinary course for an officer, 'permitted to return to his duty,' to take a passage in a sailing vessel, steering round the Cape of Good Hope. What is now called somewhat inappropriately the Overland Route, was not then open for passenger-traffic; and if it had been, it would not have held out much attraction to Arthur Conolly. He desired to return to India really by the Overland Route —that is, by the route of Russia and Persia ; and, as he has himself declared, ' the journey was undertaken upon a few days' resolve.' ' Quitting London,' he has recorded in the published account of his travels, ' on the 10th of August, 1829, I travelled through France and the North of Germany to Hamburg, and embarking on board a steam-vessel at Travemunden on the 1st of September, sailed up the Baltic and the Gulf of Finland in four days to St Petersburg.' Such is the first sentence of the two volumes of travels which Arthur Conolly has given to the world. From St Petersburg he travelled to Moscow, and thence onwards to Tiflis, whence he journeyed forward across the Persian frontier and halted at Tabreez.

It was his original intention, after having reached that

place, to strike down thence to the shores of the Persian
Gulf, and there to take ship for Bombay. But the spirit of
adventure within him grew stronger as he proceeded on
his journey, and he determined to explore at least some
portions of Central Asia. There was little known, in those
days, about Afghanistan. He might do good service by
acquiring information respecting the countries lying between Persia and India, and it suited his humour at that time
to make the effort. It was the enterprise of the Englishman more than anything else which carried him forward
in those early days. He was very young when he started
on his journey. He had numbered only twenty-two
years ; but he had courage and self-reliance of the highest
order ; and ever as he went, the desire to see more impelled
him forward to new fields of adventure. Perhaps there
was even then obscurely taking shape within him some previsions of the ' great game in Central Asia,' which he afterwards believed it was the especial privilege of Great
Britain to play.

The winter was spent pleasantly at Tabreez, where the
British Mission, of which Sir John Macdonald was then
the chief, was located; and in the early spring of 1830,
having received good encouragement and offers of valuable assistance from the minister, he made his preparation for a march to Teheran, from which place he purposed to attempt a journey, either by way of Khiva, Bokhara, and Caubul, or through Khorassan and Afghanistan,
to the Indus. ' I had the good fortune,' he said, ' to engage
as my companion Syud Keramut Ali, an unprejudiced, very
clever, and gentlemanly native of Hindostan, who had re-

sided many years in Persia, and was held in great esteem by
the English there.   I had afterwards much reason to congratulate myself upon having so agreeable a companion, and
it was chiefly owing to his assistance that I safely completed
my journey.'

Starting from Teheran on the 6th of April, the travellers made their way through Mazenderan to Astrabad,
which they reached before the end of the month.   There
Conolly determined to attempt the route to Khiva. ' Thinking it necessary,' he said, ' to have a pretence for our journey,
I assumed the character of a merchant ; the Syud was to
call himself my partner, and we purchased for the Khiva
markets red silk scarfs, Kerman shawls, furs, and some huge
bags of pepper, ginger, and other spices.'   This he afterwards confessed was a mistake, for as he did not play the
part of a merchant adroitly, the disguise caused suspicion to
alight upon him.   What befell the travellers among the
Toorkomans, Conolly has himself narrated in the first
volume of his published narrative—how they crossed the
Goorgaon and the Attruck rivers, and rode into the desert
with their pretended merchandise on camel-back ; how
they fell into the hands of thieves, who, under pretence of
protecting them, robbed them of all that they had got ; how
they narrowly escaped being murdered, or sold into hopeless
captivity ; and how at last they obtained deliverance by the
opportune arrival of a party of Persian merchants, with
whom they returned in safety to Asterabad.   He went
back *re infectâ,* but he had spent nearly a month among
the Toorkomans, and had penetrated nearly half way to
Khiva, and seen more of the country than any European

had seen before, or—with one exception, I believe—has ever visited since.

After a brief sojourn at Asterabad, Arthur Conolly, attended by Keramut Ali, travelled to Meshed, by the way of Subzawur and Nisharpoor. At the holy city he was detained, money-bound, until the middle of September, when he started, in the trail of an Afghan army under the command of Yar Mahomed, for Herat, the Afghan city which afterwards became so celebrated in Eastern history. Upon all with whom he was associated there the young English officer made a most favourable impression. Another young English officer—Eldred Pottinger—who visited the city some years afterwards, found that Arthur Conolly's name was great in Herat, and that many held him in affectionate remembrance. ' I fell in,' says the former in his journal, referring to the year 1838, ' with a number of Captain Conolly's acquaintances. Every person asked after him, and appeared disappointed when I told them I did not know him. In two places, I crossed Mr Conolly's route, and on his account received the greatest hospitality and attention—indeed, more than was pleasant, for such liberality required corresponding liberality upon my part, and my funds were not well adapted for any extraordinary demand upon them. In Herat, Mr Conolly's fame was great. In a large party where the subject of the Europeans who had visited Herat was mooted, Conolly's name being mentioned, I was asked if I knew him, and on replying, " Merely by report," Moollah Mahomed, a Sheeah Moollah of great eminence, calling to me across the room, said, ' You have a great pleasure awaiting you. When you see him, give him my salutation, and tell him that I say he has done as much to give the English nation fame in Herat as your ambassador, Mr Elphinstone, at Peshawur," and in this he was seconded by the great mass present.'

This was truly a great distinction for one so young; and it was earned, not at all as some later travellers in Mahomedan countries have earned distinction, by assuming disguises and outwardly apostatizing, but by the frankest possible assertion of the character of a Christian gentleman. Moreover, he appeared before the Heratees as a very poor one. He did not go among the Afghans as Elphinstone had gone among them, laden with gifts; but as one utterly destitute, seeking occasional small loans to help him on his way. Yet even in these most disadvantageous circumstances, the nobility of his nature spoke out most plainly; and the very Moollahs, with whom he contended on behalf of his religion, were fain to help him as though he had been one of their sect. He had many warm disputations with these people, and they seem to have honoured him all the more for bravely championing his faith. Young as he was, he felt that our national character had suffered grievously in the eyes of the people of the East by our neglect of the observances of our religion. ' I am sure,' he said, ' the bulk of the Mahomedans in this country do not believe that the Feringhees have any real religion. They hear from their friends, who visit India, that we eat abominations, and are never seen to pray; and they care not to inquire more about us. . . . . . It is, therefore, greatly to be desired that such translations of our Scriptures as may invite their study should be sent among these people, in order first to satisfy

them that we have a religion, and secondly that they may
know what our religion is; in order that they may learn to
respect us, which they do not now, and gradually to regard
us with kindlier feelings; for until they do, we shall in
vain attempt to propagate the Gospel among them;'
and then he proceeded to discourse very shrewdly and in-
telligently on some of the principal errors which had
been committed by our people in their efforts to propagate
the Christian faith—errors principally arising from our
ignorance or disregard of the national characters of those
whom we had endeavoured to instruct in the truths of the
Gospel.

From Herat, Arthur Conolly proceeded, by the route
of Ghirisk, to Candahar; and thence by the valley of
Pisheen, in which he halted for some time, to Quettah, and
through the Bolan Pass to the country of the Ameers of
Sindh.   He then journeyed to Bahwulpore and across the
great Indian Desert, to the British frontier, which he crossed
in the month of January, 1831.   At Delhi he met the
Governor-General, Lord William Bentinck, to whom he
gave an account of his wanderings, and afterwards dropped
down to Calcutta by the river route.   At the Presidency he
drew up an interesting paper on the subject of the 'Overland Invasion of India,' which he printed in one of the
Calcutta journals, and afterwards appended to his published
travels.   In those days, a paper on such a subject showing
any real knowledge of the countries traversed was a novelty;
but it was reserved for a later generation to discern the large
amount of sagacity that informed it.

During the greater part of this year Conolly was employed in arranging the information which he had collected in the course of his travels—work in which he was assisted by Mr Charles Trevelyan, then a young civilian of high promise, who drew up some joint reports with him, which appear to have been prepared partly at Delhi and partly at Meerut, from which latter place the young cavalry officer went to Kurnaul. Even at that time it was plain that nothing had made so strong an impression on the traveller's mind as the knowledge which he had obtained of the abominable man-stealing, slave-dealing practices of the Toorkoman tribes, and the misery which this vile trade inflicted upon the people of Central Asia. He saw, too, under what strong provocation Russia was labouring, and how impossible it was, with any show of reason and justice, to deny her right to push forward to the rescue of her enslaved people, and the chastisement of the States which had swept them off and sold them into slavery. 'The case of these people,' he said, 'is deplorable, and in the midst of that laudable sympathy which has been excited in this country for the condition of slaves in general, it cannot be doubted that the wretched captives who languish in the steppes of Tartary will have their share, although their situation be unhappily beyond the hope of relief; and however important it may be to check the dangerous ambition of a too aspiring nation, humanity will be inclined to wish success to the Russian cause, were it but to put a period to a system so replete with barbarity as the trade in captives at Khiva.' He was far in advance of his age when he wrote in this strain; for it was not the fashion in those days, or indeed for more than a quarter of a century afterwards, to.

look upon Russia as any other than an unscrupulous aggressor, driven onward by lust of conquest, and eager to contend with England for the mastery of Hindostan.

But the ardent philanthropist was only a regimental subaltern. It was soon time for Lieutenant Conolly to return to his military duties, so he rejoined his regiment; and, after a while, at Cawnpore, made the acquaintance of the famous missionary traveller, Joseph Wolff. 'They took sweet counsel together, and they walked in the House of the Lord as friends.' With what deep emotion has Wolff recorded his recollections of that meeting! 'From Delhi,' he says, 'I passed to Agra, and thence to various places until I reached Cawnpore. HERE I MET WITH LIEU-TENANT CONOLLY.' The words are printed in Wolff's book in capital letters, as I have printed them here. 'When I travelled first in Khorassaun, in the year 1831,' he continues, 'I heard at Meshed by the Jews, that an English traveller had preceded me there, by the name of Arthur Conolly. They described him as a man who lived in the fear of God and of religion. The moment I arrived he took me to his house, and not only showed me the greatest hospitality, but, as I was at that time short of money, he gave me every assistance in his power—and not only so—he revised my journal for me with the most unaffected kindness. He also collected the Mahomedan Moollahs to his house, and permitted me not only to discuss with them the subject of religion, but gave me most substantial aid in combating their arguments. Conolly was a man possessed of a deep Scriptural knowledge; a capital textuary. Various enemies are always found to attack the lone missionary. Nobly and well did this gallant soldier acquit himself in the church militant, both in deeds of arms and deep devotion to the cause of Christ.'* What Arthur Conolly on his part thought of his friend may be gathered from a letter written by him shortly after his departure from Cawnpore.   'Wolff

* A friend who was then at Cawnpore, writing to me of this period of Conolly's history, says : '. . . An acquaintance, which ripened into mutual regard and esteem, began in an odd way, and was improved by an odd man. I was very much charmed with his singing, and he was taken with my playing, on which he made the discovery that he had never been taught, and I had never learnt notes ; and while I was indebted to an enthusiastic bellows-blower in Chichester Cathedral, who, for sixpence a week, allowed me to operate on the old organ therein, and used to predict no end of future fame, he, too, had been encouraged by some old nurse to believe that he was a cherub, and would beat Braham yet. The odd man was Joseph Wolff. . . . . When Wolff paid Conolly a visit at Cawnpore, I was a good deal with them, and joined in their laughter. Yes, there was a good deal of laughing. Wolff was both untidy and uncleanly, and yet not unwilling to be reformed, and so, at or before breakfast, ran the lesson. From Arthur Conolly to him : " Peer Moorshid, have we put on the clean stockings ? " Then next, " Have we used the sponge and chillumchee ? " (basin.) To all of which Wolff would make good-humoured reply, adding, " Truly ye are all sons of Eezak ! " Yet there was real love in that laughing. Wolff's love and admiration of Arthur Conolly were unbounded. He could, too, break out into lofty discourse, and Arthur Conolly held his own with him. I never can forget one Sabbath conversation on the Jews, protracted till it was time for us all to go to church together, when Wolff preached on the subject—The Jews, think how great were their privileges ; Christian Englishmen, think how great are your privileges. When Wolff, in after years, went to Bokhara, and spoke of Arthur Conolly as his " moreed "—as I confidently recollect he did, though I cannot lay hold of the narrative—I feel assured his mind often went back to those days at Cawnpore.

has left us,' wrote the young Christian enthusiast on the
19th of February, 1833, 'and has taken with him the esteem
and best wishes of all who knew him. As you will shortly
see him in Calcutta, I need not enter into much detail of
his sayings and doings here, but let me again assure you
that he is neither crazy, vain, nor fantastical, but a simple-
minded, humble, rational, and sound Christian. His chief
desire is to preach to all people, Jesus Christ *crucified*, the
God, and only Saviour of mankind : he is naturally most
anxious that his own brethren should turn to the light that
has shone upon him, and therefore he seeks them in all
parts of the earth where God's wrath has scattered them,
but ever as he goes, he proclaims to the Mahomedan, and
to the idolater, the great object of his mission. On his
opinions concerning the personal reign of our Saviour on
earth during the Millennium, I am not qualified to pass
judgment, but I believe he has chiefly formed them upon a
literal interpretation of the yet to be fulfilled prophecies,
especially those contained in the 72nd Psalm and the 60th
Isaiah. . . . . And after all, though he is most decided in
his creed, he says : " I am no inspired prophet, and I may
err in my calculations and conclusions, but the book from
which I deduce them cannot be wrong—search into its
meanings, as you are commanded, with prayer and humble
diligence, and then decide according to the understanding
that God has given you ; I ask not that you should accept
my words, but that you should inquire diligently into those
which contain the assurance of a blessing to those who read
and keep them," Rev. i. 3. If this be madness, I wish he
would bite me. In his English discourses, Wolff labours

under ignorance of idioms and select expressions, and finds difficulty in well embodying and connecting the thoughts that crowd upon him, yet it is always a pleasure to hear him, for often when struggling with the words of a big sentence, he throws out a few thrillingly beautiful expressions that give light to the rest, and at times it is quite wonderful how he rises with the grandeur of his theme, and finds an uninterrupted flow of fine language. He was very clear and forcible in his exposition of the 51st Psalm, and the 9th of Acts, and the Sunday morning before he left us, he preached a homily upon Paul's address to King Agrippa, which we all felt to be sublimely beautiful throughout. . . . . Judging by the benefit we have reaped from his conversation here, we may hope that he will be made the means of doing much good wherever he goes. You will be delighted with his company in private society, for he is full of varied and most interesting anecdote; but, above all, I hope you will hear him when he appears to the greatest advantage in the pulpit, for understanding the Hebrew meanings of words in Scripture, he throws new light upon passages that are familiar to us, but chiefly he preaches truth *from* the heart, and therefore, generally, *to* the heart.'

At Cawnpore, Arthur Conolly corresponded with Alexander Burnes, who had accomplished his great journey, and was then reaping his reward. Conolly had been the first to acquire and to place on record the much-needed information relating to the country between India and Persia; but he had been slow to make his appearance before the English public, and the Bombay officer had been rising into eminence, whilst his comrade of Bengal was still almost unknown. Conolly rejoiced in the success of his brother-traveller, and, without the slightest tinge of jealousy upon his feelings, wrote to congratulate Burnes on his achievements. 'Although,' he wrote on the 20th of April, 1833, 'I may be one of the last to congratulate you upon the happy accomplishment of your journey, I beg you not to rank me amongst the least sincere, for I really compliment you upon the resolution which has carried you through the most difficult as well as the most interesting part of Central Asia, and trust that you will derive as much honour and benefit from your travels, as we doubtless shall instruction and amusement. I meant to write to you at Bombay, but hearing that you were coming round to Calcutta, I determined there to address my congratulations, and some remarks upon certain matters in which you are interested. First, I owe you an explanation of a circumstance which, if I did not describe it, might possibly induce you to entertain what was, I believe, the Governor-General's opinion— that I wished feloniously to appropriate your valuable survey of the Indus. When in Calcutta, I drew up for his Lordship a map of the countries lying between the Arras and Indus, the Aral and Indian Ocean, which, being compiled at the Surveyor-General's office from the best authorities, contained the Indus as laid down by you. In this I sketched my route from Meshed to Buhawalpore, correcting the error that appeared in my protraction by the *Bukkur* of your map. When I had written out my journal for the press, I wrote to head-quarters to know whether I might send a copy of the above-mentioned map to England to be published with my book, and I especially begged to know whether there existed objections to my using that portion of it which had been copied from your survey. I addressed myself to my relation, Mr Macnaghten, the secretary, and our mutual friend Trevelyan answered for him, in a note which I am sure he will not object to my enclosing. In consequence of its contents, I sent home to the Geographical Society, in London, as much of the map as embraced my route, copying into it from your survey a *bit* of the river about *Bukkur*, so as to place that point correctly, and mentioning that I had so done; there anticipating that a full and correct copy would be furnished me for my book. I wrote a preface to the last, in which I offered you my poor thanks for the benefit I thought to borrow from your labours. Objections were made at the Surveyor-General's office to completing the map without specific instructions from head-quarters. I wrote for these, and the Governor-General being up the country, I was occupied in alternate correspondence with his Lordship's and the Vice-Resident's secretaries for about two months, at the end of which time it was notified to me that I might use every part of the map in question except that part which had been laid down by you. I had then only to regret that I had lost so much time in consequence of his Lordship's opinion not having been correctly ascertained in the first instance, and to cancel that part of my preface which made mention of you. In this particular instance I could not see much danger of acting wrong, as I was informed that *Government* would very shortly publish a map containing *all* the latest inform-ation; but I would in no case have borrowed information from you, had I thought that you would object to my

doing so with due acknowledgment of my obligations. I
do not now apprehend that you will hold me guilty of any
evil intention, but it is proper that I should explain the circumstance, and beg your excuse for any error with which
you may deem me chargeable. . . . . I have before me
your long and kind letter, dated on the Ravee, January 26,
1832, since when you have made a grand tour. You were
right in supposing that I would willingly have undertaken such a trip with you, but, as you so well foresaw,
there were several objections to my doing so. The notes,
for which you so politely thanked me, were, I fear, too
slight to have served you much, but they were heartily at
your service, as are all those which I have collected for
publication. Permit me to offer you these, with the sketch
of my route, and the slightly altered country through which
it runs. The map which contains it, you will get at the
Surveyor-General's office, and my relation, Mr Macnaghten,
now Political Secretary, will procure for you a copy of the
roughly-printed pages which I sent home for Mr Murray
to publish. From them you may glean a few particulars
which will enable you to prove, or to complete, some of
your notes, and I beg that you will make the freest use of
all. 'Tis late to thank you for the good wishes and kind
encouragement contained in your precedingly-mentioned
letter, but you have not been travelling upon post roads,
and must, therefore, accept my present acknowledgments.
Several untoward circumstances have conspired to keep me
without the pale of the Sirkar's patronage, and my wisest
plan, I believe, would be to fold up my carpet of hope, and
betake myself to a quiet whiff at the pipe of resignation,

but I am at heart too much of a vagabond to do this, and trust yet to pitch a tent among some of our long-bearded friends of the mountains.'

But these anticipations of continued neglect were soon falsified. In 1834, Lieutenant Conolly went with his regiment to Mhow, and soon afterwards he was transferred to that great outlet for the energies of aspiring young soldiers, kept down by the seniority system—the Political Department. He was appointed an assistant to the Governor-General's agent in Rajpootana. He was consoled at the same time by receipt of intelligence from England assuring him that his book had been published, and had been well received by the critics and by the public. Burnes sent him some cuttings from the literary journals to show how well his fellow-traveller had been reviewed—an attention which Conolly gratefully acknowledged in a letter, which is interesting on many other accounts. Writing from the Sambhur Lake, May 30, 1835, he said: 'Pray accept my sincere thanks for your welcome letter of the 11th instant, containing Monsieur D'Avega's secret and confidential notice of the honours designed for us by the Geographical Society of Paris. I must endeavour, in my letter of thanks to this liberal and enlightened body, to atone for not having at first presented a copy of my book to them. It was very kind of you to do this for me, according to the hint by which I could not otherwise have profited, and I have to thank you for this friendly act as one of a series for which I am your debtor. I did not answer your London letters, because you talked of returning to the East immediately; but you may be sure that I was much gratified by the periodical notices of my work, which you were so good as to send me. They came like rays of sunshine after a cloud! There could be little doubt of your success; but as it has been hardly equalled, I may offer you my congratulations upon it. I think you did right in declining the Secretaryship to his Majesty's Embassy in Irân, because Mr Elphinstone advised you, and I hope that he saw a better field for you in Caubul or Bokhara. The attention of the home authorities has, after a long dream, been awakened to the state of their politics in Persia, and the appointment of Lord Heytesbury to the Governor-Generalship induces me to believe that British interests will no longer be neglected in Central Asia. Your fortune, of course, is not dependent upon the retention or abolition of what is termed the non-interference system with regard to our foreign affairs; you may speedily rise here to a higher station than the one above-mentioned, but, for my own part, I would rather be secretary of Embassy in Persia than the greatest magnate in any part of this *consuming* clime. It does, indeed, try both body and mind. I speak feelingly on this subject just now, for I am living in a tent on the border of the famed Salt Lake of Sambhur, ceded to us after the Joudpore war, in order that Lord William might be styled "the fountain of grace and bounty." As assistant to the Governor-General's agent in Rajpootana, I am residing here in the joint capacities of Hakim and Bunneeah, and as everything is yet in confusion and ruin, I am as hardly worked and as badly fed as Sancho was in Barrataria. The last advices from Loodianah state that Runjeet was about to close with the Afghans. I fear that

he will get the better of them somehow or other. Shah
Soojah is in the Sikh camp. I hear the Maharajah has
promised to make him King of Peshawur. Thus far may
the troops of the Royal Cyclops advance their standards,
but they will not be able to hold ground farther west: so
thinks my esteemed friend Syud Keramut Ali, who has
lately returned from Caubul, and who gives me very interesting accounts of the state in which he left the Caubul
Sirdars. The Syud advised Jubbar Khan to send his eldest
son to India for an English education. Captain Wade discovered a political mystery lying deep under this specious
pretext, and after some quarrels which occurred in consequence, my friend, as the weakest party, went to the
wall. I hope, however, to be able to show that all the
differences had rise in mistakes. He at present stands
condemned upon an *ipse dixit*, according to the equitable
system by which whites judge blacks. I have requested
my Galcutta agent to send you a copy of my book—a compliment which I could not sooner pay, and which I hope
you will accept as a mark of my high esteem.'

In the performance of his political and other duties,
Arthur Conolly worked on, until, in the month of January,
1838, he obtained a furlough to England. He did not go
home because he was sick, or because he was weary of
Indian life, but because he was drawn thither by the attrac-
tions of one to whom he had given the best affections of
his heart. He had ever, in words which I find in one of
his own letters, with reference to the character of a friend,
a great *besoin d'aimer*—and he had found one worthy to
fill the void. He had met in India a young lady, the

daughter of a man in high position there, a member of a
noble family; and he had given to her all the love of his
warm, passionate nature. But she had returned to England
with her parents; and so he followed thither, believing, as
he had good reason to believe, that their reunion would soon
be followed by their marriage.

They met again, under her father's roof; and for a while
he was supremely happy. But the fond hopes which he
had cherished were doomed to bitter disappointment. The
blight which fell upon the life of Henry Martyn fell also
upon the life of Arthur Conolly. The whole history of it
lies before me as written by himself, but it is not a history
to be publicly related. There was no fault on either side.
Nothing more is to be said of it than that it was God's
will. And no man ever bowed himself more resignedly
or reverentially to such a dispensation. He had been
resolved for her sake to sacrifice his career; never to return to India, but to go into a house of business—to accept
any honourable employment, so that he might not take
her from her family and her home. But when this hope
was unexpectedly prostrated, he turned again to the career
which lay before him, and went back into the solitude of
public life. He went back, chastened and subdued, full of
the deepest love for the one, and of boundless charity for
the many; not at all exasperated, not at all embittered,
but with a softer and more loving heart than before; with
an enlarged desire to benefit the human race, and a stronger
faith in the boundless mercy of God. The refined tenderness and delicacy of his nature could be fittingly expressed
only by the use of his own words. I know nothing more

beautiful—nothing more touching—than his letters on this subject. The entire unselfishness of his nature was manifest in every word that he spoke, up to the time when, the betrothal ended, he said to her whom he had lost, that, although there was cause for sorrow on both sides, there was none for reproach on either; that, with God's comfort, he should not fail to find happiness in single life, especially if he could feel assured of God's restoring hers; and conjured her to look up and be herself again, for the sake of all those who must grieve if she did not, and ever to feel that she had his full and undying esteem, his unpresuming friendship, and his unceasing prayers. It was all over. Thenceforth Humanity became his bride, 'and airy hopes his children.'

Happily for him, there was something in the great world of becoming magnitude to fire his imagination, to absorb his thoughts, and to invite him to energetic action. The contemplated invasion of Afghanistan was at this time occupying the minds of those members of the Cabinet whose duty it was to shape our policy in Asia, as seen both from our Western and our Eastern dominions. The information of any intelligent Englishman who had actually visited the countries, or any part of the countires, which were about to become the scene of our operations, was, therefore, eagerly sought. Alexander Burnes had returned to India, leaving behind him, however, some rich Oriental legacies; and it was no small thing in such a conjuncture, for a Secretary of State for Foreign Affairs, or a President of the India Board, whose experiences did not lie much in that direction, to be able to converse with a British officer who

had visited Herat—the famous frontier city to which the
Persians were laying siege.   Whether Arthur Conolly were
altogether the kind of man best suited to their purpose
may admit, perhaps, of a doubt.   They may have thought
him a little over-enthusiastic—a little too wild and visionary.   But sober-minded practical men were not very likely,
in those days, to make such hazardous journeys as Arthur
Conolly had made.   The man who did these things had
necessarily a dash of romance in his nature, and you might
be sure that he would not expound his views in a very
cold-blooded manner.   One thing, however, must have
satisfied them.   He was delighted with the idea of an
advance into Afghanistan.   Seeing, as he did, in the distance such grand results to be obtained by British inter-
vention, he did not scan very narrowly the means to be
immediately employed.   His view of the matter was rather
that of a grand Anti-slavery Crusade, than of a political
movement intended to check-mate the designs of another
great European power.   He grasped, in very singleness of
heart, the idea of a band of Christian heroes entering the
remote regions of Central Asia as Champions of Humanity
and Pioneers of Civilization.   Full of this thought, he drew
up a memorandum for the Home Government, in which
he expounded his views, saying : ' Now both the Russians
and Persians have the most legitimate plea for invading
Toorkistan, especially Kharasm, where numbers of their
countrymen are held in abject slavery—a plea last to be
disallowed by England !   How, then, can we frustrate the
designs of ambition which our rival will so speciously
cover ?   Possibly, by persuading the Oosbegs themselves to

do away with the grievance which gives the Russians and Persians a pretext for invading them. Let the British Government send a properly accredited Envoy to Khiva, in the first place, and thence, if advisable, across the Oxus, at once to explain our present acts in Afghanistan, and to try this only open way of checking a Russian approach, which will entail far greater trouble upon us. Since the last Russian Embassy to Bokhara, the ruler of that kingdom has actually exerted himself to suppress the sale of Russians in his territory, and nearly all the Muscovite people who remain enslaved in Toorkistan are now in Kharasm. Nothing but fear can have induced the Ameer of Bokhara to heed the Czar's remonstrances, and arguments which have proved so effectual with him should not fail with the Khan of Khiva, in the event of the latter chief's being brought to see the danger of Russo-Persian invasion nearer and greater than he has been accustomed to consider it. . . . . . The King of Bokhara would seem prepared to meet us half way in our commercial advances. When Sir A. Burnes was at his capital, "the Vizier," writes that officer, "conversed at great length on subjects of commerce relating to Bokhara and Britain, and expressed much anxiety to increase the communication between the countries, requesting that I myself would return *as a trading* ambassador to Bokhara." A similar desire for an improved trade with us was repeated to Mr Wolff, the missionary, when he visited Bokhara. The advantages of the commerce which his neighbour encourages cannot be unknown to the Khivan Khan, and few representations should be needed to convince the latter chief that he might

make his desert capital a still greater trade mart than
Bokhara, through the facility that the river Oxus offers
him.'

To remove the not unreasonable pretext for Russian
advances in Central Asia, Arthur Conolly proposed that the
British authorities should negotiate with the principal
Oosbeg chiefs, and represent to them that if they would
undertake to restrain the Turcoman tribes from carrying off
into slavery the subjects of Russia and Persia, the British
would use their influence with the Governments of those
countries to persuade them to fix their boundaries at limits
which would inspire our Government with confidence, and
insure peace to the Oosbegs themselves. On the other
hand, in treating with Russia, he contended that we should
best consult our interests by basing all our arguments on
the one broad principle of humanity. ' It might not be
amiss,' he wrote, ' frankly to put it to the Court of St
Petersburg whether they, on their part, will not desist from
a jealousy which is injuring us both, and many people connected with us. Whether, ceasing from an unworthy
policy, which seeks to keep alive a spirit of disaffection
among the thousands whom it is our high aim to settle and
enlighten, they will not generously unite with us in an
endeavour peaceably to abolish rapine and slavery; to make
safe trade roads to their own possessions near Toorkistan;
and, in the words of their servant, Baron Mejendorf, " de
faire germer, et d'étendre dans cette partie de l'Asie, les
bienfaits de la civilisation Européenne." Let us direct,' he
added, ' the vast means prepared to the accomplishment of
the greatest possible end, and while we are in a position to

speak with effect, endeavour to lay the foundation of the
grand beneficial influence that we ought to exercise over
the long-neglected tribes of Western Asia! Suppose, however, that the above great project should entirely fail; that
at the very outset the Oosbegs should reject our anti-slavery
suggestions, or the Russians haughtily decline our interference, would our labour be lost? By no means. The
cost of our mission would be well exchanged for increased
knowledge of countries, in which, sooner or later, we shall
be obliged to play some part, and for more positive notions
than we now possess of the danger against which we have
to provide; while it is probable that though the Oosbegs
might desire to be left to fight their own battles with the
Russians and Persians, they would accept overtures of a
generally amicable nature from us that might have some
way for the extension of our commercial relations beyond
Afghanistan, which we hope to settle.'

These were suggestions not to be lightly regarded, at a
time when the designs of Russia in the East were disturb-
ing the serenity of the English Cabinet, and a British army
was about to march into Central Asia. There might be
more ardour and enthusiasm in Arthur Conolly than were
likely to recommend him to official men; but there was a
good substratum of sound sense at the bottom of his recommendations, and the authorities were not disinclined to
avail themselves of the services of a man so eager to do anything and to suffer anything in so great a cause. At first,
they were minded to send him directly from England to
Toorkistan, with credentials from the Home Government;
but afterwards they determined only to recommend such a

mission to the Governor-General, and therefore they sent him to India with letters to Lord Auckland, and with £500 in his pocket for the expenses of his journey. He was to travel by the way of Vienna, Constantinople, Armenia, and the Persian Gulf, and acquire, as he went, information that might be useful to his Government, and smooth the way for his future operations on the banks of the Oxus and the Jaxartes.

On the 11th of February, 1839, Arthur Conolly left London, and made for the Austrian capital. There he had an interview with the great minister and arch-diplomatist, Metternich, to whom he explained in detail our Central-Asian policy, and thereby removed some erroneous impressions which had been made upon his mind. It happened, also, that at that time an envoy from the Shah of Persia (Hoossein Khan by name) was halting at Vienna on his way to England. It was obviously a great thing that Conolly should hold frequent communication with the Elchee, and it was desirable, at the same time, that it should be as little formal and ceremonious as possible. So the English officer quartered himself at the hotel where tne Persian minister was residing, and they soon established familiar intercourse with each other. This Hoossein Khan appears to have been a shrewd fellow, with some sense of humour in him. At one of the interviews, the details of which Conolly afterwards noted down, the English officer hinted that the Persian minister was prejudiced against Mr M'Neill. 'Not at all,' said Hoossein Khan. 'We have always been the best of friends. He has lived at my house for days together. Indeed, I owe him my highest appointment. When it was proposed to send me as Envoy to England, M'Neill represented that I had not rank enough. "Why," replied the Shah, "Hoossein Khan is of a very ancient family. He is Adjutant-General, and he is my foster-brother. Moreover, we received the other day Mr Ellis from your Crown. Now, I'll engage that the Sovereign of England has at least three hundred subjects equal in station to Mr Ellis, whilst I have not ten equal to Hoossein Khan." "Your Majesty forgets," said M'Neill, "that Mr Ellis was a Privy-Councillor." "Very well," said the Shah, "we will add this dignity to Hoossein Khan's titles," and I was made a *Preevy-Koonsillah* from that day.' *

The case was well argued upon both sides, but with no result. The Persian was as tenacious of his opinions as the Englishman; and it must be admitted that he had a way of stating the case in favour of his master, which, if not always truthful, had a very plausible appearance of truth. It is instructive to see the different glosses which two men can put upon the same event, as seen from the sides of their respective nationalities. Thus the well-known story of the seizure of the British Courier, which did so much to embitter our relations with Persia, as seen from the Persian side, was rather a wrong suffered by them than a wrong

* This conversation really took place between Mahomed Shah and Major Rawlinson, who conveyed to the royal camp at Nishapoor Mr M'Neill's protest against Hoossein Khan's appointment as minister to England.

done to the English. 'The Shah never thought,' said the Persian, ' of injuring India. He went to Herat to chastise rebels who continually murdered or sold his own subjects. Then comes your Elchee and prohibits punishment and redress, and when he finds his representations unheeded (how could the Shah prefer them to the cries of his own people?), he intrigues with the Prince of Herat, sends a messenger there secretly, and when this fellow is caught returning in Afghan clothes, like a spy as he was, and was seized as anybody in any country would have been in such circumstances,* his short imprisonment is magnified, his interested statements are taken in preference to the testimony of respectable men who were lookers-on, and knew everything, and we, who had a right to be the complainants, are made to appear the party in fault.' Again, taking a comprehensive view of the whole question, Hoossein Khan said : 'You talk of our acting against your interests, and our own real interests; but are we ever to sacrifice what we think to be ours, to your notions for us, or to your precautions for yourselves? The question of Persian policy lies in a small space, and the sooner it is reduced to its essence the better. We are situated between you and Russia, being weaker than either of you; we therefore want support from one or the other. If you will give it, good; if not, we must just take to those whom we like least, and make the most of them, whether it pleases you

---

* The Duke of Wellington is said to have observed, that if he had been in the Shah's place he should have hanged Mahomed Ali Maafee as a spy ; and nothing is more probable than that he would.

or not. The Shah will never give up his claims upon
Afghanistan: why should he resign what he can take with
ease, purely to soothe a fear of the British Government?
The whole country up to Caubul was ready to submit to
him when he left Herat, and will prove so whenever
he advances his standard again. You misinterpret his
Majesty's generosity in retiring at your request, and
think you gained your wish by sending troops to Karrak;
you encourage revolt in the South; does it not strike your
acute penetration that we can play the last game, if need
be, in Hindostan? We can; and if you provoke us too far,
we will.' To this Conolly replied: 'Your admissions now
go far to justify our proceedings in Afghanistan. Your
very threat of using your political influence against our
repose in India, is quite reason enough for us to prevent
your establishing it any nearer, by the fair way that your
hostile conduct has opened to us.' If this was an empty
threat that the Persian uttered, not a clear declaration of the
settled policy of his Government, it is certain that we did
not wait very many years to see how effectually it could be
converted into a fact.

From Vienna, Arthur Conolly made his way to Constantinople. There most propitiously it happened that he
found an Envoy from Khokund—one of the very Oosbeg
States which he desired to wean from their inhuman habits.
The chiefs of Central Asia had, and still have, unbounded
faith in the Sooltan. They believe that his power is unlimited, and that he can rescue them from all their difficulties and dangers. As I write, the Khan of Khokund has

an Envoy, if not two, at Constantinople.* To Conolly, this circumstance of the presence of the Khokundee at the Ottoman capital was one of happy augury; and he determined to turn it to the best possible account. So he soon made the acquaintance of the Envoy, and began to expound to him his views of the situation in Central Asia. 'One of the Shah's pretexts for invading Herat,' he observed, 'was that the people of that State used to carry off his subjects into slavery; but this plea was proved false by his refusing to accept our guarantee to Kamran's promise that such should not again occur. I don't think that there were many real Heratees engaged in this work.† The Hazarehs perhaps did it occasionally, in concert with the Toorkomans, and it was against the latter tribes that the Shah of Persia should have directed his arms, if he wished to put down the evil, as his father, Abbas Mirza, did at Serria. People say that there are now in Khiva, Bokhara, and other parts of your country up there, as many as thirty thousand Persians taken one time or other from the villages and high road of Irân by the Toorkomans. Is it so?' 'Thirty?' was the reply, with a hearty laugh; 'thirty! say a hundred thousand, or two, if you will; we've no end of those scoundrels; upon our parts, we find them very useful.' 'And other people also? Russians! have you many of those?' 'We haven't many, nor the Bokhara people either; at Khiva

* Written in 1865.
† He had afterwards too much reason to change his opinions on this point. In fact, Yar Mahomed, the Heratee minister, was one of the greatest slave-dealers in Central Asia.

there are a great many.' 'What do they do there?' asked Conolly. 'They do everything; work in the field—work in the houses.' 'We English, perhaps your Excellency knows, do not approve of slavery at all. Our Government, the other day, gave forty millions of ducats to buy off the slaves of its own subjects.' 'How? What do you mean?' asked the astonished Envoy. 'Why, in former times, many English subjects, possessed of estates in foreign provinces of England, had been the owners of negro slaves, who used to till their lands for the cultivation of sugar, spices, &c. Now the rule in England itself is, that no foot which touches its dust can remain for a moment longer enslaved against its will. The free people at home all cried to the throne that no English subjects should have a slave anywhere, so the Government, not to be unjust, bought off all the negroes from its own people, and declared them free for ever.' 'You wish men not to be slaves of each other, but only *bundagan khoda*, slaves of God. Good for you, if you do well. Our habits are different.' 'Yes,' said Conolly, 'as I learned in my endeavours to reach Khiva.'

A few days afterwards Arthur Conolly again visited the Envoy, and plunged deeply into the politics of Central Asia; the depths which he sought to fathom ever being those in which he touched with his foot the abominations of that vile traffic in human flesh, which he was eager to root out from the land. They talked about the complications that had recently arisen—of the movements of the Persians, the Russians, and the English, and of the dangers which beset the Oosbeg States. The Envoy asked what was to be done—what was to be the remedy. This was the opportunity which Conolly desired. 'I have no certain remedy,' he answered; 'but there is one which may be tried. The Russians will invade Khiva, and take other Oosbeg States, on the ground that they have a right to liberate their people enslaved among you. We could not say a word against this, nor would we; for, to be frank with you, if any of our people had been in the condition that theirs are, we should long ago have done what they threaten to do. You must send every Russian slave out of your territories, and never capture any more.' 'We and the Bokharians have not many Russians,' said the Envoy; 'but the Khiva Khan wouldn't find it easy to do what you propose. He has a great many.' 'How many?' 'More than a thousand, certainly. There's only one way in which I can see a likelihood of your plan being accomplished, by the Russians *buying* all their people. They are dispersed among many masters; so the Khan could not give them up if he wished.' 'I don't think the Russians would condescend to this,' returned Conolly. 'Perhaps, however, an arrangement might be made, if you promised never to capture any more. What would it cost to buy the thousands you speak of?' 'Not less than fifty or sixty thousand ducats. Perhaps you would buy the whole, and make the Russians a present of them. This would not be a great thing after your millions of ducats.' 'Well, we'll discuss all practicable means when the plan is agreed to. And the Persians! Will you let them go also, and cease from your forays?' 'Oh, you must not think of the Persians,' rejoined the Envoy, 'in such an arrangement.

There are too many of them by hundreds of thousands. Besides, we want them. For the Russians, perhaps, we might come to an arrangement.' 'Sooner or later, methinks,' said Conolly, 'you'll be obliged to satisfy both nations on this score; but it isn't for me to dictate positively on the matter. The question in all its bearings concerns you much more than it does us. We and the Russians are people likely to quarrel, if we come near each other in the East. We, please God, are well able to wage war with any nation, in any part of the world, but we don't want to quarrel with any people, because war is inhuman and expensive, and because it interrupts commerce, which is the source of our great strength. For this reason we wish to keep the Russians at a distance; the best way of doing so is to be strong and independent (for this reason we are building up the Afghans), and we don't make big professions, so we shall not make big promises. Here' (showing Burnes's map) 'is our position, there is yours; you see that we are far enough from you to prevent your entertaining the slightest apprehension of our power, though we are not so far that we cannot do you good in several ways. We should like to confer with you about the means of removing Russia's pretext for coming farther on in your direction. Hear, all of you, what we have to say, and adopt what you like. If you like none of our suggestions regarding other powers, you can open and keep open a friendly intercourse with the English Government, and draw close in commercial dealings with our people of Hindostan.' 'Very good! very good!' replied the Envoy; 'write to your ministers, and we will see the end. I, for my part, will engage that you, or any other (English) Envoy, shall go safely up there and back.'

Again and again the Envoy pressed Conolly to wait until he himself had received from the Sooltan his orders to depart, that they might travel to Khokund together; but the English officer pleaded the instructions of his own Government, and declined the invitation. In truth, he had already made a longer halt at Constantinople than was consistent with the wishes of the authorities in England, who censured him for his delay. But he had been doing good work. His conferences with the Envoy from Khokund had done much to detach that worthy from the grasp of Russian diplomacy, which would have had it all its own way, if Conolly had not been at Constantinople to exercise that benign influence which few men could resist. He parted on the best possible terms from the Oosbeg agent, carrying with him all sorts of friendly assurances and some pledges; and on the 22nd of August he left Constantinople, *en route* to Baghdad, intending to reach Samsoun as the first stage in his journey. But learning that the road thence to Diarbekir was infested with bands of plunderers, and scarcely passable, he landed at Trebizonde, and, by the Consul's advice, proceeded to Erzeroum, where he arrived early in September. After a halt of two days, he resumed his journey, furnished with letters for his safe protection to the authorities of the province, and before the end of October—having passed a week at Baghdad *en route*, where he first made the acquaintance of Major Rawlinson—he had reached Bushire in the Persian Gulf, where Major Hennell, the British Resident, not having immediately at his command a Government vessel, sent Conolly forward in a fast-sailing merchant-ship to Bombay, which place he reached on the 13th November, 1839.

From Bombay he made his way to Calcutta, saw the Governor-General, expounded his views, and received the confidences of Lord Auckland. Nothing could have been more propitious than the conjuncture. There was a bright flush of success over all our policy in Afghanistan. In Arthur Conolly's words, we had to all outward seeming 'built up the Douranee Empire' again. We had accomplished a great revolution. The *de facto* ruler of Afghanistan was beaten and a fugitive. The nationality of the country was stunned and bewildered by the roar of the British guns. More than all, the great magician, who had accomplished this mighty change, was a near relative of Conolly himself. The Envoy and Minister at the Court of Shah Soojah-ool-Moolk was his cousin, William Macnaghten, about soon to have the prefix of *Sir* to his name—a name not to be mentioned without a respectful and a tender regret, for he was a brave and an able man, who sacrificed his life in the service of his country. The Governor-General, therefore, had no very difficult part to play. As the Home Government had left it to him to find a field of adventure for Arthur Conolly, Lord Auckland also in his turn left it to the representative of British interests in Afghanistan to indicate the particular service on which his enthusiastic relative might most advantageously be employed.

So Conolly proceeded to Caubul, and in the spring of 1840 was immersed, breast-high, in the troubled stream of Afghan politics. What was then stirring in his warm heart and in his active brain may be gathered from the letters which he addressed to an old and very dear friend—a man high in place and deservedly high in honour. I do not know why, in such a work as this, designed, however feeble the execution, to do honour to the great Indian services, I should not write, in this place, the name of one who was for many years among the brightest of their ornaments. The beloved friend to whom Arthur Conolly poured out his heart more freely than to any other correspondent, was Thomas Campbell Robertson, a member of the Bengal Civil Service, who at this time was Lieutenant-Governor of the North-Western Provinces, and Provisional Governor-General of India. He had risen to this high station after a blameless career of more than thirty years of beneficent work, in many parts of the country, and in many departments of the service. With a largeness of official zeal, which ever kept him in the front rank of his contemporaries, he combined a genuine love of European literature, which was a source of unfailing refreshment to him in his non-official hours, and made him a delightful companion to the cherished few whose intercourse he sought. He had ever a high sense of justice—of that justice which has its root in a generous and sympathizing nature—and he groaned in bitterness of spirit over the inroads of that new faith which, during the later stages of his career, tended towards the absorption of the native principalities and the subversion of the ancient aristocracy of India. Few members of the enlightened service to which he belonged had larger or sounder views of Indian policy; but a physical infirmity, which crept upon him in the prime of his life, debarred him

from taking his right place in the public eye among the
Indian statesmen of his generation, at a time when the
services of Indian statesmen were in great national request.
And I am not sure whether his good old-school opinions,
which he had lived to see disowned by a new race of civilians, did not help to keep him in the background. Nothing,
at all events, could convince him that such was not the
case.

There were circumstances of a domestic nature which
caused Mr Robertson to take a deep interest in the fortunes
of the young Cavalry officer, and which bound Arthur
Conolly to the veteran civilian in bonds which at times may
have been very painful to him, but which he would not
have severed for the world. I have said that what was
stirring in the soldier's warm heart was freely communicated
to his friend, who well knew all his sorrows. No one could
understand better than Mr Robertson the yearning desire
for continual excitement which at that time was gnawing
Arthur Conolly's breast ; no one could appreciate better the
full force of every word he wrote—its tenderness, its generosity, its consideration for another—when after much that,
profoundly touching as is the interest of it, I cannot, bring
myself to make public, he proceeded to say : ' Those feelings
have more force with me than ever now, because I am
about to undertake a journey, which is not without risks to
life, and if mine should end in Tartary, I would not have
her fancy it shortened or carelessly ventured in consequence
of my disappointed love for her. You will be able, if necessary, to explain that the cause I go upon is one which
every man must be proud and eager to peril his life for—

the noblest in which he could fall; and you may without
hesitation assure her, that I have regained a cheerful mind,
and only hope that the same unfailing spirit of goodness
who has surrounded me with objects to make life a great
blessing will give her the best gifts of earth, and make her
eternally happy in heaven, where all separations and dis-
quietudes will be healed. I meant but to say a few words
on this subject when I began it, and yet after a whole sheet
was not half satisfied with what I have written. You will
divine my thoughts more clearly than I have expressed them,
and will forgive my prolixity. It was like your kindness to
answer for my motive in halting at Constantinople. I only
got reproof for setting aside Talleyrand's motto,* but I acted honestly, and the more the politics of Toorkistan open
upon us, the more am I satisfied that my conduct was wise.
I trust that I shall prove it by gaining all that you kindly
wish me to obtain on the Jaxartes. Many thanks for your
offer of Baber's Memoirs, but I have already provided myself
with a copy. It will indeed be interesting to read the history and thoughts of this great man in the land of his birth.
You ask for my sentiments on Afghan affairs as modified
by personal observation. After I had ended my late journey through the country from Sukkur to Jellalabad, I submitted the impressions which I had noted on the way to
Sir William Macnaghten, who is the person best qualified
to judge and correct them. I consider the move into this
country unavoidable and politic; but did *I not* think so, I
would exclaim against the faintest thought of going back
again. The recent hesitation is likely to embarrass greatly

* 'Surtout, monsieur, point de zèle.'

if not to ruin us, whereas if we resolutely and literally set ourselves to consolidate the nationality of the Afghans and to get them good government, we shall after some years gain a full return for our money, and see that we have been the instruments of incalculable good. I feel very confident about all our policy in Central Asia, for I think that the designs of our Government there are honest, and that they will work with a blessing from God, who seems now to be breaking up all the barriers of the long-closed East, for the introduction of Christian knowledge and peace. It is deeply interesting to watch the effects that are being produced by the exertions of the European powers—some, selfish and contrary; others, still selfish, but qualified with peace and generosity; all made instrumental to good. See the French in Africa, the English, Austrians, and Russians on the Bosphorus, forcing the Turks to be Europeans under a shadow of Mohammedanism, and providing for the peaceful settlement of the fairest and most sacred countries in the world. Will you turn aside when you go home at the end of next year to see " those blessed acres which Our Saviour trod?" Syria, it seems, is to revert to the Porte. If so, and the new Sultan acts up to the "Hatti Scherifs" (Khat-e-Shereef) which he published soon after his accession, the now eager desire of the Jews to return to the Holy Land of their fathers will find speedy gratification. Did you attentively read that Khat-e-Shereef? If not, it may interest you to peruse the copy which I enclose. It has been considerably fingered, for I have been concocting from it an address which we hoped Shah Soojah would adopt; but his Majesty, I regret to say, ran a cold eye over the production, and said it was

much too refined for his lieges; that they had too much
wind in their heads already, and that he would consider
of something brief and more suited to their cur-like understandings. This is not quite the mood for an Afghan re-
generator. Sir William Macnaghten deals very tenderly
with him, and probably this brings him round to points
which our impatient desire for reform would overleap. If
the Envoy had a *carte blanche* at the Calcutta treasury, and
could say, " I'll give your Majesty so much to do so and so,"
we should get on better and faster, but Lord A. already begins to ask when the Shah will be able to keep himself,
while the King answers that proposal with " Give me time
to see what my means really are," and looks anxiously out
for members of his body politic to which he may apply the
screw. You and Sir James Carnac must back Sir William
against the easy-going secretaries, who, quietly entrenched
within the Ditch, rave about economy, and sententiously
recommend prudence. If we treat the Toorkistan question
liberally, we shall, I think, secure the great position which
we have now gained, and make our jealousy of Russian advance in this direction the means of purifying and enriching
to our future advantage the whole of Oosbeg Tartary. You
will have heard that my route has been changed, and that I
and Major Rawlinson are to proceed in the first instance to
the head-quarters of General Per-owsky, or -offsky, there to
see that he does not exceed the Emperor's declarations, and
I hope quietly to commence the arrangement which it is
proposed to base upon Kokund. You saw the "instructions "
issued to me for my mission to the latter state, and probably
guessed that I followed the usual practice of Envoys in

drawing them up for myself.   I am very glad that you approved of their tenor.   Sir James Carnac has also written
his approval of this mission, and comforted me with expressions like yours for the jobation that I got from home for
delaying at Constantinople.   His honour, moreover, very
kindly sent me a public acknowledgment that my labours in
this journey were esteemed, the which I add to the papers
now forwarded to please my brother, who thinks more
about me than I deserve.   Lord Auckland also wrote very
kindly to me.'

It had been arranged that Captain Conolly and Major
Rawlinson should proceed together to the Russian camp at
Khiva, but the failure of General Peroffski's expedition had
caused this plan to be abandoned ; and Lord Auckland was
growing more and more distrustful of the benefits of extending the 'great game' all over Central Asia.   Eager for
action as Conolly was, the folding up of a scheme which,
according to his perceptions, embraced nothing less than a
grand Anti-slavery Confederation, was a heavy disappointment to him.   ' I was greatly disappointed,' he wrote to the
same dear old friend at the end of May, ' when Lord Auckland's prohibitory letter arrived, for I had set my heart upon
this nobly-stirring employment, and when the chance of it
seemed removed, I felt the blank that a man must feel who
has a heavy grief as the first thing to fall back upon ; but
then, this very sorrow operated to compose me, showing
that I ought to sit loose to lesser disappointments.   Now
things look promising ; but the Governor-General is so
anxious to get off without embarking in anything new, that
he may put a second veto upon it, at least on onward

progress. I send you my Toorkish notions, contained in two letters to Lord Auckland, with a continuation of the proceedings of which I inflicted a first part upon you. Please send all on, when perused, to my brother William at Saharunpore, under frank. I am ashamed of the first page now that I read its murmuring tenor, but it is dark, and just post-time, and you will forgive my groans. I never utter them to anybody else. I hope to hear from you before we start. Write me your sentiments on my Toorkistan policy. Macnaghten will forward them after me, and it will be both a satisfaction to hear from you and a benefit to hear your suggestions. You need not care to write freely, for I am sure you will write nothing to offend the Ooroos, should your letter—which is not probable—fall into their hands. I am sure that extended liberality is the policy. If you agree with me, back the scheme.'

Upon this great question of the extension of our diplomacy in Toorkistan, the highest authorities were divided. Sir Alexander Burnes was strongly opposed to the scheme, as one involving extraordinary risks ; * but Sir W. Macnagh-

---

* The letters of Burnes to Dr Lord, in 1840, are full of emphatic protests against this expedition. During the preparation of the preceding Memoir, I noted down a number of passages illustrative of his opinions upon this subject, from which I take the following as sufficient for the purpose : 'March 26. Arthur Conolly has gone to Jellalabad. He is flighty, though a very nice fellow : he is to regenerate Toorkistan, dismiss all the slaves, and looks upon our advent as a design of Providence to spread Christianity. "Khiva is subdued by Russia," said I. "Bokhara is her ally, and Kokan not inimical, if not friendly. How, then, is the league to be formed, and how are you to get two hundred thousand Kuzzilbash slaves given up for nothing ? It must be done. Yes, with the wand of a Prospero ! ! !"' 'April

ten had imbibed some of the enthusiasm of his earnest-
minded relative, and had consented to impress upon the

5. But what will you say to the astounding announcement that Arthur
Conolly and Major Rawlinson are to go to Kokan? It seems mighty
civil to take all the work out of you, and send another to reap the
honours. The *Agra* says I am to go to Turkistan with General Sale,
but I have not heard a word of it, and have my little wish to do nothing of the kind as to the Kokan journey. I replied to the Envoy
that it would be found a tough job, and I thought would only irritate
Russia the more, that Bokhara, Kokan, and Khiva were all now
under Russia's grasp, and what could we do there? That as to
Bokhara, indeed, a mission there might, if it would be received, avail
us as letting us publish our views.' ' April 15. I told you that, if an
opportunity offered, I would have my say on this crotchet of Conolly
going to Kokan, and with my " observations " I said to Macnaghten
that you were a little startled at "being superseded towards Kokan
by Conolly," as I thought it the most delicate way to convey my
coincidence with your views. I received his reply yesterday, and
send it, as it also concerns you on other points. The Envoy's logic
is very bad. Conolly, it is true, applied to go to Khiva while in
England, and Sir J. Hobhouse referred the matter to the Governor-
General for consideration. When he got to Constantinople he met a
Kokan agent, and so much was he taken that he stopped, and referred to England the propriety of bringing an Oosbeg agent to London,
and pointed out the advantages of an alliance with Kokan. For this
he got a wig for delaying at Constantinople, and the wig he gave me
to read. How, after this, Macnaghten can bring himself to believe
that "Conolly has express instructions from the home authorities to
be employed in that quarter " (Kokan), I know not. Never you
mind, the journey is not feasible ; and if it is, the *cui bono* is not apparent, and I should be sincerely sorry to see you employed on it.
. . . . Since Conolly received my "observations," I have not heard
from him, but Ferris writes that "Conolly appears bent on taking
the trip to Kokan." ' 'May 13. There is something new : Kokan
pronounced impracticable, and Conolly going on a mission to the
Russian camp, consequent on instructions from Lord Auckland to
address General Peroffski. The plan was matured when I was at

Governor-General the advantages that might ensue from Conolly's mission to Kokund. Whilst the question was still in abeyance, about the middle of July, the latter wrote to Major Rawlinson, at Candahar, saying, ' Spite of all the encouragements to persevere that Todd's letters from Abbott and Shakespear afford, Burnes persists in believing that all interference in Toorkistan on our part has been and will be " insanity." " Our rear," he says, " is not secure enough." Then make it more so. But don't, for this imperfect reason, give up as lost the important ground in front, upon the independence of which from Russian control depends your retaining the necessary footing that you have gained

Pughman, and sent out, cut and dry, to me, saying that I was the man to go, but I could not be spared, and my health had not been very good ! ! I struck all out about my health, and offered to go at once ; to prevent all mistakes, however, I wrote to the Envoy officially, and as my letter will explain much, I send it and his reply.' ' May 26. Of the Khivan expedition under Conolly I have nothing new to communicate, further than that Rawlinson and he are preparing, and their start is to be regulated by the arrival of a Khivan Elchee (God save the mark !) *viâ* Candahar. I think they cool upon it, but perhaps I am wrong, and you shall hear further particulars in my next.' . . . ' June 13. Conolly having been beaten out of Kokan . . . has chalked out for himself a mission to Bokhara to release Stoddart, but it does not seem to be entertained. He will stand a fair chance of keeping Stoddart company if he goes, but it is very disgraceful we can do nothing to release Stoddart.' ' August 26. A. Conolly now says he will start on Friday, but what he goes for it would be impossible to say, seeing that Shakespear states, in his last despatch, that the Khan of Khiva had given up to him all his Russian prisoners, and that he was about to start with them for the first Russian fort ; if so, what is A. Conolly to do ? I would not mind betting he will never go at all, and if he goes, how is he to get on with this confederacy forming ahead ?'

in Afghanistan. Our endeavour to form a peaceful and
just confederation of the Oosbeg powers for the preservation
of their independence, cannot commit us in any way, while
the knowledge gained in the endeavour (supposing a failure,
which I do not) will better enable us to resort to the *ultima
ratio*, if the Ooroos should force such an appeal upon us. I
was much gratified by a perusal of Shakespear's letter; it
shows him to be a man of ready apprehension and sound
sense, and has given Sir William a very favourable idea of
his capacity, which he will not fail to report to the Governor-General. I shall be glad to think that I have such a
fellow-labourer in the field, if I am sent to any part of it,
which appears more than ever probable, though not yet
positive—though I have no end of regret that we did not
start at once for the Jaxartes together. . . . . . I think it
must end in my going to Khokund, probably *viâ* Khiva,
with the Envoy thence, Yakoob Bai, with whom I have
established great croneyism, in order that I may communicate Sir William's last instructions to Shakespear. Perhaps
I may come round by Bokhara, if the Ameer relents upon
the last forcible appeal that Sir William is about to make to
him through two Sahibzadehs, whom Shah Soojah sends
with a letter recapitulating all that he and his allies, the
English, have done to disabuse the Commander of the
Faithful of unjust notions and unnecessary apprehensions,
religious and political, and of all the insults and injuries that
the said allied Governments have received in return; briefly
ending with a request to know whether he is considered a
friend or enemy, and begging to be the medium of a similar
question from the English Government, who, considering

the long detention of their Envoy, Colonel Stoddart, *infra* their *dig.*, will expect his honourable release as the first sign of any friendly disposition that the Ameer may feel towards them, and require explanation of his conduct in thus treating their Ambassador and missives. I should have mentioned this first, but my brain has got muddled with much copying and original scribbling, this being a very busy day, and John * having shirked clerk's work for the organization of more Jan-Bazes.'

That the mission, which he so longed to undertake, was a perilous one, was not to be disguised. Captain Abbott had gone to Khiva, and had fought for his life. Colonel Stoddart had gone to Bokhara, and had been thrown into hopeless captivity. The liberation of poor Stoddart was one of the many benevolent objects which Conolly hoped to accomplish by his embassy. It was with much grief and disappointment, therefore, that he saw the efforts of our Government to obtain the release of their officer limited to the despatch of a letter from Shah Soojah to the Ameer of Bokhara. Even this was a slow process. 'At last,' wrote Conolly, on the 24th of July, to Major Rawlinson, 'we have got the letter to the Ameer of Bokhara, through the Shah's *dufter* (office), and the two Sahibzadehs propose starting with it to-morrow, which their calendar shows to be a remarkably fortunate day. May their errand be successful! Poor Stoddart's health was drunk last night at the Ghuzni anniversary dinner, among absent English friends, after a briefly eloquent speech by Sir Alexander,

* His brother, John Conolly, who was an attaché to the Caubul Mission.

who concluded by expressing a hope that if the last of Sir William Macnaghten's amicable endeavours to bring the Ameer to reason should fail, our gallant and unfortunate countryman would be released from captivity by *Baron Bokhara.* You may imagine the accent and energy with which Burnes thundered out the two last words.' Then, after a detailed account of other uproarious incidents of the anniversary dinner, he wrote, with characteristic delicacy of feeling : ' I felt very much ashamed of myself when my Ghibre lad handed me my cap and whip ; and I thought as we rode home, in the loveliest of calm nights, how very much English gentlemen let themselves down by these vulgar outbreaks. I remain in uncertainty about the Toorkistan journey. I must go at last, and if so, I'll write all the scientific parts of my researches to you, that you may add learned notes to them.' A few days afterwards he wrote again to the same correspondent, saying : ' If I ever cool my parched brow in the Jaxartes, I'll drink a goblet of its waters to the extension of your shadow in every direction. You've a great game, a *noble* game before you, and I have strong hope that you will be able to steer through all jealousy, and caprice, and sluggishness, till the Afghans unite with your own countrymen in appreciating your labours for a fine nation's regeneration and advancement. These are not big words, strung for sound or period. I didn't know that I could well express my desire more simply, certainly not when writing at a long canter to reach the post-bag ere it closes for the night. I've been rendering English into Persian, and Persian into English, till I feel quite addled, and every half hour brings one of

Sir William's comprehensive requests in a pencil note.'
The month of August dawned auspiciously, and the
clouds soon began to disappear. On the 4th he wrote, in
the highest spirits, to Major Rawlinson, at Candahar, saying :
' Hip, hip, hurrah ! I do believe that I am fairly going now,
so accept my best thanks for your congratulations. I receive them with a pang of real regret that you are not
going with me ; but Todd bids me be comforted with the
thoughts of your realized important elevation, so I'll utter
no vain words. Nothing can be done ahead, unless Afghanistan is properly settled, and I have confident hope of your
being highly instrumental to this desirable end.'
The fact was that help had come to him from an unexpected quarter. His old friend Syud Zahid, the Khokund
Envoy, with whom he had discussed the politics of Toorkistan in Constantinople, had written him a letter reminding
him of their past acquaintance, stating that it had sufficed
to keep him out of the hands of Russia, and adding that he
had been to Khiva, where he had seen Richmond Shakespear, but that he had hoped to hear from Conolly at
Meshed. Sir William Macnaghten lost no time in sending
a translation of this letter to the Governor-General, observ-
ing : ' The evidence which this letter affords of the importance that Syud Zahid continues to attach to the
friendship of the British Government, in that he has had
opportunity of consulting with the Court of Khiva about
the results of manifested intentions of Russia towards
Toorkistan, will, I have no doubt, be judged very satisfactory by his Lordship in Council. Syud Zahid shows that
he waited a whole month at Meshed in the hope of hearing

from Captain Conolly, who gave him to expect that he himself, or some other British officer, would be appointed to join him on the Persian frontier, for the purpose of proceeding with him, *viâ* Khiva, to Khokund; and the stress that he lays upon his sacrifice of Russian offers for the sake of English connection, is so strong, that I am of opinion we should no longer hesitate to show our sense of his friendly overtures, especially since it appears, from a private letter from Lieutenant Shakespear to Major Todd, that, judging from my former notifications of an intention to depute Captain Conolly and Major Rawlinson to Khokund, he had spoken at Khiva of the expected arrival there of the two officers in company with the Khan Huzrut's Envoy to this place.'

The precise objects of the mission were, as officially noted, the establishment of a correct impression, at every place which Conolly might visit, of British policy and strength, as it bore upon Asia and on Europe (with reference especially to our interference in Afghanistan), the strengthening of amicable arrangements with the chief Oosbeg powers, which had shown a friendly disposition towards us, and endeavouring to persuade them to help themselves, and enable us to help them, by doing prompt justice to their enemies, and forming an agreement with each other to prevent or to redress future injuries done by any one party among them to Russia, so as to deprive the latter power of all pretext for interfering with their independence. Either at Khiva or Khokund, Conolly was to learn the result of Shah Soojah's mission to Bokhara to obtain the release of Colonel Stoddart. If by the influence thus exerted, or by other means, the Ameer should be induced to exhibit a decided disposition to atone for his past conduct, and to resume friendly relations with us and the Afghan King, Conolly was authorized to return to Afghanistan *viâ* Bokhara. Otherwise, his course was to be regulated by circumstances.

The general scheme of the mission having been settled and the detailed instructions issued—which, after the manner of diplomacy generally, were drafted by Conolly himself—preparations were made for the journey, not the least of which was the selection of a fitting Afghan Envoy to accompany the British officer. This gave rise to some ridiculous intrigues and complications, which Conolly described with much humour in his correspondence. One candidate for the office was said to be ' a dreadfully modest and downcast man, who had never been heard of out of the Shah's chambers, and his Majesty confessed that he was chiefly meritorious as a candle-snuffer. So he was set aside ; ' and at last the choice settled on one Allahdad Khan, of the Populzye tribe, whom Conolly described as ' a scrubby-looking, sallow little man, with a scant beard and a restless eye, which seems to indicate all the disposition of intrigue.' Spoken of by the Shah's minister, who had said that Allahdad Khan was ' such an intriguant that it would take three hundred Cashmerees to make another such one.' ' So perhaps,' said Conolly, ' I read his visage by the false light of the latter old defamer's report (he never has a good word for mortal but himself, or some one in whom he is peculiarly interested), and shall find the Khan a good representative of the Afghan monarch. I have shaken hands with him as fast friends and fellow-workers for the great end that lies before us. Our departure,' he added, ' has been delayed for another week. I am sorry, and yet on some accounts glad, for it will enable me to cram a little more useful knowledge for the route, and to take leave of my many friends in waiting. Perhaps also I may get my long coming kit, in which are many things which I desire for the approaching voyage.'

At last, everything was ready for a start; and on the 22nd of August Conolly wrote to Rawlinson at Candahar: ' We are just on the wing, and I shall make the best of my way to the two capitals for which I carry credentials. Shakespear has really done wonders, and if we can follow up the good impressions which he and Abbott have made, if the British Government will give pecuniary aid, we may keep the Russians out of Toorkistan altogether, and bring about a fine order of things there for every party concerned; and I only wish again that you were to be of the party to accomplish it; but, as I said before, you occupy a high and useful station, and can't be at two places at once. If the British Government would only play the grand game—help Russia cordially to all that she has a right to expect—shake hands with Persia—get her all possible amends from the Oosbegs, and secure her such a frontier as would both keep these men-stealers and ravagers in wholesome check—take away her pretext for pushing herself in, letting herself be pushed on to the Oxus; force the Bokhara Ameer to be just to us, the Afghans, the other Oosbeg States, and his own kingdom. But why go on, you know my—at any rate in one sense—enlarged views. Inshallah! the expediency—nay, the necessity of them will be seen, and we shall play the noble part that the first Christian nations of the world ought to fill.' This, however, was only a false start. September found him still at Caubul, 'bothered and detained; ' but on the 3rd he reported that he was at last fairly off—' King's and Company's and Oorgunjee men,' commencing their first march.

It happened that at this time great events were taking shape in Afghanistan. The deposed Ameer of Caubul, who had for some time been an exile and a fugitive, was now returning to the land of his fathers and raising the tribes of the Hindoo Koosh in a last despairing effort to recover his lost dominions. A slender detachment of troops, principally of Shah Soojah's army, posted at Bameean, was threatened by the advancing levies of the ex-Ameer, and it was necessary to send a regiment of the Company's troops to reinforce them. They started from Caubul at the very time of Conolly's departure; so he accompanied them, and was present in Brigadier Dennie's action with Dost Mahomed and the Wallee of Khooloom on the 18th of September. The victory then gained cleared the way for the advance of the British Mission; so Conolly and his party pushed on through the country of the Hazarehs, without any remarkable adventures by the way. Ever as he went there rose up before him fresh evidences of the ubiquity of the detestable traffic in human flesh, which it was the darling object of his soul to suppress. 'The articles,' he wrote in his journal, 'which the Hazarehs and Imauk take to market are *men and women*, small black oxen, cows, sheep,' &c. &c. In the neighbourhood of Maimunah he found that slaves were the representatives of value in that part of the country. One man offered him a good horse in exchange for a pony and a young male slave. When Conolly asked him if he were not ashamed of dealing in God's creatures, he apologized by saying that he did not mean a slave in the flesh, but the money-value of a slave—' showing,' said Conolly, ' that men are here a standard of barter, as sheep are among the Hazarehs.'

There was a war then raging between the Imauks and the Hazarehs, which greatly increased the difficulties and the dangers of the journey, but after some adventures, Conolly and his companions reached Merv, which is the head-quarters of the slave-trade of Toorkistan. Here the things which he saw filled his soul with measureless compassion, and excited the keenest indignation. And he suffered all the more in the presence of so much iniquity, because he felt that he was condemned to silence. ' I have found it necessary,' he said, ' to repress even the expression of our sympathies for the strangers who are so unhappily enslaved in this country, for the interference of Abbott and Shakespear for the release of the Russian captives has given rise to an idea, which has spread like wildfire through Toorkistan, that the English have come forward as deliverers of all who are in bondage there—a notion which, grateful as it may be to our national reputation, required to be corrected by all who come to Oosbeg Tartary in any political character, lest it should excite the enmity of slave-owners against all our efforts for good among them, as well as increase the unhappiness of the enslaved. To you, however, I may mention that the state

of affairs here is pitiable in the extreme, and such as to
make every Englishman who witnesses it most earnestly
reprobate the idea of our consenting to its continuance for
the sake of any political contingency whatever.' Determined, as he said, to examine into all the sins of the place,
he rode into the slave-market, and saw 'enough to shame
and sicken the coarsest heart.' Slaves of both sexes and
all ages were exposed for sale, and intending purchasers
were going about from one group to another, 'handling
them like cattle.' * But other feelings than these were

* To this Conolly adds : 'Judge only from the following note.
As we came out from visiting the Bai (governor), a party of Zekkah
Toorkomans unceremoniously entered, bearing three blackened skulls
upon the point of lances, and leading. thirty bound persons from
Kelat-i-Nadier, who, with thirty-six horses, had been recently cap-
tured in a chupao. When they had reported the success of their expedition, these bandits gave the governor two men and two horses
for his share, excusing themselves from paying the full proportion of
one in ten, on the plea that they had lost or injured some of their
own horses. They then presented the heads of their victims, and
having received five tillas for each, received orders to parade them
through the bazaar, it being market-day, where I, an hour afterwards,
saw them again hung by the beards to a pole. Determined to examine
into all the sins of this place, which had been reported by my servants, I ordered my horse when the market was warm, and riding
through every corner of it, saw enough to sicken and shame the
coarsest heart. The camel and horse fair was conducted on level
spots outside the streets of standing shops in which the necessaries of
life were displayed among a few luxuries by the resident traders. At
the doors of many of these shops females of different ages under that
at which they could no longer be recommended for their personal at-
tractions, were placed for show, tricked in good clothes put on them
for the occasion, and having their eyes streaked with antimony to set
off their countenances. Others past their prime, with children of poor

raised by the sight of the desolate grandeur of the ruins of Merv. His eager imagination grasped the idea of its restoration to its pristine glories; and he exclaimed : ' Shall we not, some of these days, exert the influences, which our grand move across the Indus has gained for us, to make Merv once more " a King of the Earth," by fixing its borders in peace between the destructively hostile parties, who now keep up useless claims to it, and by causing the desolate city to rise again, in the centre of its national fruits, as an emporium for commerce, and a link in the chain of civilizing intercourse between Europe and Asia ? '

' Our route from Merv to Khiva,' wrote Conolly in his report, ' struck into that taken before us by Shakespear. From the canal beyond the Murghab, at which we halted to lay in water, we marched seventeen miles north to camp in the desert. In the first ten miles were visible in

appearance, were grouped, males and females together, in corners of the streets, and handled like cattle ; and I saw small mud pens, a little above the height of a man, enclosed on all sides, into which intending purchasers take either male or female captives that they fancy, for the purpose of stripping them naked to see that they have no bodily defects.' So inveterate were these slave-dealing propensities among the Khivans, that even the Envoy who accompanied Conolly on the part of the Khan Huzrut, was carrying on a little quiet traffic on the road. ' Every defenceless person,' wrote Conolly, ' who can be used for labour, is carried off to the insatiable markets of Tartary. We were followed by a small kafilah of slaves from Maimunah, consisting of Sheah Huzarehs and Soonee Imauks of all ages, from five to thirty, and we actually discovered that the children of this lot had been purchased on a speculation by our colleague, the Khivan Envoy, while towards us he was reprobating the practice as irreligious and impolitic, and expressing hypocritical hope that it would soon cease out of all their countries.'

all directions the ruins of former little castles, about which
lay broken bricks and pottery. After the first two miles
we found thin drift-sand lying here and there upon the hard
clay plain, but there was none to signify, even to the end
of the stage; and it may be inferred that if, after so many
years of abandonment, so little sand has been collected
here, the annual drift in time of full habitation and tillage
would not be left. Next day we marched eighteen miles
north to the single well of Tereh, the road generally over
sand, which lay half-hoof deep upon the hard plain, though
occasionally we had to pass deep beds, gathered loosely
upon this foundation. Every now and then a patch of the
hard soil appeared quite bare, and we could observe here
and onwards to the Oxus, that in soil of this description are
set the roots of nearly all the bushes and shrubs which
cover the surface of the wilderness. . . . . . The sixth
march of twenty miles, over similar sandy and undulating
plains, took us to Tukt—a spot from which this road is
named—marked by a broad belt of bare, loose sand-hills,
which rise over each other towards the centre from the
length of twenty to eighty feet, and serve as reservoirs for
the snow and rain-water that fall upon them. We found
holes about three feet deep, dug at the bases of the most
sheltered sand-hills, containing a foot or more of filtered
and deliciously sweet water, and it was only necessary on
draining a hole to scoop a little more sand from its bottom,
and to wait a while for a fresh supply to rise into it.' The
seventh march carried him on fifteen miles with the same
excellent supply of water. The eighth took him the same
distance to the 'broad dry bed of the Oxus,' in which he

encamped 'amongst reeds and jungle-wood, near the left bank of the actual river, where the stream was six hundred and fifty yards broad, flowing in eddies, with the dirty colour of the Ganges, at the rate of two miles and three-quarters an hour. A noble stream,' he added, 'but, alas! without anything in the shape of a boat upon it.' He looked in vain for traces of civilization, and grieved over their absence.

The beginning of the new year (1841) found him at Khiva, waiting for the arrival of the ruler of that place, the 'Khan Huzrut,' who was then absent from his capital on a hunting excursion. On the return of the Khan, he received the English Envoy with becoming courtesy and respect. Conolly described him as a dignified and gentle-man-like person, about fifty years of age, gentle in his manners, kindly and affable in his address, with a low pleasant voice, and a habitual smile upon his face. In the presence of such a man Conolly soon felt himself at ease, and several lengthened conferences took place in the Khan's tent. Conolly spoke in Persian, and the Khan in Toorkish, and a native official interpreted between them. The Khan was altogether in a warlike frame of mind, and not a little boastful in his speech. 'He was determined,' he said, 'to punish the Khokundees; and as to the Persians and the Russians, let them come.' When Conolly pointed out the danger of this, he said : ' If the Persians obtain European aid to invade me, I will employ your aid to repel them.' 'The British Government,' replied Conolly, 'will doubtless do its utmost in every case to prevent the borders of Kharasm from being broken up; but it cannot take part against any of your Majesty's enemies who may come with a just ground for invasion.' 'What just ground,' asked the Khan, 'can the Persians assert?' 'One,' replied Conolly, 'which no third nation can disallow—that your Majesty's subjects carry off their men, women, and children, and sell them like four-footed beasts.' But nothing could persuade the Khan Huzrut that any real dangers beset him. He was obdurate and unimpressionable; and even when Conolly told him that, in the event of a Persian advance into Toorkistan, the whole slave population would rise against him, he still smiled at the picture that was placed before him.

It was doubted in the Council Chamber of Calcutta whether Arthur Conolly, in these conferences with the Khan Huzrut, had diplomatically played his part well. But diplomacy and philanthropy are too often divorced. It was said that British influence at Khiva was 'based on his (the Khan's) looking on us as helpers to get out of difficulties he does see. If we point out and preach about difficulties he does *not* see, he will think we create them.' But whatever may be the soundness of this—and in good truth I do not dispute it—on the whole, perhaps, it is pleasant to think of that eager, ardent humanity which would not suffer him for a moment to forget the foul traffic in human flesh, which was the shame of the Oosbeg States, and, as he believed, of every nation that passively permitted it. But it was plain that Arthur Conolly was drifting into danger; and one who was at the same time his relative, his dear friend, and his honoured political chief, wrote to him in the hope of saving him. 'I have told you, in several of my late letters,' wrote Sir William Macnaghten, 'that I feared your zeal would lead you into difficulties, and I have implored you not to attempt too much either in the cause of Policy or Humanity. Inveterate habits arc not to be got rid of by any sudden exertion of diplomatic skill. You are considered as being a great deal too high in your language and too visionary in your views. You must adapt yourself to the sober and unambitious tone of the Council Board.' And then came an extract, to the effect indicated above, from the letter of a member of the Supreme Council. But Macnaghten's letter never reached Arthur Conolly. By what process it came into my hands I know not; but ît lies before me as clean and as little travel-stained as if it had been written yesterday in Belgravia.

During his sojourn here, Conolly wrote a long and interesting letter to Major Rawlinson, in which he said: ' I have resumed my communications to Sir J. Hobhouse, lest I should be thought sulky at the hard blows sent to me from Cannon-row, since the days in which I experienced his great kindness there. I feel comforted under these severities by a conviction that I acted honestly and by a strong notion that I acted rightly, which is not saying a very great deal for myself, since it is natural that a moderate capacity which has had its attention directed to a subject for several years should form a more extensive view of it than the mind of the greatest genius upon whom it comes in all its complications with suddenness. Sir J. H., though fiery and somewhat resolved in his first opinions, is a generous-hearted and just man, and when at the end he sees that the Secret Committee has been too rigid, he will, I doubt not, cause all possible amends to be made. If this consummation should not reward my submission, I must just close the account, as the Khan does that of his troubles, by placing against the balance—*Kismut!* Some rubs have been inflicted which don't heal, but leave scars on the heart that go to a longer settling day. Those who give concise verdicts should remember this before they accuse a man of anything approaching to deception, as some confidential clerk did in my case with three flourishes of a goose-quill ere stepping into his omnibus for Putney. . . . . I shall be anxious to know how Sir Alexander (Burnes) treats this matter. He judged the missions of Abbott and Shakespear to be measures of "perfect insanity;" but now they have been productive of much good result, I trust that he will see the expediency of "going ahead" to make the most of the work. Or will he say that the Ides of March are not yet past, and still hook on a caution to my impatient wheels? I do believe that but for Burnes's "khabburdar" (take care) to Lord Auckland, I should ere this have taken measure of the Jaxartes; but when he succeeds to the ministerial chair at Caubul, he will see much farther over the Hindoo Koosh than he can be expected to do in a seat which gives him no reins to hold, and I shall look for his patronage of my largest plan. You will see that in my letter to Sir William I have taken the liberty of quoting your opinion as well as Todd's about the supposed sanction to the advance. I have done this in self-defence, lest it should be made to appear that I have marked Khokund as a point on the face of the earth

which I, Arthur Conolly, must reach, be it for good or
be it for evil. It really is not so. I have already given
reasons enough to you for wishing to proceed; but I will
cheerfully go to any one of the cardinal points that remain,
if the authorities that be so order my steps. I don't understand Lord Auckland's revoke, unless the question has
become a duel between the political chief of Caubul and
the political secretary in Calcutta. . . ,. . . Our mission
was to Khiva and Khokund; the despatch does not mention the first place with a limitation, and the Envoy's loving
friends display such an indefinite acquaintance with the
country beyond the Hindoo Koosh, in which troops were
to be placed to prevent the spreading of false rumours,
that it is not to be inferred from their communications that
they did not mean us to go the whole hog, if such a simile
may, without offence, be applied to a Mahomedan country.'
. . . . . 'Men who think at all about the events which
cast their shadows before them,' wrote Conolly, in conclusion, ' must foresee such questions. Is it fair, is it politic,
to send one of their agents half-a-dozen vague expressions
which make him a stammerer where he should be decided,
instead of manfully summing up the contingencies, and
saying in such and such case we would do so and so, and
you may give assurance to this extent? The Khan Huzrut
will be in in a few days, and I shall be able to discover
what he thinks of the demands for hostages. I don't
anticipate his making any difficulty. It's quite in the
Tartar way, and occasionally affords a convenient mode of
providing for troublesome members of the Royal Family.
His Majesty of Khiva must now know pretty well that the

Emperor would not kill or maim his lease of pledges in the event of a quarrel, so they would be no more than resident ambassadors. The Czar might indeed send such persons to Siberia on their chief's offending; but perhaps the Khan Huzrut would not care much about their banishment, and they themselves would probably have no great choice, so long as they got plenty of tea, which abounds in all Russia. Indeed, according to Captain Cochrane, Siberia is an exceedingly pleasant place. But what shall we say for Russia's return to the barbarism out of which she has been striving in so many ways to grow? Unless Count Nesselrode abandons the point of the treaty, he will be compared to the cannibal woman of New Holland, who, after having been restrained from the evil propensity of her girlish days, and made to educate a whole colony of white children with the utmost tenderness, fell sick beyond physician's healing, and was told that she might eat anything she took a fancy to, when she with dying accents expressed a longing for the arm of a young baby. Give a dog a bad name, and you know the consequence. We do our worst to prevent the intellectual advance of the Russians by abusing them.'

Authentic intelligence of the traveller here halts a little. That Conolly was in Khiva in the first week of January, 1841, and that he then believed that his departure would not be much longer delayed, is certain. The statement of the Akhond-Zadeh, Saleh Mahomed, the accuracy of which, so far as it goes, is generally admitted, supplies no dates. But he says that he remained at Khiva with Captain Conolly seven months; that Conolly then sent him to Caubul with

despatches; and that when he returned to Khiva the English gentleman had gone on to Khokund. At the latter
place he received a letter from Colonel Stoddart, written at
the request of the Khan of Bokhara, inviting him to that
city. This letter must have been written before July, for
on the 7th of that month Colonel Stoddart wrote to Major
Rawlinson, saying: 'Conolly is not yet here from Khokund,
nor have my messengers to him yet returned. They conveyed the orders from Caubul, and an invitation from the
Ameer to return by this route.' * At what time this letter
reached him is uncertain; and there is some doubt respecting the date at which he entered Bokhara. In one of his
last letters from that city,† he said: 'The Khan treacherously caused Stoddart to invite me here on his own *Imanut-*

* Captain Grover says : 'Encouraged by the kind and courteous
terms in which the Ameer granted his' request, Captain Conolly, after
much trouble, succeeded in obtaining the permission of the King of
Kokan, Mohammed Ali, which was only granted on condition that
he went round by Tashkend, so that he might not become acquainted
with the road the Ameer would have to follow to reach Kokan.
After many difficulties, in consequence of the state of the country,
Captain Conolly succeeded in reaching Djizakh, where the governor
informed him that the Ameer was at Hodjend. He hastened there,
expecting a kind reception ; the Ameer had, however, already left
that town, and Captain Conolly overtook him at a place called Meh-
ram. The Ameer being informed of Captain Conolly's arrival,
ordered his immediate attendance. He was conducted to a tent without a carpet, where he was allowed to remain two hours unnoticed.
An order then came from the Ameer that he was to go to the Naib,
Abd-ool Samet Khan, who accompanied the army ; and this man
was ordered to convey him immediately to Bokhara, where they
arrived on the 9th of November, 1841.'
† Given entire at page 366 *et seq.*

nameh; and after Stoddart had given him a translation of
a letter from Lord Palmerston, containing nothing but
friendly assurances, which he could have verified with our
entire consent at the Russian Embassy, he pent us both up
here to pay him, as a kidnapper, for our release, or to die
by slow rot.'

I have always conceived that this happened a little
before Christmas, 1841, because at the end of February
Conolly wrote that he had been seventy-one days in confinement. But the Russian Colonel Bouteneff, who was
at Bokhara at the time, in an official report to his Government, says : 'Colonel Conolly was arrested on his arrival
here in October last, and all his effects were sold in public;
with him was imprisoned for the second time Lieutenant-
Colonel Stoddart. The Emir, however, before their arrest,
promised me that they should be allowed to accompany me
back to Bokhara.'*

Notwithstanding this high authority, I am still disposed
to think that Conolly was not thrown into prison before
the third week of December. Saleh Mahomed said that
he reached the Bokhara frontier about the middle of
December, and was then told that two days before his arrival the English gentlemen had been seized and confined.
And one of Conolly's own servants distinctly stated that
his master was not imprisoned until after the arrival of
intelligence of the November outbreak at Caubul. For
now all Afghanistan was in a blaze. The 'great game'
had exploded. The Afghans had risen as one man against
their deliverers. Sekundur Burnes, who had visited Bokhara

* Mitchel's 'Russians in Central Asia.'

some years before, had been killed, and all his countrymen were in deadly peril. What, then, could the Feringhees, who were plainly at their last gasp, do either to liberate Stoddart and Conolly, or to avenge their deaths? So it happened that about the time when Sir William Macnaghten was slain by the hand of Akbar Khan, his kinsman, Arthur Conolly, was cast into hopeless and most miserable captivity.

January passed, and February passed, and there were occasional gleams of hope, and the captives bore up right manfully, in spite of all their sufferings. Conolly contrived to save some sheets of Russian paper and apparently a reed pen, with which, in very small characters, he kept a record of what passed. The journal is so interesting, that I give the principal part of it. The following are the entries of January and February: ' January 2, 1842. Allahdad Khan's servants arrived from Karshee: they were brought up to the court outside the wall of our prison, with his horses and baggage, and in the evening they were sent down to the town, to our late residence, we were assured, but we had no opportunity of verifying the statement. We learned from our guardians that the Walee's man, Moolla Shums, had been brought back with A. Khan's people, but let go again—— 8th. The brother of the Topshee-Bashee, who felt pity for us, told me in confidence that Akhond-Zadeh, Saleh Mahomed, was confined without his servants in the Topshee-Bashee's office, and that he remained very ill; also that a messenger had been sent out as far as Kara-Kool to meet him and to take away his letters.   Got intelligence conveyed by the old man to the Akhond-Zadeh that we were in prison near him—— 29th. A humble friend of Stoddart's, " Long Joseph," [   ] to the Ameer, very boldly and kindly came on some pretence to the Topshee-Bashee's house, and looking in upon us, said, hastily, " All the Afghans have been given their head." We judged that he meant our servants, who had been in prison and dismissed, though our guardians and the Topshee-Bashee said that our people remained in our late residence—— 31st. This morning a Mehrum came to desire that we would minutely describe the city and castle of Caubul, and also give an account of Herat. Allahdad Khan drew a plan of the first place ; Stoddart was named as the one who best knew the second, but the Mehrum did not take his account of it. We next day learned that he had been sent to the Akhond-Zadeh, who had drawn a large plan of his native city—— February 9th. Moolla Nasir came to ask if we had seen the Peacock Throne of India. As every lettered Asiatic should know that Nadir Shah carried that throne away to Persia, and Moolla Nasir's manner was pointedly kind, we judged that the question he had been sent to ask was merely a pretence, and that the Ameer desired an opening for a return to proper treatment of us. Stoddart, therefore, gave him this, by speaking of his position here as British Agent, and expressing regret that he had not been able to relieve the Huzrut's mind from the doubts which he seemed to entertain of the English Government's friendship. We showed the sad state of our clothes (Stoddart had been obliged to put aside his shirt in consequence of the roof's having leaked over him the night before);

and expressed a hope that the Ameer would soon improve
our condition.   But we both spoke cheerfully, that the King
might not think we entertained resentment for his treatment
of us—— 13th. Last day of A. H. 1257. At sunset Allahdad
Khan was taken away from us ; the Topshee-Bashee first
said, to his office, afterwards to the Dustan Kanchee's house.
The old [   ] afterwards told us that the Akhond-
Zadeh had been removed also to the Dustan Kanchee's, but
we have doubts regarding both statements, for the accounts
which our keepers give of my late colleague's quarters vary,
and a servant of Colonel Stoddart's, who had been sent to
the Russian Ambassador's openly with a book, and was said
to have been detained at the same Prime Minister's house,
came back, after twenty-five days, with his back cruelly
scored by the heavy-stick flogging in practice here, to say
that he had been confined all the time in the " Kenneh-
khameh," or Bughouse of the gaol—— 15th. A boy
Mehrum came with one of my thermometers to ask how
much cold there had been in the night, stating that it had
been observed to the mark of four degrees below zero.
We mentioned that we had been unable to sleep all night
for the cold.   This day " Long Joseph " gallantly darted
into our room, and carried off a note which we had written
to Colonel Bouteneff to inform him of our situation——
16th. " Long Joseph" having won a servant of the Topshee-
Bashee's, conveyed to us a note from the gaoler.   I sent it
to him, Stoddart writing to Government through Sir J.
M'Neill.   We hoped from Moolla Nasir's visit, and that of
the page who brought my thermometer, that the Ameer
was relenting, but nothing has since occurred to favour this.

idea; on the contrary, the chief would appear to find
pleasure in his servants' accounts of our discomforts, which
may be imagined from the fact that we have now been
seventy-one days and nights without means of changing or
washing our linen, which is hanging in filthy tatters from
our persons. The Topshee-Bashee, who looks in upon us
every seven or eight days, replies to our entreaties for an improvement in this respect, that our state must be well known
to the Huzrut, whose mind retains thoughts of the greatest
and least matters, and that nothing can be said to his Majesty
about us till he opens the subject. The Topshee-Bashee
has, I believe, been as kind to us as he has dared to be.
We have had quite enough firing and food throughout the
cold season we have passed in his house, and continue, thank
God, in good health! We sometimes think, from the
Ameer's keeping back Said's and the Akhond-Zadeh's
packets, that he must have received the Governor-General's
communication, and that he is acting big in irritation at
not having been answered from the English throne; but it
is impossible to form certain conclusions from his conduct,
for it is very often influenced by caprice, which is not very
far from madness. We hope that all is well in Afghanistan,
and that, soon as the Hindoo-Koosh roads become open,
the Ameer will receive some communication which will
induce him to properly treat or dismiss us. We beg that
Government will convey its sentiments to the Ameer in
Persian, as he will not take our word for what is written
in English any longer than it suits him; and also that no
allusion may be made to the above details, for if the King
knew that we were able to send intelligence he might treat

us worse, and perhaps kill everybody about us. The
Russians propose to go about No-roz. We kept Colonel
Bouteneff informed of our proceedings up to the date of our
seizure, and if he should reach Europe ere our release he
may be able to enlarge this abstract, which is necessarily
very imperfect. I took the accounts of my mission in
English up to the time of our leaving Khokund from
Augustin, who kept the whole in Greek. My memoranda
or his may be recovered. Augustin is a very honest and
worthy man. Having myself no money, and thinking that
Stoddart was about to be sent away immediately, I took
from Naib Abdool Sammud three thousand tillas, which he
wished to have invested in Company's paper. The greatest
part of this remained in Augustin's hands when we were
seized. My Afghan servants have all behaved well. I
reported that Shah Mahomed Khan, Adum Khan, and
Mousa, with one of Allahdad Khan's men, were completely
stripped in the Ameer's camp when they carried our letters
to his Majesty announcing our coming from Khokund.
None of their property was restored to them. My notes
from Khiva to Khokund and this place were in charge of
my faithful servant (formerly Shakespear's), Gool Mahomed : perhaps he was able to preserve them. In the portion
not made up, for every minute of progress one hundred and
seventeen yards is to be allowed, the pace of my horse,
where not otherwise noted, having been calculated at four
miles per hour. In my observations of the sun's meridional
altitude, the *lower* limb was always taken.' *

* On one side of the paper containing the above were written the
following notes :

In the second week of March, Arthur Conolly's powers of physical endurance gave way. Fever seized upon him, and believing that his days were numbered, he wrote to his brother John at Caubul, saying : ' From our Prison in the Bokhara Citadel, 11th of March, 1842. This will probably be my last note hence, so I dedicate it to you, who now, alas ! stand next to me. We both dedicate everything we feel warmest to William, whom may God bless in all belonging to him, for his long and untiring brotherly affection to us all. Send my best love to Henry and to all our dear sisters. This is the eighty-third day that we have been denied the means of getting a change of linen from the

---

' Bokhara, February 28, 1842.

' To the Secretary of the Government of India, &c.

' SIR,—The Governor-General in Council will be informed by the accompanying abstract how far my position here [and that of Captain Conolly] has been sacrificed.

' I have the honour to be, &c. &c.

' C. STODDART.

' P.S. This is left open for the perusal of the Envoy and Minister at Caubul.'

The words in brackets were erased by Conolly.

' MY DEAR JOHN,—Keep all friends informed of my health, and don't let them be disturbed by rumours.

' Yours affectionately,

'A. C.'

' Bokhara, February 28, 1842.

' MY DEAREST JANE,—Best love to you all. Say something very kind for me to all at Chilham. . . . Kind remembrances to all. Don't believe all you hear or may hear.

' Your ever affectionate brother,

'CHARLES STODDART.

' To Miss Stoddart, Norwich.'

rags and vermin that cover us; and yesterday, when we
begged for an amendment in this respect, the Topshee-
Bashee, who had before come occasionally to our host to
speak encouragingly, set his face like a flint to our request,
showing that he was merely a vane to the withering
wind of his heartless master, and could not help us thus,
so that we need not ask him to do so. This, at first,
astonished and defeated us; we had viewed the Ameer's
conduct as perhaps dictated by mad caprice; but now,
looking back upon the whole, we saw instead that it had
been just the deliberate malice of a demon, questioning and
raising our hopes, and ascertaining our condition, only to
see how our hearts were going on, in the process of breaking. I did not think to shed one warm tear among such
cold-blooded men, but yesterday evening, as I looked upon
Stoddart's half-naked and nail-lacerated body, conceiving
that I was the special object of the King's hatred, because
of my having come to him after visiting Khiva and Khokund,* and told him that the British Government was too

---

* It has been said that Conolly had no authority to go beyond
Kokund, and that he brought all his troubles on himself by exceeding
his instructions. But this is a mistake. Full permission for the
journey was granted by the Supreme Government. ' As in the present
aspect of affairs,' wrote the Chief Secretary (Dec. 28, 1840) to Sir
William Macnaghten, ' it does not seem necessary to continue the
restriction which had at first been imposed, the Governor-General in
Council authorizes you to permit Captain Conolly to proceed from
Khiva to Khokund, if he should think it expedient, and if he
finds that he can do so without exciting serious distrust and jealousy
at the former place. In his personal intercourse with the Khan of
Khokund he will be guided by the instructions which have been
issued prescribing the purport of his written communications. Cap-

great to stir up secret enmity against any of its enemies, I
wept on entreating one of our keepers, the gunner's brother,
to have conveyed to the Chief my humble request that he
would direct his anger upon me, and not further destroy,
by it, my poor brother Stoddart, who had suffered so much
and so meekly here for three years. My earnest words were
answered by a " Don't cry and distress yourself; " he also
could do nothing. So we turned and kissed each other, and
prayed together, and then said, in the words of the Kokun-
dees, " My-bish! " Let him do as he likes! he is a demon,
but God is stronger than the devil himself, and can certainly
release us from the hands of this fiend, whose heart he has,
perhaps, hardened to work out great ends by it; and we
have risen again from bed with hearts comforted, as if an
angel had spoken to them, resolved, please God, to wear
our English honesty and dignity to the last, within all the
filth and misery that this monster may try to degrade us
with. We hope that, though the Ameer should now dismiss us with gold clothing, the British and Afghan Governments will treat him as an enemy; and this out of no feeling of revenge. He treacherously caused Stoddart to invite
me here on his own Imanut-nameh; and after Stoddart had
given him a translation of a letter from Lord Palmerston,
containing nothing but friendly assurances, which he could
have verified, with our entire consent, at the Russian Em-

tain Conolly may in such a journey find increased means of using an
useful influence at Bokhara for the release of Colonel Stoddart, and
his Lordship in Council need not add that he would wish every such
means to be employed with the utmost earnestness and diligence for
that purpose.'

bassy, he pent us both up here, because we would not pay
him as a kidnapper for our release, to die by slow rot, if it
should appear that he might venture at last to put us altogether out of the way.   We hope and pray that God may
forgive him his sins in the next world ; but we also trust
that some human power will soon put him down from his
oppressive throne at this capital, whence emanates the law
by which the Khivans harry and desolate the roads and
homes of the Persians.   He wishes every soul to crouch
before him, and not breathe God's air freely without his
leave, nor dare to be happy or at ease.   For instance (and
we are at the fountain-head of police report), a poor wretch,
confined without food for three days and nights in the Bughouse, an infernal hole used for severe imprisonment, said
incautiously, on being taken out, that he was alive and well.
" He is, is he ? " said the Ameer, on the report, " then put
him in for three days and nights more."   Again, the other
night fifty-six grooms assembled at a house outside the city,
to make merry on pilau and tea, with money liberally given
by one of the Oosbeg men, Rahman Kool Tosh-aba, to his
head groom, who acted as master of the feast ; they were
convicted of having got together, so all that the police-
master could seize received seventy-five blows each on his
back with a heavy thorn stick ; and because one man un-
complainingly bore his punishment, which was inflicted on
all before the King, he had him hoisted for seventy-five
more, saying, " He must have been struck softly."   " But
what was the crime in this innocent meeting of poor
grooms ? " we asked our gaolers.   " Who knows ?—he is a
King, and gave the order."   The master of the entertain-

ment stood with his dagger against some thirty policemen, till he was felled by a stone thrown at his head, to let all who could escape; for this heavier offence he was condemned to be thrown from a part of the citadel wall, which gives a culprit a chance of escape with only the fracture of a limb, because it has a slope; he threatened to pull down with him any who should approach the brink to throw him off, and, leaping boldly down, came to the ground with whole bones, and lives, let us hope, for many a happy meeting yet with his friends in this now oppressed city. This is how the Ameer would treat such ambassadors as he dares insult, who do not bend reverently enough before him ; but the days for such despotism are passing quick, and he must himself be made to go down before the strong spirit of western civilization. Stoddart has asked me to put on paper my notions as to the measures that should now be adopted for the settlement and independent happiness of the Central Asian States ;—here they are, briefly and freely ; those of a man born and bred, thank God! in Protestant England, who has seen Russia, Persia, and Afghanistan, and all the three Oosbeg States. Turn out the horrible Wuzeer Yar Mahomed Khan, who has sold twelve thousand men, women, and children, since he obliged the Persians to retire from Herat, and buy out Kamran's family from that principality. Kamran himself forfeited all his kingly right here by his letter to the Khan Huzrut of Khiva, which the latter chief gave me in return for my frank communication to him, and which I sent to Sir William Macnaghten. Thus will be gained the only point from which the Afghan nation can lend its weight to the preservation of peace and the advancement of civilization in Toorkistan, protect its weakest subjects from being stolen or sold away, and properly guard its own and India's frontier. Next, let Pottinger come in attendance upon Shah Soojah's heir-apparent, Shahzadah Timour, with a few thousand select Afghan horsemen of both the tribes, half Douranee and half Ghilzye, to blow down the gate of the citadel, which unjustly imprisoned us, against the rights of all nations, except those the Oosbegs profess. The Ameer scornfully says that the Afghans and English are one people; let him feel that they really are so in a good cause. I really do believe that if Shahzadah Timour were to return, after such a proceeding, to assume the actual exercise of government at his father's capital, taking back with him all real Afghans now enslaved in Toorkistan, whose orthodoxy, according to the Soonees, is unquestionable, and who might easily be collected for a friendly offering, the Afghans would so thoroughly like him and understand us, that every English and Indian soldier might be withdrawn to Hindostan. Let the Shah-i-Shah of Persia at the same time write these few words to the Court of the faithful at Bokhara, sending copies of his letter by friendly and high ambassadors to Khiva and Khokund: "I want all my enslaved subjects who are not willing to remain in Bokhara, and I am now coming, in reliance upon the only God of justice, to free them, and to destroy the law of thy Mooftehed, by which people who pray towards the same Kebla are sold as cattle." Let Mahomed Shah lithograph this, and send a copy to be stuck up at every mosque where his authority or influence can reach, in Persia, Afghanistan, and Tartary. This writing will tell the Ameer that his king-

dom has been weighed and found wanting ; it will do much
to soften and liberalize Mahomedan feeling wherever it is
read ; and if the Persian nation are informed that it comes to
them recommended by English sympathy, they will dismiss
all irritation of mind that was caused by our checking their
military career at Herat. I feel confident that this great
and most necessary measure of Persian emancipation may
be effected at once, without shedding one drop of blood. I
never uttered a word of hostility against the Ameer, either
at Khiva or Khokund ; but now I am authorized to show
how I thought the rulers of these States, who both hate him,
may be made to end or lessen their own foolish enmity by
his removing from between them. Let the Shah of Persia
send a firman to Syud Mahomed Zahed, Kurruck Kojeh at
Khokund, whom he knows, saying : " Tell the Khan Huzrut of Khokund, who I am happy to find does not deal
in my people, that I am about to liberate all those oppressed
men and women who are unwillingly detained as slaves in
Bokhara. I don't want that country ; and if you will send
Lushkur Begglerbeggee, or Mahomed Shereff Atalik, with
the Khokund army about the same time to Samarcand, my
prime minister shall make it over to him by treaty, as the
capital of Mawarulneh. I shall give up Merve to the Khan
Huzrut of Khiva, to be made the capital of Kharasm, on
condition of his doing all he can to restore and content my
unfortunate people, whom his tribes have carried off during
my wars in other directions." The best Oosbeg troops are
mere rubbish as opponents to Persian regulars and cannon,
and they all know it. Allah Kouli Khan is the best and
most sensible man in his country, and he will remain quiet

while Mahomed Shah comes against Bokhara, if Shake-spear can be empowered to tell him that this is a reform which must be effected, and which Persia is determined now to effect, with the consent of England and Russia. Shake-spear can mediate between the Khan Huzrut and Mohamed Shah for the gentle emancipation of those who may wish to return home in the next four or five years, or to settle in the fine waste land of Merve, and perhaps Mahomed Shah may give to Allah Kouli Khan the very large colony of Merve handicraftsmen now settled here, who really yet long for the home of their fathers ; this, and my securing to the Khokan frontier up the Oxus to Balkh, perhaps leaving the Khan of it his easy tributary, would make him agree to all that the Afghans need for the formation of their frontier from Persian Khorassan to the Oxus. England and Russia may then agree about immutable frontiers for Persia, Af-ghanistan, Mawarulneh, and Kharasm, in the spirit which becomes two of the first European nations in the world in the year 1842 of Jesus Christ, the God incarnate of all peace and wisdom. May this pure and peaceable religion be soon extended all over the world !—— March 12. I beg that fifty tillas may be given to Tooma Bai, the servant who will convey this to Long Joseph. (Let the utmost caution be used always in mentioning their names while this Ameer lives or reigns.) As for Long Joseph, I don't know what reward to propose for him. He has risked his life for us in the most gallant manner, as few men would, except for a brother ; and he is a noble fellow. I feel sure that Govern-ment will forgive me for not being able to make an ac-count of my stewardship during my Toorkish mission, and that it will use every exertion to get free and to reward all who have suffered with me, but remained alive. Allahdad Khan had some four hundred tillas in cash when he was brought back, besides his baggage and horses. Akhond-Zadeh, Saleh Mahomed, has served too well to make it necessary for me to recommend him. I trust that God has preserved his life.'

Thus ever, as he lay rotting in his noisome cell, he forgot his own sufferings and his own sorrows, and all the great sympathy and compassion of his nature expended themselves on the woes of others. Not only in all this is displayed that tender, loving thoughtfulness for his companions in misfortune, which made him ever eager to leave behind him a record of the claims of those who had done good and faithful service and suffered for their fidelity, but he strove mightily to make his dying voice heard in righteous condemnation of the cruelty which condemned so many of his oppressed brethren to hopeless slavery. For to Arthur Conolly all men were brethren, and it was a solace to him to think that his death, which then seemed to be close at hand, might give power to his words, and that if his utterances could but reach those to whom they were addressed, he might yet accomplish that which had so long been the object of his life. But he had other consolations. ' Stoddart and I,' he wrote at the end of this long letter, ' will comfort each other in every way till we die, when may our brotherhood be renewed in heaven, through Jesus Christ our Saviour. Send this assurance to all our friends, and do you, my dear John, stand on this faith. It is the only thing that can enable a man to bear up against the trials of this

life, and lead him to the noblest state of existence in the
next. Farewell! Farewell!'

He thought that this letter would be his last, but his release, by the gate of Death, was not so near as then, in the
restlessness and agony of a burning fever, it seemed. The
paroxysms passed away, and left him, though very weak,
on the way to the recovery of such health as was possible
amidst all the noxious influences of that miserable dungeon;
and he soon again resumed his journal. On the 22nd of
March he wrote: 'Our last note from this prison, dated
28th ultimo, was written for Shah Mahomed Khan to take
to Caubul.* Apparently he could not get off with it till
about a week ago. The Naib, to whom he applied for
money for his travelling expenses, first required to see both
our names written in English on the back of the note, as if
he had been led to doubt whether we were still alive. He
then made Ismael, one of his people, who can read English
characters, copy from a spelling-book, in which Stoddart
had noted the Persian meaning over different words: " *So
am I to go, I am to go in, so do ye,*" inducing us to guess that
he anticipated the Ameer's sending us away in his charge,
and finally he refused aid to Shah Mahomed Khan, who

* There is something not very intelligible in this, as it is
obvious that Conolly had written, at considerable length, on the
11th and 12th of March. The journals, which are now printed
entire—as far, at least, as they are recoverable—are written in
very minute characters; in many places they are defaced by damp
and attrition, so that it has been a task of difficulty to decipher
them. It happens that this part of the manuscript is remarkably
distinct, or I might have thought that there had been some error in
transcribing it.

borrowed ten tillas elsewhere, and started with a caravan. Shah Mahomed Khan has throughout behaved very well, and will, I hope, be especially provided for. Our business here has been chiefly conducted by Stoddart's faithful servant, Ibraheem, a lad of Herat, who has raised a claim to be particularly taken care of. On the 4th of March, Futoollah Beg sent word that the Naib had taken away his letter for Teheran and given it to Nooroollah Khan (a Persian lad of good family, formerly a pupil of Stoddart's), who was about to return to Persia by the same caravan— an uncalled-for act of interference, for which we did not thank our military acquaintance, but we felt assured that Futoollah Beg would not be allowed to suffer from it. After sending a page with my thermometer on the 15th ultimo (February), to ask how much cold it indicated, as detailed in my last letter, the Ameer took no notice of us till the 13th of this month, when he sent the gold chronometer which I had given him, to show that its chain was broken, and to ask if we could repair it—a pretence, the Topshee-Bashee said, to ascertain what state we were in. We had both become ill a few days before from a sudden cold change of weather and the discomfort of filthy clothing; and I, who had given in most to the sickness, owing to anxiety of mind regarding the many persons whom I had been the means of bringing into the Ameer's tyrannous hands, was lying weak in bed with fever when the last page came. The Topshee-Bashee, who for some time spoke encouragingly about changing our clothes, had by this time caused us plainly to understand that he neither dared himself to amend our position in this respect, nor

even to represent it to the Ameer. He now tried to save us
by telling the page that I had been confined to my bed
eight days, and by remarking upon the wretched state of
our apparel after eighty-five days' and nights' wear. I
showed the Mehrum that Stoddart had been obliged to
cast away all his under-clothing, and was suffering much
from cold on the chest. I experienced hope that the
Ameer would take some pity upon us, and especially upon
such of my late travelling companions and people as might
be suffering under his displeasure. The page said that he
would make a representation ' if the Huzrut questioned
him ; and he afterwards told the Topshee-Bashee that
on the Ameer's doing so, he had stated that the King's
last-come slave, Kan-Ali (Conolly), had been very ill for
eight or nine days; to which the Huzrut had replied:
" May he not die (or I suppose he won't die) for the three
or four days that remain till his going." We thought from
this that the Ameer proposed to send us away with the
Russians, who were said to be preparing to depart after the
No-roz. Nothing else has since transpired regarding ourselves; but through the indefatigable Long Joseph, we
have learnt the following items of intelligence about our
friends. On the 13th instant Ibraheem wrote : ' With re-
gard to Caubul, *be quite at ease;* thirty thousand persons
(rebels ?) have been slaughtered there. Allahdad Khan, the
Akhond-Zadeh Eusoff Khan (Augustin), the Jemadar, and
Meer Akhor, with Bolund Khan, Kurreem Khan, and Gool
Mahomed, remain in the black-hole of the gaol; Mahomed
Ali and Summud Khan are gone to Caubul ; Mohammed
Meer Akhor " (the man formerly in Dr Gerrard's service,

enslaved ten years ago, whom I ransomed at Khiva by order of Government) " has become your sacrifice; the rest are dispersed. All the papers, except the books, have been burned, and by the Ameer's order, Nazir Khan (Nazir Khira-Oollah) has brought the remainder of the property for two hundred tillas." In the next three days Ibraheem sent word that Augustin, Bolund Khan, Kurreem Khan, and Gool Mahomed had been released—news for which we sincerely thanked God: their sufferings, poor fellows, in that horrible dungeon must have been great. We desired Long Joseph to keep quite away from them for some days, judging it probable that they would be closely watched, only sending them word to keep a good heart, and to stand fast till after the departure of the Russians, with whom it was possible that we might be sent, and we remain ignorant of the fate of the other prisoners. Long Joseph's information of the 29th January, " that all the *Afghans* had been given their head," must have referred to the Soonee Mahomedan servants of my party, between whom and the Sheeahs of Caubul and Herat a religious distinction was apparently made. Our suspicions regarding the worse treatment of Allahdad Khan and the Akhond-Zadeh were but too well founded; the reasons for it do not yet appear. On the 23rd we were made further happy by the verbal intelligence of Long Joseph, that Allahdad Khan and the rest of our people had been released—— 24th. This forenoon the Topshee-Bashee, coming to see us, said with a cheerful manner : " Sewonchee—reward me for glad tidings. I represented your great want of clothes, and proposed to buy shirts and trousers for you from the bazaar, but the

future, if the Shah would be a good neighbour to him,
while he had sent to Merve a positive prohibition against
Alamanee, and he, Budub, mentioned that he had himself
met the Khan Naib, a relation of the [obscure], carried off
last year from Mondooran, on his way back to Meshed.
Budub added that [   ] the Jew was with the English
Elchee, whom he described as a young, tall man; he concluded, therefore, that England and Russia had decided to
come forward together to effect a complete settlement of
Persia's claims upon Toorkistan, associating in the design
the Khalifah of Room as the man who can, with the highest right, denounce to these tribes the inhuman practices for
which they pretend to have a religious warrant.   The news
made us very glad.   Our old friend now informed us, on
the authority of his Afghan acquaintance, Meer Hyder, that
all our people had left Bokhara on hearing that they had
been inquired about.   This made it seem as though the old
man, at any rate, had treated us fairly in his former account.
Perhaps the Topshee-Bashee wanted to find Eusoff a province, in order to question him about the Elchee from that
place, said to have come with the other three from the
west.   Possibly the Ameer really did mean to send us away
at the time of his marching, but deferred to do so on hearing that we had no servants left here, or from one of his
incalculable caprices.   I had noted, in a detailed report of
our proceedings after leaving Khokund, which when we
were seized I was waiting the Ameer's permission to despatch
by a courier to Caubul, an expression which the Naib heard
his Majesty had uttered in his camp after my arrival, to the
effect that he would give the English a few rubs more, and

page who had brought the chronometer on the 13th, came this morning with a parcel of my medicines to desire that I would describe their properties. We felt at a loss how to interpret this visit, as I had, on our first being brought to this prison, given an account of the said medicines, and my labels remained on most of the bottles; but I wrote fresh descriptions for the page, whom the Ameer, perhaps, sent to ascertain our condition without taking pains to satisfy his curiosity delicately—— 28th. Meerza Ismael Mehrum came this morning with some more of my medicines to desire that I would note the proportions in which they should be given, as the labels only mentioned in what diseases they were used. He said that the Huzrut would now show us favour, and our keepers ' . . . .

A portion of the journal here seems to be missing, but on that same day (March 28) Conolly wrote a letter to his brother John, in which he again implored him to do all that was possible to protect and reward his servants and followers. In that letter he expressed some little glimmering of hope that the exertions then being made, honestly and strenuously, by the Russian Mission, might be crowned with success. 'We have been comforted by intelligence that the Ameer has released Allahdad Khan* and all my people from the gaol into which he so unjustly and cruelly confined them. . . . .† The Ameer has lately been talking, we hear, of sending us away, and though we do

* The Caubul Envoy.
† The passages omitted are repetitions of the recommendations on behalf of his followers, already given in his letter of March 11.—12.

not set much store by his words, we think it possible he may give us to the Russian Mission, who are about to depart. . . . . I wrote you a longish letter on the 11th of this month, when I was in a high state of excitement, from fever and several nights of sleepless anxiety. The burden of it was an entreaty to the last effect regarding my poor people, and a hope that the British Government would seize the opportunity which the Ameer's faithlessness had given them to come forward with Persia to put him down, and give his country to Kharasm and Khokund, on condition of the entire suppression of the Persian and Afghan slave trade in Toorkistan. If that paper (which I shall endeavour to recover) should reach you, compress its words into this purport and destroy it, reserving my last good wishes for the friends to whom I addressed them, thinking that I might not live much longer. I am now, thank God, almost well in health again, and the news regarding our people has set my mind at rest. Stoddart, also, who was suffering awhile from severe cold, is, I rejoice to say, convalescent. We are both in a very uncomfortable state, as you may imagine, having been ninety-nine days and nights without a change of clothes ; but we are together. Stoddart is such a friend as a man would desire to have in adversity, and our searchers having missed the little Prayer-book which George Macgregor gave us (tell him), we are able to read and pray, as well as to converse together. God bless you, my dear John. Send my love to everybody.'

The journal is resumed on the 5th of April. At this time the officers of the Russian Mission were preparing for their departure, and Colonel Bouteneff was still making

honourable efforts to obtain the liberation of the English
gentlemen. Among the final demands which he made was
one for " permission for Stoddart and Conolly to return with
him in accordance with the promise made by the Ameer."
But the answer given to this was, that the Englishmen had
presented a letter to the Ameer saying that their Queen
desired to be on friendly terms with Bokhara, in consequence of which he had himself written to the Queen, and,
on receiving an answer, would despatch them both direct
to England.' * Vague tidings of these good Russian efforts
reached the prisoners in their dungeon, but soon all hope
of release was gone. ' April 5. A note received this
morning from Ibraheem informs us that the Jemadar and
Meer Akhor were only released yesterday from the terrible
dungeon. He adds that they were much depressed by their
imprisonment, and that, like the rest of our men who remain
in the city, they have to support themselves by begging.
There has been a little difference between the verbal reports
which Long Joseph sent us through Tooma Bai and those
which Ibraheem has written. I thought that Gool Mahomed and Kurreem Khan had gone on the 28th, and I
wrote a note for them addressed to my brother John, in
which I begged him to destroy a letter which I had written
to him on the 11th of March, if it should reach Caubul.
Ibraheem now writes that they propose departing in three
days hence with Ibraheem Candaharee, another young man
in my service who has behaved very well; and they request
me to give them a letter. We have resolved, therefore, to
send this journal by their hands, and I take the opportunity

* Mitchel.

of explaining that my letter of the 11th of March was written when I was very ill with fever. Thinking that he might possibly be sent away without me on the departure of the Russians (as they had brought a request for his dismissal), or that we might be otherwise separated, Stoddart had begged me to give him a memorandum of my opinions regarding the policy to be pursued towards these States, and I wrote off a hasty summary of these notions which were running in my head, with many things that I was anxious to say about my unfortunate servants and to my friends, when under excitement, which must have made my expressions very wild and incoherent. I hoped that the paper containing them remained in the hands of Long Joseph ; but he, misunderstanding our instructions, instead of keeping it, gave it to Eusoffee-i-Roomee (Augustin), who apparently went off with it at once to Caubul. When I got better, I drew up for Stoddart the memorandum which he had asked for, and which he now decides on forwarding. It is written in a more calm and less indignant tone than the letter aforesaid, but allowance must be made for the brevity and freedom of the propositions, for we were so liable to be interrupted and discovered, that I could only pen my opinions by snatches, and paper is a scarce article with us. Part of the paper also is a repetition of what I wrote some time ago to Sir William Macnaghten. When I came here, Stoddart did his utmost to put me forward ; but now, as long as the Ameer detains him, I shall refer to him, as the accredited British agent, every communication on business that the Ameer may make to me, whether we should be together or separated. He well knows all the people here, and the dignity of our Government is safe in his hands. We have heard that the Russians are about to depart, and that they take their enslaved people with them, but we cannot get at the truth of this statement. Report also says that the Ameer will march with his army seven or eight days hence. There is no doubt that he is preparing for an early move; but though Tashkend and Khokund are named as his points of attack, it is not certain that he will go eastward. This is the hundred and seventh day of our confinement, without change of clothes; but the weather having become warmer, we can do without the garments that most harboured the vermin that we found so distressing, and we are both now, thank God! quite well. We trust that our friends will be informed of our well-being. We have desired all our servants, except Ibraheem (who remains behind to keep up correspondence), to return to their homes as soon as their strength enables them to travel, begging them to make their way anyhow, and to rest assured that everything due will be made up to them on their reaching Caubul. I gave some of my people notes on Caubul instead of pay in cash: these bills may have been taken from them; if so, I hope that their words will be taken for the sums due to them. Hoossein, a carrier, whom I put on the escort-list at the pay of twenty rupees per mensem, instead of one of the dismissed Indian troopers, lost two ponies when I sent him from Khokund with Mousa Adum Khan, and Shah Mahomed Khan, and Allahdad Khan's man, Huneefa, to announce our coming to the Ameer. The last persons lost everything belonging to them, and they are all entitled to *reward*, moreover, for the risk they ran on that service. Allahdad Khan had three or four hundred tillas in his bag when brought back from Kaishee: probably this has been appropriated by the Ameer with my colleague's horses, arms, &c. Allahdad Khan behaved very firmly in refusing to allow that he was the servant of a Feringhee servant, as the Ameer wished him to do, and did justice both to the dignity of his royal master and to the policy of the British Government in Afghanistan. I beg that his conduct may be mentioned to Shah Soojah, and I trust that all his losses will be made up to him; but if the preparation of the account is left to him, he will make it a very large one, and part of the settlement may, perhaps, be deferred till it is decided whether or not the Ameer is to be called upon for repayment.'

A trusty messenger was found to convey these writings to Caubul, and then a new journal was commenced. 'When our last packet was despatched,' wrote Conolly in the same minute characters, 'we deemed it not impossible, from the Ameer's expressions, which had been reported to us, that his Majesty designed to send us away with the Russian Mission. Our keepers rather inclined to the idea that Huzrut would dismiss us about the same time by the route of Persia, and the Topshee-Bashee's old brother talked seriously about performing a pilgrimage to the holy city of Meshed in our company.——April 13. We heard that the Russians had been dismissed with presents of honour,* that Khodiyar Beg, Karrawool-Beggee, ranking as captain or commander

---

* This tallies with the report of Colonel Bouteneff, who says that the khelats were received by the Russian Mission on the 12th of April.

of one hundred, had been attached to Colonel Bouteneff as
the Ameer's Envoy to St Petersburg, and that the Huzrut
had promised to promote him to the grade of Tok-Suba,
commander of one thousand, privileged to bear a cow-tail
banner on his return after the performance of good service.
The Ameer's own arrangements were said to be completed,
and the direction of it certainly to the eastward. An Envoy
from Khokund, who arrived two days ago, was not received, but was told to go about his own business wherever
he listed.   Our informant mentioned at the same time that
the last Envoy from Khiva had been dismissed a fortnight
before with extraordinary honour, all his servants getting
dresses.   We now also learned that the heir of the Koondooz Chief had sent an Envoy to the Ameer, who had
ordered one of his officers, a Khojeh, styled Selim Aghassi,
to accompany that agent to Koondooz on his return.   It
was thought, we were told, that the Koojeh of Balkh would
endeavour to take Koondooz on Meer Morad's death, and
the heir may, in this apprehension, have been alert to put
himself under the Ameer's protection.   This morning the
Ameer showed the Topshee-Bashee an especial mark of
favour by sending him a loaf of refined sugar from the
palace.   Towards evening, his Majesty rode four miles to a
place of pilgrimage, and on his return at night had the
Topshee-Bashee up to give him some orders.   Early next
morning (the 14th) the Ameer marched out to the sound
of his palace kettle-drums and trumpets, leaving us in the
filthy clothes which we had worn for one hundred and
fifteen days and nights!   We said to the gunner's old
brother, when he mentioned the Ameer's having departed,

"Then the Meshed caravan apparently stands fast." "No," was his reply; "please God it will go soon. I asked the Topshee-Bashee last night if nothing had been settled about you, and he replied, 'When the Russians got out a march or so, the Dustan Kanchee will make a petition about them, and they will be dismissed.'" The old man also remarked, probably from what he had heard his brother say, that the Ameer had expressed himself to the effect that he knew the Russian Elchee was led to get us in order to make a boast of having procured our release, which made it seem as though Colonel Bouteneff had been endeavouring to obtain our dismissal. Our old keeper persisted for some days in assuring us of his belief that our immediate dismissal was designed, and on the 18th said that he was going down into the city to seek out my Dewan Beggee, Eusoff Khan (Augustin), to set his mind at ease about us; he returned, saying that he had been referred from place to place without finding Eusoff Khan, or any of our people, but that one Meer Hyder and another shopkeeper of his acquaintance, had assured him that they were all in the town, and that four or five of them were in the habit of coming occasionally at night to a certain quarter to hear books read. We had thought the Gunners might have received orders to collect some of our people in order to our respectable dismissal; but knowing that all our men, except Ibraheem, had left Bokhara, we concluded that the Topshee-Bashee had made use of his old brother to deceive us, in order to keep us hopeful and quiet for another period, as he said nothing about changing our clothes, and kept himself quite aloof from us, which he would hardly have done had he believed what he reported in the Ameer's name. Just before the Ameer's departure, we heard that a British Elchee had arrived at Merve on his way hither. We could get no further accounts of the said Elchee, but judged that it might be Shakespear on his way to Khiva.' . . . [Defaced.]

'From the 4th to the 7th of May,' continues the prison journal, 'the palace drums and trumpets were continually sounding for intelligence that Khokund had been taken after a faint endeavour at resistance under the famed Khokund General Guda Bai; that the latter had been taken prisoner, and that the rebellious town had been given up to plunder,' &c. . . . [Defaced.] 'On the morning of the 18th, however, Selim Beg, the one-eyed Mehrum who was sent at the end of last January to ask us about the castles of Caubul and Herat, arrived direct from the Ameer, announcing that Khokund had been taken late on the afternoon of the 11th. The city, he reported, had been defended awhile by Mahomed Ali Khan's Subaz regular infantry—probably some of the citizens in the fort—in skirmishing with whom the Naib had been led into the battle which the Huzrut had turned into so great a victory by ordering all his army on to the support. A great many of these soldiers, he said, had been killed by the Naib's men, and the Bokharians poured into the city, but the Ameer, on entering the Khan's Palace after sunset, had stopped plundering, and proclaimed peace to all who would be quiet, and he was waited upon by the high and low of the place. The Khan and his brother were reported missing. This news was followed on the 22nd by intelligence that the brothers had been taken and brought in, and that the Ameer had put them both to death in cold blood, together with the Khan's son and his maternal uncle, while he had given all persons in the city of Khokund, not natives of the place, a week in which to settle their affairs and depart to their several countries.   On the 24th, some of the Ameer's officers were named as having been appointed to the Governments of Khokund, Tashkend, and [   ], and it is said that his Majesty intended to march back to Bokhara after the despatch of another week's business.   We had expressed to our old guardian a wish to get some money from Meshed, with which to reward him for his kindness, and to get him privately to buy us a few necessaries in the event of our further detention, and, liking the idea, he, on the 19th instant (May), brought secretly to see us his son-in-law Budub, employed as a caravan-bashee between Bokhara and the Holy City, who agreed to act as agent in the business after another week.   Inquiring the news from Budub, we heard that Kamran was said to be confined in Herat by Yar Mahomed Khan—that the English remained as before at Candahar and Caubul—and that four Elchees, English, Russian, Persian, and Turkish, had gone together to Khiva, each displaying his national flag, and told the Khan Huzrut that he had the choice of quietly giving up plundering and slave-dealing, or of meeting the Shah of Persia, who had assembled a large army for the redress of his people, and waited for their report in order to decide upon his movements.   Akousi Khan was said to have expressed himself willing to give up all Persia's slaves in the course of two years, and to keep peace for the

future, if the Shah would be a good neighbour to him,
while he had sent to Merve a positive prohibition against
Alamanee, and he, Budub, mentioned that he had himself
met the Khan Naib, a relation of the [obscure], carried off
last year from Mondooran, on his way back to Meshed.
Budub added that [   ] the Jew was with the English
Elchee, whom he described as a young, tall man; he concluded, therefore, that England and Russia had decided to
come forward together to effect a complete settlement of
Persia's claims upon Toorkistan, associating in the design
the Khalifah of Room as the man who can, with the highest right, denounce to these tribes the inhuman practices for
which they pretend to have a religious warrant.   The news
made us very glad.   Our old friend now informed us, on
the authority of his Afghan acquaintance, Meer Hyder, that
all our people had left Bokhara on hearing that they had
been inquired about.   This made it seem as though the old
man, at any rate, had treated us fairly in his former account.
Perhaps the Topshee-Bashee wanted to find Eusoff a province, in order to question him about the Elchee from that
place, said to have come with the other three from the
west.   Possibly the Ameer really did mean to send us away
at the time of his marching, but deferred to do so on hearing that we had no servants left here, or from one of his
incalculable caprices.   I had noted, in a detailed report of
our proceedings after leaving Khokund, which when we
were seized I was waiting the Ameer's permission to despatch
by a courier to Caubul, an expression which the Naib heard
his Majesty had uttered in his camp after my arrival, to the
effect that he would give the English a few rubs more, and

then be friends with them again. Though we were not sure
that the Ameer had so spoken, the plan seems one likely to
be entertained by an ignorant and weak man, anxious to give
an imposing impression of his greatness and confidence;
and to it I partly attributed the ungraciousness of my public
reception in camp, though I was the Naib's honoured guest;
the failure of the Huzrut to recover the horses and the
property of my servants, which had been plundered at his
outposts, when bringing letters to him, and the hauteur
with which, at the first joint reception of Stoddart and
myself here, he caused it to be signified to us that as in old
times there had been friendship between the Mussulmans
and infidels, there existed no objection to the establishment
of friendly relations between the states of Bokhara and
England; but that the Huzrut desired to know whether
we (the English) had been travellers all over Toorkistan
to spy the land with a view to take it, as we had taken
Caubul, or for other purposes; and wished all our designs
to be unveiled, in order that if they were friendly they
might become apparent, and that if hostile they might still
be known. The Government of India, knowing what
communications it has sent to Bokhara, will be able to
judge the Ameer's conduct better then we can.

'On the 19th (May) the Topshee-Bashee paid us a visit
of a few moments, after keeping away for two months.
He mentioned that a man with a name like Noor Mohum-
nud had come three or four days before from Persia, bringing a load of things for Stoddart, of which the Dustan
Kanchee had forwarded a list to the Ameer—probably the
articles which should have accompanied Lord Palmerston's

letter. The Huzrut, the Topshee-Bashee said, would doubtless, on his return, be gracious to us, and give us fine robes of honour, and treat us even better than before. About sunset on the 23rd, as Stoddart and myself were pacing up and down a small court of twenty feet long, which encloses our prison, one of the citadel door-keepers came and desired us both to sit down in a corner; we complied, wondering what would follow, and presently saw heads peering at us from the adjoining roofs, when we understood that the Ameer's heir, a youth of seventeen, had taken this way of getting a sight of the Feringhee Elchees. We must have given him but a poor impression in the remains of our clothes, and with heads and beards uncombed for more than five months. On the 23rd, Tooma Bai was accosted by a man named Makhzoom, known to Stoddart, who gave him a token, and a note written in such bad grammar as scarcely to be understood, in which he said one Juleb arrived lately from Khiva, mentioned that he saw Pottinger Sahib there, and another person named Mooza having come, bringing a letter from Pottinger Sahib, who, he says, is at Khiva, with the Elchee of Mahomed Shah. We tried to get the said letter, but on the 26th heard from Mikhroun that the messenger would not give it up. They had heard, they told him, that we had been made away with, and would wait till the return of the Huzrut, in whose camp they had a friend who could, with certainty, satisfy their fears, and certainly communicate with us, and thought that Mooza might possibly be one of my late servants, who went from this on leave with my dismissed Hindostanees, but he did not understand half the sign which I sent him. We consoled ourselves for the delay by attributing it to the caution of our trusty agent Ibraheem, who knowing Mikhroun not to be a man of solid character like " Long Joseph," would desire to put as little of our business as possible into his hands. Our new agent's aid did not slacken, for he wrote us another note to say that a man had come bringing a letter which *Shah Mahomed Khan* had despatched after his arrival at Caubul, the which he also insisted on keeping till the Huzrut's return, and that one of the men from Khiva was about to return thither. We then sent him a packet, containing nearly the preceding journal and the notes belonging to it, to be forwarded by the latter messenger to the English Elchee at Allah Kouli Khan's Court, and begged him to remain quiet, letting the other comers have their own way. All the men named by him must have been careless to let him learn so much of their business, and knowing the cautiousness of Afghans, and that the Ameer has news-writers at Caubul, we beg that all my released people, as well as Allahdad Khan's servants, may be enjoined not to name a single person who befriended them or us here, or to allude to the coming and going of Cossids between Afghanistan and Bokhara.'

This is the very last record, in my possession, in the hand-writing of Arthur Conolly himself. But I have an autograph letter from Colonel Stoddart, dated May 28, 1842, the last, perhaps, from those brother-prisoners which ever reached the outer world. In this Stoddart speaks, with some detail, of the war between Bokhara and Khokund, and concludes his letter by saying : ' No change has taken place in our treatment, though hopes, so long found to be deceitful, are held out to us, on the return of the Chief, said to be about to take place very soon.' And a week or two afterwards the Ameer returned, flushed with conquest, from the war against the Khokundees; and one of the first acts by which he celebrated his victory was the execution of the English captives.

The last scene of this sad tragedy is believed to have been performed on the 17th of June. It has been described by different persons. I am still inclined to think that the most trustworthy story is that of the Akhond-Zadeh Saleh Mahomed, of whom mention has already been made in this narrative. He said that he derived his information from one of the executioners, and that he had seen the graves of the murdered men. On that 17th of June, 1842, it is said, they were taken out of their miserable dungeon and conducted into an open square, where a multitude of people were assembled to witness the execution of the Feringhees. With their hands bound before them, they stood for some time, whilst their graves were made ready for them. Stoddart was first called forth to die. Crying aloud against the tyranny of the Ameer, he knelt down, and his head was cut off with a huge knife. Then Conolly was told to prepare himself for death; but life was offered to him, if he would abjure Christianity and adopt the religion of Mahomed. To this he is said to have replied indignantly, 'Stoddart became a Mussulman, and yet you have killed him. I am prepared to die.' Then he knelt down, stretched forth his neck, and died by the hand of the executioner.

Another version of the closing scene is this. When Joseph Wolff, afterwards, moved more than aught else by the strength of his love for Arthur Conolly, journeyed to Bokhara to learn the history of his fate, if dead, or to endeavour to rescue him from captivity, if alive, he was told that 'both Captain Conolly and Colonel Stoddart were brought with their hands tied, behind the ark, or palace of the King, when Colonel Stoddart and Captain Conolly kissed each other, and Stoddart said to Mekram Saadut, "Tell the Ameer that I die a disbeliever in Mahomet, but a believer in Jesus—that I am a Christian, and a Christian I die." And Conolly said, "Stoddart, we shall see each other in Paradise, near Jesus." Then Saadut gave the order to cut off, first the head of Stoddart, which was done; and in the same manner the head of Conolly was cut off.'

And so Arthur Conolly, pure of heart, chastened by affliction, the most loving and unselfish of men, passed out of great tribulation with his garments washed white in the blood of the LAMB.

It must be admitted that some uncertainty still obscures the death of Arthur Conolly and his companion in misfortune. It has been contended that the sacrifice was not consummated until the year 1843. Dr Wolff, after all his explorations and inquiries on the spot, was for some time in a state of incertitude as to the date of their execution, and at last arrived at the conclusion that they were butchered in the early part of 1843. 'On my arrival at Teheran,' he said in his published book, 'Colonel Shiel asked me whether Colonel Stoddart and Captain Conolly had been put to death in 1259 of the Hejirah (1843), or 1258 (1842).* I told him that the Naib had said 1259, but that twenty months had elapsed between the time of my arrival and their execution. I told him on a second occasion that, according to this calculation, the execution was in 1258 (1842), to which he agreed. On leaving, however, for Tabreez, Abbas Kouli Khan and myself had some conversation on this subject, and he then said, " I made most accurate inquiries pursuant to my official instructions. You may depend upon it that the information I have obtained about their execution is more correct than your own. Stoddart and Conolly were put to death eleven months before your arrival." He then said, emphatically, " They were put to death as the Naib told you at the first, in the year 1259; not 1258." And,' adds Dr Wolff, ' as it is certain that Shakespear's note, with the letter of Lord Ellenborough, arrived before their execution, the information of Abbas Kouli Khan, and the first official statement of the King and Abdul Samut Khan, is correct.' But that which Dr Wolff here says is ' certain,' is anything but certain. If Lord Ellenborough's letter to the Khan of Bokhara, which bears date October 1, 1842, was received before the death of Stoddart and Conolly, it is certain that they were not executed in June. But the principal authority for this statement appears to have been one Hadjee Ibrahim (a brother of Abdul Samut Khan), of whom it is said that ' cunning and knavery were depicted in his very

* The year 1258 commenced Feb. 11, 1842. See *ante*, page 363.

look.' This man told Dr Wolff that 'Conolly came with letters from the Ambassador at Caubul. He was put in prison. Then a letter came from the Sultan. The Ameer cast it away with disdain, and said, "The Sultan is half a Kafir. I want a letter from the Queen of England." Some time after a letter arrived from the Sirkar of Hind (the Governor-General). 'This letter,' said he, with a sneer, 'stated that Stoddart and Conolly were "*innocent travellers.*" Upon which the Ameer was so angry that he put them to death; and I have this account from my brother, Abdul Samut Khan.' In Lord Ellenborough's letter the prisoners were described as 'innocent travellers.' But as the Bokhara authorities were naturally anxious to justify the execution of the prisoners, and as the official repudiation of them by the Governor-General placed them before the Ameer in the position of spies and impostors, there was an evident purpose in representing that the letter had been received before their death.

I am not inclined to accept such interested authority, in the face of all conflicting evidence which points to the date already indicated. I have not been able to trace anything written, either by Conolly or Stoddart, of a later date than the 28th of May, 1842. The British Army of Retribution, under General Pollock, was at Caubul up to the 12th of October in that year, so that later letters might have been received by our people, if they had been despatched to them from Bokhara. But on the morning of the 16th of September Major Rawlinson met one of Stoddart's servants near Caubul, and the man informed him that he had come from Bokhara, where his master had been executed shortly before his departure. There is reason also to believe that the Ameer caused his English prisoners to be put to death very soon after his return from the expedition against the Khokundees, and this certainly took place in the early part of June, 1842. The evidence, indeed, was sufficiently strong to convince the Government, both of the Queen and the Company, that Death scored the names of their officers from the Army Lists on that miserable 17th of June.

POSTSCRIPT. ARTHUR CONOLLY'S PRAYER-BOOK.

In the journal from which I have quoted so freely in the foregoing Memoir, mention is made of the little Prayer-book given by George Macgregor to Arthur Conolly, which had been so great a comfort to the prisoners. This little book, which has been almost miraculously preserved, served a double purpose. Spiritually it yielded consolation to them in their affliction, and materially it received from day to day, along its margins and on all its blank pages, a record of the prison-life of the captives. 'Thank God,' wrote Conolly, in one place, 'that this book was left to me. Stoddart and I have found it a great comfort. We did not fully know before this affliction what was in the Psalms, or how beautiful are the prayers of our Church. Nothing but the spirit of Christianity can heal the wickedness and misery of these countries.' And in another place: 'Desiring that the circumstances of our last treatment at Bokhara should become known, and conceiving that a record made in this book has a better chance of preservation than one made upon loose paper, I herein note the chief occurrences since my arrival.'

Many of the entries in this interesting journal are identical with those which constitute the journal-letters, already quoted, which Arthur Conolly wrote to his brother John. But the Prayer-book supplies an important omission relating to the date and circumstances of the first seizure and imprisonment of Stoddart and Conolly. The record commences with this retrospective statement: 'On the 10th of November, 1841, Stoddart joined me at the Naib's, and on the 19th we removed thence to a good house, given to us by the Ameer, in the city, where we were well entertained for a month. At our first audience, the Ameer expressed his resolve to send Stoddart away immediately, and to keep me as British Agent, seeming only to hesitate a little on account of the non-arrival of a reply to his letter to the Queen; but we at this time received friendly intimations that we were both distrusted, and the Chief, after sounding us by different questions as to the way by which I should go, decided to keep us both awhile. We had four or five interviews with the Ameer that month, in all of which he cross-examined me and Allahdad Khan about the object of our journey to Khiva and Khokund, and expressed impatience for a reply to his letter to the Queen—once proposing that I should go home *via* Russia to ascertain why it had not been sent. . . . . . Towards the end of November reports came that Shah Soojah had been deposed at Caubul, ... and that, in a word, our influence in Afghanistan had been quite destroyed. The Ameer questioned us about these rumours; we could only express doubt of their truth. But they evidently gained hold of his Majesty's mind, and encouraged him to think that we had been cut off from our support; for after summoning us to Court on the 2nd of December, he, after a loose and querulous complaint that our policy was not clear, suddenly attacked me about our missions to Khiva and Khokund, saying, in an overbearing and contemptuous manner, he perfectly understood that the object of our dealing with those states was only to incite them to enmity against him; but that we must not think, because we had got five or six Afghan houses, that we could play the same game here, for that Toorkistan could not bear it. I replied that the English Government never urged underhand war; that it was able, please God, to encounter any enemy in its own strength, and that where it designed hostility, it would declare the same openly, but that it had from the first really entertained towards his Majesty the friendly desires which it had through every channel professed. The Ameer on this accused me of talking big, said he would imprison me, and then an army might come and see what it could do.'

It appeared, however, at the time, that this was an idle threat. The English gentlemen received assurances from different quarters that the Ameer had only designed to sift them, and that he was satisfied with the result. Friendly messages came asking them about the time and manner of their departure. On the 10th, Colonel Stoddart received a despatch from Lord Palmerston, the contents of which were made known to the Ameer, who again expressed disappointment that there was no letter from the Queen. 'On the 19th,' continues the record in the Prayer-book, ' the Ameer summoned Stoddart and myself to Court, and talked long and graciously with us about the continued bad rumours from Caubul. As we were leaving the citadel, a Mehrum came after us to say that the King had heard that I possessed a very superior watch, and that his Majesty would like to see it. I went home and returned alone with my gold M'Cabe chronometer, which on a second interview I presented to his Majesty. He graciously accepted it, and for some time conversed with me very kindly about the superiority of English manufactures.' These favourable appearances, however, were deceptive. On the following day they were told to fix a period at which they would guarantee the receipt of an answer to the Ameer's letter, or else provide ransom-money to the amount of ten or twenty thousand tillahs, in which case they would receive safe conduct across the Oxus. Otherwise they could only look for imprisonment. ' We answered,' wrote Conolly in the Prayer-book, ' that although we had reason to believe that the fullest letters were on the road, we could not undertake to say positively when they would arrive, that we did not understand upon what point the mind of the Ameer required to be satisfied, but that if the assurances his Majesty desired could be had either from Persia or from Caubul, we thought that they could be obtained in the course of two months. We said that we were not authorized to give money for our release, and would not consent to do so, as that would be tantamount to an acknowledgment that we had committed crime against the Ameer, whereas we had only been the bearers of kind communications from the British Government; and we begged him to be good enough to await the arrival of the letter which the English Minister, Lord Palmerston, had announced the Governor-General would write to his Majesty. But this reply was not satisfactory, and on that day—the 20th of December—at sunset, they were 'conducted to the house of the Topshee-Bashee, or master gunner of the citadel,' where they were 'confined together in a small room, where the brother and the nephew of the Topshee-Bashee slept to guard them.' This removes all doubt with respect to the accuracy of the previous statement that Stoddart and Conolly were cast into prison in the third week of December.

This record contains also the following narrative of the circumstances of the first attempt made to induce Conolly to apostatize. It happened on the evening of the 27th of December: 'The Meer-shub came down to our room with the Topshee-Bashee, and ordered me, in a rough manner, to take off my coat and neckcloth. We thought he had been sent to put me to death, and Stoddart, who knew him, conjured him to say what was intended. He replied that nothing was designed against either of our lives, but that I had incurred the Khan Huzrut's displeasure, and that in this case clothes like mine were out of place. Then causing me to go on disrobing, till I stood in my shirt and drawers, he called for a torn and stinking sheepskin cloak and a cotton girdle cloth to match, which he made me put on, and departed, telling Stoddart that he might remain as he was, for that he and his clothes were all right. When the

doors of the house had been barred for the night, we heard
a knocking without, and the Topshee-Bashee presently
came into the room, bearing his axe of office, and after a
few moments of serious silence turned to me, and asked if
I would become a Mussulman, and remain in the enjoyment of favour at Bokhara. We both thought that he had
been sent to announce death as the alternative; therefore,
to avoid argument, by which he might hope to persuade
me, I told him most decidedly that my religion was a
matter between me and my God, and that I would suffer
death rather than change. All the world knew, I said
that a forced profession of Mahomedanism was null, and
that Colonel Stoddart had consented to repeat the Kulna at
a time when his character was not rightly understood here,
solely to avoid bloodshed and disorder; but that I had
come to Bokhara on the invitation of the Huzrut, against
whom I had committed no fault, and that there must be
no more of this work. The Topshee-Bashee seemed to
assent to what I had said, and told me that the proposal
had not come from the Ameer, but that a certain person
had suggested it to him. I said I was glad to hear
that, but begged him distinctly to understand that, come
from whence it might, nothing should induce me to accept it.'

This little Prayer-book contained also Arthur Conolly's
will. He was very anxious that all his debts should be
paid, and that his servants and followers, who had shared
the perils of his journey, should be provided for from the
residue of his estate. He thought also, with tenderest
compassion, of some more helpless dependents, saying:

'Among my private servants is a negro whom I ransomed at Khiva. I beg my brother John to keep him, or to get him into some other service, in case of my death. Mohamed, the Afghan boy, whom I was obliged to buy, as reported in one of my letters to Sir William Macnaghten from Khiva, is a willing lad, and I hope some Englishman will take him into service, if he escapes hence to Caubul. He has a mother at Herat, but were he to be sent back in the Ameer's time he would only be sold again. . . . There is an old man in London known to Mrs Orr, and to Mr Allen, the publisher of Leadenhall-street, to whom I intended to give half-a-crown weekly for the rest of his life. I send home a year's allowance, and Mrs Orr promised me the pittance should not fail. In the event of my death, pray let his allowance be continued to him by some of the family. He is a worthy old man.' He then bethought himself of many far-off friends, to whom he wished to send his affectionate remembrances. 'A great many valued friends,' he wrote, 'to whom I should like to express my love, come to mind; but I cannot now particularize them. If you meet Henry Graham of the Bengal Engineers, and Mansell of the Civil Service, remember me most kindly to them; also Robert Farquharson and Parry Woodcock; Robertson, late Governor of Agra, and our mutual friend of the same name in the 13th. Write also my best remembrance to Mr Mack, late of the Russian Mission, and thank him for his letters to me from Meshed. I did not think it necessary to name Mr Marjoribanks at the head of the list. He well knows my grateful attachment to him.' And so to the last, in the midst of his own

sufferings, he was loving, and compassionate, and thoughtful for others.   Self had been utterly crucified within him.

The little book in which the preceding entries were
made found its way, after Arthur Conolly's death, into one
of the bazaars of Bokhara, whence it was recovered by a
Russian prisoner, who consigned it to General Ignatieff,
when the mission under that officer visited Bokhara in
1858.   On returning to the Russian frontier and proceeding
to Orenburg, the General intrusted the little book to the
care of Major Salatzki, a member of his mission, with the
view, originally, of its presentation to the Geographical
Society of Great Britain.   But when it was subsequently
discovered that the notes were of a personal rather than a
scientific character, it was rightly considered that it would
be a more appropriate gift to the family of the deceased
owner.   So one day in 1862—twenty years after Arthur
Conolly's death—it was left at the door of his sister, Mrs
Macnaghten, in Eaton-place.

MAJOR ELDRED POTTINGER.

[BORN 1811.—DIED 1843.]

THE father of Eldred Pottinger was an Irish gentleman —Thomas Pottinger, of Mount Pottinger, in the county of Down, who married Charlotte, the only child of James Moore, another Irish gentleman, whose place of residence, however, was for the most part in the Danish capital. This lady had many and great accomplishments, and strong literary tastes, which might have borne good fruit, but that death cut short her early promise; she passed away from the scene, after a few years of wedded happiness, leaving behind her an only son, the subject of this Memoir.

Eldred Pottinger was born on the 12th of August, 1811. He was scarcely two years old when his mother died. But he seems to have inherited from her a love of letters and a readiness in the acquisition of languages, which was very serviceable to him in later days. He was docile, and in all things quick to learn; but it was soon apparent that there was a sturdiness of character and a love of enterprise in him, which rendered it more likely that the tendencies of his manhood would be towards a life of strenuous action than to one of studious repose. His father took a second wife,

and little Eldred, after a time, went to live with his step-
mother, who in due course had children of her own.   But
Eldred was ever to her as her own son, and he loved her
tenderly as a mother.   He was very affectionate and very
sociable, and often, when his father was absent in his yacht,
the pleasant companionship of the boy was a source of
comfort to Mrs Pottinger never to be forgotten.   It is an
undiscriminating injustice that makes step-mothers the *bêtes
noires* of domestic history.   The 'injusta noverca' is in real
life a rarer personage than is commonly supposed.   At all
events, the relationship at Mount Pottinger had nothing
that was not beautiful about it.   No distinctions were ever
recognized there.   The gentleness and tenderness, the forbearance and self-denial, of young Eldred towards his little
brothers and sisters is still gratefully remembered ;· and I
am assured by one of the latter, that not until she had nearly
reached the age of womanhood was she aware that Eldred
was not her own brother.

High-spirited and adventurous as he was, he was very
tractable, and, save in one particular, seldom got himself
into any boyish scrapes.   He was very fond of playing with
gunpowder ; and once very nearly blew himself up together
with his brother John.   His military instincts were even then
developing themselves, for nothing delighted him more in
his play-hours than to erect mimic fortifications, and to act
little dramas of warlike attack and defence.   One of these
last had nearly a tragic termination ; for having, in execution
of some warlike project or other, heaped up a number of
heavy stones on the crest of the garden wall, some of them
fell upon and well-nigh killed an old man or woman who

was seated on the other side. But though forward ever in active adventure, he was by no means an inapt or inattentive scholar, and he pursued his studies in his father's house, under a private tutor, with very commendable success. It happened, however, that, on one occasion, when in his fourteenth year, he fell out with his preceptor on some point either of discipline or of learning, and the tutor threatened him with personal chastisement. The high spirit of the boy could not brook this, and he declared that, if the threat were carried into execution, he would run away and seek his fortune in some remote place. The time, indeed, had passed for home teaching. The instincts of young Eldred turned towards foreign travel and military adventure. He delighted to peruse the records of great battles, and it is remarkable that of all the books which he read in his youth, the one which made the deepest impression upon him was Drinkwater's narrative of the siege of Gibraltar. For a youth of this temper, it seemed that the Indian Army opened out a field admirably calculated to develop his powers. So a nomination was obtained for him to the Company's military seminary at Addiscombe.

[I went, not long ago, with a very dear friend, to Addiscombe. The ploughshare had passed over it. It no longer exists; no longer exists as it was in the old days of Pitt and Jenkinson; no longer exists as it was when it flourished as a great nursery of Indian captains. All the old associations and traditions have been materially effaced by the despoiling hand of speculative builders. But a sort of moral odour of Indian heroism still pervades the place, for the desolators have named all the new roads and villas, which have cut

the old place to pieces, after such men as Canning and
Outram, Clyde and Lawrence. I thank them for this.
But it was a sad sight still to see the utter obliteration of
all that has twice been memorable in our history—memorable in the days of the *Rolliad,* and again in the best days
of our Indian history. With the former such a work as
this has little or nothing to do. But the Company's Military Seminary at Addiscombe was, in its time, a remarkable institution, and, in spite of all its defects, it sent forth
many remarkable men. It was established first as a training-
school under civil government. Lord Liverpool's house
near Croydon became an academy self-contained. But after
a while it expanded into a cluster of barracks and study-halls,
and the military governor occupied the ' mansion.' It has
the proud distinction of having sent forth the finest race of
Engineer and Artillery officers that the world has ever yet
seen—men whose pre-eminent merits have been recognized
by such heroes as Hardinge and Napier and Clyde, who,
having risen from the other service, were at least not prejudiced in favour of the Company's corps. There were many
grave errors in the system—very grave they were in my
time; * but there is scarcely an Addiscombe cadet now
living who does not look back with affectionate remembrances
to the years which he spent in those barracks and study-halls,
and who does not admit, in spite of much which his mature
reason condemns, that he grew there in knowledge and in
manliness, and passed out with the making of a first-rate

---

* After that time, some of the graver errors were, I believe,
remedied. I hope that I had something to do with the reform. At
all events, I *tried.*

officer in him. If it were only for the friendships which I formed there—some of which death only has severed, whilst others, after the lapse of a third part of a century, are as green as they were in our youth—there are very few years of my life which I would less willingly suffer to slide out of the calendar of the Past.

That the civil and military services of the East India Company, from the time of the establishment of the Haileybury College and the Addiscombe Seminary, increased greatly in general efficiency, is a bare historical fact. Men such as Elphinstone and Metcalfe, Malcolm and Munro, were independent of such aids. I speak of the general mass of the Civil and Military services of the Company. And if it had been only for the fine sense of comradeship which these institutions developed, they would have greatly enhanced the efficiency of the Services. Men who have known each other in youth, and have kindred associations, work together with a heartiness of zeal less rarely engendered between strangers who have reached the same point by different paths. And even where contemporary limits are passed, and there is no personal knowledge, there is often association through common friends, a traditionary familiarity with character and conduct, and a general feeling of clanship, which are almost as potent as actual acquaintance in the flesh. It is certain, also, that these institutions, which sent forth many accomplished scholars and men of science, did much to improve the general character of Anglo-Indian society, by imparting to it a literary tone, which had been scarcely apparent before. The teachings of Empson and Malthus, Le Bas and Jones, of Cape and Bordwine, Bissett and Straith, and in the important departments of Oriental literature, Ouseley, Williams, and Eastwick in one institution, Shakespear and Haughton in the other, all bore their good fruit; and among those good fruits was a greater softness of manner, which developed itself in an increased regard for the feelings of the natives of the country. Indeed, these seats of learning, with all their faults, were laden with much good to the two Services, and I cannot, now that they have passed into traditions, refuse them a few words of affectionate regret.]

Eldred Pottinger was but fourteen when he went to Addiscombe. Young as he was, he took a good place in his class. But he was esteemed among his comrades rather as an active, manly, courageous boy; very honourable, truthful, trustworthy, and staunch. Even in his childish days, it had been observed that he could keep a secret better than most grown people. He was sure to keep it if the interests of others were concerned. When he was at Addiscombe he committed a grave academical offence. The story has been variously told to me, and I am afraid that the balance of evidence is not much on the side of the more favourable version of it. It is traditionary in his family that he invented a new kind of shell—said to have been something very clever for a youngster of his years—and that he exploded it one day to the consternation of the authorities, and very probably to the extreme peril of his comrades. But his Addiscombe contemporaries believe that he was moved to this exploit less by a love of science than by a love of mischief, and that in reality he merely charged an old shell with gunpowder, and fired it from a mortar in the college grounds. Fortunately, the question is one which it is not material to decide. There was as much good promise in the mischief as there would have been in the scientific ardour of the young artilleryman ; and it is far more important to note, that though others were inplicated with him, Gentleman-Cadet Pottinger took upon himself all the responsibility of the breach of college rules, and tried to bear all the punishment. It well-nigh cost him his commission ; but nothing would induce him to give up the names of those who were associated with him in the affair of the shell.

After the usual period of two years spent at Addiscombe, Eldred Pottinger went up for his final examination, and came out as a cadet of Artillery. He selected the Bombay Presidency, because his uncle, Colonel Henry Pottinger, was fast rising to distinction under that Government. Having joined the head-quarters of his regiment, he devoted himself very assiduously to the duty of mastering professional details both military and scientific. In the knowledge of these he made rapid progress ; and in due course was appointed quarter-master of a battalion. Having served thus, for some time, on the Regimental Staff, he was, through the good offices of his uncle, who then represented British interests in Sindh and Beloochistan, appointed to the Political Department as an assistant to his distinguished relative.* Though he had at no time any great amount of

---

* There is an anecdote current respecting this period of Eldred Pottinger's service, which is worthy of narration, though I do not vouch for the absolute correctness of the words in which it is here narrated. One day, Eldred appeared before his uncle in a great state

Oriental book-learning, he had a considerable colloquial knowledge of the native languages, which he improved under his uncle's superintendence. But an eager longing for active employment had taken possession of him, and there was that, in the political atmosphere at the time, which rendered it likely that the coveted opportunity would soon present itself. And it soon came. Events were taking shape in the countries between India and Persia, which made it a matter of no small importance to the British Government in the East that they should obtain accurate information relating to all that was passing in Afghanistan; and as Eldred Pottinger was willing to penetrate that country as an independent traveller, his uncle the Resident was well disposed to accept the offer. It was, in truth, precisely the kind of service which the adventurous spirit of the young artilleryman was most eager to embrace; and so he went forth, full of hope and expectancy, as one loving danger and excitement for its own sake, and longing to be of service to his country; but moved little by personal ambition, for he had none of the vanity of youth, and self-seeking was far from him. His enthusiasm was of a sturdy, stubborn kind. It cannot be said that he had much imagination;

of excitement, declaring that he had been grossly insulted by a native —a horsekeeper, or some other inferior person—on which Henry Pottinger, amused by his young relative's earnestness, said, smilingly, to him, 'So, I suppose you killed him, Eldred?' 'No,' replied the young subaltern; 'but *I will*, uncle.' Thinking that this was an instruction from higher authority, he was quite earnest in his declaration. It need not be added that the joke exploded, and that the retributive hand was restrained.

but he had something still better, an abiding sense of his duty to his country.

He started in the disguise of a Cutch horse-dealer, and journeyed onwards towards Caubul, with a most unostentatious retinue, and attracted little attention as he went. The route which he took was that of Shikarpore, Dehra Ismael Khan, and Peshawur. At Caubul he determined to push his way on, through the difficult country inhabited by the Imauk and Hazareh hordes, to Herat, the famous frontier city of Afghanistan, assuming for this purpose the disguise of a ' Syud,' or holy man, from the lower part of the country.

Here his adventures commenced. He was eager to explore this rugged and inhospitable hill-country, knowing well the dangers of the route, but knowing also the importance of obtaining correct information relating to it. ' As I had made up my mind,' he wrote in his journal, ' against the advice of the few acquaintances I had in Caubul, and there was some suspicion that Dost Mahomed would prevent my proceeding to Herat, on quitting the place I gave out that I was going out with Syud Ahmed to see the defile of the Logur River. After dark I left the house on foot, having some days previously sent the horses to a caravanserai, and thence ordered those I intended taking to join me at the bridge, where my guide also met and escorted us to his house at Vizierabad, a few miles from the city.'

He had not proceeded far before he fell in with a man who had known Sir Alexander Burnes, and who strongly suspected that Pottinger was a Feringhee. 'We here met a traveller from the opposite direction,' he wrote in his journal, 'an acquaintance of my guide, who had been a pack-horse driver with the kafila, which Sir A. Burnes accompanied to Balkh. He was struck by the fuss my guide was making about me, and appeared to discover me. He joined us, and commenced talking of the " Feringhees" and "Sekundur Burnes." He told me that officer had employed him to collect old coins at Balkh, and, praising his liberality, gave me several hints that he expected I would be equally so, and give him a present. But to all I turned a deaf ear, and would not be recognized, though I listened with all complacency to his stories, and chimed in with the usual explanations in his pauses, so that, as his acquaintance would give him no information, he finally took leave of us, evidently in much doubt as to the correctness of the surmise.' A few days afterwards he was again suspected. A Kuzzilbash asked him whence he came—if from Lucknow. ' I feared,' said Pottinger, 'he had been there, so said " from near Shahjehanabad ;" upon which he informed me that Lucknow was a very fine city, and the only place in India which the Feringhees had not taken ; that he had never been there himself, but knew a person who had. Seeing him pause for an answer, I replied that he, doubtless, was right ; that I myself had the honour of being acquainted with a Syud whose friend had been to Lucknow.' *

But a far more serious difficulty awaited him in Yakoob Beg's country. This man was a noted Hazareh chief, who

* These and all the following extracts are from the unpublished journals of Eldred Pottinger.'

was wont to levy black mail upon all travellers, and, if it
suited his purpose, to sell them off into slavery. He was
not a bad man, after his kind, but he was surrounded and
influenced by a crew of unscrupulous ruffians, and Pottinger
and his companions were for some time in danger of losing
either their liberties or their lives. Detained for several
days in Yakoob Beg's fort, the young English officer was
rigorously examined, and was often at his wits' end to
answer the questions that were put to him. Of the dangers
and difficulties by which he was surrounded he has given
an interesting account in his journal. ' The chief,' he says,
' was the finest Hazareh I had seen, and appeared a well-
meaning, sensible person. He, however, was quite in the
hands of his cousin, an ill-favoured, sullen, and treacherous-
looking rascal. I, by way of covering my silence, and
to avoid much questioning, took to my beads, and kept
telling them with great perseverance, no doubt much to
the increase of my reputation as a holy personage. Syud
Ahmed did the same to cover his ignorance of the Sheeah
forms. This turned the conversation on religious subjects,
and I found that these people knew more than we gave
them credit for, and though on abstruser points I could
throw dust in their eyes, yet on the subject of every-day
duties I was completely brought to a stand-still by my ignorance of the Sheeah faith, and fear lest I should, by mentioning Soonee rules, cause a discovery. Syud Ahmed was
equally puzzled, and felt in full the false position I was in,
and the want of a skilful and clever aid to take the brunt
off my shoulders. Hoosain did all he could, but he was
too distant to prompt me, and by several blunders, or

rather inappropriate attempts of his to support me, I was regularly floored, and at last had to declare that I had not a proper knowledge of these things. I had been a soldier and had not studied, but would do so now. The confusion I showed, and the ignorance of some of my answers, raised the suspicion of the chief's cousin, who, on one of the party asking if the Feringhees had not conquered all Hindostan, said: "Why, he may be a Feringhee himself. I have always heard that the Hindostanees are black, and this man is fairer than we are." I am sure we must all have shown signs of confusion at this. For my own part, I felt my cheeks tingle, and my presence of mind fast failing me, particularly as the whole assembly turned towards me. I had, however, no time for observation, and found I must say something for myself. Hoosain had at once commenced a vigorous denial, in which he was joined by the Caubul merchant; yet the chief, a shrewd fellow, paid no attention to them, and evidently appeared to think there was some truth in it; and the multitude, ever prone for the wonderful, were already talking of the Feringhee in no very complimentary terms, scarcely one paying attention to my defenders. I, therefore, addressing the chief, said that such inhospitality had never before been heard of; that here I had come as a pilgrim trusting to his aid; that I had chosen an unfrequented and barren road because inhabited by the Mussulmans, in preference to the easier road, as it is well known the Afghan people treat them well, and only tyrannize over the sect of Ali, the lawful Caliph; that in India there were Moguls, Pathans, and all sorts of people from cold climates; that, truly, much of it was hot, but that parts were cold to the north, and snow always lay on the mountains, and that if he asked my friends, they would tell him that I was a Kohistanee and a true believer. The chief appeared satisfied with this, and turned his attention to Syud Ahmed and the others, who were all talking together at the top of their voices; and the multitude, on finding me speak as others did, and that I had no monstrosity about me, as they doubtless fancied a Feringhee should have, had gradually turned their attention to those who made most noise; and I, having succeeded in satisfying the demand for an answer, was glad to be silent. My companions, however, carried their explanations too far, and the accuser, besides being obliged to make an apology, was taunted and badgered so much, that even a much less rancorous man would have been irritated and vowed vengeance, and seeing that my attempts to quiet them only added to his anger, I was obliged to hold my peace. It being now sunset, the chief got up and said, " I'll not prevent you from saying your prayers; as soon as I have finished mine, I will return." We immediately broke up, and set to performing the necessary ablutions, and then commenced prayers. I had no taste for this mockery, and not considering it proper, never before having attempted it, was rather afraid of observation. I fortunately, however, by the aid of Hoosain, got through properly, at least unremarked, and then had recourse to the beads till the rest had finished. Syud Ahmed, however, got into a scrape; the Caubulee detected him as a Soonee, but. he was pacified on Hoosain acknowledging that the other was but a new convert going to Meshed for instruction.'

Days passed; Pottinger and his companions were still detained; so they began to meditate flight. The operation, however, was a hazardous one, and it seemed better to wait a little longer, in the hope of receiving the chief's permission for their departure. Meanwhile, there was no little danger of the real character of the party being discovered, for their baggage was subjected to a search, and many of the articles in Pottinger's possession were such as, if rightly understood, clearly to divulge his European origin. Among these was a copy of Elphinstone's *Caubul*, which puzzled them greatly. ' On the 6th,' wrote Pottinger in his journal, ' the chief had evidently an idle day—he came before breakfast, and afterwards coming a second time, examined our loads. There was a small tin can with medicines in it, which attracted his attention; but the danger of it was escaped by saying we were merely transporting it. The printed books were at first passed over, but, being unwatched, one of the meddlers hanging about took Elphinstone's *Caubul* up, and happened to open at a print. We were nearly floored at once, the whole party declaring it was an idol. Hoosain, however, swore that it was not, and that the houses of Kuzzilbashes in Caubul were full of such pictures. A small parcel of reeds next struck their attention, and they would not rest satisfied till opened, when they found some pencils and a pair of compasses, which I had tied there to preserve their points. They were lost in astonishment, and when I said the compasses were for the study of astronomy, a pursuit which the Persian sect, for the purposes of astrology, pay much attention to, I was surprised to find it was in the Hazareh estimation a forbidden science. However, a few names and assertions got us over that. The hangers-on had, in the mean time, got hold of a note-book of mine, in which was a catalogue of generic terms in English, and the equivalents in Persian and Pushtoo. This puzzled them greatly, and the party being joined by a neighbouring chief, the brother-in-law of Meer Yakoob, and a Syud, both of whom could read, there was a general examination of the writing, and no explanation would satisfy them; at last, tired of guessing, they gave it up and retired. . . . The chief asked me how I would like to live with him, and on my replying that if in the summer I found it so cold, what would I do in the winter, he said, " Such a delicate person as you would die in a week. It is only we" (pointing to his miserable half-starved clansmen) " who can stand the cold." The chief here made a slight mistake (from judging by himself, I suppose) : he was certainly a well-fed, hearty-looking fellow, who could have stood or given a buffet with a right good will. As for the others, they were melancholy anatomies, apparently made but to prove in what misery, brutality, and ignorance the human kind can exist. The half-clothed barbarians of Southern Asia have an idea that all persons of fair complexion must be delicate, while we in general attribute delicacy to a dark skin. Their poor—from the want of clothing—expose their bodies to the vicissitudes of the weather, and it becomes tanned, and consequently they think it a mark of hardiness, while their wealthy and great, always covered and housed, retain, in a great measure, their lightness of colour. Hence it is considered the badge of delicacy and effeminacy,'

His prospects were now anything but cheering. His companions were taken ill, and there seemed to be too much reason to apprehend that he would be detected and imprisoned. Another source of disquietude was the extreme dislike of his honest truthful nature to the imposture which he was compelled to act. ' In the evening,' so he wrote in his journal, ' Hoosain was also taken ill with intermittent fever, and Syud Ahmed fancied that he had a relapse. I was, therefore, more alone than usual, and at the time I should have avoided reflection; but I was obliged to review the actions of the day, which had, indeed, followed so fast upon each other, that I had not a previous moment to consider the results. Now that I looked back, well knowing the imposition I had been practising, I could not conceal from myself the true state of the case, and that a discovery had really been made; but that hitherto good fortune had saved us. For the barbarians were not certain in their own mind, though a grain more evidence or the speech of a bold man would probably have decided the affair. I also felt my total incompetency to meet them alone, from my inadequate knowledge of their language and customs; and, as people in my situation generally do, I blackened my prospect a great deal more than it deserved.' Thus he meditated for a while; but he was a man naturally of a cheerful and sanguine nature, so he cast away unavailing anxieties, and fortified himself for the work before him. ' At last,' he continued, ' finding that I could do nothing, I judged it better to join Hoosain's servant in an inroad on our provision-bag, which he was very vigorously undertaking, than pursue such bootless ruminations.' And, indeed,

as he said, his prospects were not so bad as they seemed;
for, on the following day, the morning of the 7th of August,
the Hazareh chief yielded to the persuasions of the strangers
and suffered them to depart in peace.   They had scarcely,
however, recommenced their march, when, to their dismay,
they were summoned back again.   What followed may
best be told in Pottinger's own words. It must be premised
that he had propitiated Yakoob Beg by the gift of a de-
tonator gun.   ' We, congratulating ourselves on getting off,
were gladly climbing the rocky glen which led down to
the castle, and had nearly reached the top of the mountains,
when we were aware of several men running after us at
speed and shouting for us to turn back.   We had no choice
left, so obeyed.   I never saw such a change come over a
party, particularly as the slave-dealers were let go, and we
alone called back, the messengers specifying that the chief
wanted me.   I made up my mind that I was to be detained, and certainly was too annoyed for further talk; it,
however, struck me the chief might want a turnscrew or
bullet-mould, and I left Syud Ahmed behind to unload the
pony, and, if he could find them, send them after.   For
this purpose we halted opposite the strangers' hut, and left
our cattle.   Hoosain and I having made this arrangement,
and charged the others to be cool, with as much unconcern
as we could muster, proceeded on alone.   We had got
then within a few yards of the esplanade in front of the
castle where the chief was, when we heard a shot, and then
a shout of exultation.   What this meant we could not
make out; but whatever it was, it had the effect a good
shout always has of raising my spirits, and I felt that it

would have been a great relief to give so joyful a hurrah myself; but as I thought, we reached the open space, and a few yards took us within speaking distance of the chief, who, in answer to " Peace be unto you," replied, " You may go now,—I don't want you ; I only sent for you to make the gun go off, but it is gone off." I turned to be off too, wishing him most devoutly a passage to Tartarus, but Hoosain had been too seriously frightened to let him go off so quietly, and burst out into so eloquent an oration that he perfectly delighted me, and astonished the Hazarehs. He asked the chief, among other things, " Do you expect that we are to return from Herat, if you choose to send every time your gun misses fire? " He, in fact, quite over-threw the chief by his heat, and that worthy only appeared anxious to get out of reach of such a tongue.'

Without much further adventure, the travellers reached Herat on the 18th of August, having been twenty-six days on the road, eight of which were days of detention. Soon after their arrival they narrowly escaped being carried off and sold into slavery. ' On our first arrival,' wrote Pottin-ger on the 20th of August, ' we went about unarmed; but happening to go to the Musula, a building about eight hun-dred yards from the gate of Muluk, built by Gowhur Shah Begum, the wife of Shah Rook Sooltan, as an academy, without the walls, we were very nearly carried off by the people who live near it in a rendezvous for slaveholders. We were only saved by Syud's Ahmed's presence of mind, who, on being questioned, said we had come with a party to a neighbouring garden to pass the day, and that our com-panions were coming after us. On this they went off, and

we made the best of our way back to the city, with a firm
resolution never again to venture out without our arms; and
it is a rule every one should follow in these countries, unless
attended by an armed escort. However, in any case, a
sword should always be carried, if not by yourself, by an
attendant. So universal and necessary is the custom, that
the Moolahs always travel armed even with an army.'

At this time, Shah Kamran, the reigning Prince of Herat, with his Wuzeer, Yar Mahomed, was absent from his
capital, on a campaign in the still-disputed territory of Seis-
tan. On the 17th of September they returned to Herat,
and all the population of the place went forth to greet them.
They had scarcely arrived, when news came that Mahomed
Shah, the King of Persia, was making preparations for an
advance on Herat; and soon it became obvious that the
Heratees must gird themselves up to stand a siege. Yar
Mahomed was a base, bad man; but he was not a weak
one. He was a man-stealer, a slave-dealer of the worst
type; a wretch altogether without a scruple of conscience
or an instinct of humanity. But he was, after his kind, a
wise statesman and a good soldier; and he threw himself
into the defence of Herat with an amount of vigour and
resolution worthy of a hero of a higher class. Shah Kamran was little more than a puppet in his hands. To this
man, Pottinger, in the crisis which had arisen, deemed it
right to make himself known. The fall of Herat would
manifestly be an event injurious to British interests. He
was an artillery officer, skilled in the use of ordnance, and
knew something of the attack and defence of fortified
cities, from the lessons of Straith and Bordwine. Might he

not be of some use in this emergency? The first step to be
taken was to make the acquaintance of Yar Mahomed. So
he went to his quarters. 'He received me,' wrote Pottinger, 'most graciously; rose on my entrance, and bade me
be seated beside himself. He was seated in an alcove in
the dressing-room of his bath. As it is not customary to go
empty-handed before such people, I presented my detonat-
ing pistols, which were the only things I had worth giving.
After this interview I went about everywhere boldly, and
was very seldom recognized as a European. A few days
afterwards, I paid a visit, by desire, to the King.' From this
time, the disguise which had sat so unpleasantly upon him
—which had, indeed, been a thorn in the flesh of his honesty and truthfulness—was abandoned. He was under the
protection of the King and the Wuzeer, and, save by their
authority, no man dared to molest him.

Eldred Pottinger was the least egotistical of men. He
was provokingly reticent about himself in all the entries in
his journal. In some men this might have been traced to
caution; for his papers might have fallen into hands for
which they were never intended. But, in him, it was simply the modesty of his nature. It is not to be gathered,
from what he has written, in what manner the Wuzeer of
Herat and the young English officer first became friends
and allies, or what was the exact character of the relations
established between them. Yar Mahomed was far too as-
tute a man not to see clearly that the presence of an English
officer in the besieged city might be turned to profitable account; whilst Pottinger, on his part, saw before him a grand
opportunity of gratifying the strong desire which had glowed

within him ever since he was a child. The Persians invested Herat, and his work began. It need not be said that the young artilleryman held no recognized position, either of a military or a political character. He was merely a volunteer. But there were Russian engineers in the Persian camp; and there was never, perhaps, a time when a little European skill and knowledge were more needed for the direction of the rude energies of an Oriental army. There was much in the mode of defence which excited Pottinger's contempt; much which also evoked his indignation. The following passage from his journal illustrates both the want of humanity and the want of wisdom they displayed : ' I have not thought it necessary to recount the number of heads that were brought in daily, nor indeed do I know. I never could speak of this barbarous, disgusting, and inhuman conduct with any temper. The number, however, was al· ways in these sorties insignificant, and the collecting them invariably broke the vigour of the pursuit, and prevented the destruction of the trenches. There is no doubt that great terror was inspired by the mutilation of the bodies, amongst their comrades; but there must have been, at least, equal indignation, and a corresponding exultation was felt by the victors at the sight of these barbarous trophies and the spoils brought in. From the latter, great benefit was derived, as it induced many to go out who otherwise never would have gone out willingly; great benefit was derived from the arms and tools brought in on these occasions ; but though the Afghan chiefs fully acknowledged and felt the value of proper combination for this purpose, they were too irregular to carry through any arrangement. It always appeared to me desirable that every sortie should consist of three distinct bodies : one of unencumbered light troops to break in on and chase off the attackers, the second body to be kept together as a reserve to support the first in case of a check, but not to follow them farther than to a position sufficiently advanced to cover the third party, which should be armed with strong swords or axes, and be ordered to destroy the works and carry off as many tools or arms as possible on the return of the sortie. If successful, the prize property should be equally divided and given to the men on the spot. It is worthy of remark, that all the sorties were made with swords alone, and that, though many slight wounds were given, very few men were killed outright; and that the Afghans, having apparently exhausted the stimulus that carried them on at first, or wanting confidence in their weapons, never once attempted to meet the Persian reserves, the first shot from which was invariably the signal for a general retreat.'

Affairs were obviously now in a bad way; and, three days before Christmas, Yar Mahomed, not knowing what to do, sought the young English officer's advice. ' Mirza Ibrahim,' wrote Pottinger in his journal, ' the Wuzeer's private secretary (I may call him), came to talk quietly over our prospects. I suggested that some one should be sent to the Persian camp to sound the chiefs, and I would go with him ; and he told me no Afghan would venture, and that no Sheeah would be trusted; but he would see what the Wuzeer said. It was our idea at this time that the city must eventually fall. All hopes of diversion until the equinox had failed. For my own part, I could not understand what kept the Persians back. They had an open breach, and no obstacle which would have checked British troops for a single moment. The Afghans were badly armed, and their fire of small-arms could easily have been kept down, while the scattered and desultory exertions of a few swordsmen against a column could have availed little. The Persians, however, had begun scientifically, and in their wisdom did not comprehend what was to be done when the enemy held out after they had established themselves on the counterscarp. Their practice under our officers did not go further, and in this unheard-of case they were at a loss, and the European officers still with them did not appear to have influence enough or skill enough to direct the attacks further.'

The new year found the siege still dragging wearily on, and the Afghans within the walls wondering how it happened that they continued to hold out. Not expecting, however, that this state of things could last much longer, the Shah and his Minister again bethought themselves of sending Pottinger as a negotiator into the Persian camp. On the 19th of January, the young English officer had a lengthy interview with Kamran, in the course of which the King instructed Pottinger with respect to the language —strange language, half entreaty and half threat—which it was desirable to address to the Persian monarch. But a day or two afterwards the King withdrew his sanction to the proposed negotiation, and it was not until the end of the first week of February that Pottinger set forth on his mission. The story is thus told by himself: 'On the 8th of February I went into the Persian camp. I took leave of the Wuzeer in the public bath of the city. He was in company with the Arz-Begy, Ata Mahomed Khan, the Topshee-Bashee, Nujeeb Allah Khan, and his private Mirza (*i. e.* secretary), sitting at breakfast on the floor of the bath. Not one of the party had a rag of clothing on him except a cloth round their waists, while their servants, officers, and messengers from the ramparts stood round armed to the teeth. At the same time the temperature of the Humman was so hot that I burst into a profuse sweat on entering, and it was so overpowering that I would not sit down or join in their meal, bùt hurried off as quickly as I could. The Wuzeer begged me to tell Hadjee Aghasy, the Persian Wuzeer, "that ever since he had been honoured by the title of son, and the Hadjee had assumed that of his father, he had been most desirous of showing his filial affection, and had endeavoured to do so, but the Hadjee, in a most un-paternal manner, had brought the Shah-in-Shah with an army to besiege Herat, and he, by his salt, was bound to stand by his old master; if, however, they would return to Persia, he would follow and show his obedience as a son to the Hadjee and a servant to the Shah-in-Shah; and further, whatever might be his own wish, the Afghans would never surrender, nor dare he propose such a thing to them. That they had heard of the bad treatment the Afghans who had joined Mahomed Shah met with, and that they and he were all frightened by that from joining his Persian Majesty." I then left the city by the gate of Kootoob Chak, accompanied by a small party who went with me to within musket-shot of the village of Baharan, on the west of the town, which the Persian picquets occupy at night. Having left the Afghans, who stood watching my progress and shouting their good wishes, I pursued my way, accompanied by Syud Ahmud, to the Kasid, whom I had mounted on a baggage-pony. The village was unoccupied, and we had to push on through twisting narrow lanes, bounded by high mud walls, and I every moment expected a bullet from some sentinel, as we were approaching in a manner calculated to excite suspicion. The Afghan and Persian plunderers having frequent skirmishes amongst these gardens, all the walls had breaches made so as to favour the approach or retreat of men on foot passing these gaps. I kept a good look-out, and fortunately I did so, as through one I observed the Persians running to occupy the road we were following. I therefore stopped, and made Syud Ahmud wave his turban, for want of a better flag of truce. The Persians, on this, came towards us in a most irregular manner, so much so, that if twenty horsemen had been there, the whole picquet might have been cut off. Some were loading as they ran, and one valiant hero, who came up in the rear, after he had ascertained who we were—to prevent danger, I suppose—loaded his musket and fixed his bayonet. They were a most ragged-looking set, and from their dress and want of beard looked inferior to the Afghans. They were delighted at my coming, and the English appeared great favourites with them. A fancy got abroad that I was come with proposals to surrender, and made the great majority lose all command of themselves at the prospect of revisiting their country so soon. They crowded round, some patting my legs and others my horse, while those who were not successful in

getting near enough, contented themselves with Ahmud
Shah and the Kasid, the whole, however, shouting: "Afreen!
Afreen! Khoosh Amudyd; Anglish humisheh Dostani
Shah-in-Shah!"—"Bravo! Bravo! Welcome. The English were always friends of the King of Kings!" The
officer who commanded the picquet was a Major. He had
been under Major Hart, and knew all the English in Persia,
and when Yar Mahomed was a prisoner in Mushud he
had been in charge of him, so we were soon friends. He
told me he had charge of this post during the day, but that at
night he went to the trenches, and that two hundred men
were sent to this point to relieve him; he invited me into
his quarters, which were in a howze (covered reservoir);
the basin had been filled up, and it now made a very nice
guard-room. I told this man that I had a message for
Mahomed Shah from Kamran Shah, and he apologized for
having to delay me, saying, that as I was a soldier I must
be aware that discipline required I should first be taken to
the Major-General commanding the attack; moreover, I
learnt he belonged to the Russian regiment, and that I
was to be taken before Samson Khan. We only stopped
in the Yavur's (Major's) quarters till a kallyan was produced, and as I did not smoke, the others were hurried
over their pleasure, and we resumed our way to General
Samson's quarters; the way lay through gardens and vine-
yards, in which not even the roots of the trees or shrubs
were left. . Samson received me very civilly, taking me for
an Afghan, and was a good deal surprised at finding I was
a European. He sent for tea and kallyans, and after par-
taking of the tea, sent me on to camp in charge of the

Yavur. News of my arrival had reached the camp before
I did; who or what I was no one knew, but the report
went abroad that I was the Moojhtehed of Herat (a title
only used by Sheeahs, and, therefore, quite out of place
with regard to Herat), and that I had brought the submission of Kamran to Mahomed Shah's terms; the whole of
the camp, therefore, crowded to meet us. As we advanced,
the crowd got denser, and in the main street of the camp
we would have been stopped by the pressure if the escort
had not taken their iron ramrods and laid about them, by
aid of which discipline we reached the tents of Hadjee
Aghasy, the Persian Wuzeer. I was received with considerable civility as an envoy from the town, and after the
usual salutations the Hadjee asked my business. I told
him I was an English traveller, that H.M. Shah Kamran
had sent me with a message to Mahomed Shah, that
Wuzeer Yar Mahomed Khan had charged me with a
message to his Excellency, and that I had brought letters
from the Government of India for Colonel Stoddart, which
had been brought into the town, and the Afghan Government had permitted me to take to Colonel Stoddart. I
further said I wished to see Colonel Stoddart immediately,
as I believed the letters were of importance. To this he
assented, and said that with regard to the message for the
King he would request orders. I then proceeded to Colonel
Stoddart's tent, who I found in the greatest astonishment
possible, as his servants, taking up the general report of my
rank, had announced me as the Moojhtehed of Herat. He
had been undressed, and pulling on his coat to do honour
to the high dignitary, gave me time to enter his tent before

he could get out, so we met at the door, where he over-
whelmed me with a most affectionate Persian welcome, to
which I, to his great surprise, replied in English.   No
one who has not experienced it can understand the pleasure
which countrymen enjoy when they thus meet, particularly
when of the same profession and pursuing the same object.
We had hardly got rid of the crowd who accompanied me,
and got seated, when one of Hadjee Aghasy's servants
arrived and summoned me.   He was rather impertinent,
interrupting our conversation to hasten us, and as he paid
no attention to my answers that I would pay the Hadjee a
visit as soon as I had drunk my coffee, it became necessary
to tell him plainly the longer he stayed the more delay
would occur, as I should not make any preparation to move
while the tent was occupied by strangers.   He was, therefore, obliged to leave.   I was anxious to delay my visit as
long as possible, as I fancied the Hadjee, who is a keen
debater, would enter into long arguments in no way connected with the points at issue, and I was anxious to make
the most of my time and see how the tide of politics was
running.   It must be recollected that I was an Afghan
emissary, and had nothing to do with British politics.   I
had calculated on the Persians making this a plea to prevent my communicating with Colonel Stoddart, and had,
therefore, brought the Kasid (courier) to insure the letters
reaching him, but my unexpected appearance and language
had taken Hadjee Aghasy by surprise, and he unthinkingly
allowed me to go where I was nearly a free agent.   When
I was ready, Colonel Stoddart accompanied me to the
Hadjee's tents.   After we were seated, and the usual com-

pliments passed, the Hadjee asked me to tell him my
message to the King of Kings from Prince Kamran, and
his own one from Yar Mahomed. I replied that the
message from the Afghan King was to the Persian King,
and I could not deliver it to any one else; that regarding
his own message, probably a smaller number of auditors
would be desirable. Assenting to this, he ordered the tent
to be cleared. One young man sat a little longer than the
rest, evidently wishing to remain. The Hadjee, who was
apparently excessively bilious and out of temper, no sooner
saw this than he attacked him with abuse, and his breath
being expended without satisfying his rage, he, no longer
able to speak, spat after the offender, who slunk out of the
tent pale and frightened with the storm he had witlessly
raised. The Hadjee, a small thin man, twisted himself
into a thousand contortions, and anything but dignified. I
delivered my message, and though we talked until past four
o'clock on the subject, we did not get any nearer an agreement. The Hadjee would not listen to the Afghan proposals, as might have been and was expected, nor would
his proposal have suited the Afghans. During the visit he
called for our last map to prove that the British allowed
Herat to be a Persian province. Burnes's map was in consequence produced (with the names of places written on it
in Persian); it, however, proved the Hadjee wrong. He
was very indignant at this, and said the British Government
had never told him, and asked Colonel Stoddart (who,
when the tent was cleared, had been asked to stay) why he
had not heard. Colonel Stoddart replied that he had no
instructions which would explain the point, but he would

refer the case to the Envoy at Teheran; however, he was
not himself aware the British Government had ever received
official information from the Persian Government of Herat
being annexed to that State, while a branch of the Sudozay
monarchy, which family the British Government had
acknowledged (in conjunction with Futteh Ali Shah) as
sovereign in Afghanistan, still held possession of and
claimed it. The Hadjee told both Colonel Stoddart and
myself, on going away, that Mahomed Shah would send
for us *both* in a few minutes. We had scarcely got back
to Colonel Stoddart's tent when the Shah's messenger
arrived. We accompanied him across the esplanade; in
front of the King's tent a large working party was employed
in carving stone shells out of the grave-stones, which they
appeared tolerably expert at. Around the Shah's tents was
the usual serai-purdah, or screen, about eight feet high, of
red canvas. We entered by a narrow door, and found the
Shah seated almost immediately opposite us in a European
arm-chair, under the fly of a large double-poled tent. He
was plainly dressed in a shawl vest, with the black Persian
cap on his head. His personal servants stood at the
opposite end of the diagonal of the tent, with heads bent
and arms folded. The Shah heard Kamran's message, and
replied to it by stating his complaints against Herat, and
added he was determined to take it. He never would be
satisfied till he had a garrison in the citadel. At first he
spoke with much dignity, and he made the most of the
just grounds of complaint which he had. Finally, however,
he talked himself into a passion, and said Kamran was a
treacherous liar. After an audience of half or three-quarters

of an hour, we were given permission to leave. In the evening a tremendous storm set in, attended with sleet and rain; this continued all night. In the morning of the 9th it still continued; about noon the sleet and rain changed to snow, and it continued till dark, when the clouds broke, and it began to freeze hard, which continued all night, and next day, the 10th. The bad weather on the 9th prevented my return to the city, so, after breakfast on the 10th, I mounted, and riding out by the flank of the Persian line, I returned to the city, the gate I came out at, and so avoided the points where hostilities were going on. On my coming back the whole town was in a ferment. What they had expected I do not pretend to know, but from the instant I entered the gate I was surrounded by messengers requesting information. I, however, referred them all to the Wuzeer, and went there myself. After a short interview, I was summoned by a messenger from the Shah. His Majesty having seen my return with his glass, was awaiting my arrival, anxious to hear Mahomed Shah's message. When he had heard it, he replied by a gasconading speech, in which he abused every one. During the storm on the 9th the Afghans mustered to sortie, trusting the inclemency of the weather would make success rest on cold steel. However, on account of my being in the camp they gave up their intention. It was a great pity, as a powerful sortie at this period of the siege would have had a great effect on the after negotiations which took place, while the Persians had an idea the Afghans were much reduced.'

So negotiation having failed, the siege went on, but with very little result on the one side or the other.

Although Mahomed Shah had used such high language, he was really well inclined to come to terms, and he thought it expedient that it should be known in Herat that if the Heratees would admit his rights of sovereignty, he would hold them in abeyance, and abandon the idea of planting a Persian garrison in the place. Above all things, he wished them to get rid of the Englishman, and in future to negotiate for themselves. Only a few days had elapsed, therefore, before a Persian envoy appeared in Herat. The incident is thus narrated by Pottinger in his journal : ' On the 12th, the Persian officer whom I first met, Yavur Agha Jan, was sent in by the Persians to try and talk the Afghans over. He had instructions to represent how much better it would be for them to settle their differences between themselves than càll in the infidels ; the man was also instructed to say that warning should be taken from our conduct in India, where we had pretended friendship and trade to cover our ambition, and, finally, by such deceit, had mastered all India. The Yavur was taken up into the citadel and prevented from communicating with any one of the eunuchs, either Hadjee Firoz Khan or Wuly Khan being always with him. The Persian fire did not in the least diminish on account of their envoy. Indeed, it could scarcely have done so without stopping altogether. In the evening we had another snow-storm, which lasted all night. In the morning (February 13th) the whole country was covered : but at sunrise a thaw commenced, accompanied by sleet, which finally changed to rain, that lasted till three in the afternoon, when it cleared up, and the garrison sent out the Yavur with promises calculated to deceive, but stipulating that, as the Persians were the stronger, they should retire a short distance, as a proof that they really intended peace. . . . The Yavur confidently assured the Afghan chiefs that Mahomed Shah had no wish to interfere in the internal affairs of their country ; he wanted them to supply his armies with soldiers as they had done Nadir; his aim in the present expedition was not Herat, but India ; that it behoved them as Mahomedans to support the Persian King ; that he would pay them liberally, and lead them to the plunder of India and Toorkistan.*

It happened, however, that nothing came of these overtures, There was mutual distrust. The Afghans especially declared that they had no faith in the Persians,

* Under this date (February 13), Pottinger records that he obtained some money on the preceding day from a merchant, in a manner very honourable to the British character. ' As I was sending off a cossid last night,' he wrote, ' a Candahary trader, whom I had never before seen, came and requested me to give him an order on Candahar, offering to pay me gold here. Being in want of money I accepted his offer, and gave him a note to Major Leech, of the Bombay Engineers, an old acquaintance of mine, requesting him to pay the amount, explaining to the man that I was not certain if Major Leech were in Candahar or not, and if not, he must follow him. Though the man couldn't understand a word of English, and no one but myself in Herat could read the note, he implicitly trusted me, for he had learned from the Hindoos and others that I was an English officer. I found a great change in my position for the better when it became known that I was in the British service, and not an impostor personating a European ; for in general the genus Feringhee is expected to wear a cocked-hat, tight pantaloons, and a feather. There are other distinguishing marks also fancied, but they are not agreed to by all, while the above three, as far as I could discover, are universally allowed ; I therefore mention them alone.'

but that if the latter would place their affairs in the hands of Colonel Stoddart, the Heratees would delegate the power of peace-making to Pottinger, and so a satisfactory issue might be attained.   Meanwhile, the siege was continued, with no very material results; and the young English officer was constantly present on the works, advising the Wuzeer or other leading chiefs, and assisting them as much by his resolute example as by his professional skill.

But he did not disguise from himself that his position was one of much difficulty and delicacy, and he doubted sometimes not only whether, as an officer of a Government which, at that time, was a neutral power, he ought to take an active part in the defence, but also whether his presence at Herat might not really be prejudicial to the Afghans. ' It might be alleged,' he wrote, ' from my having a commission in the Indian Army, that I was a secret agent for Government, whereas I was a free agent, Government having most liberally given me a *carte blanche* as to leave and action, in return for which I offered to lay before it my acquisitions in geography and statistics; and I was very apprehensive that my actions might be disapproved of, and I should not have remained in Herat but for the pressing invitations of the Herat Government, which used the argument so persuasive amongst themselves, viz. " that a guest should not leave his host at the approach of danger, but help him through it, so as to congratulate him at the end on his escape." '   Moreover, he felt that his Afghan friends were not altogether free from suspicion that his presence at Herat might not be quite accidental, and that the English had a covert design to possess themselves of the Afghan

country. One passage in Pottinger's journal, which bears
upon this subject, is worth quoting, for it shows the mixed
feelings with which at that time the anticipated interference
of the English in the affairs of Afghanistan was regarded :
' On the 15th (of April) I was invited, in walking through
the works, to stop in an Afghan officer's quarters. He
fancied the English wished to take Afghanistan preparatory
to attacking Persia and Russia, and his gasconading as to
what the Afghans' prowess would be when they were employed by us was quite overpowering. With a great deal
of trouble, I explained to him that the English had no wish
to extend their frontier ; they merely wished to be let alone,
and instead of wanting the Afghans to plunder and attack
their neighbours, they wanted them to stay quietly at home
and eat the produce of their own fields. After considering
a little, my acquaintance replied that it was very fine and
proper, but an impossibility, " for we won't let each other do
so. No Afghan in power will elbow another out of
power to possess wealth, lest it be used to remove him
from his situation ; and all the Alekozyes here have merely
come from necessity. We were turned off our land at
Candahar by the Barukzyes. We have there of hereditary
lands quite sufficient to make us wealthy and influential ;
if we could get them back we would return to-morrow,
and until we can we must live here by plundering others."
I suggested that if the British Government interfered it
would of course endeavour to bring about a settlement of
these claims, though such matters, being of an internal
nature, it did not appear proper a foreign Government should
interfere. He interrupted me testily, saying : " What is the

use of talking? If you interfere in one point, you must in all, for no one will act till you do, and it is nonsense talking of advice and persuasion. Your Vakeels and Elchees will and can do nothing with us till you frighten us. March ten or fifteen regiments to Kelat, and then tell the Sirdars what you want done and they will obey implicitly; till then, no one will fear you." '

But there were times, also, when the young English officer was necessitated to defend his country from the imputation of weakness and insignificance in comparison with the power of other European States. It falls to the lot of all our isolated countrymen in remote Eastern regions to be called upon to disabuse men's minds of strangely erroneous impressions of the geography and the politics of the Western world; and the entries in their journals which relate to these explanations are not among the least interesting of such records. How Eldred Pottinger combated the ignorance of his Afghan friends may be gathered from the following : ' On the 16th the Persians fired from the two-gun battery at the gate of Kooshk all day, and damaged the parapets about the gate a good deal. A small party assembled at Sooltan Khan's post, opposite the Karadaghy attack, to see the firing. The conversation turned upon Europe. ·Sooltan Khan is a very inquisitive, sharp person for his rank, and knows more than Asiatics generally do regarding Europe. He had been reading of Napoleon, and ·had heard from the Persians that the Russians had defeated him, and conquered all Europe but England. After a good deal of trouble, I succeeded in making my auditors understand that Napoleon had been Emperor of the French

nation; that that nation had been tyrannized over by its
sovereigns until they rose up and overturned the monarchy;
that great disturbances and excesses had taken place, and
that the whole of Europe had combined to check the
people and restore the monarchy; that in the ensuing war
Napoleon's talents had saved his country as Nadir did Persia;
and, finally, in the same manner, he had been chosen
Emperor, and had beaten the whole of Europe but England,
which had only been saved by the impossibility of gettiug
to it, our ships having swept the ocean, and completely
prevented an enemy approaching our shores; that the war
had thus raged for many years, and Napoleon, being dis-
pleased with the Emperor of Russia, resolved to dethrone
him, in pursuance of which he marched the greatest part of
his army into Russia, but the Russians, having burnt the
capital with all its stores, left the French monarch, at the
beginning of winter, under the necessity of retracing his
steps or starving, and that in the bitter cold of the Russian
winter his army had perished. The other European nations,
as soon as they found the French army destroyed, rose up
and attacked the Emperor, and he was obliged to succumb
to the universal combination, particularly as many in France
itself opposed him. That so far from France being a province
of Russia, it was a far more powerful Government, and had
a much larger and more effective army than any European
nation whatever. In the numerous disputes and conversations I had with well-informed natives, I always made
it a rule to give them as much information as I possessed
myself, and I studiously avoided any attempts to underrate
the power of any nations in opposition to the English.

When such attempts were made as regards England by the Europeans in the service of Persia and others, and the natives requested me to answer them, or taunted me for not replying, I generally contented myself by remarking that if England were so powerless and insignificant as represented, it was curious that people should take so much trouble to decry its power, in comparison with the powerful states mentioned; that every one thought the best of his own country, and results were all that could be judged by.' *

The monotony of the siege was now and then broken by some exciting incidents, which Pottinger has detailed in his diary with the unadorned accuracy of a soldier's pen. The following may be taken as a fair sample of the whole,

---

* Another sample of this kind of conversation may be given in a note : ' He ' (a Persian messenger) ' amused me much by the manner in which he dilated on the immense extent of Russia, and the number of its arms, which he contrasted with England. After a more than usually high-flown description of Russia, he turned to me and said : " You know that in comparison with Russia there is no use speaking of England. It is only forty parsangs wide, and sixty parsangs long (*i.e.* one hundred and sixty miles, and two hundred and forty) ; it has got no army ; all its wealth is derived from shopkeeping ; and it keeps its position by paying money to other Governments." I did not reply till the worthy's volubility ran him out of breath, when I remarked that the size of England or the number of its armies were of but little consequence, whether it had ten soldiers or ten lakhs was immaterial, for every one knew that no State in the world ever attempted any act of importance in opposition to England, and that only a few years ago the disapproval of the English Government, when mentioned to the Russian Government, had been sufficient to stop the march of the Russian Army on Teheran, and to preserve the King of Kings from becoming a vassal of that empire.'

and it derives an additional interest from the fact that it exhibits the danger to which the young Englishman, ever in the front, was continually exposed: 'April 18. The Wuzeer ordered the Afghans to cease firing, and sit down under cover; they, however, though beaten with the musketry, drew their swords, brandished them above their heads, shouting to the Persians to come on. As might have been expected in such a storm of musket-balls, this bravado caused several casualties. Several men received bullets through the hands and arms. One fellow, more foolhardy than the rest, kept brandishing his huge Afghan knife, after the others had complied with repeated orders to sheathe their weapons, and had the knife destroyed by a bullet, which struck it just above his hand. I had gone down to the spot to see the mine sprung, and was sitting on the banquette with the Wuzeer and a party of chiefs, who, while he was preparing, were bantering the man whose knife was broken, and who came to beg a sword instead, when a bullet came in through a loophole over my head, and smashing a brick used for stopping it, lodged in Aga Ruhyia's lungs, who was standing opposite, one of the splinters of the brick at the same time wounding him in the face. The poor fellow was a eunuch of Yar Mahomed's, and was always to be seen wherever any danger was; he died in two or three days. I had been but the moment before looking through the clods on the top of the parapet, with my breast resting against the loophole, watching the Persians, who were trying to establish themselves in the crater of the mine, and the Afghans in the counterscarp, who were trying to grapple the gabions and overset them, so that the scene was very interesting, and I had not sat down with the chiefs until Dyn Mahomed Khan actually pulled me down by my cloak, to listen to the jokes passed on the man who had his knife destroyed, and thus I escaped Aga Ruhyia's bullet.'

And here the story of this memorable siege enters another phase, and new interests are awakened. The English Minister at the Persian Court, accompanied by Major D'Arcy Todd, an officer of the Bengal Artillery, of whom some account appears in the third volume, was now in the camp of the besiegers; and it was soon manifest that negotiations would be reopened for an amicable adjustment of the differences between Persia and Herat. On the evening of the very day on which Eldred Pottinger had thus narrowly escaped death, news came that D'Arcy Todd was seeking admittance within the works. 'In the evening,' wrote Pottinger, 'the Persians at No. 2 attack announced that an Englishman wanted to come in. The Afghans received the announcement with peals of abuse, fancying it was some of the Europeans in the Persian service. After a great deal of trouble a Persian note was sent in, saying that Major Todd, the Naib of the English Ambassador, had arrived in the Persian trenches, and wanted entrance, and begged the person who might receive the note to inform Yar Mahomed Khan. As soon as the Wuzeer received the note he sent it to me, and I immediately joined him. The greater number of chiefs were assembled in the upper fausse-braie of the west side near the breach. On my arrival I was much disappointed at not seeing any European, as I fully expected to have met Major Todd. The Wuzeer, making room for me on the charpoy where he was sitting, laughingly remarked : " Don't be angry ; I have thrown ashes on it, and blackened its face myself." I begged for an explanation, and learned that he had sent back word that the Afghans neither wanted the Turks, the Russians, nor the English to interfere ; they trusted to their swords, and at that hour of the evening they wouldn't let the Shah-in-Shah in himself; moreover, at that point no person should enter; but if the English Naib would go in the morning to the south-east angle he would be let in. I was much annoyed, and told him he had probably prevented the English Ambassador interfering, and he excused himself by saying that he acted so to make the Persians think he was not solicitous for the English to interfere.'

This, however, was mere gasconading, for which the Afghans of Herat had an unquestionable genius : and on the following day the British emissary was received with all honour. Pottinger's account of his reception is interesting : ' I was sitting with the Wuzeer in Hadjee Firoz Khan's mosque, in the citadel, when the head [of a Persian] was brought up and the report made of the fight, and as it was the point that Major Todd had been directed to enter by, I feared they would not let him in, so went down myself, and just arrived in time, as the Afghans told him to keep away till the evening. The fact was, the explosion of the mine had cut off the retreat of several of the Persian miners without destroying the place they were in. The Afghans were, therefore, digging away on one side to make prisoners of them, and the Persians were doing so on the other side to release their comrades, they themselves working hard for the same purpose. My arrival was most opportune to persuade the Afghans, who thereon ceased firing, and all hostilities above ground, but nothing would induce the miners to be quiet; their blood was up, and digging, they insisted, was not fighting, so the point had to be yielded; and as soon as I ascertained that it was really Major Todd, he was told to come in. Futteh Mahomed Khan, who was an old acquaintance of Major Todd's, invited him into the tent, and had tea made, according to custom. He detained us till the fausse-braie was filled up by a strong body of men, who were thrown in for the edification of a Persian who accompanied Major Todd. Without this, the crowding of the inhabitants of the town to see the Feringhee was sufficient to have astonished any person. Major Todd was, I fancy, the first European who ever appeared in costume in Herat, and the cocked-hat, epaulets, &c. &c., caused great admiration. In narrow streets a small number of persons appears very great, so the crowd to-day appeared tremendous, particularly as the inhabitants of the houses along the line of streets followed were mounted on the roofs to see the procession. Major Todd was sent in by the British Minister to offer the mediation of the British Government between Persia and Herat, and to announce that Mahomed Shah having requested this interference, Shah Kamran's consent was all he now required. Shah Kamran was delighted with the offer, and told Major Todd to request the British Envoy to act as his plenipotentiary, and whatever arrangement was decided on by him the Herat Government would sanction; moreover, he begged Sir John M'Neill would come into the city and talk affairs

over with him. After Major Todd left the presence of
the Shah, his Majesty took off his cloak, and sent it by
Yar Mahomed Khan to Major Todd—a mark of the
highest consideration in the Afghan territories, and one but
seldom paid. A horse was also given ; but Major Todd
was as anxious not to accept presents as the Afghans were
to make them, so he would . not wait for the horse, notwithstanding they set about cutting away the parapet of
the fausse-braie, and making a ramp up the counterscarp to
get the nag out.'

On the same evening—sooner, indeed, than the most
sanguine had dared to expect—Sir John M'Neill sought
admittance into the beleaguered city. There had been a
meeting of chiefs, which Pottinger had attended, and the
discussions had been of a more than commonly warlike
character, when tidings arrived that the British Minister
was coming. 'The assembly,' wrote Pottinger, 'had just
broken up, when a man came in to say that the British
Minister had arrived at the edge of the ditch and wanted entrance. The man was not sent, and had only heard the
report, and ran on to be the first with good news. As
he could not give any intelligence we disbelieved him, and
were composing ourselves to sleep, when the real messenger arrived, with notes from his Excellency for Yar Mahomed and myself. I immediately went down to the south-
west angle, while Yar Mahomed sent to collect some chiefs
to receive the guest with proper honour. On reaching Futteh
Mahomed Khan's post, I found Sir John M'Neill had just
entered the fausse-braie. The chief, who was Kamran's
ambassador to Teheran, knew Sir John, and having re-

ceived much kindness from him, no sooner heard of his Excellency's arrival than he went and brought him into the fortifications, so almost the first person met at the post was the Envoy. After sitting a short time with Futteh Khan we proceeded to the city. We met Dyn Mahomed Khan on the way to Futteh Khan's post to welcome the Envoy, and, accompanied by him, proceeded to the gate of the citadel, where Yar Mahomed met us, and, after embracing the Envoy, led him to his quarters. Here the greater part of the night was spent in discussing the Persian and Afghan propositions; after which Sir John M‘Neill accompanied me to my quarters. When I lay down the day had dawned, and I was a good deal surprised on awaking at half-past six to see the Envoy already up and busy writing. At seven, according to engagement, I sent to let the Wuzeer know that his Excellency was ready to receive him. Yar Mahomed was asleep when the message arrived, but they awoke him, and he joined us in a short time with a whole posse of chiefs. On my meeting him at the door, he asked me was it customary for our Ministers not to sleep at night, declaring that he had scarcely closed his eyes when he was told Sir John M‘Neill was waiting for him; and further remarked : "I do not wonder your affairs prosper, when men of such high rank as your Minister Plenipotentiary work harder than an Afghan private soldier would do even under the eye of the Shah." Yar Mahomed brought a message to Sir John from Shah Kamran inviting him to an interview, and his Excellency immediately proceeded to the citadel, where he had a long interview with his Majesty, who placed everything at his disposal, and promised to agree to everything he decided on, and gave him the fullest powers to negotiate with the Persians. After the interview, the British Minister was requested to partake of the Afghan hospitality, and in the afternoon his Excellency left the city and the armistice ceased. The breaches being open and practicable, and the garrison making no efforts to stop them, the Persian fire was not resumed, and everything remained quiet.' Yar Mahomed was a shrewd man though a bad one, but he seldom said a shrewder thing than that set down in the above extract from Pottinger. Truly is it no wonder that our affairs prosper, when men of the highest rank, far away from the eye of their sovereign, work as hard as a common soldier in the presence of the Shah. It is by conscientious laboriousness of this kind— this duty-doing for duty's sake, so little understood by Asiatics, that we owe our prodigious successes in the East.

But this visit of the British Minister was of no avail. All our efforts at negotiation, breaking down under the characteristic insincerity of the Persians,* failed; and the siege dragged wearily on—all through the months of April and May and June. Now and then a new interest was awakened by pretences of Russian mediation, which were productive of no results. The language, at least, of Yar Mahomed in this case was dignified and becoming. He said that if the first offer of mediation had come from the Russians it might have been accepted by Herat, but that having admitted the arbitration of the British Ambassador, it would

---

* Compare with this statement the opinions expressed by Major Todd, vol. iii. page 44.

not be right that he should turn to the representatives of another country.

It would demand the space of a volume to narrate in detail the incidents of this protracted siege. Throughout many long months, the young English artilleryman was the life and soul of the defence. But there were many great advantages on the side of the Persians, and at last, towards the end of June, the Heratees were almost at their last gasp. Yar Mahomed was beginning to despond, and his followers were almost in a state of prostration. Food was scarce; money was scarce. There was a lack of everything, but of the stubborn courage which continued to animate and sustain the solitary Englishman. On the 25th of June, the Persians made a desperate attempt to carry the place by assault; but Yar Mahomed was incredulous of danger. 'The Wuzeer,' wrote Pottinger in his journal, 'would not take warning, remaining quietly at his quarters, which deceived the garrison, and made many think that the signs of the assault were illusory. Indeed, most of the men had gone to sleep, when suddenly the report of two or three guns and the whiz of a rocket in the air was heard. The enemy immediately opened a heavy fire, but the musketry was feeble : it gradually, however, became more sustained, and the roar of the cannon on all sides was continued. The Wuzeer, on the first alarm, repaired to the gate of Mulick with a small body of men as a sort of reserve.' He soon found that the peril was imminent; and then 'the Wuzeer mounted and went by the gate of Kandahar to the Fausse-braie, sending orders for different chiefs to go to the aid of those on the summit of the breach. In spite of all advice, and even entreaty, his own party was allowed to struggle on in advance, and he arrived nearly alone. Sooltan Mahomed Khan at the same time arrived on the rampart to his brother's assistance, and gave him most opportune aid. The Wuzeer and his party, arriving at the traverses about a third of the way from the end of the upper Fausse-. braie, found the men retreating by twos and threes, and others going off with the wounded : these were stopped. The Wuzeer, however, was alarmed. At first, he sat down about half way, whence, after some trouble, those about him insisted on his going on or sending his son. He chose the former, and sent the latter to the gate of Kandahar to stop stragglers and skulkers and attend to orders. The Wuzeer himself then went on past two traverses, to the last one held by the garrison ; but on finding the men at a stand-still and insensible to his orders or entreaties to fight, he turned back to go for aid. The moment he turned, the men began to give way. He made his way to the first place he had sat down at. There, by showing him the men retreating and the evident ruin that must follow, he became persuaded to stop. Then they succeeded in bringing him back to the first traverse, which having but a narrow passage, his people and those about could turn back those who were coward-like retreating. From this he sent for aid ; but foolishly, in spite of all advice, again allowed the men to go on by twos and threes, so that they did nothing. At last, a Sooltan arrived with about fifty men, when, on a short consultation, it was resolved to send him down into the lower Fausse-braie, to push along, that while those on the rampart were ordered to attempt an attack down the breach, those on the Fausse-braies on the east side should push on the other flank of the Persian column. Pursuant to this, Yar Mahomed, after much entreaty and even abuse, advanced the third time, and finally ventured past the last traverse, where, seeing the men inactive, he seized on a large staff, and rushing on the hindermost, by dint of blows he drove on the reluctant. Some, crowding up in narrow parts, seeing no escape, wildly jumped over the parapet and ran down the exterior slope, and some straight forward; the people on the other side making their rush at the same time. The Persians were seized with a sudden panic; abandoning their position they fled outright down the exterior slope and out of the lower Fausse-braie; after which the business ceased. . . . . The Wuzeer did not behave so well as expected; he was not collected, nor had he presence of mind to act in combination; the Urz-begy was greatly frightened, and did much harm by un-nerving the Wuzeer, who with difficulty could be prevented from following his suggestions, to leave the Fausse-braie and muster the men in the city. The defenders—the people about *—abused, and several times had to lay hold of the Wuzeer and point to him the men, who turned as soon as he did. At last he got furious, and laid on as before-mentioned, without even knowing whom he struck. The alarming state of things at this point, and the frequent

* By 'those about him,' here and in the preceding page, the reader is to understand Eldred Pottinger. It is known that he seized Yar Mahomed by the wrist, dragged him forward, and implored him to make one more effort to save Herat.

messages for aid, put in motion nearly half the garrison and all the chiefs of distinction, so that when the business was over, men came pouring in so as to fill the upper Faussebraie; but the men appointed for the defence of the Faussebraies were so panic-struck, that they took advantage of the watch being temporarily removed from the gates to abscond, and it was with great difficulty that a sufficient number of the garrison could be procured to defend the point.'

It is not to be doubted that the Heratees owed it to the young Englishman that Herat did not at this time fall into the hands of the Persians. But this can be gathered only incidentally from Pottinger's journal. Two days afterwards I find him thus expressing his astonishment at the result. ' A man arrived from Kurookh ; he said he had left a detachment of six thousand Orgunjees, who only waited for orders to foray, or even attack the Persian outposts ; I was surprised to find my share of the business of the 25th had reached Kurookh. The moment the man arrived, he seized and kissed my hands, saying he was rejoiced he made so great a pilgrimage.' But it was not all fame. The great things which had been done by the individual gallantry of this one English gentleman increased the difficulties of his position. It was soon plain that the Heratees really wished to get rid of him. The entries in his diary show the perplexities in which he was placed : ' July 8th. Had a visit from the head Jews, to thank me for my interference, and found that they were still in fear. . . . . The Persians wrote to Yar Mahomed Khan, that they would give up Herat to the Wuzeer, if he would but send Kamran and me to them as prisoners; I told him he had nothing to do but to tell me to go, and I would go to them of myself, if they said that was all they wanted. He appeared to perfectly understand the deceitful nature of the offering. 25th. The Wuzeer received a letter from Hadjee Abdool Mahomed in the Persian camp, *upbraiding him for joining with infidels against Islam,* and for holding on by the skirt of the English, from whom he could never receive any advantage; that they would flatter him and give money as long as suited their interest, as they do in India, and when they had made a party in the country and knew all its secrets they would take it for themselves; that the Government found such was what they wanted to do in Persia, but had on the discovery prevented it by turning them away; and that until the Envoy of these blasphemers—myself—was also turned out of the city, they would not allow the Mooshtuhid to venture into the city. A note to the same effect was received from the Wuzeer's brother, with the addition that the Russian Envoy would not send his agent till I left.——July 6th. In the morning, the Afghans had a consultation of what they would answer. At last it was resolved the Wuzeer should write in answer, that the Englishman is a stranger and guest, that he had come to the city, and in the present state of affairs the Afghans could not think of turning him out of the city; for in the distracted state of the country he could not arrive in safety in his own country, and if anything happened to him it would be a lasting disgrace to the Afghan name, and as a guest he must go or stay according to his own pleasure; moreover, the Wuzeer wrote that he did not hold out in expectation of aid from the English, that he had no wish to join that state against Persia (Iran), from his connection with which he had no wish to tear himself, but that the Persians would give him no choice, but surrendering or fighting, which he did from necessity and not from being so absurd as to wait for aid from London.——August 6th. In the evening, when the Persians had gone, went to the assembly. The Wuzeer told me that, the whole business being upon me, the Persians made a point of obtaining my dismissal, without which they would not treat. They were so pressing that he said he never before guessed my importance, and that the Afghan envoys, who had gone to camp, had told him they had always thought me one man, but the importance the Persians attached to my departure showed I was equal to an army. The Afghans were very complimentary, and expressed loudly their gratitude to the British Government, to the exertions of which they attributed the change in the tone of the Persians; they, however, did not give the decided answer they should have, but put the question off by saying I was a guest——August 30th. The movement of the Persians is spoken of with increased positiveness, but no certain intelligence could be procured, notwithstanding the Afghans were grumbling at the delay of the English, and Yar Mahomed himself was one of the agitators of this feeling, he giving out in public that, in his opinion, the English Government intended to drop the connection, that it wanted merely to destroy the Persian power, and did not care if the Herat power was at the same time rooted up. All sorts of absurd rumours were rife; but a very general opinion, originating from the Persian zealots, was that the

British and Russian Governments were in alliance to destroy
Mahomedanism and partition off the country, dividing India
from Russia, between them.'

Soon after this, the siege was raised. The Persians,
moved by their repeated failures, and by the demonstration
made by the British in the Persian Gulf, struck their camp,
and Herat was saved—saved, as we may believe, under
Providence, by the wonderful energy of the young artilleryman, who had done so much to direct the defence and to
animate the defenders. We shall never very accurately
know the full extent of the service which Eldred Pottinger
rendered to the beleaguered Heratees ; and for this reason
(as I have before said), that the extreme modesty of the
journal, which lies before me, has greatly obscured the
truth. He was at all times slow to speak of himself and his
doings ; and it can be gathered only inferentially from his
narrative of the siege, that he virtually conducted the operations of the garrison. That the Persians believed this is
certain ; and it is equally clear that, although Yar Mahomed
and other Heratee chiefs, being naturally of a boastful, vain-
glorious character, endeavoured to claim to themselves the
chief credit of the victory, the people in the surrounding
country knew well that it was to the personal gallantry of
the young Englishman that they owed their salvation from
the Persian yoke. But he was himself greatly surprised at
the result, and when the siege was over declared it to be the
strangest thing in the world that such a place and such a
garrison could have held out for so many months against
the whole Persian army, aided, if not directed, by European
officers, and under the inspiring influence of the personal

presence of the Shah. In an elaborate report upon Herat, which he drew up nearly two years afterwards, he said: ' It is my firm belief that Mahomed Shah might have carried the city by assault the very first day that he reached Herat, and that even when the garrison gained confidence, and were flushed with the success of their sorties, he might have, by a proper use of the means at his disposal, taken the place in twenty-four hours. His troops were infinitely better soldiers than ours, and twice as good troops as the Afghans. The non-success of their efforts was the fault of their generals. . . . . The men worked very well at the trenches, considering they were not trained sappers, and the practice of their artillery was really superb. They simply wanted engineers and a general to have proved a most formidable force.'

There was now a season of repose for Herat, but it was the repose of utter prostration. The long-protracted siege, and the exactions which had attended it, had reduced the people to a condition of unexampled misery. The resources of the state were exhausted; the people were starving; and Yar Mahomed was endeavouring to recruit his finances by the old and cherished means of slave-dealing. In this crisis Pottinger put forth all his energies a second time for the defence of Herat. By obtaining from his Government advances of money he was enabled to restore both trade and cultivation, which had been well-nigh suspended, and thus large numbers of people, who had emigrated in despair, were induced to return to their homes. The ascendancy which he thus obtained enabled him to exert his influence for the suppression of the horrible traffic in human flesh—good work, in which he was aided by Colonel Stoddart, who remained for some time at Herat with him. But these and other humane efforts for the protection of the people were distasteful in the extreme to Yar Mahomed, and a few months after the raising of the siege the English officers were openly insulted and outraged. Colonel Stoddart quitted Herat for Bokhara in the month of January; and Pottinger, after the insults he had received, would have gone also, but he was earnestly implored by Shah Kamran to remain, and he knew that it was the wish of his Government that he should not quit his post.

In the mean while, the Government of India were equipping the Army of the Indus, and maturing their measures for the restoration of Shah Soojah to ' the throne of his ancestors.' Their first manifesto was put forth on the 1st of October, at which time intelligence of the retreat of the Persians from before Herat had not reached Lord Auckland. At the end of this manifesto there was a notification distributing the agency by which our diplomatic operations in Afghanistan were to be conducted, and Lieutenant Eldred Pottinger was then appointed senior Political Assistant to the Envoy and Minister. But, after a little while, news came that the siege had been raised, and another public announcement was put forth, declaring that although the British Government regarded the retreat of the Persians as a just cause of congratulation, it was still intended to prosecute with vigour the measures which had been announced, ' with a view to the substitution of a friendly for a hostile power ' in Afghanistan, and to the establishment of a permanent barrier against schemes of aggression on our North-Western Frontier. And then the Governor-General proceeded to render honour to Eldred Pottinger in these becoming terms: ' The Right Honourable the Governor-General is pleased to appoint Lieutenant Eldred Pottinger, of the Bombay Artillery, to be Political Agent at Herat, subject to the orders of the Envoy and Minister at the Court of Shah Soojah-ool-Moolk. This appointment is to have effect from the 9th of September last, the date on which the siege of Herat was raised by the Shah of Persia. In conferring the above appointment on Lieutenant Pottinger, the Governor-General is glad of the opportunity afforded him of bestowing the high applause which is due to the signal merits of that officer, who was present in Herat during the whole of the protracted siege, and who, under circumstances of peculiar danger and difficulty, has by his fortitude, ability, and judgment, honourably sustained the reputation and interests of his country.'

So Eldred Pottinger continued to dwell at Herat until September, 1839, by which time Major D'Arcy Todd had arrived on a special mission, of which mention is made in a subsequent Memoir. Pottinger then made his way by the route of Bameean to Caubul, where he found the British Army encamped, and the British Embassy, under Macnaghten, established. After a brief residence there, he quitted the Afghan territory, and went down to meet the Governor-General in the Upper Provinces of India. He was warmly welcomed by Lord Auckland, who received with the liveliest interest the information with which he was laden, and would have heard with warmer admiration his narrative of the stirring scenes in which he had been engaged, if he had spoken more of himself and his actions. He was of course invited to join the Government circle at dinner; but nothing was known of his arrival until the guests were assembling in the great dinner-tent. Then it was observed that a 'native,' in the Afghan costume, was leaning against one of the poles of the tent; obviously a shy, reserved man, with somewhat of a downcast look; and the Government-House Staff looked askance at him, whispered to each other, wondered what intruder he was, and suggested to each other that it would be well for some one to bid him to depart. But the 'some one' was not found; and presently the Governor-General entered, and leading his sister, Miss Eden, up to the stranger, said, 'Let me present you to the hero of Herat.' And then, of course, there was a great commotion in the tent, and, in spite of etiquette, the assembly burst into something like a cheer.

Then Eldred Pottinger went down to Calcutta and remained there for some time, during which he drew up certain valuable reports on Herat and the adjacent country. In the mean while, Major Todd was doing the work of the Political Agency, to which Pottinger in the first instance had been appointed, and it was not thought expedient to disturb the arrangement. So another post was found for the young Bombay Artilleryman, and the year 1841 found him again serving in Afghanistan. He had been appointed Political Agent on the Turkistan frontier, and his head-quarters were in Kohistan, or the country above Caubul, where he dwelt, with a small staff of officers and a native escort, in what was known as the Lughmanee Castle.

As the autumn advanced, Pottinger saw most clearly that there was mischief in the air; that the measures of retrenchment, so injurious to the interests of the Kohistanee as of other chiefs, were fast relaxing the only hold which we had upon their forbearance. The tie which bound them to us was the tie of gratified avarice. But now our great system of bribery was beginning to collapse. When Pottinger knew what had been done, he scented the danger at once, and he wrote several letters of earnest remonstrance to Sir William Macnaghten. 'In September,' wrote Pottinger, 'the Envoy sent several back; not understanding the reason why, I remonstrated with him, and he then informed me that he was ordered by Government to make retrenchments, and that it had been resolved to diminish the gross amount of pay to the military throughout the country by one-third. Immediately on the receipt of this I wrote as strongly as, it appeared to me, became my situation, to the Envoy, and pointed out the danger likely to accrue from irritating the minds of people in a province so surrounded by rebellious districts, and particularly the gross breach of public faith which would be committed if this measure were carried into effect throughout the Kohistan, and begged he would, at least, spare the chiefs installed last year (1840). The Envoy replied that he could not help the reduction, as his orders were peremptory, but he informed me that the chiefs who were advanced under our knowledge during the past year should be considered as excused.' Day after day appearances became more threatening. It was plainly necessary to do something. If we could not any longer purchase the submission of the chiefs, we might overawe them by a display of force. So Pottinger went to Caubul, and urged upon the Envoy the expediency of sending an expedition into the Nijrow country, and 'getting rid of some of the most dangerous of our enemies.' To this Sir William Macnaghten was averse. 'He, however, wrote Pottinger, 'referred me to General Elphinstone, and told me that if the General would consent, he would. On visiting the General, I found that he had received such reports of the country, that he would not permit an expedition without further information; whereupon I offered to take any officers the General might select and show them the country, as my presence in the Kohistan was necessary. I returned there before anything was determined.'

During the early part of October, the Kohistanees remained outwardly quiet; but day after day brought new rumours of coming insurrection, which Pottinger duly reported to head-quarters. But both Macnaghten and Burnes said that they could see no grounds of alarm—no cause for suspicion. 'Notwithstanding,' said Pottinger, 'by the end of the month my suspicions were so aroused, that I felt it my duty to recommend that hostages should be demanded from the Kohistanee chiefs. To this measure the Envoy reluctantly consented, and I only succeeded in procuring them by the end of the month, when everything betokened a speedy rupture.' The enemy were then gathering around him; and though many of the chiefs came to him with professions of friendship and offerings of service on their lips, he clearly saw the necessity of strengthening his position and taking precautions against a sudden attack. But it was necessary, at the same time, to veil his suspicions, and therefore, as he said, his defensive operations were restricted to half-measures.

It has already been told how on the second day of November the storm burst furiously over Caubul. It soon swept into the Kohistan. On the morning of the third, it was plain, from the number of armed men that were gathering round the Lughmanee Castle, that the crisis was close at hand. The chiefs, however, still professed friendship, and clamoured for rewards. Pottinger then told the principal men that if they would render the service required from them they should have not only rewards, but dresses of honour from the King. They appeared to be satisfied, but said it was necessary that this should be explained to the petty chiefs who were in the adjacent garden. On this, Pottinger sent out his Assistant, Lieutenant Rattray, to commune with them. Soon conscious that foul play was designed, Rattray was about to leave the assembly, when he was shot down. A friendly Afghan had run to the castle to apprize Pottinger that treachery was around him. 'He had scarcely made me comprehend his meaning,' wrote Eldred, 'as he spoke by hints, when the sound of shots alarmed us. The chiefs with me rose and fled, and I escaped into the castle through the postern-gate, which being secured, I ran on the terre-plain of the ramparts, and thence saw Mr Rattray lying badly wounded about three hundred yards distant, and the late tenderers of service making off in all directions with the plunder of the camp. Before I was master of these facts, a party of the enemy crossing the field observed Mr Rattray, and running up to him, one put his gun to his head and despatched him, whilst several others fired their pieces into different parts of his body.'

And now what was to be done? The enemy were swarming around him; and those of his own people, who remained faithful among the faithless, were few. Captain Codrington was then with Pottinger in Lughman, but his regiment was three miles off, at Charekur. The alarm, however, had been given; and in the course of the afternoon, young Haughton, the Adjutant of the Ghoorkhas, a gallant soldier, who has well fulfilled the promise of his youth, appeared with two companies of the regiment, and then Codrington, mustering what men he could, made a sortie and joined him. There was then some sharp fighting, and the gardens were cleared. By this time night was falling. It was the duty both of Codrington and Haughton to return to Charekur; but they left Pottinger some sixty men, which made up his entire garrison to a hundred, all the ammunition at his disposal amounting to only fifteen rounds a man. But his friends of the Ghoorkha regiment promised to bring him fresh supplies and new reinforcements of men on the morrow; so he determined, with God's will, to maintain his post.

But it was not so ordained. The attempted relief failed. Codrington sent out four companies of the Ghoorkhas and a six-pounder gun; and if the gallantry of the young officers, Haughton and Salisbury, could have insured success, the desired succour would have been conveyed to the Lughmanee Castle. But the enemy were numerous, and some of our troops were young and impetuous. The detachment was, therefore, compelled to fall back with

466 MAJOR ELDRED POTTINGER. [1841.

heavy loss. Salisbury was killed, and Haughton was obliged to take back the remains of his disheartened party to Charekur. 'On perceiving the retreat,' wrote Pottinger, 'I concluded Captain Codrington would not again attempt to relieve me, and as I had no ammunition beyond the supply in the men's pouches, I determined to retreat on Charekur after dark; but the better to hide my intention, ordered grain to be brought into the castle.'

By wise arrangements, which eluded the vigilance of the enemy, Pottinger with a few followers contrived to make good his retreat to Charekur, under the shadow of the night. He had scarcely thrown himself into that place, when the enemy began to rage furiously against the people of the King and his supporters. The time for negotiation had passed; so Pottinger, divesting himself of his political character, took command of the guns, and prepared to resist the insurgents.

The little garrison had stout hearts, and they fought manfully, making frequent sorties against the enemy, but prevailing not against the crowds that were gathering around them. In one of these sorties Pottinger was wounded by a musket-shot in the leg; and soon afterwards, Captain Codrington, who commanded, was killed. Then young Haughton took the command, and against fearful odds performed feats of heroic gallantry, which won the admiration and perhaps excited the not ungenerous envy of his disabled comrade.*

* After the death of Captain Codrington, wrote Pottinger in his Budeeabad report, the enemy were 'repulsed with loss from the barracks, when Mr Haughton, on whom had devolved the command,

There was, however, an enemy which it was impossible to resist. The little garrison held out manfully against vastly superior numbers, but they were perishing from thirst. The insurgents had cut off their supplies of water, and there was no hope for them. Reduced to this strait, they were summoned to surrender. The condition to secure their safety was that Christians and Hindoos alike should accept the Mahomedan faith. ' We came to a Mahomedan country,' answered Pottinger, ' to aid a Mahomedan sovereign in the recovery of his rights. We are, therefore, within the pale of Islam, and exempt from coercion on the score of religion.' They told him that the King had ordered the attack, and he replied, ' Bring me his written orders. I can do nothing without them.'

But the thirst was destroying them. The last drop of water had been served out ; and when they endeavoured to steal out in the night to obtain a little of the precious moisture from a neighbouring spring, the enemy discovered them and shot them down like sheep. There was failure after failure, and then the disciplined fighting men became a disorganized rabble. The few that remained staunch were very weak, and they had but a few rounds of ammunition

followed up the success and drove the enemy back by a sortie far beyond the gardens occupied in the morning, and maintained the ground despite the incessant attacks of the enemy, who did not desist till dark.' And again : ' On the 9th, the enemy blew up a part of the south-west tower, owing to the carelessness of the guard. Before, however, the enemy could profit by the breach and the panic of our men, Mr Haughton rallied the fugitives, and leading them back, secured the top of the parapet with a barricade of board and sand-bags.'

in their pouches. With this little body of Ghoorkha troops, Pottinger and Haughton, having taken counsel together, determined to fight their way to Caubul. The story of their escape shall be told in Pottinger's own words: 'On the 12th,' he wrote, 'after dark, Mr Haughton ordered out a party to cover the water-carriers in an attempt to get water. The Sepoys, however, left the ranks to supply themselves, and dispersed on being fired at; in consequence, the water-carriers failed in their object. A sortie, consisting of two companies, under Ensign Rose, was then ordered: one company separated, and the men left their officers in search of water; the other company, under Mr Rose himself, fell on a post of the besiegers, and put every man of it to death. They, however, became unaccountably panic-struck (lest the enemy should come down in force), and fled back to the barrack. Mr Rose, being left nearly alone, was obliged to return without gaining his object. Mr Haughton having apprized me of these circumstances, and that the corps was nearly disorganized from the privations it had suffered, the utter inefficiency of the native officers (who had no sort of control over the soldiers), the exhaustion of the men from constant duty, the total want of water and provisions, I considered that one only chance of saving any portion of the regiment was a retreat on Caubul, and though that was abundantly perilous, I entertained a hope that the most active men, who were not encumbered with wives and children, might reach it in safety. Mr Haughton coincided, but lest the enemy should hear of our intention, we resolved that the men should not be informed till paraded for starting. In the afternoon of the 13th, Mr Haughton discovered amongst the Punjab artillerymen two men who had deserted from that body a few days previous, and, while apprehending them, the Jemadar of artillery snatched a sword from a bystander, and before aid could be given cut down and severely wounded that officer. He then, followed by the artillerymen, and the greater number of the Mahomedans in the castle (barracks), taking advantage of the opportunity, ran off at the same time. This caused such a tumult, that, at first, I feared the enemy had attacked and were driving our men from the walls; under this impression I had myself hurried to the main gate, but found on arrival that Dr Grant had secured that, and rallied the men. The native officers immediately gathered round with many of the Sepoys, to assure me of their fidelity; but the latter were evidently disorganized, which may be judged of from the fact of their having plundered the treasure and Captain Codrington's quarters the moment I left them, and, in face of the enemy's fire, pulled down the officers' boxes which had been piled up as traverses to cover the doorways, broken them open, and pillaged them. In the evening (Dr Grant having previously spiked all the guns with his own hands), we marched out of the barracks by the postern. The advance was led by myself (as Mr Haughton, who accompanied me, was unable to do more than sit on his horse), Dr Grant brought out the main body, and Ensign Rose, with the quartermaster-sergeant, brought up the rear. I found it totally impossible to preserve any order after leaving the gate, and in vain attempted leading the men to besiege a building generally occupied by the enemy after nightfall, so that we might cover the exit of the main body from the barracks;

and it was not without much difficulty I eventually succeeded
in halting the men about half a mile from the barracks, till
Mr Rose, with the rear, closed up. . Dr Grant, however,
was missing, and was never afterwards seen. After this we
proceeded in a disorderly crowd along the road to Sinjitdereh,
on which I knew we should soonest find water. At the
first place we did so; a great delay took place, and I, with
the advance, suddenly found we were separated from the
main body, but after some search I rejoined them. Below
Sinjitdereh we were obliged to leave the road, lest alarm
should be taken, and were considerably delayed before we
found the road again on the other side of the village. On
reaching Istalif we were obliged to do the same thing, when
finding very few men inclined to push on, and that I was
getting exhausted with the pain of my wound and fatigue,
I determined pushing on with Mr Haughton, and trying to
reach Caubul before daylight. Neither of us was capable
of the exertion or of sustaining the fatigue consequent on
the slow movements of the regiment; we, therefore, rode
on, but having no guide, we got into so many difficulties,
that day was breaking when we reached the range of
mountains about half way between Charekur and Caubul,
where, at Mr Haughton's advice, our horses and selves being
quite exhausted, we halted in a deep and dry ravine. Our
other companions were a Sepoy of the regiment, my English
writer, and the regimental bunya. In the forenoon we
were alarmed by firing in the mountains above us, but
otherwise we passed the day undisturbed. At dusk we
resumed our route. Being prevented by watch-fire attempt-
ing to gain the high road, we followed a sheep-path over

the mountain into the plain of Altifat, which we crossed, avoiding the castle of that name, and leaving the main road; from that plain crossed the remaining range of hills by a footpath descending into the Caubul plain behind the lake, round the southern end of which we took our road, intending to cross the cultivated land to cantonments by the back of the Shah's garden at Kila-boleno. Where we should have branched off, I missed the turn, and as we were within the enemy's sentinels I feared to attract observation by turning (when I discovered my mistake); this obliged me to make for Deh-Afghan, intending to try that road, but on reaching that we found the place occupied, and ourselves so urgently challenged by the sentinels, that we were obliged to pass on to the city, which having gained without interruption, we pursued our way through the lanes and bazaar along the river-bank till we gained the skirts of the city, where we found a picket. We had nearly passed, when we were observed and called on to stop, and as we did not do so, several pursued us, but as the horses gained on them, they fired, and we received a volley from the now aroused picket, fortunately without any injury, and a few hundred yards farther carried us to our own entrenched cantonment, which we found besieged. My wound had become so painful and irritated from want of dressing and exertion, that I was obliged to keep my bed for some time.'

I have suffered Eldred Pottinger to tell his own story, but one incident omitted from the narrative must be told here to complete the recital. When they were not far from Caubul, Haughton feeling utterly exhausted from pain, loss of blood, fatigue, and want of food, implored Pottinger to leave him to die and to save his own life. Pottinger said that he would die with his comrade, but that he would never desert him; and after resting awhile, both contrived to struggle on, and were, almost miraculously, saved.

When Eldred Pottinger reached Caubul, he was compelled, for some time, to nurse his wounds; but, before long, the great crisis of the insurrection brought him again to the front. Sir William Macnaghten, who was at the head of the British Mission, was slain by Akbar Khan; and every man in camp then felt that Pottinger was the man above all others to rescue the English from the difficulties which hemmed them in as with a ring of fire. It was on the 23rd of December, 1841, that the Envoy was killed. On the 25th, Pottinger wrote to Major Macgregor, who was Political Agent at Jellalabad:

'Caubul, December 25, 1841.

'My dear Macgregor,—We have had a sad Comedy of Errors, or rather tragedy, here. Macnaghten was called out to a conference and murdered. We have interchanged terms on the ground he was treating on for leaving the country; but things are not finally settled. However, we are to fall back on Jellalabad to-morrow or next day. In the present disturbed state of the country we may expect opposition on the road, and we are likely to suffer much from the cold and hunger, as we expect to have no carriage for tents and superfluities. I have taken charge of the Mission. Mackenzie, Lawrence, and Conolly are all seized.

The first two I fear for. The latter is quite safe. The cantonment is now attacked.

> ' Yours, very truly,
> ' ELDRED POTTINGER.

Five days afterwards he wrote to Captain Mackeson, at Peshawur—disguising the language of his letter in French, and signing his name in Greek, because there were those in the enemy's camp who could read English :

'Cantonnements à Cabool, 30me de Décembre, 1841.

' MON CHER MACKESON,—J'ai eu le plaisir de recevoir votre lettre du 12me au feu Envoyé. Notre situation ici est des plus dangereuses. L'Envoyé était tué à une conférence, qui avait lieu hors d'ici, le 23 de ce mois. Quand je prenais charge je trouvais qu'il avait engagé du part du gouvernement de quitter Afghanistan, et de donner *hostages* pour que le Dost soyait mis en liberté, aussi que pour préliminaires il avait rendu le *Balla Hissar* et les forts qui dominent les cantonnements. *Ces acts* et le manque des vivres faisaient les cantonnements untenable, et les quatre officiers militaires supérieurs disaient qu'il fallait résumer le traité au lieu de forcer une marche rétrograde sur Jellalabad. Nous avons aujourd'hui finis les termes du traité, et nous espérons partir d'ici demain ou après demain. De leur promesses je m'en doute, malgré que les ordres ont été expédiés pour que nos troupes quittent Candahar et Ghizny. Il faut que vous tenez ouvert le Khyber, et que vous soyez prêt nous aider le passage ; car si nous ne sommes pas protégés, il nous serait impossible faire halte en route pour

que les troupes se refraichissent, sans laquelle j'ai peur qu'ils
soient désorganisés.

> ' Votre ami,
>
> ' Ελδρεδ Ποττινγερ.

' Après aujourd'hui j'écrirai mon nom en lettres
Grecques. Lorsque le Cossid vous remettra cette lettre
vous lui donnerez trois cent rupees.'

It is hard to say what Eldred Pottinger suffered when
he found himself compelled to negotiate with the enemy
for the surrender of Caubul and the evacuation of the
country. He vehemently opposed himself to the weak
policy, which had been agreed upon before he was placed
in the direction of affairs. He protested; he remonstrated;
but all in vain. The military authorities had determined
that they could fight no longer, and that there was nothing
to be done but to make an ignominious retreat from the
country which they had so proudly invaded. The explanation of the circumstances which at last compelled him,
sorely against the promptings of his own courageous heart,
to negotiate with the Afghan chiefs for a safe-conduct, is
on record. ' We received,' he wrote, in a report to Government drawn up at a subsequent period, ' a tender from
Mahomed Oosman Khan, offering to escort the army to
Peshawur for the sum of five lakhs of rupees, as had been
offered him (he said) by Sir W. Macnaghten. At the
same time, letters from Captains Macgregor and Mackeson
were received, urging Sir William to hold out, and informing us of the reinforcements which were on their way from

India. The information from the city showed that feuds. were running high there, and that Shah Soojah appeared to be getting up a respectable party for himself. When I informed General Elphinstone of these facts, he summoned a council of war, consisting of Brigadier Shelton, Brigadier Anquetil, Lieut.-Colonel Chambers, Captain. Bellew, and Captain Grant. At the Major-General's request I laid the above-mentioned facts, and the enemy's tenders, before these officers, and also my own opinion that we should not treat with the enemy, because —*firstly*, I had every reason to believe that the enemy were deceiving us; *secondly*, I considered it our duty to hold aloof from all measures which would tie the hands of Government as to its future acts; and *thirdly*, that we had no right to sacrifice so large a sum of public money (amounting to nineteen lakhs) to purchase our own safety—or to order other commanding officers to give up the trusts confided to them—for it was especially laid down by writers on international law, that a General had no authority to make any treaty, unless he were able to enforce the conditions, and that he could not treat for the future, but only for the present. The council of war, however, unanimously decided that remaining at Caubul and forcing a retreat were alike impracticable, and that nothing remained for us but endeavouring to release the army, by agreeing to the tenders offered by the enemy; and that any sum, in addition to what had already been promised by Sir William Macnaghten, if it tended to secure the safety of the army, would be well expended, and that our right to negotiate on these terms was proved by Sir William Macnaghten having agreed to them before his assassination. Under these circumstances, as the Major-General coincided with the officers of the council, and refused to attempt occupying the Balla Hissar, and as his second in command, who had been there, declared it impracticable, I considered it my duty, notwithstanding my repugnance to and disproval of the measure, to yield, and attempt to carry on a negotiation. For the reasons of the military authorities I must refer you to themselves.'

In a letter of a more private character, addressed to Captain Macgregor, our Political Agent at Jellalabad, Pottinger thus stated the necessities which had driven him to work out the capitulation, however distasteful to his individual manhood. 'There are many points,' he wrote, 'that my character requires me to explain, particularly that we continued our negotiations with the enemy in direct opposition to my advice, and that we were prevented from going into the Balla Hissar by the obstinacy of Brigadier Shelton, who declared the attempt impracticable. The General (Elphinstone), from his illness, was incapable of making up his mind, and the constant assertion of the impossibility by his second in command, outweighed the entreaties of the Envoy when alive (who was always afraid to commit himself in military matters), and of mine afterwards; and a retreat on Jellalabad was the only thing they would hear of; and, notwithstanding that I pointed out the very doubtful character of any engagement we might make with the heads of the insurgents, and the probability they could not make it good, and begged that they would spare us the dishonour and guard the loss which any negotiation must

entail. In a council of war held at the General's house—
Shelton, Anquetil, Chambers, Grant, and Bellew present
—every one voted to the contrary; so, seeing I could do
nothing, I consented. At the time we had but two courses
open to us, which, in my opinion, promised a chance of
saving our honour and part of the army. One was to
occupy the Balla Hissar, and hold it till spring. By this
we should have had the best chance of success. The other
was to have abandoned our camp and baggage and encum-
brances, and forced our way down. This was perilous but
practicable. However, I could not persuade them to
sacrifice baggage; and that was eventually one of the
chief causes of our disasters. You may conceive my
anxiety to have this properly made known to Government.'

But when there was no longer any hope of that honourable resistance which Pottinger so persistently counselled,
when the nobler and the manlier course was impossible to
him in the face of this great military defection, Eldred
Pottinger conceived it to be, as doubtless it was, his duty
to do his best to extricate his countrymen from the perils
which environed them. He had no special power or
authority, which the military chiefs would have acknowledged, had he endeavoured to overrule their decision.
He did not, by the death of the Envoy and Minister, succeed to the plenipotentiary chair. He was simply an
'Assistant-Political,' of no very long standing in the department; he was only a Lieutenant of Artillery; all his
weight in those wretched councils was derived, therefore,
from his brave deeds; and those were times when, though
there were some noble hearts among our people at Caubul,

a great depression had come upon the Many, and simple manliness was not potential for the preservation of the honour of the nation. If, then, those were times when the young Artilleryman thought that an appeal might be made to the Army against the decree of the military leader, he soon felt that it was better to suppress the heroic aspiration. There was nothing, indeed, left for him but to endeavour to save his country from worse disasters than had already befallen it. So he bowed to the decision of the military chiefs.

'As soon as this was decided upon,' he wrote afterwards, 'I commenced negotiating. The enemy's first demand (on complying with which they promised to agree to the terms we offered on the 25th) was, that we should settle with the Hindoos they brought forward regarding the payment of the money the Envoy had promised, *i.e.* which the Council of War had decided should be paid. * * * I would willingly have avoided the payment of such; but the enemy, by stopping our supplies, obliged me to suffer the imposition, as the military authorities were urgent to prevent a renewal of hostilities, cost what it might. These sums were promised in the name of Sir William Macnaghten, by his agent (the Naib Ameer), to the different chiefs, to bring about a treaty and support it when formed. Major-General Elphinstone recollected the Envoy having informed him of his having authorized the agent to make the promises, as also did Captain Skinner.'

So the name of 'Eldred Pottinger, Major,' * was

---

* He had been promoted to a brevet majority, and created a Companion of the Bath, for his services at Herat.

attached to the Treaty; and on the 6th of January, 1842, the British army was under arms to march out of Caubul. But the escort, which the Afghan chiefs had promised for the protection of the conquered, had not been sent. 'The military authorities, however,' wrote Pottinger, in the report above quoted, 'refused to wait; and notwithstanding my advice to the contrary, marched out of our entrenchments.' There was nothing but death before them; for the snow had fallen heavily, and the wretched Hindostanee soldiers could not bear up against the rigours of the Northern winter. Pottinger clearly foresaw this, and endeavoured to impress upon the military authorities the importance of so clothing the Sepoys as to resist the severities of the winter, and enable them to escape the destructive bitings of the frost. 'Major Pottinger' (it is narrated by Sir Henry Lawrence) 'told us that when the retreat was decided on, and no attention was paid to his, Lawrence's, and Conolly's advice, to concentrate in the Balla Hissar, he urged the officers to have all the old horse-clothing, &c., cut into strips and rolled round the soldiers' feet and ankles after the Afghan fashion, as a better protection against snow than the mere hard leather of shoes. This he repeatedly urged, but in vain, and within a few hours the frost did its work. Major Pottinger said that there was not an Afghan around them who had not his legs swathed in rags as soon as the snow began to fall.'

Then came that memorable retreat through the dreadful snow, of which history has but few parallels. The Afghans, whom there was no one to hold in restraint, swarmed down upon our unhappy people, and massacred them, benumbed and helpless as they were, almost without resistance. At last, the Barukzye chief, Akbar Khan, who had slain Sir William Macnaghten, appeared upon the scene, and promised to escort the remnant of the Army safely to the British frontier, if three hostages were given up to him as a guarantee for the evacuation of our outposts in other parts of the country. Brigadier Shelton and Captain Lawrence were named; but Shelton refused to go; so Pottinger offered to take his place, and the offer was accepted. George Lawrence and Colin Mackenzie were his companions.

From that time, in the early part of January, to the September of the same year (1842), Eldred Pottinger remained a prisoner in the hands of Akbar Khan. All the circumstances of this memorable captivity are well known, for there are few who have not read the interesting journals of Vincent Eyre and Florentia Sale. It is sufficient to write briefly of this period of suffering. From the middle of January to the middle of April the prisoners were confined in the fort of Budeeabad. There Pottinger drew up for Government an elaborate report of the circumstances, so far as he was himself connected with them, of the rising in the Kohistan and of the subsequent Caubul capitulation, from which document I have quoted freely in the course of this narrative. From Budeeabad they were removed to a fort on the Loghur river, a few miles from Caubul, where they enjoyed comparative comfort and freedom. Although a prisoner, and as such incapable, in a strict sense, of official action, he was still recognized both by captive and captor as the responsible political authority, and was in frequent communication both with Akbar Khan and with General

Pollock respecting the terms of a mutual surrender of prisoners. It was natural and right that, in such circumstances, Pollock, who was advancing with his Army of Retribution upon Caubul, should have been suspicious of overtures made by the enemy through a prisoner who was completely at his mercy. And it is curious to observe in the correspondence between the old and the young soldier, how two brave and honourable men, regarding from different stand-points this matter of negotiation, looked with very different eyes upon the same manifestations. Pollock could not but regard the murderer of the British Envoy as a blood-stained criminal with whom it was sore distress, and indeed almost humiliation, to treat upon anything like equal terms. But Pottinger, who had lived too long in intimate relations with the Afghans to feel very sensitive on this score, told the General that his communications to the Sirdar were considered most offensive, and deprecated the tone of Pollock's letters. It was, undoubtedly, a difficult conjuncture, for many believed that if Akbar Khan were driven to despair, he would in revenge massacre the prisoners. But General Pollock judged, and judged rightly, that the bolder and more defiant the attitude which we assumed, the greater would be the safety of the prisoners; for in Afghanistan every man's hand was against his neighbour, and it was certain that there would be found those whose interest it would be, for their own sake, to side with the English who were advancing upon the capital.

It was at this period, in the summer of 1842, when Pottinger, Troup, and Colin Mackenzie were separated from the other prisoners, and in the immediate custody of

Akbar Khan, that an incident occurred so characteristic of
Pottinger's indomitable courage, that no record of his life
would be complete without its recital. The bills which he
had drawn upon India for the purpose of extricating the
British Army from the toils that surrounded them, after
the military leaders had determined to retreat, were repudiated by the Government. When intelligence of this
reached the leading Afghan Sirdars, they were exceedingly
wroth, and they determined that Pottinger should be compelled to draw fresh bills upon his Government. The
chiefs who assailed him were Ameenoollah Khan, who had
instigated the murder of Burnes; Mahomed Shah Khan,
Akbar's father-in-law, who was the very main-spring of the
insurrection; and another of some note. Suddenly entering the cell in which the three Englishmen were confined,
they told Pottinger that his bills had been protested, and
with fierce and insolent menaces told him that he must
immediately sign others. At first he tried to persuade
them of the inutility of such an act, as the new bills would
meet with the same fate as the old. They would not accept the plea, and renewed their threats; so he turned a
grim, stern face upon them, and said, 'You may cut off my
head if you will, but I will never sign the bills.' The chiefs
took counsel with each other, and hastily leaving the room
went to Akbar Khan, who was in an apartment above, and
asked what was to be done. But that chief knew too well
the kind of man with whom he had to deal to attempt
personal violence, which was certain to have no effect in
inducing him to swerve from his resolution.*

* Whilst in this tower, Pottinger, learning that there was a

To the bold front which Eldred Pottinger assumed, when tidings came that General Pollock was advancing victoriously upon Caubul, the captives owed it mainly, under Providence, that they finally obtained their release. From the neighbourhood of Caubul the captives were carried off to Bameean. As briefly told by the historian of the war, there is something almost ludicrous in the confidence of this little band of Englishmen. For we are told that, at Bameean, ' they deposed the governor of the place, and appointed a more friendly chief in his stead. They levied contributions on a party of Lohanee merchants who were passing that way, and so supplied themselves with funds. And, to crown all, Major Pottinger began to issue proclamations, calling upon all the neighbouring chiefs to come in and make their salaam; he granted remissions of revenue; and all the decent clothes in the possession of the party were collected to bestow as *khelats* (dresses of honour).' And there was wisdom in this; for so true is the old adage, ' Possunt qui posse videntur.' *

The account of these proceedings, which Pottinger has

supply of powder stored in it, proposed to take advantage of the opportunity when Akbar Khan and some of the leading chiefs were in the upper rooms, to set fire to a train and blow up the place, the Englishmen taking their chance of escaping disguised in the confusion. But his more prudent companions protested against the scheme.

* His services as chief political officer with the Caubul prisoners were highly appreciated by those who shared his captivity, and they subscribed to present him, after their release, with a testimonial, which he never lived to receive. But it was requested by the subscribers, who one and all mourned his decease, that it might be kept as an heirloom in his family.

officially recorded, is of the most inornate character; but as such, so characteristic that I am induced to insert it. No man's reputation ever owed less to his own utterances. He was quite incapable of a flourish.

'TO MAJOR-GENERAL POLLOCK, C.B., COMMANDING IN AFGHANISTAN.

'Caubul—Camp Racecourse, September 21, 1842.

'Sir,—I have the honour to report my arrival in your camp, and beg to lay before you the following statement of the measures we had recourse to at Bameean to effect our release. On the 10th of this month, Syed Moortiza Kashmeeree, an agent of Ali Reza Khan Kuzilbash, arrived in Bameean: he had received from Moonshee Mohun Lal verbal assurances that all those who would engage in effecting our release should be handsomely rewarded, and that a pension should be paid to himself and Saleh Mahomed Khan, who commanded the Afghan regiment sent to escort the prisoners to Toorkistan. Syed Moortiza brought urgent letters from the Kuzilbash chiefs to their clansman, Saleh Mahomed, and having gained over his brother, Mahomed Sadig Khan, paid him fifty out of a hundred rupees which had been furnished by Moonshee Mohun Lal, and carried him along with himself. They alighted at the dwelling of Mahomed Turym Beg, the chief of the Bameean Tajiks, and Syed Moortiza thence sent Mahomed Sadig to speak with Saleh Mahomed; the result was, an interview between Syed Moortiza and Saleh Mahomed, when the latter declared that he would only consent to treat with myself and the other English officers.

'Saleh Mahomed then had an interview with me, and afterwards Captains Lawrence, Johnson, and myself had a meeting with him and Syed Moortiza, in which we agreed to give him a present of twenty thousand rupees, and to continue to him the command of his regiment on his present salary of one thousand rupees a month, granting him a full pardon for all past offences, and that we should sign a paper to this effect. Having so far discovered the sentiments of Saleh Mahomed Khan, we brought him to Major-General Shelton, and laid before that officer and Colonel Palmer the plan: both these officers declined affixing their signature to any such paper, lest they should implicate themselves with Mahomed Akbar Khan, whereupon we consulted with Major Griffiths and the rest of the prisoners, and resolved to attempt the plan at all risks, and that if we found it were an attempt to overreach us, we should try to seize the weapons of the guard, and hold out in the forts till succour arrived.

'As soon as this arrangement had been completed, we sent off Syed Moortiza to Mir Mowhib (chief of the Fowlady Hazarehs), to invite his aid, and he came the next day, i. e. the 12th, whereupon Naib Zoolfikar, the governor, sent a message to say he was willing to join us, and I requested, as a mark of his friendship, he would send arms for our party, which, however, he did not. The Mir Akhor Ahmed Khan also received a letter ordering us to be marched into Toorkistan, but Saleh Mahomed Khan refused to obey the order to start that day, as the men wanted pay.

I received a letter from Naib Zoolfikar, offering service, and replied by requesting arms to be sent. As he did not send any, nor show any friendly feeling, but was said to be consulting with Ahmed Khan to attack us, I gave an order to Dyn Mahomed Khan, the former governor of Bameean (on the part of Khan Shireen Khan), to assume the government, employed men to frighten the Mir Akhor by telling him (as if from friendship) we had resolved to seize him, and promised the three companies a gratuity of four months' pay. These steps, joined to the arrival of Mir Kelb Ali of Besewt to join us, had the desired effect; the governor sent his brother to proffer service, and the Mir Akhowr fled, carrying off the Ghilzie firelock-men with him. On the 15th, news of the van of the British troops having advanced was received, and the Naib Zoolfikar came in, and personally visited us, on my saying I would go and see him if he did not come to me. I could not persuade him to give us arms, but as it appeared imprudent to turn him into an enemy, I directed Dyn Mahomed Khan to hold the order I had given him in abeyance till the conduct of Naib Zoolfikar might be further developed. On the 15th, I received a note from Mirza Shahjy, informing me of the defeat of the Afghan troops at Jugduluk, and our advance from Ghuzni, also that the Kuzilbash tribes had risen in Caubul, which determined us to march the next day.

'On the 16th we marched to Topchi Bala, and encamped with the castles in our front, so that we could occupy them if need be. On the morning of the 17th I received a letter from Sir Richmond Shakespear, informing me that he had reached Sir-i-Cheshmeh with six hundred and ten Kuzilbash horse, to our aid.   We immediately crossed the Kaloo Pass, and marched to the castle of Mir Morad Beg, near the foot of the Hajykek Pass, where we were joined by Sir Richmond Shakespear with the Kuzilbash horsemen, who had marched ninety miles from Caubul over that mountainous country in two marches.   The 18th, being supplied with seventy-seven horses by the Kuzilbash, and twelve by the Hazarehs, we managed to march to Gurdendewal; at that place we learned that a body of horse and foot from the Shekhali and Ghorebund districts had marched on Kaloo to intercept us.   On the 19th, with the same assistance as before, we marched to Thikaneh, where we heard that the pass of Sufeyd Khak was occupied by the Afghans, intending to check us.   Sir R. Shakespear immediately wrote to request that the British officer—who, report also told us, was advancing in that direction—would occupy the pass, and to say we would, if opposed, hold out in some of the castles about till relieved.   On the morning of the 20th we marched, and found the cavalry of Sir R. Sale's detachment at Kote Ashroo, and his infantry holding the heights, and had the pleasure of joining his camp at Urghendeh, whence I proceeded with Major-General Nott's camp, and, remaining there during the night, joined yours this morning.   I have given the Hazareh chiefs who joined us at first, remissions on their revenue, and on our march back I paid for the necessary supplies to the party, by orders on the revenue, to the amount of the supplies furnished.*

' In concluding this, I venture to request your support-

* Some passages relating to the services of certain chiefs are omitted.

ing the steps I have taken, and recommending them to Government, and trust that my assuming the powers of a political agent under the circumstances of the case may be pardoned, for I believe in no other way would the release of our captives have been achieved, though I could with ease have effected my own escape. With regard to the pension of a thousand rupees, the prisoners have agreed to pay the amount if Government consider it too large, but considering that the man was then in receipt of that sum monthly, and that he may be obliged to flee the country if the Barukzyes regain power, I trust you will not consider it too large a sum to recommend the payment of.

' I have, &c.,

' ELDRED POTTINGER (Major).'

But when General Pollock's army marched back triumphantly to the British Provinces, it was a matter of official necessity that the conduct of Major Pottinger, who had signed a treaty for the evacuation of Afghanistan, and had drawn bills to a large amount on the British Government in payment to the enemy, should be submitted to investigation. A Court of Inquiry was therefore held, over which Mr George Clerk * presided, and of which the members where Sir Harry Smith, Adjutant-General of Queen's Troops ; General Lumley, Adjutant-General of the Bengal Army ; Colonel Monteath,† who had distinguished himself

---

* Now (1867) Sir George Clerk, G.C.S.I., K.C.B., Member of the Council of India.

† Now Sir Monteath Douglas, K.C.B.

in the defence of Jellalabad ; and Colonel Wymer, an old Bengal officer, who had also done good service in Afghanistan. The inquiry commenced on Sunday, the 1st of January, 1843. Extracts from several official documents, including the Budeeabad Report, were read, but the only oral evid: ıce taken was that of Pottinger himself. Some questions were put to him regarding events previous to the death of Jir William Macnaghten, to which he replied that his opinions differed so much from those of the Envoy that there'was very little confidential intercourse between them. He said that when he assumed charge of the Mission,* he was ignorant of very much that had taken place before the death of the Envoy ; and when he was asked what course he pursued when he became aware of existing circumstances, he replied : ' I waited upon General Elphinstone to ascertain his views, and applied for an officer to assist me in taking charge of the late Envoy's office. At that interview with the General (several officers of rank being present), it was decided that if nothing were heard regarding the Envoy by a certain time, we should abandon our position at Caubul and march upon Jellalabad. I recommended that, at any rate, a decided course should be adopted : that we should either take possession of the Balla Hissar, or retire at once upon Jellalabad, waiting for no further communication with the enemy. In the afternoon I was again in consultation with the General, the officers attached to the Staff being present. A letter was received at that time from the

---

* Being asked why he assumed charge, he said that not only was he senior officer of the Mission, but that he ' was especially requested by General Elphinstone to take charge.'

enemy, containing overtures which the General said were the same as those to which the Envoy had agreed, with the exception of four additional clauses. To take this letter into consideration, the General sent for General Shelton, Brigadier Anquetil, and Colonel Chambers. I may add that this letter was accompanied by a note from Captain Lawrence, acquainting us for the first time with the death of the Envoy. I should also mention that Sir William Macnaghten, some time previously to his death, had told me that his letters from Government were of such a nature as to induce him to believe that although going into the Balla Hissar was probably our best course, still, if we remained there throughout the winter, we would in spring have eventually to force our way down to Jellalabad ; that he thought Government would be glad of what had occurred, as forming a pretext to shake off its connection with the country. Remembering this observation of the Envoy's, I did not oppose taking into consideration the enemy's letter, but as it contained terms to which we could not agree, a proposal was made to the enemy to discuss the matter the next day, and it was further notified to them that it would be necessary to omit or alter the objectionable clauses, which were—calling upon us to give up our treasure, the ladies, our cannon, and the arms in store. The next morning I received a letter directed to the Envoy from Captain Macgregor, at Jellalabad, and Captain Mackeson, at Peshawur, to the effect that reinforcements were on their way from India, which, setting my mind at rest as to the chance of being abandoned, decided me to recommend the course described in my official despatch, dated the 1st of February, to the address of the Secretary to the Government.'

When questions were put to him regarding the bills, he replied : ' In the Council of War it was decided that nineteen lakhs should be paid to the Afghan chiefs, on the understanding that they were to give their aid in making the treaty, and in escorting the troops safely to Peshawur. Fourteen lakhs of this sum of money had been previously promised to the above chief. bv Sir William Macnaghten's agent, in his name, tor the same purpose ; and five more lakhs were added by the Council of War, for the purpose of purchasing Mahomed Othman Khan's escort to Peshawur. I objected to the whole of this outlay, but being overruled by the consentient voices of the rest of the Council, I subsequently, as the agent of the Council of War, drew the bills in the usual official form on the Indian Government. In the first instance, the bills were made payable to the Afghan chiefs, perfectly understanding that they were only payable on the safe arrival of the Army at Peshawur, but the Hindoos refused to negotiate the bills in this form : they were consequently returned, and I was then directed by the General to draw them out in favour of the Hindoos, which was done, agents of the Hindostanees being warned, at the time of receiving the bills, of the circumstances under which they were drawn. It is also necessary to add that, shortly afterwards, when the news of the destruction of the Army reached Caubul, the Government agent at that place, Lieutenant John Conolly, expressly warned the Hindoos that the conditions on which the bills were granted having been

infringed, payment would certainly be refused by Government. Lieutenant Conolly's report upon this head to
Government is, I believe, before the Court; and he in
formed me personally that he had so reported, and that he
warned the people.'

The Court assembled again on the 2nd of January,
when General Shelton, who had been second in command
at Caubul, and Captain George Lawrence,* Sir William
Macnaghten's secretary, were examined. General Shelton,
when asked if Pottinger coincided in the opinion of the
Council of War, that the Army should retire on Jellalabad,
said : 'To the best of my recollection Major Pottinger did
not coincide.' The evidence of Captain Lawrence related
principally to the circumstances in which the bills upon
Government were drawn. The Court then decided that
no further evidence was necessary. The members then,
beginning, according to rule, with the junior member of the
Court, expressed their opinions—and these opinions varied
—as to the official competency of Major Pottinger to draw
such bills—not with respect to his conduct in drawing them.
The final decision of the Court was what every one felt in
his inmost heart that it must be. It only shed fresh lustre
on Eldred Pottinger's reputation. 'The Court,' it stands
on record, 'cannot conclude its proceedings without expressing a strong conviction that throughout the whole
period of the painful position in which Major Pottinger
was so unexpectedly placed, his conduct was marked by a
degree of energy and manly firmness that stamps his character as one worthy of high admiration.'

* Now General Sir George Lawrence, K.S.I.

Then Eldred Pottinger went down to Calcutta; and after a brief residence there, determined on a visit to his family in Europe. During his residence at the Presidency, as I well remember, the attempts to lionize him were very unsuccessful. Everybody was struck by the extreme modesty of his demeanour. He was shy and reserved, and unwilling to speak of himself. The impression which he made upon society generally was not favourable. He did not realize, either in his person, his conversation, or his manner, their ideal of a youthful hero, and, therefore, thoughtless people were disappointed. But to the more thoughtful few he appeared to be precisely the kind of man from whom such good deeds as had made him famous were to have been expected. Heroism takes many shapes. In Eldred Pottinger it took the shape of a sturdy and indomitable perseverance—a courage, great in resistance to apparently overwhelming odds; but there was nothing impetuous, nothing showy about it. ' And in all these respects the personal aspect and demeanour of the man represented his inward qualities.

What he might have done, had it pleased God to give him length of life, can only be conjectured; but even then he was nearly approaching the close of his earthly career. His uncle, Sir Henry Pottinger, was then at the head of the British Mission in China. Moved by feelings of affection and gratitude, Eldred resolved to pay his distinguished relative a visit; and during this visit, in a disastrous hour, he caught the Hong-Kong fever, and on the 15th of November, 1843, a career of the brightest promise was cut short by untimely death. It has been said that his life was embittered and his health impaired by the neglect—if it were only neglect—with which he had been treated on his return to India by Lord Ellenborough, whose prejudices against the Afghan Politicals were strong and deep. I know not how this was. It little matters now. The verdict of no ruler of a day can avail anything against the national judgment. The romance of Indian History has few more interesting chapters than the story of Eldred Pottinger—the Defender of Herat.